UNSOLVED MYSTERIES

PAST AND PRESENT

W9-BNA-186

UNSOLVED MYSTERIES

PAST AND PRESENT

COLIN WILSON
and Damon Wilson

CB

CONTEMPORARY
BOOKS

CHICAGO

Library of Congress Cataloging-in-Publication Data

Unsolved mysteries past and present / Colin Wilson and Damon Wilson.

p.   cm.

Includes index.

ISBN 0-8092-4091-2 (pbk.)

1. Curiosities and wonders.   I. Wilson, Damon.   II. Title.

AG243.W55   1992

031.02—dc20   92-4008

CIP

Copyright © 1992 by Colin Wilson and Damon Wilson
All rights reserved
Published by Contemporary Books, Inc.
180 North Michigan Avenue, Chicago, Illinois 60601
Manufactured in the United States of America
International Standard Book Number: 0-8092-4091-2

Contents

Acknowledgments ───────────────────── ix

Introduction ───────────────────────── xi

1 King Arthur and Merlin: Legend or Reality? ──────── 1

2 The Baader-Meinhof Gang: Suicide or Murder? ───── 15

3 The Basa Murder: The Voice from the Grave ──────── 26

4 The Canning Mystery: The Eighteenth Century's
Most Notorious Cause Célèbre ──────────────── 31

5 The Cleveland Torso Murders: Who Was
"the Mad Butcher"? ──────────────────── 42

6 Crop Circles: UFOs, Whirlwinds, or Hoaxers? ─────── 50

7 Was Philip K. Dick Possessed by an Angel? ──────── 57

8 The Dogon and the Ancient Astronauts:
Evidence of Visitors from Space? ─────────────── 69

9 Fairies: Are the "Little People" Just a Fairy Tale? ──── 77

10 The Forgotten Children: The Strange Story
of the Railway Children ──────────────────── 96

11 The Glozel Mystery: Archaeological Riddle
or Fraud? ───────────────────────── 99

12 Victor Grayson: The Strange Case of the
Disappearing Member of Parliament ———— 105
13 Rudolf Hess: Was It Hitler's Deputy Who Died in
Spandau Prison? ———————————— 124
14 The Disappearance of Harold Holt: Was the
Australian Prime Minister a Chinese Spy? ——— 136
15 Homer and the Fall of Troy: Are They Both
a Myth? ———————————————— 145
16 The Hope Diamond: The Famous Cursed Jewel —— 171
17 The Mystery of Hypnosis: Real-Life Svengalis
and the Telepathy Theory ———————— 176
18 Jack the Ripper: Shedding New Light on the World's
Most Infamous Serial Killer ——————— 195
19 Junius: Who Was the Eighteenth Century's Most
Feared Satirist? ——————————— 215
20 The Death of Meriwether Lewis: Suicide
or Murder? ————————————— 234
21 Fedor Kuzmich: Did the Tsar Die an
Unknown Monk? ———————————— 242
22 Glenn Miller: The Strange Disappearance of a
Bandleader ————————————— 254
23 The Missing Link: The Unsolved Mystery of
Human Evolution ——————————— 266
24 Joan Norkot: The Case of the Bleeding Corpse —— 280
25 The *Oera Linda Book:* The Forgotten History of
a Lost Continent ——————————— 286
26 Possession by the Dead: Myth or Reality? ——— 294
27 Richard III: Murderer or Scapegoat? ———— 324
28 The Sea Kings of 6000 B.C.: The Maps That
Contradict the History Books ——————— 337
29 Sea Monsters: Unknown Giants of the Deep ——— 347

30 The Skull of Doom: The Strange Tale of the
   Crystal Skull —————————————— 358
31 Vampires: Do They Exist? ————————— 368
32 Vortices: The Bridge Between the Natural and
   the Supernatural? ———————————— 401
33 Zombies: The Evidence for the Walking Dead ——— 413
   Index ————————————————— 418

Acknowledgments

W e owe a debt of gratitude to many friends who have either read parts of the manuscript or provided information. These include Geoffrey Ashe, Dennis Stacy, Robert Temple, Lois Bourne, Elaine Watkins, Christopher Logue, Robin Odell, Wilbur Wright, Ray Hurt, Donald Seaman, Frank Smyth, Dr. Ian R. Hill, Hamish McAlpine—and also two friends who are now dead, Joe Gaute and Anita Gregory. We also wish to thank Diana Peterson of Contemporary Books for her patience and support.

C.W. and D.W.

Introduction

The part of England where I live, Cornwall, is conducive to an interest in unsolved mysteries. It has more legends and ghost stories than most of the rest of England put together and dozens of those mysterious megaliths and "stone circles" whose precise purpose is still unknown. When I first came here, more than thirty years ago, I assumed that its peculiar atmosphere was simply a matter of "local color"—of spectacular cliffs and pretty harbors and bleak open moorland. Since then, I have come to recognize that it is no accident that the place is so full of oddly menacing fairy stories—stories of abductions and betrayals—as well as tales of demons and legends of the battles of King Arthur and of a land called Lyonesse that has been engulfed by the sea.

The realization began to dawn when I learned that I could use a dowsing, or divining, rod. A friend who was an expert dowser asked me to drive him down to the megalithic stone circle known as the Merry Maidens, near Penzance, and I watched with astonishment as he walked among the stones holding a dowsing rod (in fact, two narrow strips of plastic tied together at one end with string), which kept twisting violently in his hands. He held out the rod to me: "You try it."

"No, these things never work for me."

"Show me how you hold the rod." I did so, holding the ends of the two plastic strips between each forefinger and thumb. "No, that's no good. You've got to *bend* the two ends so they've got a spring on them."

He made me bend both ends of the rod into U shapes. Then, holding it awkwardly, I walked toward one of the standing stones. To my astonishment, it twisted upward in my hands. At first I assumed that I had "done it myself" by changing the pressure on the rod, but half a dozen more tries convinced me that the rod was acting of its own accord. When I came close to a stone, it twisted upward; when I moved away, it fell again. And when I walked across the circle, I noticed that the "force" seemed to be particularly powerful in the middle.

This, I suspect, is why our ancestors of four or five thousand years ago built these circles. They recognized the spots where the ground possesses some odd "magnetic" force and deliberately placed the stones there to capture and channel the force, much as an acupuncturist sticks his needles into the body's meridians, the crossing points of its lines of force.

But what did they then *do* within these stone "temples," of which Stonehenge (in Wiltshire) is the most spectacular example? It seems certain that the structures were used for some form of ritual worship associated with the earth's fertility and that this worship often involved dancing. We know that the Druids performed such rituals many centuries later. The stones were probably also used for healing. (T. C. Lethbridge, whom we shall meet in chapters 16 and 32, thought that the dancing "charged up" the stones, like accumulators.)

After I had learned that I could dowse, I began to notice that I seemed more sensitive to the local "atmosphere." This may, of course, have been sheer self-deception. I noticed it, for example, in Lamorna Cove, near the Merry Maidens, where there is a legend of a cobbler named Lenine who made a bargain with, and managed to cheat, the Devil. But the Devil remained in the cottage, making it impossible to keep a roof on the building, until he was finally exorcised by the local parson, the Reverend Corker, a famous huntsman who was also reputed to be skilled in the magic arts. It is not that I accept the truth of the legend, or believe in the Devil as a personal entity; but I can believe that *something* happened in that curiously atmospheric area that became transformed into the tale of diabolic forces.

Less than a mile away is a house called Rose Merryn that belonged to the novelist Crosbie Garstin (whose mysterious disappearance deserves to appear in a sequel to this volume) that has a curious underground passage known as a *fougou*, where ancient ceremonies were undoubtedly performed (and, in more recent centuries, witches' sabbats) and that caused my dowsing rod to respond violently. Many of its tenants have committed suicide or died under peculiar circumstances, but its present owner is convinced that this is not because it is somehow "cursed." He believes that the ground is permeated by powerful forces and that anyone who can learn to "tune in" to these forces, to harmonize with them, so to speak, can somehow make use of them for his own spiritual evolution. Those who are "out of tune" experience a sense of menace and confusion that can bring disaster (for, like me, he is inclined to believe that disasters come when we induce them with negative attitudes).

Now it is necessary to explain that I was trained as a scientist and that from the age of eleven I dreamed of becoming a nuclear physicist as other boys dream of becoming engine drivers. My favorite writer was H. G. Wells, because he was also possessed by this vision of science as the most exciting and romantic thing in the world. An earlier interest in ghosts and Spiritualism evaporated like a bad dream. If you had pressed me, I would probably have admitted that there was a strong probability that ghosts existed; but I would have insisted that they were uninteresting compared to the problem of the expanding universe. I lost interest in the idea of becoming a scientist because, when I left school at sixteen, I went to work in a factory and was so miserable that I began to devote all my free time to reading poetry and listening to music. As I began to experience the magic that "fills/The soul with longing for dim hills/And faint horizons,"* I began to find science horribly cold and one-sided. It was obvious that the world of literature and music was as exciting—and as intellectually

---

*Rupert Brooke, "Song of the Pilgrims."

valid—as the world of stars and atoms. Yet there was no question of rejecting science, only of trying to find some wider form of knowledge that could embrace *both* worlds.

When, a quarter of a century later, I was commissioned to write a book on "the occult," I approached it with the same skepticism I had felt at age fifteen. Within a week or two I had come to recognize that skepticism is merely a name for intellectual laziness. Precognition, telepathy, out-of-body experiences, "second sight," and poltergeist hauntings are all undoubtedly real. But how could they be fitted into a scientific framework?

Fortunately, I happened to be staying in Majorca that winter, in a little village named Deya, whose most celebrated inhabitant was the poet and novelist Robert Graves.

In 1944 Graves had written a book of such apparently wild eccentricity that it was turned down by a number of publishers, one of whom hinted that he had gone off his head. It was called *The White Goddess*, and its basic theme is that the kind of knowledge taught in our universities is as crude and impersonal as a railway timetable: that there is a *totally different kind of knowledge* and a totally different way of knowing. During his school days Graves had noted that a boy named Smilley could solve complex mathematical problems *instantaneously*: "It just came to me." The mathematics master found this so disturbing that he caned the boy until the faculty went away.

The odd thing is that this faculty, which all "mathematical prodigies" possess, enables its "owners" to solve problems that should be logically insoluble. A prime number is a number that cannot be divided exactly. (Five and seven are primes, but nine is not because it can be divided by three.) If a number is huge, there is no mathematical shortcut to discovering whether it is a prime or not. Yet a mathematical prodigy named Zerah Colburn was able to announce, after a few seconds, that one ten-digit number was not a prime because it could be divided by 641; it just "came" to him. As a schoolboy, Graves himself had a "mystical insight" which, he remained convinced, solved the whole problem of the universe and human existence. It lasted for twenty-four hours but vanished when he tried to write it down. Graves called this type of intuitive understanding "lunar knowledge," while our ordinary rational understanding he termed "solar knowledge."

In the mid-1960s a scholar named John Michell stumbled on a series of closely related insights. He discovered a book entitled *Feng Shui* by the Reverend E. J. Eitel, about the ancient Chinese science of wind and water, which aims to establish harmonious relations between people and their natural surroundings. He went on to rediscover the work of an English brewer, Alfred Watkins, who in 1921 had been the first to observe the curious network of footpaths and farm tracks that connect British "sacred sites" such as churches and stone circles. Watkins called them "ley lines" and believed they were simply ancient trade routes—although it was not clear why trade routes should connect churches and sacred sites. Michell became convinced that they were lines of "earth force," which the Chinese called *lung mei*, or dragon paths. Ancient man, he came to believe, was intuitively aware of these strange earth forces. Michell was also interested in the phenomenon of "flying saucers," declining to accept that they are merely a sign of hysteria, and he observed that UFO phenomena often seem to occur most frequently in areas where ley lines intersect. Watkins had already noted that sacred sites like Stonehenge may be multiple crossing points.

Around 1960 science was finally able to place this paradox of "lunar" and "solar" knowledge on a rational foundation. It happened when an American psychologist named Roger Sperry realized that man literally has *two* brains in his skull—or, rather, that the human brain consists of two identical halves that can operate independently. These two halves—the left and the right cerebral hemispheres—deal respectively with "lunar" and "solar" knowledge. (See also chapter 17.)

The two hemispheres are joined by a knot of nerves called the *corpus callosum*, or commissure, and if the commissure is severed—as it sometimes is to cure epilepsy—the patient begins to act literally like two people. A "split-brain patient" might try to zip up his fly with one hand while trying to undo it with the other; one such patient tried to hit his wife with one hand while the other held it back.

For some unknown reason, the left side of our body is connected to the right side of our brain, and vice versa, and the same
applies to the visual field of our eyes. If a split-brain patient was
shown an apple with the left eye and an orange with the right and
asked what he had just seen, he would reply, "Orange." Asked to
write down with his *left* hand what he had just seen, he would
write, "Apple." Asked what he had just written, he would reply,
"Orange." A split-brain patient who was shown an indecent picture with the right side of her brain blushed; asked why she was
blushing she replied, "I don't know." Clearly, the *I*—the person
you call "I"—lives in the left side of the brain; the person who
lives in the other side is a stranger.

Sperry also discovered that the left-brain "you" is the rationalist, the scientist, the person who copes with your everyday life.
The right-brain "you" is the artist; he operates on intuition. He is
the one who enjoys music and appreciates beautiful scenery. It
was Smilley's right-brain "self" that could somehow leap to the
solutions of problems in a flash without having to go through the
slow process of working them out rationally. And, as we have
seen, this right-brain person can, to some extent, *defy* the normal
laws of reason and "see" that a number is not a prime when a
computer would have to do it by the long, rational method.

There is also evidence that when we dowse it is that "other
person" in the right brain who picks up the vibrations of underground water or standing stones and unconsciously causes the
muscles to react and make the rod twist.

So the scientist who dismisses all "lunar knowledge" as pure
superstition is not a true scientist, for he is ignoring the scientific
facts about the right cerebral hemisphere.

It also follows that the kind of person who enjoys reading about
unsolved mysteries has no reason to be ashamed of his taste. The
craving to explore the unknown is the evolutionary urge in its
purest form. It is true, of course, that some people are too uncrit-
ical, but that is no reason to try to seal off whole areas of human
knowledge.

I must admit that some of the most vociferous skeptics are
friends of mine and that—except in one case, that of the scientific
journalist Martin Gardner—their attitude has in no way disturbed

our friendship. Melvin Harris—who, like myself, is interested in the problem of Jack the Ripper—is the author of a book entitled *Sorry You've Been Duped*, which begins by demolishing the case of "the Amityville horror," which is indeed as fraudulent as he says it is. He then goes on to other subjects, such as psychic detection and hypnotic regression to past lives, and makes short work of them too. But the one case in which I was personally involved, the disappearance of a schoolgirl named Genette Tate, is presented in Harris's book in a way that is lopsided.

The point is that I know Melvin Harris to be a decent and generous person; I also know that he is not willfully distorting the facts out of sheer malice. And he emphasizes at the beginning of his book that he is not engaged in a crusade against the paranormal but is merely recording the results of his investigations. The fact remains that the book *is* an attack on the paranormal and that, as such, it sets out to do something that is logically impossible: to dismiss the *whole* subject on the evidence of a few well-chosen examples that can be shown to be dubious.

The same applies to another old friend, Professor Marcello Truzzi, who founded a magazine called *The Zetetic Scholar* to investigate and explode "claims of the paranormal." He later became one of the founders of CSICOP, the Committee for the Scientific Investigation of Claims of the Paranormal, whose attitude toward the paranormal is as intolerant as the attitude of the House Un-American Activities committee was toward Communists. Unfortunately, Truzzi proved to be too honest and open-minded a man to be able to live with the passionately "true unbelievers" on the committee, and after a scandal in which they tried to repress some evidence favorable to the paranormal, he resigned.

More recently he has coauthored a book on "psychic detection" entitled *The Blue Sense*, which spends much of its time debunking psychics like Peter Hurkos and Gerard Croiset. So is it another attack on the whole subject of the paranormal? No. In fact, he recounts many other cases in which the aid of psychics in solving criminal cases cannot be dismissed and concludes by admitting that he cannot state with confidence that psychic detection is a fraud. Yet even in going just this far, he has effectively abandoned the position of CSICOP—that the whole thing is a contemptible fraud and that all psychics are fools or crooks.

The career of another friend, Ian Wilson, has also provided me with a great deal of wry amusement. A Roman Catholic convert, he began by writing an important book that argues that the "holy shroud of Turin" is genuine. He followed this with a book about reincarnation entitled *Mind Out of Time*, which brilliantly attacked a number of cases of alleged "memories of past lives," like the famous Bridey Murphy case. (The Catholic church has officially condemned the notion of reincarnation.) He was then asked to participate in a television series based on the files of the Society for Psychical Research, and although he was again able to use his debunking technique to considerable effect in cases like that of the "Croglin vampire," he had to admit that in other cases—particularly those involving "ghosts"—the evidence simply could not be dismissed. When Wilson turned his attention to "the after-death experience" (in a book of the same title), the same thing happened, and even after dismissing much of the evidence as fraudulent, he ended by acknowledging that the overall case for "survival" is very powerful indeed. A more recent book of Wilson's, *Superself*, concerns unusual powers of the mind, including dowsing and healing, and ends by acknowledging the reality of what might be called the "superconscious mind." Here, as in the case of Marcello Truzzi, we have an example of a man who has the patience and honesty to study many cases of apparently paranormal powers in some detail and who ends with his skepticism deeply eroded—although, like Truzzi, he finds himself too embarrassed to come out openly and admit that he has, in effect, made a 180-degree turn.

An interesting example of the "wholesale" attitude toward paranormal phenomena can be found in a book entitled *Secrets of the Supernatural* by Joe Nickell and John Fischer. The authors' aim is to solve a number of mysteries through the investigative approach. The first chapter describes an investigation into a haunting at Mackenzie House, in Toronto. They cite various witnesses who claim to have seen ghosts over the years and some who have heard spooky noises at night. They then describe how they spoke to the caretaker of the house next door, who demonstrated that various noises made in the basement were "telegraphed" to the "haunted house." The authors leave us in no doubt that many of the "spooky" noises in Mackenzie House were the result of a rumbling boiler. But this, of course, fails to explain the ghost sightings of the witnesses. The tacit assumption is that the demonstration about the noises allows us to dismiss these sightings. In fact, however, it may or it may not. If you happen to believe, as I do, that there *are* such things as ghosts, then you would require a further demonstration that the sightings of a shadowy woman and a man in a frock coat were also the result of the rumbling boiler.

Skeptical investigators all seem to make this same curious logical error. William James pointed out that if you want to disprove that all crows are black, you do not have to try and prove that no crows are black; you only have to produce one single white crow. So a bookful of cases of fraud or excessive gullibility proves nothing except that those particular cases are fraudulent. But one single case of a paranormal event for which the evidence is overwhelming *does* demolish the argument that the paranormal is, by definition, fraudulent.

When I saw that Nickell and Fischer had a chapter on the mystery of the Barbados coffins, I turned to it eagerly. This mystery has always baffled me because it seems to break all the rules that even convinced "believers" accept. Every time the Chase family vault was opened up, the coffins were found in disorder; on each such occasion the vault was carefully sealed so that no intruder could enter without leaving telltale signs. Yet the coffins continued to be thrown around by some unknown force until the family decided to stop using the vault. Natural explanations such as flooding or earth tremors had to be ruled out. Yet supernatural explanations such as poltergeists were also implausible, since poltergeists seem to require some kind of energy source, usually a disturbed teenager. Sir Arthur Conan Doyle made the weird suggestion that some kind of "effluvium" was responsible, without explaining what he meant.

Nickell studied the accounts of the disturbances by various eyewitnesses, and although he noted a few contradictions he was unable to prove actual dishonesty. Then light dawned. In investigating an account of lost silver mines in Kentucky, he had noted the statement that the alleged discoverer had marked a tree with symbols that Nickell recognized as Masonic. He then learned that the silver mine was supposed to have been discovered in 1788, the year Freemasonry came to Kentucky. The silver mine, it seemed, was not a real one but merely a symbol for Freemasonry.

Was it possible that the whole Barbados vault story was simply a Masonic allegory—that is, a lie invented to symbolize the truths of Freemasonry? That seems an odd assumption. The coffins were finally moved elsewhere in 1820, and the first account of the case, by Sir J. E. Alexander, dates from 1833. The Reverend Thomas H. Orderson, the vicar of Christ Church during the whole period, wrote out his own account of the affair several times for different people; not surprisingly, a few minor inaccuracies (such as dates) crept into some of his accounts, but they are otherwise consistent. The Hon. Nathan Lucas wrote an eyewitness account of the last opening of the tomb. Sir Robert Schomburgk described the events in his *History of Barbados* in 1848, less than thirty years later.

Nickell observes that the Reverend Orderson's brother Isaac wrote his own memoirs of Barbados (1842) and failed to mention the incident. Would this have been likely, he asks, if it were true? The answer is: Yes, if Isaac Orderson disliked ghost stories or even if he felt that a ghost story was inappropriate in another kind of narrative. In *Man Eaters of Kumaon*, tiger hunter Jim Corbett mentions in passing that a certain bungalow had been associated with a supernatural incident but that that book was not the place in which to describe it. And my own attempts to track the story down through Corbett's sister and his publisher were total failures—his publisher admitted he knew the story but refused to repeat it. I find it very easy to believe that Isaac Orderson decided not to include a "ghost story" for similar reasons.

Were any of the people involved in the Barbados mystery Freemasons? An investigation revealed that Lord Combermere, the governor of the island, who had opened the vault in 1820, was later a Grand Master. But did this apply to any of the others—for example, the Reverend Orderson? Nickell's attempts to find out were unsuccessful, except in one case of an alleged eyewitness, Sir R. Boucher Clark, who proved to be a Past Master. But he decided that the Reverend Orderson's account was full of Masonic symbols, such as right angles and "the northeast corner."

What about Sir Arthur Conan Doyle, who later commented on the case? Research revealed that Doyle had also been a Mason and that the word *effluvia* appears in the Master Mason's degree.

And so, concludes Nickell, his case is more or less proven. The case of the Barbados coffins was an invention of the Freemasons. But *why*? Why should a number of respectable and presumably truthful people invent a mystery in order to symbolize Freemasonry? To communicate some secret to other Masons? That sounds absurd. And would a clergyman not only participate in the fraud but go on repeating his lie over the years?

But what is surely most absurd of all is the notion that Doyle, a spiritualist and a man of known integrity would have deliberately introduced the Masonic word *effluvia* into his own attempted explanation—presumably to indicate to other Masons that the whole thing was a fraud.

Nickell certainly has to be given an A for effort. But as an "explanation" of the mystery, his theory is a failure. He could, of course, be right, and the Barbados vault story could be some kind of hoax. But his own attempt to explode it is more unbelievable than the original mystery.

For me, the really interesting problem is why investigators like Joe Nickell are so anxious to prove that paranormal phenomena simply cannot occur. They explain that people who accept the paranormal are trying to escape their hidden fears—for example, the fear of death. But they do not explain why they themselves are so determined that the universe is a normal, solid place with no secrets that cannot be solved in the laboratory.

In fact, we *know* that this is not the case. Newspapers from early June 1991 contained photographs taken by the world's most powerful telescope, at La Silla, in the Chilean Andes. They show galaxies whose existence has never been suspected. "The picture has baffled cosmologists," wrote the *Daily Telegraph*. "No one had expected to find so many galaxies at this distance, and it suggests that there may be many more than hitherto believed. It will therefore lengthen estimates of the age of the universe."

The last sentence has a comforting sound; although the universe turns out to be far bigger than we thought, scientists are already working on the problem. We needn't worry—everything is under control. For a moment, even I feel lulled into a sense of security. Then I glance again at that picture full of things that look like exploding galaxies, and I realize that "security" is an illusion. So the universe is bigger than we thought, and those galaxies are receding at 90 percent of the speed of light. And what are they expanding *into*? Space, presumably. And since I can conceive of the universe expanding forever, then presumably space goes on forever? But that simply contradicts my basic experience of space and time. Periods of time last for just so long, and objects—or the space in which they exist—extend just so far.

Since this notion of something going on *forever* contradicts my basic experience, I can only assume that my experience is, in some way, a liar. Kant tried to solve the problem by explaining that space and time are categories invented by our own minds. That seems to imply that if I could understand the way my mind works, I would understand where space ends. Whatever the explanation, I have to assume that my "natural standpoint" is somehow a *mistake*, an error.

Now I turn to one of my favorite anecdotes: how Charles Dickens one day dreamed about meeting a lady in a red shawl who introduced herself as Miss Napier. As he shaved, he thought how odd it was to have such a circumstantial dream about someone who did not exist. That night (May 30, 1863), after he had given a reading, some friends came into his dressing room with the "lady in red," who was introduced as Miss Napier.

That is impossible—at least, in our commonsense universe; you cannot dream of events that have not yet taken place. My skeptical friends would look for natural explanations, such as that Dickens *had* met her earlier, but forgotten her, etc. . . .

Do I have an alternative explanation? No. All I can say is this: that after thinking for five minutes about that picture of distant galaxies and all that it implies, Dickens's story no longer affronts my sense of reality; on the contrary, it only confirms my vague sense that our normal, comfortable view of reality is laughably inadequate. And—*pace* Melvin Harris, Ian Wilson, and Joe Nickell—that until we stop clinging, like frightened children, to that normal and comfortable view, it will remain laughably inadequate.

Colin Wilson

1

King Arthur and Merlin: Legend or Reality?

King Arthur and his magician, Merlin, are two of the most popular figures in world mythology. But did either of them really exist? Or are they merely characters in a charming fairy tale?

We can understand, of course, why historians would cast doubt on the existence of Merlin. But some modern scholars have even doubted that King Arthur was a real historical character. This is obviously a question that must be settled before we go any further.

We first hear about Arthur and Merlin in a book entitled *History of the Kings of Britain*, written around 1135 by a Welsh bishop named Geoffrey of Monmouth—whose reliableness may be judged by his opening chapter, in which he explains how Britain was named after the warrior Brutus, who sailed there from the siege of Troy. A hundred or so pages later, Geoffrey describes how a king named Vortigern—who was a real historical character— ordered an impregnable tower to be built on Mount Snowdon, in Wales. The tower kept collapsing, whereupon some soothsayers told him that if he wanted the tower to remain standing, he would have to sprinkle the stones with the blood of a boy who had no father. His messengers traveled throughout the kingdom in search of such a youth, until they overheard two boys quarreling and one of them jeering that the other had no father. The fatherless boy was named Merlin.

King Vortigern sent for Merlin and his mother, who proved to be the daughter of the king of South Wales. She described how she had been seduced by a handsome youth who subsequently vanished into thin air—although she sometimes heard his voice speaking to her when she was alone. Vortigern then explained that since Merlin was literally fatherless, he had to sacrifice him and sprinkle his blood on the foundations of the tower. Merlin promptly offered to prove that the soothsayers were liars and asked to have them brought before him. "Do you know why the tower keeps on collapsing?" he asked them. They shook their heads. "Because there is a pool underneath it which makes the earth soggy." Vortigern's men were ordered to dig and found the pool. Merlin then went on to foretell that if they drained it they would find two dragons (or serpents). And when this also proved to be true, Vortigern decided to spare his life. Merlin then went on to make a series of prophecies—including the augury that Vortigern would be burned to death in a tower. This came about just as Merlin foretold, when a king named Aurelius Ambrosius—the rightful heir to the throne—invaded Britain and set fire to Vortigern's tower.

When Aurelius was poisoned his brother, Uther Pendragon, became king. After conquering Scotland, he invited all the nobles of his realm to a feast to witness his coronation. Among these were Duke Gorlois of Cornwall and his beautiful wife, Igerna. Uther fell madly in love with Igerna, and when Gorlois realized this he hurried back to Cornwall. This insulted the King, who pursued Gorlois with an army. Gorlois forestalled the rape of his wife by hiding her away in the castle of Tintagel, which was virtually impregnable, for it stood on an island that was approached only by a narrow neck of land. When he learned about this, Uther Pendragon fell into a deep depression, for he could think about nothing but possessing Igerna.

The problem was solved by Merlin, who used his magic to transform Uther into Duke Gorlois's double. Uther went to the castle of Tintagel and was immediately admitted. That night, in Igerna's arms, he conceived the boy who would become King Arthur.

While Uther was away his men attacked the castle in which Gorlois had taken refuge. Gorlois was killed, and Uther Pendragon married Igerna and made her queen. He reigned for another fifteen years until he was also poisoned, and then Arthur became king.

Readers of Geoffrey of Monmouth (whose book is still in print in a popular edition) will wonder what happened to the sword in the stone, the Knights of the Round Table, and other famous parts of the legend. The answer is that they were added by later (mostly French) chroniclers and given their definitive form in one of the first printed books, Sir Thomas Malory's *Morte D'Arthur*, printed by William Caxton in 1485. Little was known about its author until 1926, when literary research revealed—to the dismay of scholars—that Malory was a robber chief who sacked monasteries and rustled cattle, and who raped a woman named Joan Smyth, the wife of one Hugh Smyth, on at least two occasions. He apparently wrote *Morte D'Arthur* in Newgate Prison, where he is buried.

But if Arthur was a teenager when his father died, why should he have had to prove his right to the throne by pulling a sword out of a stone (or an anvil set in a stone, as Malory tells the story)? Malory overcomes this problem by having Merlin take charge of Arthur from the moment he is born; Merlin then hands the baby over to a knight named Sir Ector, whose wife suckles Arthur.

It all sounds so absurd that it is not surprising that some scholars have dismissed Arthur as a legend. They point out, for example, that one of the main sources of information on Arthur's period is a monk named St. Gildas who wrote a bitter and disgruntled book entitled *The Downfall and Conquest of Great Britain (De excidio et conquestu Britanniae)* and who does not even mention Arthur—although he speaks of the Battle of Badon, which is Arthur's most famous battle.

But a biography of Gildas by Caradoc of Llancarfan mentions that Arthur killed Gildas's brother, Hueil, who fought against him; that in itself would obviously explain why Gildas could not even bring himself to mention Arthur's name.

So what do we actually know about the legendary hero called King Arthur? Well, to begin with, he was not a king but a general. He did not ride around on a white charger dressed in a suit of medieval armor, because he belonged to a far earlier period—he was probably born about A.D. 470, during the period when the Romans had just left Britain. He was, in fact, a Roman—or at least a Roman citizen. So his horse would have been a small Roman horse, about the size of a modern pony, and his sword would have been a short Roman sword, not a long broadsword like the legendary Excalibur.

Around A.D. 410 the Romans decided to pull out of Britain—they needed all their forces to defend Rome from the barbarians. A chieftain named Vortigern set himself up as king of Britain but soon encountered trouble with the wild Picts from north of the Scottish border; around 443 he invited Saxon mercenaries from the Continent to come and fight for him. They did, but when Vortigern ran out of money to pay them, they decided to stay and conquer Britain. The original Britons—whom we now call Celts—were slowly driven west into Wales, Cornwall, and Scotland. However, an ex-Roman warrior named Ambrosius Aurelianus rallied the Celts and went to war with Roman thoroughness, inflicting many defeats on the invaders. When he died, his brother, Uther Pendragon, replaced him. And one of his most brilliant generals was a young man named Artorius, the legendary King Arthur—who may or may not have been the son of Uther Pendragon.

It was Arthur who brought the Saxon invasion to a standstill in a series of twelve great battles, the last of which, the Battle of Badon, took place about A.D. 518. This established him as the Dark Age equivalent of General Montgomery or General Eisenhower. If his allies had remained loyal, it seems probable that the Saxons would have been driven back to the Continent, and it would now be Arthur's Celtic descendants who rule Britain, not the Anglo-Saxons.

Unfortunately, Arthur's former allies now fell to squabbling among themselves, and Arthur spent the remainder of his life trying to avoid being stabbed in the back. When he finally died, in the Battle of Camlann—which, according to Geoffrey, took place near the River Camel in Cornwall—he was fighting his own nephew Mordred, not the Saxon invaders. According to Geoffrey of Monmouth, Arthur's body was carried off to the "Isle of Avalon," which has been identified as Glastonbury, a small town in the west of England with a famous abbey and a tor—a hill surmounted by a tower. (Although Glastonbury is now inland, there was a time when it was surrounded by the waters of the Bristol Channel.) Because the burial was secret, to prevent the Saxons from finding the body, a widespread story soon arose that Arthur was not really dead but would return to help Britain in her hour of need.

In the summer of 1113, about twenty years before Geoffrey of Monmouth wrote his *History*, a group of French priests came to Bodmin, in Cornwall, carrying holy relics. When one of the locals mentioned that Arthur was still alive and was expected to return any day, the servant of one of the clerics was tactless enough to sneer. This caused a violent confrontation, and a group of armed Cornishmen burst into the church with the intention of teaching the skeptical foreigners a lesson; it was only with some difficulty that they were pacified. This seems to demonstrate that Arthur was already a legendary figure before Geoffrey of Monmouth wrote his bestseller.

In fact, Arthur is mentioned many times in various Welsh poems written within a century of his death. But the next major reference to him comes in a confused collection of historical material compiled by a monk named Nennius some time between A.D. 800 and 820. The earliest material about Arthur that Nennius quotes is a collection of Welsh "Easter Annals," tables of the dates of Easter (which is a movable feast) compiled by monks. These tables have wide margins, and in one of these—for the year A.D. 518—there is a jotting (in Latin): "Battle of Badon in which Arthur carried the cross of Our Lord Jesus on his shoulders for three days and three nights and the Britons were victors." And another, for the year A.D. 539 reads: "The strife of Camlann in which Arthur and Modred [sic] perished." So if we can believe the Easter Annals, Arthur ruled for twenty-one years after the Battle of Badon.

But the most dramatic incident in the story of Arthur occurred about thirty years after the death of Geoffrey of Monmouth (in A.D. 1154), during the reign of Henry II—the king who is best remembered in connection with the murder of Archbishop Thomas à Becket. Henry was an indefatigable traveler, and on one of his trips to Wales he met a Welsh bard, a "singer of the past," who told him that King Arthur was buried in the grounds of Glastonbury Abbey. To protect the body from the Saxons, said the bard, it had been buried sixteen feet deep. He even mentioned the exact location—between two "pyramids."

The king was naturally delighted, for Geoffrey of Monmouth's *History* had represented Arthur as one of the greatest conquerors since Julius Caesar. (According to Geoffrey, Arthur had conquered Ireland, Scandinavia, and France and was about to march on Rome when news of Mordred's rebellion forced him to return to England.) He was also relieved to hear that Arthur *was* buried in Glastonbury. As the great-grandson of William the Conqueror, he was familiar with the legend that Arthur would return in England's hour of need. If he could prove that Arthur was well and truly dead, the latter would cease to be a rallying cry for rebels like the men of Bodmin.

Besides, Henry had an affection for Glastonbury, because the abbot Henry of Blois had played a part in making him king. So Henry went to call on the abbot to tell him the good news.

Oddly enough, the abbot was not as pleased as he might have been. Glastonbury Abbey was already one of the richest in England; it didn't need any more fame to attract pilgrims. And "between two pyramids" might mean anything.

Then the situation changed dramatically. On May 25, 1184, the abbey caught fire and was left in ruins. The encouraging thing about it was that the image of Our Lady of Glastonbury had survived undamaged, which suggested that God still had great things in store for the abbey. Henry II produced funds to start rebuilding; many nobles contributed. And in 1191 one of the monks died after expressing a wish to be buried on the grounds, between two crosses. These stood on two marble pillars that tapered toward the top and might have been described as tall pyramids. For some reason—perhaps because they remembered the words of the Welsh bard—the monks went on digging below six feet and at seven feet encountered a stone slab. They prized it up. On its underside was a leaden cross, with a Latin inscription that read: *Hic jacet sepultus inclytus Rex Artorius in insula*

Avalonia ("Here lies buried the renowned King Arthur in the Isle of Avalon").

They went on digging—it probably took days to make a hole sixteen feet deep and wide enough to allow several diggers to operate. But at sixteen feet, just as the old bard had foretold, the mattocks struck wood. An enormous coffin, hollowed out of oak, was unearthed. Inside, they found the huge skeleton of a man, whose skull had been smashed by heavy blows. A monk saw a lock of yellow hair and leaned over to grab it. It dissolved in his fingers, and the monk fell into the coffin. Later, they identified fragments of a smaller skeleton and realized that the hair was that of Arthur's wife, Guinevere. One chronicler, Giraldus Cambrensis (Gerald of Wales), who actually saw the bones and the cross in the following year, says the inscription on the cross also mentioned "Queen Wenneveria" (Guinevere).

From that moment on, the abbey became the most popular tourist site in England, if not in Europe. The abbey was soon rebuilt on a magnificent scale.

Scholars have accused the monks of Glastonbury of inventing the whole story, yet this seems unlikely. Giraldus Cambrensis seems to have been an honest man—he was one of the few to denounce Geoffrey of Monmouth's *History* as a pack of lies—and he specifically claims to have seen both skeletons and the leaden cross. This cross was still around for many centuries, and in 1607 an antiquarian named William Camden published a picture of it. His text spells Arthur *Arturius*, an ancient form that was in use in the time of King Arthur but had not been used since. (Even the Easter Annals spell his name *Arthur.*)

Moreover, a reexcavation of the site in 1963 by C. A. Radford showed that the monks were telling the truth about digging down sixteen feet. Besides, as the Arthurian scholar Geoffrey Ashe has pointed out, Glastonbury is also supposed to be the burial site of Joseph of Arimathea, the man who gave Jesus a decent burial; if the monks faked the grave of Arthur, why did they not go on and fake Saint Joseph's too?

So, on the whole, there can be no doubt that King Arthur—or rather, General Arturius—really existed and that he deserved his reputation as a great hero. Dozens of questions still remain, but some of these are slowly being answered. For example, many scholars believe that we now know the location of King Arthur's court at Camelot. In 1542 a writer named John Leland wrote that a fortified hill in South Cadbury, Somerset, was, in fact, "Camallate, sometime a famous town or castle . . . Arthur much resorted to Camallate." In 1966 excavations were begun at Cadbury Castle (not a castle in the medieval sense, but a fortified hill). On top of Roman remains were found the foundations of impressive buildings that were clearly occupied, in Arthur's period, by a chieftain of considerable power and authority.

Even Geoffrey of Monmouth's absurd story about Tintagel Castle begins to look as if it has some foundation. The present Tintagel Castle was built around 1140, at the time of Geoffrey's *History*. Historians have pointed out that in the time of King Arthur there was only a Celtic monastery on the site. In 1924 the "visionary" Rudolf Steiner visited Tintagel and devoted a lecture to it, identifying various places as the Hall of the Round Table, the sleeping place of the knights, and so on. It all sounded like pure fantasy.

But in the dry summer of 1983 a fire on the island destroyed the grass, and wind and rain went on to reveal the foundations of more than a hundred small rectangular buildings and of a hall more than eighty feet long. Down below, at the foot of the cliff, is a small natural harbor, and pottery discovered on the island indicated that large quantities of wine and oil were once imported. (There is more imported pottery on the site than on all the other British and Irish sites put together.) A stone "footprint" on the opposite side of the island looks out over old Celtic Christian burial mounds; such a "footprint" was often made by a chieftain who planted his foot and surveyed his kingdom. (In this case, he would have looked across to the graves of his ancestors.) All this sounds as if Tintagel were once the fortress of a considerable chieftain, not simply a monastery. The objection that Tintagel was essentially uninhabited in the time of Arthur cannot be sustained.

So the evidence for the real historical existence of King Arthur is very strong indeed. In a book entitled *Arthur: Roman Britain's*

Last Champion, Beram Saklatvala has even argued that there is evidence for the existence of the sword Excalibur and of the Holy Grail. The Latin word for stone is *saxo*, which is close to "Saxon." If some early chronicle mentioned Arthur taking a sword from a Saxon—some warrior he had killed—then it could well have been the origin of the legend of the sword in the stone. Geoffrey of Monmouth calls Arthur's sword *Caliburn*; and *Caliburn* is a combination of two words for "river"—the Celtic *cale* and the Saxon *burn*. Swords need, of course, to be tempered in cold water, and as the Anglo-Saxon word *cale* means "cold," *caliburn* could be translated as "the cold stream." So Arthur's sword could have been named after the stream it was tempered in, the Cale, near Sturminster, in Dorset.

As to the Grail—the cup that Jesus was supposed to have used at the Last Supper and that Joseph of Arimathea is said to have brought to Glastonbury—this was probably a much larger vessel, too large for a drinking cup, that was used for ritual purposes. In 1959 a large marble urn was found during excavations of a Roman palace in North Africa; the palace dated from the same period as did Arthur. The urn had a cross carved on it, and the lid had rivet holes in the shape of a cross, indicating that it had once had a metal cross on it. The urn probably contained the bones of a saint and was almost certainly used for administering oaths, as we now swear on the Bible. A libation hole suggests that it was used in some special ritual. Arthur would fairly certainly have had a similar urn in his own chapel for the administering of oaths. If this sacred vessel had been captured during one of Arthur's many wars, Saklatvala suggests, then the quest for the Grail could well have been based on fact.

But what of the magician Merlin? Surely *he* was an invention of Geoffrey of Monmouth? In fact, Geoffrey followed up his successful *History* with a *Life of Merlin*, a poem written for a smaller audience. If Geoffrey had invented Merlin, we would expect the poet more or less to repeat the story as told in the *History*—or at least, not to contradict it. Merlin was obviously a great deal older than Arthur, for he was a boy when King Vortigern was alive—and the monk Gildas tells us that Vortigern made the fatal mistake of inviting the Saxons into England in A.D. 443. Yet in the Merlin poem, Geoffrey has Merlin fighting with a king named Rodarcus against a Scottish king named Guennolous—and these real historical characters lived a century later, *after* the death of Arthur. Geoffrey is aware of this and explains it by saying that Merlin lived to a phenomenally old age—more than a century. But it looks as if Geoffrey has found material about Merlin that obliges him to try to explain why his original dates were wrong.

The explanation that is accepted by most scholars is that Merlin was based on a Welsh bard named Myrddin, who was alive after A.D. 573. The Welsh language only came into existence after the death of Arthur, so Myrddin could not have been older than Arthur. This identification of Merlin with Myrddin is accepted by Robert Graves in his mythological study *The White Goddess* (1948) and by Nicolai Tolstoy in *The Quest for Merlin* (1985). But it is obviously a somewhat disappointing theory, for if it is correct, Merlin was not even called Merlin. (The usual view is that Geoffrey of Monmouth changed Myrddin to Merlin because *merde* in French means "shit," and a magician named Myrddin would have invited ridicule in an age when England was ruled by the French.) Moreover, Myrddin cannot have known Arthur, for even if their lives overlapped, he would only have been a child at the time of Arthur's death. Geoffrey Ashe agrees that Merlin is Myrddin and that Geoffrey of Monmouth made him Arthur's senior merely for the sake of a good story.

The American professor Norma Lorre Goodrich rejects this notion in her book *Merlin* (1988) and argues convincingly that Merlin *was* a real person who was about thirty years older than Arthur, although she agrees that some of the legends of Myrddin have been incorporated into the Merlin story. She suggests that Arthur's Merlin was born in Wales and buried in Scotland. In fact, she ends by suggesting that "Merlin" was a title rather than a name (a merlin is a type of hawk) and that the original Merlin was a bishop named Dubricius, who crowned Arthur. Myrddin, on the other hand, was a "Wild Man of the Woods," a poet who went mad, lived in the wilderness, and achieved certain magical powers. *This* Merlin is, in fact, the one Geoffrey of Monmouth learned about after writing his *History*. His *Life of Merlin* is, indeed, about a Welsh leader and prophet who went mad after fighting in a battle against a Scottish king and who became a wanderer in the wilderness, delivering a great many prophecies. The Merlin of the *History* is also, we may recall, a prophet: in fact, Geoffrey published a book of Merlin's prophecies first, then incorporated them into the *History*. It sounds as if he learned about the Welsh prophet Myrddin after writing the *History* and decided that Myrddin and Merlin must be the same person. Nicolai Tolstoy agrees with this theory and devotes much of his *Quest for Merlin* to an analysis of various poems and legends that tell of the "Wild Man of the Woods."

It would seem, then, that we have two contesting theories: that there were two Merlins, a view first suggested by Giraldus Cambrensis; and that there was only one Merlin, who was really called Myrddin and who was a Welsh bard and soothsayer. Yet Goodrich and Tolstoy both argue their theories so brilliantly that it seems a pity to have to choose one or the other. Goodrich is most convincing on the subject of the two Merlins and in her argument that the original Merlin *was* the counselor of King Arthur. But Tolstoy has some profoundly important things to say about Merlin the Wizard.

To understand what he is suggesting, we have to forget our modern images of wizards and magicians, derived from Shakespeare's Prospero, Tolkien's Gandalf, and T. H. White's amiable and bumbling Merlin. These are recent inventions. In the age of Arthur a magician would have been a combination of a priest and a witch doctor, a *shaman*.

For an account of a magician in action, it is necessary to turn to *A Pattern of Islands*, Arthur Grimble's account of his years as Land Commissioner in the Gilbert Islands in the South Pacific. Told that he ought to eat porpoise flesh, Grimble inquired how he could obtain some. He was told that some islanders farther up the coast were the hereditary porpoise-callers of the island and that his informant's cousin could also call them. Grimble was invited to the village, where a feast was laid out. The fat and friendly porpoise-caller retired into his hut, and for several hours there was silence. Then the man rushed out and fell on his face, crying, "They come, they come!" The villagers all rushed into the water and stood breast-deep, and to Grimble's amazement, hundreds of porpoises began to swim in to the shore. It seemed that they were in a trance. The "hypnotized" porpoises were then gently lifted into boats, taken ashore, and slaughtered.

It is not difficult to hypnotize animals, and it has been argued elsewhere in this book (see chapter 17) that hypnosis may involve a kind of telepathy. But "hypnosis" of porpoises from a distance sounds absurd.

Absurd or not, it seems fairly clear that this *is* a power possessed by many primitive witch doctors and shamans. The study of modern primitives leaves no doubt that Stone Age cave drawings of "magicians" dressed in animal skins are not a form of Palaeolithic art but are dipictions of rituals that were designed to attract animals into the vicinity of the hunters, exactly as Grimble's shaman summoned porpoises. A remarkable book, *Wizard of the Upper Amazon* by F. Bruce Lamb, describes the experiences of a Peruvian named Manuel Cordova, who was kidnapped by Amahuaca Indians and spent his life among them. Lamb makes it clear that the primitive hunters of the twentieth century use exactly the same techniques as their Stone Age counterparts. Cordova describes how the hunters kill the sow who leads a herd of pigs, then bury the head with ritual chants, to ensure that the herd will always return that way. And in one remarkable sequence he describes how the Indians drink a "vision extract" called *hini xuma*, and how they then shared visions of snakes, birds, and animals; a black leopard appears among them at the height of the ceremony but does no one any harm.

In another firsthand narrative of years spent among the natives of Papua, New Guinea, *Mitsinari* (1954), Father André Dupreyat gives an account of a sorcerer named Isidoro who can turn himself into a cassowary (a kind of ostrich) and is consequently able to make a five-hour journey over a mountain in two hours. He also describes his own clash with sorcerers who place him under a "snake curse," after which snakes attack him on several occasions. (Snakes will normally do their best to escape from the vicinity of human beings.)*

---

*These and many similar cases are discussed in my 1981 book *Poltergeist*, in the chapter entitled "The Black Magic Connection."

So it is a mistake to think of a magician as a Walt Disney cartoon character wearing a tall conical hat with stars painted on it. Real sorcerers are closely related to modern "spirit mediums"; they assert that their power comes from spirits. Modern "magicians"—such as the notorious Aleister Crowley—believe that power can be obtained over spirits by the use of certain precise rituals, which must be performed with punctilious accuracy.

The traditional role of tribal witch doctors and shamans is as intermediaries between human beings and the spirit world, and their chief function is to ensure good hunting or good harvests. Celtic druids belonged to this tradition. Druidism was a form of nature worship; it came to Britain around 600 B.C. with the Celts, but many older forms of nature religion had existed long before that: Stonehenge, for example, was a temple for such worship and is precisely aligned to the stars.

Nicolai Tolstoy is convinced that Merlin was "the last of the druids." Druidism was driven into Wales with the Celts and survived there long after Christianity had stamped it out in the rest of the British Isles. Tolstoy points out that the Myrddin stories—particularly those of bards like Taliesin—are full of clues that link the magician with druidism. He invokes sacred apple trees (the druids worshiped in sacred groves) and has as familiars a pig and a wolf. He takes on many of the characteristics of the horned god of pagan mythology. Tolstoy places the "wood of Calidon," to which Merlin fled after going mad, in Scotland, near Hart Fell, where the rivers Annan and Clyde both have their source. And, according to Tolstoy, Merlin fulfilled his own prophecy that he would meet a "threefold death," clubbed, speared, and drowned. After being beaten for days by shepherds, he slipped into the river Tweed and was impaled on a stake before he drowned.

Professor Goodrich prefers the traditional story, in which Merlin is murdered by a maiden named Ninian or Nimue, the Lady of the Lake (also called Vivian), of whom he becomes enamored and to whom he offers to teach magic. She refuses to become his mistress and finally uses one of his own spells to bind him and entomb him in a cave under an enormous rock. Another commentator has argued that the maiden Nimue is actually the Christian Saint Nimue and that the story of her final triumph over

Merlin is really the triumph of Christianity over paganism.

The books by Nicolai Tolstoy and Norma Lorre Goodrich are rich and complex detective stories that will leave most readers in a state of "enlightened confusion." The final picture that emerges is of a real King Arthur, who was one of the greatest generals of the Dark Ages, and of a real Merlin, a shaman and druid, who was Arthur's counselor and adviser. Both were men of such remarkable stature that, even within a few decades of their deaths, they became the subject of endless legends. The legends have blurred the reality to such an extent that it is now virtually impossible to discern the outline of the real men who lived sometime between A.D. 450 and 550. But the outcome of all the detective work is at least a certainty that they actually existed.

2

The Baader-Meinhof Gang:
Suicide or Murder?

On the afternoon of Thursday, October 13, 1977, four Palestinians seized control of Lufthansa Flight LH181 as it flew from Majorca to Frankfurt. Two men and two women held the passengers and crew at gunpoint and forced the pilot to change course for Rome's Leonardo da Vinci Airport. After wiring the aircraft with explosive charges, they issued their demands in the name of the Struggle Against World Imperialism Organization.

Few informed sources were surprised when the Palestinian hijackers' main demand turned out to be the release of "all German political prisoners"; it was an open secret that Palestinian paramilitary organizations had close links with the left-wing revolutionary terrorists in West Germany. The demand was later reduced to the release of eleven high-ranking members of the Red Army Faction (RAF; generally referred to by the nickname Baader-Meinhof) then in custody in the GDR.

Over the next three days the hijacked jet was flown on to Cyprus and then Dubai to keep the security forces from launching an attack. Then, on Friday, October 16, only hours before the ransom deadline expired, it was flown to Aden in Yemen.

Shortly after landing, the pilot, Jürgen Schumann, asked permission to inspect the front landing gear, which he thought had been damaged by the last touchdown. He checked the gear, found it to be still serviceable, and started to walk back, but on the way he made the mistake of speaking to a group of airport security men. As he reentered the aircraft he was made to kneel down and was "executed" in front of the other hostages with a shot through the back of the head. Schumann's body was dumped onto the runway, and the copilot was forced to fly them to Mogadishu Airport in Somalia.

As the deadline the terrorists had set for the destruction of the jet approached, the West German government played for time. They offered to release the eleven prisoners and fly them to Mogadishu to join the Palestinians; they would then be given a substantial sum of money and a jet to fly them wherever they chose. The leader of the hijackers, who called himself Martyr Mahmoud, agreed to extend the deadline to facilitate the arrangements but added, "There must be no tricks. This will not be another Entebbe."

By "Entebbe" he was referring to a similar hijacking that had taken place a year earlier. An Air France jet had been seized on a flight from Tel Aviv to Paris and had been flown to Entebbe Airport in Uganda. The hijackers, five Arabs and two Germans, had negotiated with the president of Uganda, Idi Amin, demanding the release of fifty-three pro-Palestinian terrorists held in Israel and around the world; these had included two members of the Baader-Meinhof gang and four from the affiliated Second June Movement, imprisoned in West Germany.

Two days later three army transport planes had landed unannounced at Entebbe; several squads of Israeli commandos had poured out onto the runway and gone on to storm both the hijacked jet and the airport's main building. During the hour's fighting that ensued, twenty Ugandan soldiers, one Israeli commando, three hostages, and all seven hijackers had been killed. The remaining hostages had been rescued.

Martyr Mahmoud's misgivings in the case of the Mogadishu hijacking proved justified. At two o'clock on the morning of Tuesday, October 18, the newly formed West German antiterrorist squad, the GSG-9, stormed the hijacked airliner. Lighting an oil drum under the front of the aircraft to distract the terrorists, they forced the rear emergency exits and tossed in stun grenades. In the resulting confusion they engaged the hijackers in gunfire over the heads of the crouching passengers. Within minutes three of the terrorists were dead, including the leader, and the fourth was badly wounded. This time only one of the ninety hostages was hurt in the cross fire, and the GSG-9 squad suffered no casualties.

The Mogadishu hijack was the third attempt within a year to force the German authorities to free members of the Baader-Meinhof gang. Entebbe had been the first. The second had occurred five weeks before the Mogadishu incident. On September 5, 1977, a sixty-one-year-old German industrialist, Dr. Hans-Martin Schleyer, had been kidnapped in Cologne by the RAF; his driver was killed by submachine gun fire; so were three armed guards who were driving immediately behind him. His ransom demand included the same eleven RAF members later demanded by the Mogadishu hijackers. (In fact, both ransom notes proved to have been written on the same typewriter.)

The Mogadishu hijack ended at 2:15 on the morning of Tuesday, October 18, 1977. Shortly after 7:30 the same morning, guards at Stammheim Prison in Stuttgart, West Germany, began to take breakfast around to the prisoners in the seventh-floor cells. Baader-Meinhof terrorist Jan-Carl Raspe, who was serving a life sentence for the murder of four American soldiers in a bombing incident, was found propped up in bed with a bullet wound in his head. He was still alive but died a few hours later. Three cells away, Andreas Baader, the leader of the gang, was found dead with a gun lying beside him. Gudrun Ensslin, Baader's mistress, was found hanging from the barred window of her cell. The fourth RAF terrorist, Irmgard Moller, was found lying in bed with four stab wounds in her chest. She underwent emergency surgery and survived.

That evening the West German minister of justice, Traugott Bender, announced that the three RAF leaders were dead and that a fourth was seriously ill. They had apparently entered into a suicide pact when the news from Mogadishu had made it plain that they had no immediate hope of release. And although Bender insisted that there was no suspicion of foul play, most of the world press took the view that the terrorists had been "executed" to circumvent further hijackings or kidnappings. In fact, Schleyer was murdered by his kidnappers a few hours later—they shot him three times in the head and cut his throat—and his body was found in a car trunk in Mulhouse, France, the next day.

The Baader-Meinhof story, which ended so abruptly that October morning in 1977, began in the late sixties, with the death of a student named Benno Ohnesorg, who was shot by a West Berlin policeman in a protest demonstration against the visit of the shah of Iran. This event soured the whole tone of political debate in Germany. The sixties had been marked by left-wing protest—against the atom bomb, against the Vietnam War, against capitalism in general—but it had remained basically peaceful.

Ohnesorg's killer, Detective Sergeant Kurras, was tried on a manslaughter charge seven months later but was acquitted on a plea that the heat of events at the protest had affected his judgment. The radical Left was incensed by the verdict, which confirmed their view that Germany was still a fascist state. On the day after the shooting, Gudrun Ensslin, a tall, attractive blond dressed in the habitual black sweater and jeans of the revolutionary Left, addressed a meeting of the Socialist German Students Union (SDS) in Berlin. Shrilly emotional to the point of tears, she insisted that the "fascist state" was out to kill them all. It was stupid to aim for a peaceful resolution, she told them; in order to survive they would have to fight violence with violence: "It's the generation of Auschwitz—you can't argue with them!"

Ensslin, born in 1940, was the daughter of an Evangelical pastor who was also a Communist. She had studied philosophy at Tübingen, then moved to Berlin with the left-wing writer Bernward Vesper, with whom she had a son.

In 1967, not long after her impassioned address to the German students, Ensslin met a good-looking, dark-eyed young man named Andreas Baader at a demonstration. At the time Baader was living with—and off—a female action painter named Elly Michell, who bore him a daughter. But this did not prevent him from spending the night with Gudrun Ensslin, who had recently acted in a porno movie called *Das Abonnement* (Subscription).

Baader was entirely without political convictions; he was more interested in fast cars and women. But his own lack of money and success made him an easy convert to the notion that society was rotten and could be improved only by bloody revolution. He deserted his action painter, Ensslin deserted her writer-lover, and together they moved to Frankfurt, where the leftist student movement operated on a more sophisticated level than its Berlin counterpart. Ensslin tended to do the talking at the meetings while Baader, still out of his depth, maintained a tough but silent image. Ensslin was very much the intellectually dominant partner and referred to Baader as her "baby."

It was soon decided, however, that action must replace words. On April 2, 1968, Baader and Ensslin entered the Schneider department store just before closing time. They exited shortly, leaving behind their shopping bags. At midnight fire broke out on three floors but was soon put out by the fire brigade. The following evening Baader and Ensslin were arrested at the apartment of a friend—the police spoke of a "concrete denunciation"—and identified by employees at the department store. Two other militants—Thorwald Proll and Horst Sohnlein—who at the same time had planted a bomb that failed to go off in another department store were also arrested. All four were sentenced to three years' imprisonment for arson. At the trial Ensslin declared, "We don't care about burned mattresses. We are worried about burned children in Vietnam."

Fourteen months later all four were released pending the outcome of an appeal. They now discovered that they had become heroes within extreme-Left circles. When the time came to hear the appeal-court verdict, only Sohnlein turned up; the others—Baader, Ensslin, and Proll—had fled to Switzerland. They returned secretly in 1970, and in April of that year Baader was arrested as he was on his way to dig up a cache of arms hidden in a cemetery. This time he was sent to Tegel Prison in West Berlin.

There he was visited by a well-known left-wing journalist named Ulrike Meinhof, who had covered the arson trial and interviewed Ensslin and Baader at the time. In a subsequent article she had stated: "It is better to burn a department store than to own one."

At thirty-six—nine years Baader's senior—the divorced Ulrike was something of a celebrity; she had written plays for radio and television, was a popular talk-show guest, and was the mother of twin daughters. In recent years, while lecturing part-time at Berlin's Free University, she had become increasingly involved in extreme-Left student groups. Her apartment was frequently used for their meetings, and these were often attended by associates of Baader and Ensslin. Among these was Horst Mahler, Baader's defense lawyer and the founder of the RAF. (Baader had been in Mahler's car when arrested.) It was Mahler, together with the still-fugitive Ensslin, who convinced Meinhof to help in a plan to free Baader.

The authorities had given Baader permission to write a book on maladjusted juveniles and to conduct his research at the German Institute for Social Questions in the West Berlin suburb of Dahlem—a concession that hardly seems to support Ensslin's assertion that they were confronting a ruthless fascist state.

Another member of the rescue group, Peter Homann, later claimed that no political motive was behind the plan. Gudrun Ensslin desperately wanted her "baby" back, and the others wanted to help her, that was all. It was only later, when they were all on the run, that the idea of becoming full-time revolutionary terrorists seems to have occurred to them, partly through the logic of necessity.

On May 14, 1970, Ulrike Meinhof walked into the German Institute for Social Questions. The librarian who opened the door told her it was closed that morning. Meinhof replied that she already knew this; she had been given permission to work with Andreas Baader on his book. Since she was a well-known journalist, the librarian took her word for it. Baader was brought in and his handcuffs removed. Soon the doorbell rang again, and two young women entered, explaining that they needed to do some research. Moments later a masked man rushed into the room waving a gun; the two women produced guns from their bags, and in the gunfire that followed—mostly aimed at the floor—Baader and Meinhof leapt from a window and into an Alfa Romeo, driven by Thorwald Proll's sister, Astrid. A librarian had been seriously wounded in the gunfire.

Mahler now arranged for the group—which included Baader, Meinhof, Ensslin, and himself—to escape from Germany to the

Middle East, where they were trained in terrorist tactics by the Popular Front for the Liberation of Palestine (PFLP). It was at this point that they decided to call their movement the Red Army Faction, after the Japanese Red Army terrorist group.

Back in Germany, Mahler organized bank raids to finance the movement. Mahler himself was arrested in October 1970. In May 1972 the RAF planted bombs at the headquarters of the U.S. Fifth Army Corps in Frankfurt, killing a colonel and injuring thirteen others. Damage was estimated at more than a million dollars. An anonymous phone call stated that the bombing was in retaliation for Vietnam. The following day suitcases containing time bombs exploded in the police station in Augsburg, Bavaria, injuring five policemen. Three days later the wife of a judge was injured by a car bomb in Karlsruhe. On May 19 two time bombs exploded in the offices of the right-wing publishing house of Springer in Hamburg. And on May 25, 1972, bomb explosions at the American army base in Heidelberg killed three and injured five.

Soon after the Heidelberg bombing, the Frankfurt police received a tip-off that led them to the garage of an apartment building in the north of the city. Bomb-making equipment was seized and bombs defused. And when Andreas Baader reached the garage in the early hours of June 1, 1972, driving a lilac Porsche, he was met by armed police. In the car with him were Jan-Carl Raspe and another terrorist, Holger Meins. Raspe opened fire and tried to escape but was overpowered. Baader and Meins shut themselves in the garage but were overcome by tear-gas grenades. Baader was shot in the thigh, and Meins emerged in his underpants, with his hands held high.

Six days later Gudrun Ensslin was arrested in a Hamburg boutique—an assistant had noticed a gun in her pocket and called the police.

Ulrike Meinhof was arrested in Hanover a week later, as a result of a tip-off from a left-wing teacher who felt that the terrorists were harming the leftist cause. On June 25 a Briton named Ian MacLeod was shot and killed as police tried to arrest him in Stuttgart; he is believed to have been negotiating an arms deal for the gang.

The gang members were placed in Stuttgart's top-security

Stammheim Jail; the trial would be delayed for another three years, until an escape-proof top-security courtroom could be built. Meanwhile, evidence that the terrorist threat was as menacing as ever was provided at the Munich Olympics, when Arab terrorists from the Black September movement took nine Israeli athletes hostage and shot two more; the nine hostages died in a gun battle at the military airport, together with five terrorists. The terrorists' demands had included the release of the Baader-Meinhof gang.

Terrorist outrages continued. In June 1974 an extremist named Ulrich Schmucker was executed by fellow gang members, accused of betraying a plot to blow up the Turkish embassy in Bonn in reprisal for the execution of three Turkish terrorists. And after the death by hunger strike of Holger Meins, on November 9, 1974, a judge named Gunter von Drenckmann was shot down by flower-bearing terrorists when he answered the door on his birthday.

Judges and leading industrialists were now forced to live in a state of siege. On February 27, 1975, terrorists seized Peter Lorenz, leader of the Christian Democratic Party, as he was being driven to his West Berlin office. The release of six terrorists was demanded in exchange for his life; these included Horst Mahler but not, oddly enough, Baader or Meinhof. The West German government caved in; five terrorists were released and flown out of Germany; perhaps sick of being on the run, Horst Mahler declined to accompany them. Lorenz was freed unharmed.

The success of the escapade suggested that the next kidnapping would involve a demand for the release of the Baader-Meinhof gang. In fact, on April 24, 1975, six terrorists who called themselves the "Holger Meins commando" seized the West German embassy in Stockholm and threatened a massacre of hostages unless the Baader-Meinhof gang was released and half a million dollars paid in ransom. To emphasize their seriousness they shot to death the military attaché, Baron von Mirbach. The Bonn government refused to meet the terrorists' demands but offered them safe passage out of the country in exchange for releasing the hostages. Before further negotiations could take place, there was a tremendous explosion on the top floor of the embassy—explosives placed in a refrigerator had been set off accidentally. One terrorist was killed; the hostages made their way out of the building through the smoke. Five terrorists were caught as they tried to escape through a window. One of them died from the aftereffects of the explosion; the others were imprisoned in Germany.

Finally, on May 21, 1975, the Baader-Meinhof trial began in a building that was virtually a fortress. Objections and harangues from the four defendants—Baader, Meinhof, Ensslin, and Raspe—threatened to reduce it to a farce. But when, almost a year later, on May 4, 1976, Gudrun Ensslin claimed responsibility for three of the four bombings, it was all virtually over.

Five days later, on May 9, Ulrike Meinhof was found hanging from her cell window bars, her neck encircled by a noose made from her sheets. An autopsy led to a verdict of suicide. But a second autopsy, carried out at her family's behest, threw doubt on the verdict. Traces of semen were alleged to have been found on her underwear. Bruises on the inside of her thighs also suggested rape. A saliva track ran from her breast to her navel, suggesting that she had been unclothed at the time of her death and had been dressed later. A group of medical experts later agreed that throttling during rape could not be ruled out.

The trial dragged on until April 1977, when the three remaining defendants each were given life plus fifteen years' imprisonment. (Mahler had been sentenced to fourteen years for bank robbery in 1972.)

Six months later, in October 1977, the Lufthansa airliner was hijacked at Palma, Majorca, and the last act of the drama began; it ended with the "suicides" of Baader, Ensslin, and Raspe on October 18. The German Left was quick to accuse the government of murder, and even the Right had to concede that it was highly likely—in fact, that it was the only logical solution to the problem of further attempts to free the gang.

It looked as if one person now held the solution to the mystery: Irmgard Moller. If the others had been murdered, then clearly the killers had made a serious mistake in leaving her alive. It seemed that she owed her life to the shortness of the knife blade that had stabbed her but that had failed to reach her heart. But when Moller was able to speak, her testimony was disappointing. She brought criminal charges of murder against an "unknown person," and in a hearing in January 1978, denied that she had attempted suicide or that the four had been able to communicate with one another during the Mogadishu hijacking. But she was unable to describe how she came to be found unconscious—she could only recall hearing "two soft popping noises" and a voice saying, "Baader and Ensslin are dead already." Her ninety-minute appearance ended when she was dragged out of court as she tried to confer with her lawyers. In 1979 she was again sentenced to life imprisonment.

Ingrid Schubert, one of the women who had helped free Baader in 1970, and who had been jailed for her part in bank robberies, was found hanging in her cell on November 5, 1977, three weeks after the deaths of Baader, Ensslin, and Raspe.

Was the Baader-Meinhof gang "executed" by its captors? The Bonn government denied it. There had, they insisted, been a suicide pact, whose aim was to fuel the revolutionary fervor of the comrades outside. (Even during the trial there had been another murder—of chief federal prosecutor Siegfried Bruback, on April 7, 1977, and soon after the trial, on July 30, 1977, Jürgen Ponto was murdered by his own goddaughter, Susanne Albrecht.) A portable transistor radio *had* been discovered in the cell of Raspe, and the wires left in the walls of the gang members' cells could have been used as a primitive signaling device. Explosives found in the cells were alleged to have been smuggled in to the gang members at the same time as the pistols that had killed Baader and Raspe. The aim, said the official statement, had been to make suicide look like murder. Baader even wrote a letter to a Stuttgart court insisting that he would never commit suicide—although there was no particular need for this admission. Similarly, Ensslin had sent for two clergymen and indicated that she thought she might be murdered. All this, like Moller's accusation, could certainly be interpreted as evidence of a plot to embarrass the authorities with a final act of desperation and defiance.

The evidence against this view is sparse yet highly disturbing: the semen stains on Ulrike Meinhof's underwear; and the stab wounds—made with a blunt butter knife—in Irmgard Moller's chest. One expert stated that there would be an overwhelming inhibition against the self-infliction of such wounds.

The irony of the Baader-Meinhof story is that nearly all the protagonists came from comfortable middle-class backgrounds and had little firsthand experience of poverty or injustice. If they had been living under Hitler or Stalin, it would be easier to sympathize with the violence of their reactions. But in the democratic regime of West Germany, the argument that they were fighting "the generation of Auschwitz" sounds somehow exaggerated. One student leader commented about Gudrun Ensslin's "Auschwitz" speech: "She was too hysterical." Andreas Baader, who had always been cynically nonpolitical, allowed Ensslin's hysteria to draw him into the fire-bombing. From then on, like some character in Sophocles or Shakespeare, he was drawn into a whirlpool of events over which he had no control and that made him the central figure in a grotesque tragedy that involved the whole country. The verdict of history on the Baader-Meinhof orgy of terrorism will probably be: It was all so unnecessary.

3

The Basa Murder:
The Voice from the Grave

There have been many folktales in which the dead have returned to give evidence against their murderers; but there is only one example that has been authenticated beyond all shadow of a doubt. It is the case of a Filippino physical therapist named Teresita Basa, who was stabbed to death in Chicago on February 21, 1977.

Toward 8:30 on the evening of that day, the Chicago fire department was called to put out a blaze in a high-rise apartment building on the North Side. Two fire fighters crawled into Apartment 15B through black smoke and saw that the fire was in the bedroom. A mattress lying at the foot of the bed was blazing. Within minutes the firemen had put the blaze out and opened the windows to let out the smoke. When they lifted the waterlogged mattress, they found the naked body of a woman, with her legs spread apart and a knife sticking out of her chest.

Forty-eight-year-old Teresita Basa had been born in the city of Damaguete, in the Philippines, the daughter of a judge. She had become a physical therapist specializing in respiratory problems—perhaps because her father had died of a respiratory illness—and was working at Edgewater Hospital in Chicago at the time of her death.

Forensic examination postulated that Teresita had answered the door to someone she knew—she had been talking to a friend on the telephone when the doorbell rang. The intruder had encircled her neck from behind with his arm and choked her until she lost consciousness. He then had taken money from her handbag and ransacked the apartment. After that he had stripped off all her clothes, taken a butcher knife from the kitchen drawer, and driven it virtually through her body. Then he had set the mattress on fire with a piece of burning paper, dumped it on top of her, and hurried out of the apartment. The fire alarm had sounded before he had gone more than a few blocks.

Forensic investigation also revealed that there had been no sexual assault. Teresita Basa had died a virgin.

Although Remy (short for Remibias) Chua, another Filippino, had worked with Teresita Basa in the respiratory therapy department of Edgewater Hospital, the two had been only slightly acquainted. Two weeks after the murder, during the course of a conversation, Chua remarked, only half seriously, "If there is no solution to her murder, she can come to me in a dream." She then went for a brief nap in the hospital locker room—it was two o'clock in the morning. As she was dozing on a chair, her feet propped on another, something made her open her eyes. She had to suppress a scream as she saw Teresita Basa—looking as solid as a living person—standing in front of her. She lost no time in running out of the room.

During the course of the next few weeks, two of Mrs. Chua's fellow employees jokingly remarked that she looked—and behaved—like Teresita Basa. Her husband, Dr. José Chua, also noticed that his wife seemed to have undergone a personality change. Normally sunny and good-natured, she had become oddly peremptory and moody. Teresita Basa had also been prone to moods.

In late July, five months after the murder, Remy Chua was working with a hospital orderly named Allan Showery when she found herself experiencing an inexplicable panic. Showery was a sinewy but powerfully built black man with an open and confident manner. When Showery was standing behind Mrs. Chua, she caught a movement out of the corner of her eye—just as Teresita

Basa may have when her killer stepped up behind her to lock his forearm round her neck—and, inexplicably, her heart began to pound violently. She decided that she was suffering from nervous problems and asked for time off from work.

That night her husband heard her talking in her sleep—she was repeating, "Al—Al—Al . . ." She told him later that she had dreamed of being in a smoke-filled room. The next day she felt so ill that she asked her parents to come over. After taking a strong sedative, she climbed into bed. But after a few hours' sleep she began to babble in Spanish—a language Remy Chua did not speak. Her husband knelt beside the bed and asked, "How are you?" His wife replied, "I am Teresita Basa." When José Chua asked what she wanted, the voice replied, "I want help . . . Nothing has been done about the man who killed me." A few minutes later "Teresita" disappeared and Remy Chua was herself again.

Two days later Remy Chua felt a pain in her chest, followed by a heavy sensation, "as if someone was stepping into her body." She told her mother (who was still with them), "Terrie is here again."

When her husband returned he found his wife in bed. The voice of Teresita Basa issued from her mouth, asking accusingly, "Did you talk to the police?" José Chua acknowledged that he hadn't, because he needed proof. "Allan killed me" insisted the voice. "I let Al into the apartment and he killed me."

The strain of Remy Chua's "possession" was beginning to adversely affect the whole family (the Chuas had four children). José Chua finally went to his boss at Franklin Park Hospital, Dr. Winograd, and told him the whole story; Dr. Winograd took the "possession" seriously but believed that the police would dismiss it as an absurdity. He advised Dr. Chua to write them an anonymous letter.

The "possessing entity" had other ideas. The next time Remy Chua went into a trancelike state, the voice demanded to know why José Chua had not done as she asked. He explained that he had no proof. "Dr. Chua," said the voice, "the man Allan Showery stole my jewelry and gave it to his girlfriend. They live together."

"But how could it be identified?"

"My cousins, Ron Somera and Ken Basa, could identify it. So could my friends, Richard Pessoti and Ray King." She went on to give Dr. Chua Ron Somera's telephone number. After that she told him, "Al came to fix my television and he killed me and burned me. Tell the police."

Dr. Chua finally decided to do as she asked; he telephoned the Evanston police headquarters. On August 8, 1977, Investigator Joseph Stachula was assigned to interview the Chuas. Their story left him stunned, yet he had an intuitive certainty that they were not cranks. All the same, he could see no obvious way to make use of what they had told him. He could hardly walk up to Allan Showery and arrest him on the grounds that his victim had come back from the dead to accuse him.

A check on Showery revealed that he might well be the killer. He had a long criminal record that included two rapes, each of which had taken place in the victim's apartment. Moreover, he had lived only four blocks from Teresita Basa.

Showery was brought to the police station, and was asked if it were true that he had agreed to repair Teresita Basa's television on the evening of her murder. He acknowledged that it was but insisted that he had gone to a local bar for a drink and simply forgotten. Asked if he had ever been in the Basa apartment, he denied it. Then, when asked for fingerprint samples to compare with some found in the apartment, he changed his mind and acknowledged that he had been there some months earlier. Finally, he admitted that he had been there on the evening of her death but claimed that he had left immediately because he did not have a circuit plan for that particular television.

Now the suspect was obviously nervous, and the interviewers left him alone while they went back to talk to Yanka. She recalled that on the evening of the murder—she remembered it because the fire engine had passed her window—Showery had come home early. Asked by the interviewers if he had recently given her any jewelry, she showed them an antique cocktail ring. She was asked to accompany them back to the police station, together with her jewelry box. Meanwhile, Teresita Basa's two friends, Richard Pessoti and Ray King, were brought to the station. As soon as Pessoti glimpsed the ring on Yanka's finger, he recognized it as one belonging to Teresita Basa. The two were also able to identify other jewelry in Yanka's jewelry box.

Stachula's partner, Detective Lee Epplen, confronted Showery and told him, "It's all over." Showery screamed angrily, "You cops are trying to frame me." When shown the jewelry, he insisted that he had bought it at a pawnshop but had failed to get a receipt. Minutes later he realized that the evidence against him was overwhelming. He asked to speak to Yanka, and in the presence of the detectives said, "Yanka, I have something to tell you. I killed Teresita Basa."

He had believed that Teresita was rich and that robbing her would solve all his financial problems. But after killing her, he found that her purse contained only thirty dollars. In order to make the murder look like a sex crime he had undressed her and spread her legs apart. Then he had stabbed her with the butcher knife and set the mattress on fire, hoping that the fire would destroy any clues he might have left behind.

The "Voice from the Grave" case made national headlines. Showery came to trial on January 21, 1979, before Judge Frank W. Barbero. But the story of the "possession" of Remy Chua was so astounding that the jury was unable to agree on a verdict. The defense also objected that the evidence of a ghost was not admissible in a court of law. Five days later a mistrial was declared. But on February 23, 1979, Allan Showery acknowledged that he was guilty of the murder of Teresita Basa. He was sentenced to fourteen years for murder and to four years each on charges of armed robbery and arson.

4

The Canning Mystery:
The Eighteenth Century's
Most Notorious Cause Célèbre

One of the finest detective stories of the twentieth century, Josephine Tey's *The Franchise Affair*, is based on a real-life mystery that is as baffling today as it was more than two centuries ago.

In *The Franchise Affair*, two women—a mother and a daughter—are startled when the police arrive at their front door and accuse them of kidnapping a young girl. The girl, a pretty teenager, alleges that she was abducted by the women, who then removed all her clothes except her underwear and forced her to work as a servant. The two women kept her in a locked bedroom, and she was beaten and half-starved until she finally succeeded in escaping. The girl identifies an attic bedroom as her prison—and the police are impressed by the accuracy of her description, as well as by her knowledge of other parts of the house. Severe bruises and scratches support the girl's story of being beaten. As absurd and incomprehensible as it seems, the case against the two women looks airtight. Both are charged with abducting the girl. The Franchise affair (the house is called Franchise) arouses such hostility in the local town that people begin smearing hate slogans on the women's house and breaking the windows.

The women approach a local lawyer; although initially unwilling to take on a criminal case, he finally agrees. It is an uphill battle, for all the evidence points to the guilt of his clients. Little by little, however, he begins to see glimmers of light. For example, the house—Franchise—is surrounded by a high wall and its gates kept locked; yet the girl had described its garden with considerable accuracy. The lawyer learns that a double-decker bus once passed the house regularly and that the girl could have seen the garden from its upper deck.

After that the solutions come thick and fast, and at the trial he is able to show that the girl obtained her knowledge of the inside of the house from a maidservant who had been dismissed for theft. The two girls had invented the accusations of kidnapping. In fact, the "victim" had spent time having an affair with a commercial traveler, whose wife had invaded their "love nest" and administered the beating. The girl's fear of her parents had led her to invent the story of her abduction.

Josephine Tey's solution of the mystery is brilliant. Unfortunately, it totally fails to explain the real-life mystery upon which she based her classic novel.

Elizabeth Canning was neither pretty nor promiscuous; at the age of eighteen she was five feet tall and had the healthy complexion of a country girl, although her face was disfigured by pockmarks. Apparently she had not a single male admirer. In the year 1753 she was living in the City of London and working for a carpenter named Mr. Lyon. Her mother, a widow with five children (of whom Elizabeth—known as Bet—was the eldest), lived nearby in a street called Aldermanbury.

It was on New Year's Day 1753 that Elizabeth disappeared. She put on her best clothes and went to see her mother. She gave pennies to three of her little brothers and sisters but did not give one to the fourth, a boy, because he had irritated her. She repented, however, and bought him a mince pie. Clearly Elizabeth was a sweet-natured girl and a good elder sister. After this she went to see her Uncle Colley, who lived near the London docks, and had supper with him and his family. Toward ten o'clock the Colleys escorted her back as far as Houndsditch, a mere ten-minute walk from home. But she failed to reach her home. It looked very much as if she had been abducted—perhaps killed—

for the "purple masquerade gown" she wore and the half guinea she had in her pocket.

Her disappearance caused quite a stir and made her mother frantic. Jails and hospitals were searched without result. Neighbors raised enough money for a two-guinea reward, and an advertisement was placed in a newspaper that described her as "fresh coloured, pitted with the small-pox, has a high forehead, light eyebrows, about five feet high, eighteen years of age, well set; had on a masquerade purple stuff gown, a black petticoat, a white chip hat bound round with green, a white apron and handkerchief, blue stockings and leather shoes." This led to a woman offering the information that she had heard a shriek coming from a hackney coach near Elizabeth's home, but the questioning of a number of coachmen led nowhere.

Exactly four weeks after her disappearance, on January 29, 1753, Elizabeth walked into her mother's house. She was in a sorry state—battered, bruised, and limping, and wearing only an underskirt. A bloody rag was bound around her head, and she had a wound on her ear.

The news soon spread, and curious neighbors poured into the house. The tale Elizabeth had to tell was one of robbery and abduction. Soon after leaving her uncle and aunt, she had been attacked by two men, who had robbed her of her half-guinea and removed her dress and apron. One of them hit her on the head, and she lost consciousness. When she recovered she was being dragged along, and after half an hour she was taken into a house, where there was an old woman and two young ones. The old woman asked if she would "go their way"—presumably meaning "become a prostitute"—and she refused. So the old woman cut off Elizabeth's stays—by cutting the laces—then slapped her face and pushed her upstairs into a dark room.

There she lived for the next four weeks, seeing no one. She kept herself alive by eating some bread that was in the room and drinking a pitcher of water. She also ate the mince pie intended for her brother. Finally, she succeeded in breaking down some boards nailed across a window and making her escape.

Asked if she had any idea where she had been kept, she replied that she knew it was on Hertford Road—Hertford being a small town northeast of London—because she had peeped out of a crack in the window and had seen a coachman whom she knew and who drove the Hertford coach. (Presumably she meant she saw the coach driving past.) On hearing this, a neighbor by the name of Robert Scarratt exclaimed that she had probably been kept at the house of a gypsy named Mother Wells, known as a house of ill repute. Elizabeth said that she *had* heard the name Wells or Wills mentioned.

A retinue of friends and supporters immediately set out on horseback for Mother Wells's house, which was about ten miles away, in Enfield, halfway to Hertford. They rushed in and took possession of the place. Some went upstairs and found a room that seemed like the one Elizabeth had described—long and dark, with one of the windows boarded up. There was hay on the floor, which Elizabeth had failed to mention. But when one of them rode back and met Elizabeth, she said that there *had* been hay on the floor. Also in the long, dark room were a water pitcher, a saddle, an old picture, and a cask, all of which Elizabeth had mentioned earlier. But it lacked the fire grate that she had described.

When Elizabeth arrived, she immediately identified the room as the one she had been kept in and pointed out that the view from the unboarded window was just as she had described.

Elizabeth was taken into a downstairs room in which the inhabitants of the house were gathered. She ignored Mother Wells and walked straight up to an incredibly ugly old gypsy woman named Mary Squires, who had a huge nose and a lower lip that was "almost as big as a child's arm." Elizabeth said, "That is the old woman that robbed me." The gypsy leapt to her feet and protested that she had never seen Elizabeth before. "When did I rob you?" she wanted to know, and when Elizabeth said, "On New Year's Day," she replied, "I was a hundred and twenty miles away then."

Two younger gypsies were also in the room, a dark-haired girl named Lucy Squires—Mary Squires's daughter—and a blond prostitute incongruously named Virtue Hall. These, it seemed, were the two younger women mentioned. There was also a man named George Hall, who was Mary Squires's son. They were all— plus Mother Wells—taken to the house of a local magistrate, where Mary Squires and Mother Wells were charged and carried off to jail.

At this point, the great novelist Henry Fielding enters the story. Fielding was nearing the end of his life. The author of *Tom Jones* had never succeeded in making a comfortable living from his books and had been a magistrate since 1740. Most magistrates used the job to line their pockets by taking bribes; Fielding was rigidly honest. Later in this same year, 1753, he would create the Bow Street Runners and thereby halt London's crime wave almost single-handed. But in February, these achievements still lay in the future.

It was on February 6 that Virtue Hall and a woman named Judith Natus were brought before Fielding to be questioned about the Elizabeth Canning affair. Even before he saw Virtue Hall, Fielding was informed that she wanted to confess everything. She entered in tears; Fielding made sympathetic noises and told her that if she confessed he would do everything possible to see that she came to no harm. But it soon became clear that Virtue had no intention of "coming clean," and her equivocations finally exasperated Fielding to the point of threatening to have her thrown in jail unless she told the truth. This had the effect of making her declare that Elizabeth Canning *had* been brought to Mother Wells's house by two gypsies. Fielding was later accused of behaving disgracefully and bullying Virtue into making a statement to save herself from prison; yet it is hard to blame him for losing his temper with a woman who plainly had no intention of telling the truth. Fielding later pointed out that Virtue Hall's story tallied very closely with that of Elizabeth Canning, although neither had had a chance to hear what the other said.

Two weeks later Mother Wells and Mary Squires went on trial. Elizabeth repeated her story of having been robbed by two men and hit on the head when she had begun to scream. This, she says, caused her to have a fit—she had suffered from them for the past three or four years—and when she recovered her senses, she was being dragged along the road by the two men. In fact, a turnpike keeper named Robert Beals would later describe how he saw two men forcing a sobbing girl to walk along with them, and how he heard one of them say, "Come along, you bitch, you're drunk."

They had to lift her over a stile; then all three of them disappeared in the direction of Enfield.

The chief defense of the two women was that Mary Squires was not in the house that night and therefore could not have been involved in robbing Elizabeth of her stays. Mary Squires called three male witnesses to prove that she was in Abbotsbury, Dorset, on New Year's Eve. But the jury did not believe the witnesses— Virtue Hall's evidence for the prosecution playing an important part in strengthening their doubts—and found both prisoners guilty. When called up for sentencing, Mary Squires made her case worse by insisting that she was not in Abbotsbury on New Year's Day but in Coombe, some miles away. She was then sentenced to death, while Mother Wells was sentenced to be branded on the hand and to spend six months in Newgate Prison. To the delight of the mob, Mother Wells was branded on the spot.

And that, one might suppose, would be the end of the affair. But the lord mayor of London, Sir Crispe Gascoyne, was not happy with the verdict. He couldn't see why the three Dorset witnesses should lie about Mary Squires to provide her with an alibi. They had struck him as honest men. As to the contradiction about dates, the British calendar had been changed recently, and Christmas Day had been moved by twelve days; Mary Squires had probably been reckoning by the old calendar. So the lord mayor wrote to the vicar of Abbotsbury to ask him to make inquiries. The result confirmed his feeling that the Dorset men had been telling the truth: many reputable people, including the schoolmaster and churchwarden, confirmed Mary Squires's alibi.

Next he talked to Virtue Hall, and she admitted that she had given false evidence out of fear of going to prison; she gave a new account of what had happened on New Year's Day in which there was no mention of Elizabeth Canning. The lord mayor then went to see Mother Wells in prison and asked her about New Year's Day. Her account confirmed Virtue Hall's new story. As a result of the lord mayor's efforts, Mary Squires was pardoned on the day before she was due to be executed, and Mother Wells was also released.

The case had now attained the status of a cause célèbre, England's equivalent of the Dreyfus case, which was to divide France more than a century later. You were either a "Canningite" or an

"Egyptian." (Gypsies were so called because they were believed to have originated in Egypt.) Every man and woman in England took one side or the other. To the Canningites, it was obvious that Elizabeth had been kidnapped by evildoers who wanted to turn her into a prostitute. To the Egyptians, it was equally obvious that, whoever had abducted Elizabeth, it was not the unfortunate Mary Squires. Pamphlets flooded the market, one of which was even called *Canning's Magazine*. And the accused gypsies were encouraged by their supporters to take legal action against Elizabeth. The case was thrown out. The Canningites now prosecuted the witnesses from Dorset for perjury; that case was also thrown out. The Canningites tried a second time but failed to produce any convincing evidence. When the controversy had raged for more than a year, the Egyptians finally succeeded in having Elizabeth indicted for perjury. Her trial took place in May 1754.

The prosecution called thirty-six witnesses to prove Mary Squires's alibi. Then Alderman Chitty, who had been the first official to interview Elizabeth, appeared for the prosecution, pinpointing some inconsistencies in her statement, such as the date on which she claimed she had finished the pitcher of water. He also claimed that Elizabeth had told him that she climbed out of the window onto a penthouse roof, and he pointed out that there *was* no penthouse roof under the bedroom at Mother Wells's house. Other witnesses made similar points: for example, that there was no fire grate in the room in Mother Wells's house, although Elizabeth had mentioned one in her original evidence.

Elizabeth's witnesses included the turnpike man, Robert Beals, who had seen a crying girl being carried over a stile, and two other people who said they had seen a poor, distressed girl in her underslip making her way back from Enfield to London four weeks later. Some raised the question of what Elizabeth had done about going to the toilet during her four weeks' imprisonment and her mother declared that she had often been constipated for two weeks at a time.

And so it went on, witness after witness after witness—no fewer than twenty-six of them setting out to prove that the gypsies *had* been in Enfield when they claimed to be in Dorset. The problem for the jury was that they had no sooner heard what sounded like a reliable piece of evidence than the other side produced a witness who threw doubt on it, or on the character of the person who had given it.

The jury's final verdict reflected their confusion. They declared that Elizabeth Canning *was* guilty of perjury but not "willful or corrupt" perjury. That appeared to mean that the jurors did not believe her whole story but that they absolved her of deliberate malice in telling it. Clearly they meant her to be acquitted. The judge declined to accept such a verdict and sent them back for more deliberation. Now faced with the question of whether to go back on their previous verdict and find her innocent, they chose the coward's expedient of finding her guilty—but adding a strong recommendation for mercy. The judge ignored this and sentenced her to seven years' exile in New England. Some members of the jury compounded the impression of incompetence by signing an affidavit declaring that they believed most of Elizabeth's story but not the date on which she had finished the pitcher of water.

What finally became of Elizabeth is not clear. She was transported on July 31, 1754, and *Gentleman's Magazine* for July 22, 1773, declares that she had become a schoolmistress, had married a wealthy Quaker, and had died recently. (She would have been thirty-eight at the time.) Another account declares that she returned to England and received a legacy of £500 from a sympathizer—an old woman from Newington Green. If so, it would have given her an income for life (£500 in those days being worth about $15,000 in the currency of the late twentieth century).

The fascination of the case lies in its power to arouse in us the same emotions it aroused in the Canningites and the Egyptians. The first thing that is self-evident is that Elizabeth was not faking her abduction. Her wretched state when she finally staggered into her mother's house makes that impossible to doubt. So the fictional solution offered by Josephine Tey in *The Franchise Affair* is totally implausible; Elizabeth did not spend the month with a lover, and she did not run away to seek an abortion. It seems virtually certain that she was abducted, as she says, by two men. It is what happened next that is open to doubt.

The evidence of the Dorset men—and the clergyman who later supported it—makes it equally clear that Mary Squires was not guilty. Elizabeth declared that the old woman who robbed her was "tall, black, and swarthy," and Mother Wells was short. But if the robber was Mary Squires, then surely Elizabeth would have mentioned her enormous nose and pendulous lower lip? In short, quite apart from the evidence of the Dorset witnesses, it seems apparent that Mary Squires was not guilty.

Then how do we explain the manifold contradictions of the case? If Elizabeth *was* kidnapped and *was* badly treated, then who did it?

The main problem with Elizabeth's story—as many hostile pamphleteers pointed out—is that the gypsies would have had no motive for keeping her locked in a room for a month. They would have ended up with a corpse on their hands and the problem of disposing of it.

Let us try applying the deductive method of Sherlock Holmes. We are reasonably certain that Elizabeth was robbed and kidnapped. By whom? The story of a girl screaming from a coach may have some foundation. But if the evidence of the turnpike keeper is to be believed, the culprits were two men.

It was a very dark night—the turnpike keeper says it was pitch-black. So Elizabeth would not have known where she was taken to. But the turnpike was within three miles of the place where she was attacked, and Mother Wells's house was another seven miles away. It is difficult to believe that two men forced her to walk ten miles. Surely it is more likely that the house to which she was taken was nearer home. Elizabeth had originally said the journey took half an hour. Her return walk points to the same conclusion, for it seems unlikely that a young woman who was weak from starvation would be able to walk ten miles back home.

It is easy enough to understand why she allowed herself to be drawn into confirming the story that she had been imprisoned in Mother Wells's house. She was a plain eighteen-year-old servant girl without a single admirer; then suddenly she was a celebrity, surrounded by enthusiastic supporters. She would have had no desire to upset and disappoint the Canningites. If she had arrived at Mother Wells's house and told them, "No, this is not the place," it would have been an anticlimax. On the other hand, if it *had* been the place, surely she would have said so emphatically as soon as she saw it: "Yes, this is where I was held." Instead, she seems to have said little except enough to identify the upstairs room. It looks, then, as if she *did* allow herself to be drawn into committing perjury.

We have to go to the heart of the matter and ask: If she was not telling the whole truth about her abduction, what was she trying to hide?

Here it is necessary to return to her story of the abduction: that two men attacked her, robbed her of her best gown and her half-guinea, and then—instead of leaving her—proceeded to drag her ten miles. Why? We know that the two men had stripped her of most of her clothes, with the exception of a black petticoat and blue stockings, and that when one of them hit her, she lost consciousness. We only have to envisage the scene, with a half-naked teenager lying on the pavement, to imagine the next thought that came into their heads—in fact, that had probably come into their heads as they were undressing her. We can probably assume that, in this particular, human nature was much the same then as now.

But at ten o'clock in the evening, in the City of London, there must have been many people still about. If the men were intent on sexual ravishment, then it would be necessary to take her elsewhere to avoid being interrupted.

Now in the eighteenth century, rape was not considered as serious a crime as it became later. In cases where the rapist was a member of the upper classes, the punishment might be no more than a fine. But rape accompanied by robbery was a hanging offense, and once she had been taken to a house, Elizabeth might be able to identify it. And so, the rape completed, they must have felt that she had to be kept prisoner. And during the course of her month in the room, she may have been raped more than once. The midwife who examined her shift declared that she had not been ravished, but she was only making this inference from the lack of bloodstains. And this lack could be explained if the shift had been pulled above her head or removed entirely.

An eighteen-year-old girl would have every reason to be silent about a rape—particularly multiple rape by two men. Telling about it would make her an object of lewd curiosity and would ruin her chances of ever finding a husband. So, as curious neighbors crowded around her, one of her most insistent thoughts must have been to deny that she was no longer a virgin.

Yet without the rape, her story becomes incomprehensible. Why would two men drag her for many miles, then keep her imprisoned for a month, when they had already robbed her of virtually everything she possessed? To force her to become a prostitute? They may have made that suggestion at some later stage, and she may well have indignantly refused. That would explain why they starved her. But on the night of her abduction, why else should they have dragged her for many miles?

If this view is correct, then Elizabeth must have breathed a sigh of relief when her supporters suggested that the house was in Enfield. (She had only said it was on Hertford Road.) When Robert Scarratt exclaimed that he would lay a guinea to a farthing that she had been at Mother Wells's establishment, Elizabeth eagerly confirmed that she had heard the name "Wills" or "Wells" mentioned. But she also claimed she was left alone for a month and saw no one. Then when did she hear the name mentioned? And surely, *if* she had heard the name mentioned, wouldn't she have said so immediately, since it was a vital clue, and not waited to be prompted by Scarratt?

If this is the solution, then both the Canningites and the Egyptians were correct. Elizabeth *was* abducted and shamefully treated, and she *did* escape as she claims. But Mother Wells and Mary Squires were innocent. The investigators should have looked for the "house of ill fame" much closer to London.

It follows, of course, that the judge who sentenced her to seven years' exile in the colonies was also correct. Her determination to keep her secret almost cost an innocent woman her life. But if *Gentleman's Magazine* is accurate, we can also feel a certain satisfaction that her ordeal had a fairy-tale ending: Elizabeth Canning ended her life as a happily married woman.

5

The Cleveland Torso Murders:
Who Was "the Mad Butcher"?

The American equivalent of the Jack the Ripper murders (described in chapter 18) was the Cleveland Torso case. The Cleveland murders were more numerous, and in some ways—as will be seen—more horrific, than their Victorian counterparts.

On a warm September afternoon in 1935, two boys on their way home from school walked along a dusty, sooty gully known as Kingsbury Run, in the heart of Cleveland, Ohio. On a weed-covered slope known as Jackass Hill, one challenged the other to a race, and they hurtled sixty feet down the slope to the bottom. Sixteen-year-old James Wagner was the winner, and as he halted, panting, he noticed something white in the bushes a few yards away. A closer look revealed that it was a naked body and that it was headless.

The police who arrived soon after found the body of a young white male clad only in black socks; the genitals had been removed. It lay on its back, with the legs stretched out and the arms by the sides, as if laid out for a funeral. Thirty feet away the policemen found another body, that of an older man, lying in the same position; it had also been decapitated and emasculated.

Hair sticking out of the ground revealed one of the missing heads buried a few yards away; the second proved to be buried nearby. Both sets of genitals were also found lying nearby, as if thrown away by the killer.

One curious feature of the crimes was that there was no blood on the ground or on the bodies, which were quite clean. It looked as if the victims had been killed and beheaded elsewhere, then carefully washed when they had ceased to bleed.

Forensic examination revealed even more baffling evidence. The older corpse was badly decomposed and the skin discolored; the pathologists discovered that this was due to some unidentifiable chemical substance, perhaps used by the killer in an attempt to preserve the body. The man had been dead about two weeks. The younger man had only been dead three days. His fingerprints enabled the police to identify him as twenty-eight-year-old Edward Andrassy, who had a minor police record for carrying concealed weapons. He lived near Kingsbury Run and had a reputation as a drunken brawler.

But the most chilling discovery was that Andrassy had actually died as a result of decapitation. Rope marks on his wrists revealed that he had been tied and had struggled violently. The killer had apparently cut off his head with a knife. The skill with which the operation had been performed suggested a butcher—or possibly a surgeon.

It proved impossible to identify the older man. But the identification of Andrassy led the police to hope that it would not be too difficult to trace his killer. Andrassy had spent his nights gambling and drinking in a slummy part of town—the third precinct—and was known as a pimp. Further investigation also revealed that he had had male lovers. Lead after lead looked extremely promising. The husband of a married woman with whom he had had an affair had sworn to kill him. But the man was able to prove his innocence. So were various shady characters who might have borne a grudge. Lengthy police investigation led to a dead end—as it did in another ten cases involving the killer who became known as "the Mad Butcher of Kingsbury Run."

Four months later, on a raw January Sunday, the howling of a dog finally led a woman who lived on East Twentieth Street—not far from Kingsbury Run—to go and investigate. She found the chained animal trying to get at a basket standing near a factory wall. Minutes later she told a passing neighbor that the basket contained hams. But the neighbor soon recognized the "hams" as being parts of a human arm. A burlap bag proved to contain the female torso. The head was missing, as were the left arm and the lower parts of both legs. But fingerprints again enabled the police to trace the victim, who had a record as a prostitute. She proved to be forty-one-year-old Florence ("Flo") Polillo, a squat, double-chinned woman who was well known in the neighborhood bars.

Again, there were plenty of leads, and again, all of them petered out. Two weeks later the victim's left arm and lower legs were found in a vacant lot. The head was never recovered.

The murder of Flo Polillo raised an unwelcome question. The first two murders had convinced the police that they were looking for a homosexual sadist, which at least simplified the investigation; this latest crime made it look as if the killer was quite simply a sadist—like Peter Kürten, the Düsseldorf killer executed in 1931; he had killed men, women, and children indiscriminately, and he was not remotely homosexual. The pathologist also recalled that a year before that first double murder, the torso of an unknown woman had been found on the edge of Lake Erie. It began to look as if the Mad Butcher was a psychopath who was simply obsessed with the dissection of human corpses, as some boys enjoy pulling the wings off flies.

Cleveland residents felt they had one thing in their favor, however. Since the double killing, the famous Eliot Ness had been appointed Cleveland's director of public safety. Ness and his "Untouchables" had cleared up Chicago's Prohibition rackets, and in 1934 Ness had moved to Cleveland to fight its gangsters. With Ness in charge, the newspapers were confident that the Head Hunter of Kingsbury Run—another press sobriquet—would find himself becoming the hunted.

But it was soon clear to Ness that hunting a sadistic pervert was totally unlike hunting professional gangsters. The killer struck at random, and unless he was careless enough to leave behind a clue—like a fingerprint—then the only hope was to catch him in the act. And Ness soon became convinced that the Mad Butcher took great pleasure in feeling that he was several steps ahead of the police.

The Head Hunter waited until the summer before killing again, then lived up to his name by leaving the head of a young man, wrapped in a pair of trousers, under a bridge in Kingsbury Run; again, two boys found it—on June 22, 1936. The body was found a quarter of a mile away, and it was obvious from the blood that the man had been killed where he lay. Again, medical examination revealed that the victim had died as a result of decapitation—though it was not clear how the killer had prevented the victim from struggling while he removed his head. The victim was about twenty-five and heavily tattooed. There was no record of his fingerprints in police files. Three weeks later a young female hiker discovered another decapitated male body in a gully, with the head lying nearby. The decomposition made it clear that this man had been killed before the previously discovered victim.

The last "butchery" of 1936 was that of a man of about thirty, who was also found in Kingsbury Run; the body had been cut in two and emasculated. A hat found nearby led to a partial identification: a housewife recalled giving it to a young tramp. Not far away was a "hobo camp" where down-and-outs slept; this was obviously where the Butcher had found his latest victim.

The fact that Cleveland had been the scene of a Republican convention and was now the site of a Great Exposition led to even more frantic police activity and much press criticism. The murders were reported all over the world, and in Nazi Germany and Fascist Italy they were cited as proof of the decadence of the New World.

As month after month went by with no further grisly discoveries, Clevelanders began to believe they had heard the last of the Mad Butcher. But in February 1937 that hope proved unfounded when the killer left the body of a young woman in a chopped-up pile on the shores of Lake Erie. She was never identified. The eighth victim *was* identified from her teeth as Mrs. Rose Wallace, age forty; only the skeleton remained, and it looked as if she might have been killed in the previous year.

Victim number nine was male and had been dismembered; when his body was fished out of the river, the head was missing, and it was never found. This time the killer had gone even further in his mutilations, disemboweling the corpse in the manner of

Jack the Ripper. It was impossible to identify the victim. It was believed that two men seen in a boat might be the Butcher and an accomplice, but this suggestion led nowhere.

The killer now seemed to take a rest for nine months. Then the lower part of a leg was pulled out of the river. Three weeks later two burlap bags found in the river proved to contain more body fragments, which enabled the pathologist to announce that the victim was a brunette female of about twenty-five. She was never identified.

The killer was to strike twice more. More than a year after the last discovery, in August 1938, the dismembered torso of a woman was found at a dump on the lakefront, and a search of the area revealed the bones of a second victim, a male. A quilt in which the remains of this twelfth victim were wrapped was identified as one that had been given to a junkman. Neither body could be identified.

One thing was now obvious: the Butcher was selecting his victims from vagrants and down-and-outs. Ness decided to take the only kind of action that seemed left to him: two days after the last find police raided the shantytown near Kingsbury Run, arrested hundreds of vagrants, and burned it down. Whether by coincidence or not, the murders ceased.

Two of the most efficient of the man hunters, Detectives Merylo and Zalewski, had spent a great deal of time searching for the killer's "laboratory." At one point they thought they had found it, when a negative left behind by one of the earliest victims, Edward Andrassy, was developed and showed Andrassy lounging on a bed in an unknown room. The photograph was published in newspapers and the room was finally identified by a petty crook as being the bedroom of a middle-aged homosexual who lived with his two sisters. Upon investigation, blood was found on the floor of the room, and a large butcher knife was discovered in a trunk. But the blood proved to be the suspect's own—he was subject to nosebleeds—and the butcher knife showed no trace of blood. And when another body turned up while the suspect was in jail for sodomy, it became clear that he was not the Torso killer.

Next the investigators discovered that Flo Polillo and Rose Wallace had frequented the same saloon and that Andrassy had been a regular there too. They also learned of a middle-aged man named Frank Dolezal who carried knives and threatened people with them when drunk. When they learned that this man had also been living with Flo Polillo, they believed they had finally identified the killer. Dolezal was arrested, and police discovered a brown substance resembling dried blood in the cracks of his bathroom floor. Knives with dried bloodstains on them provided further incriminating evidence. Under intensive questioning, Dolezal, a bleary-eyed, unkempt man, confessed to the murder of Flo Polillo, and the newspapers triumphantly announced the capture of the Butcher. Then things began to go wrong. Forensic tests showed that the "dried blood" in the bathroom was not blood after all. Dolezal's "confession" proved to be full of errors about the corpse and the method of disposal. And when, in August 1939, Dolezal hanged himself in jail, the autopsy revealed that he had two cracked ribs, which suggested that his confession had been obtained by force.

The two victims of August 1938 proved to be the Butcher's last—at least in Cleveland. In Pittsburgh in 1940 three decapitated bodies were found in old boxcars. Members of Ness's team went to investigate, but no clue to the treble murder was ever discovered. The Mad Butcher was also blamed for the Black Dahlia killing in Hollywood in 1947, when an aspiring film actress named Elizabeth Short was dissected, like victim number seven. It seems highly unlikely, however, that the Mad Butcher survived that long; a large percentage of sadistic killers commit suicide.

Steven Nickel's book on the case, *Torso* (1989), makes it clear that there were many suspects in Cleveland who might have been capable of committing the murders. One man, nicknamed the "Chicken Freak," was known to the prostitutes of the third precinct because he could achieve orgasm only when watching a chicken being decapitated; he would go to a brothel with two live chickens and a large butcher knife. Naked prostitutes would be asked to behead the chickens while he looked on and masturbated; if he failed to reach a climax, the bloody knife had to be rubbed against his throat. Finally arrested, the "Chicken Freak" proved to be a truck driver who admitted that he made a habit of intercourse with chickens. But he was so obviously nauseated when shown photographs of the Torso victims that he was allowed to go.

Why have the Torso murders never achieved the same grim celebrity as the crimes of Jack the Ripper? The reason is that Cleveland in the mid-1930s was a far more violent city than London in the 1880s and the crimes made far less impact on the public imagination than the Ripper's sadistic murder of prostitutes in Victorian London. Ten years before the Cleveland murders began, six decapitated male bodies were found in a swamp near New Castle, a small town ninety miles southeast of Cleveland. The victims were never identified; the local police concluded that they had been killed by gangsters in the course of bootleg wars and that the swamp was a convenient dumping ground.

Sadly, the last decade of Eliot Ness's life—he died in 1957, at the age of fifty-four—was full of poverty and disappointment. He resigned as Cleveland's Safety Director in April 1941, after a scandal involving a hit-and-run accident. In 1947 he was heavily defeated when he ran for the post of mayor of Cleveland. A year later he was even turned down for a sixty-dollar-a-week job. "He simply ran out of gas" said one friend. In 1953, after five years of obscurity and poverty, he became involved with a paper-making company tottering on the verge of bankruptcy. But it was through a friend in the company that Ness met a journalist named Oscar Fraley and began telling him the story of his anti-bootlegging days. In the course of their conversations, Ness told Fraley that he was reasonably certain that he knew the identity of the Torso killer and that he had driven him out of Cleveland.

Ness told Fraley the following: He had reasoned that the killer was a man who had a house of his own in which he could dismember the bodies and a car in which he could transport them. So he was *not*, after all, a down-and-out. The skill of the mutilations suggested medical training, or at least a certain degree of medical knowledge. The fact that some of the victims had been strong men suggested that the Butcher had to be big and powerful—a conclusion supported by a size-12 footprint near one of the bodies.

Ness had three of his top agents, Virginia Allen, Barney Davis, and Jim Manski, make inquiries among the upper levels of Cleveland society. Virginia was a sophisticated woman with contacts among Cleveland socialites, and it was she who learned about a man who sounded like the ideal suspect. The suspect, whom Ness was to call "Gaylord Sundheim," was a big man from a well-to-do family who had a history of psychiatric problems. He had also studied medicine. When the three "Untouchables" called on him, he leered sarcastically at Virginia and closed the door in their faces. Ness invited him—pressingly—to lunch, and he came under protest. He refused either to admit or deny having performed the murders. Ness persuaded him to take a lie detector test, and "Sundheim's" answers to questions about the murders were registered by the stylus as lies. When Ness finally told him he believed he was the Torso killer—hoping that shock tactics might trigger a confession—"Sundheim" sneered, "Prove it."

Soon after this, "Sundheim" had himself committed to a mental institution. Ness knew *he* was now "untouchable," for even if Ness could prove his guilt, he could plead insanity.

Ness went on to collaborate with Fraley on a book entitled *The Untouchables*. It came out in 1957 and was an immense success, becoming a bestseller and leading to a famous TV series. But Ness never knew about its success; he had died of a heart attack on May 16, 1957, six months before *The Untouchables* was published.

6

Crop Circles:
UFOs, Whirlwinds, or Hoaxers?

On August 15, 1980, the *Wiltshire Times* carried an odd report concerning the apparently wanton vandalism of a field of oats near Westbury in Wiltshire, England. The owner of the field, John Scull, had found his oats crushed to the ground in three separate areas, all within sight of the famous White Horse of Westbury, a hillside figure cut into the chalk. It seemed obvious to Scull that the crops had been damaged by people rather than natural phenomena since the areas were identical in shape and size: almost perfect circles, each sixty feet in diameter.

It was also noted that the circles had apparently been produced manually rather than mechanically, since there was no sign that any kind of machinery had been moved through the field. In fact, there seemed to be no evidence of *anything* crossing the field; the circles were surrounded by undamaged oats, with no paths that would indicate intruders. One speculation was that the vandals had used stilts.

Close examination of the flattened cereal revealed that the circles had not been made at the same time—that in fact, the damage had been spread over a period of two or three months, probably between May and the end of July. The edges of the circles were sharply defined, and all the grain within the circles was flattened in the same direction, creating a clockwise swirling effect around the centers. None of the oats had been cut—merely flattened. The effect might have been produced by a very tall, strong man standing in the center of each circle and swinging a heavy weight around on a long piece of rope.

Dr. Terence Meaden, an atmospheric physicist from nearby Bradford-on-Avon and a senior member of the Tornado and Storm Research Organization (TORRO), suggested that the circles had been produced by a summer whirlwind. Such wind effects are not uncommon on open farmland. But Dr. Meaden had to admit that he had never seen or heard of a whirlwind creating circles. Whirlwinds tend to scud about randomly, pausing for only a few seconds in any one place, so one might expect a random pathway through the crop.

Another interesting fact was noted by Ian Mrzyglod, editor of the "anomaly" magazine *The PROBE Report.* The "center point" on all three circles was actually off-center by as much as four feet. The swirling patterns around these points were therefore oval, not circular. This seemed to contradict the vandal theory—vandals would hardly go to the trouble of creating precise ellipses. It also made Meaden's whirlwind explanation seem less plausible.

Almost exactly a year later, on August 19, 1981, another three-circle formation appeared in a wheatfield below Cheesefoot Head, near Winchester in Hampshire. These circles had been created simultaneously and, unlike the widely dispersed circles in Wiltshire, were in close formation—one circle sixty feet across with two twenty-five-foot circles on either side. But the sides of these circles had the same precise edges as the Wiltshire circles, and again, the swirl of the flattened plants was slightly off-center, creating ellipses. And again there were no paths through the grain to indicate intruders.

The new evidence seemed to undermine the natural-causes theory. Instead of a neat, stationary whirlwind creating only one circle, Meaden now had to argue the existence of an atmospheric disturbance that hopscotched across the landscape and produced circles of different sizes. Meaden suggested that perhaps peculiarities of terrain created this effect—the field in question was on a concave, "punchbowl" slope, and this might indeed have caused the vortex to "jump."

There were a few isolated reports of similar incidents in 1982, but they were unspectacular and excited little attention. As if to make up for it, a series of five-circle phenomena began in 1983, one of them at Bratton, again close to the White Horse of West-bury. These were clearly not caused by whirlwinds, for they con-sisted of one large circle with four smaller ones spaced around it like the number five on a die. A "quintuplet" appeared in Cley Hill, near Warminster—a town that, in earlier years, had had more than its share of "flying saucer" sightings. Another appeared in a field below Ridgeway near Wantage in Oxfordshire. Quintu-plets were no longer freaks but were virtually the norm.

Now the national press began to cover the phenomena. The British press often refer to the summer as the "silly season" because, for some odd reason, there is often a shortage of good news stories in the hot months of the year, and newspapers tend to make up for the deficiency by blowing up trivia into major news stories. Crop circles answered the need perfectly, with the result that the British public soon became familiar with the strange circle formations. UFO enthusiasts appeared on television explain-ing their view that the phenomena could be explained only by flying saucers. Skeptics preferred the notion of fraud.

This latter view seemed to be confirmed when a second quintu-plet found at Bratton turned out to be a hoax sponsored by the *Daily Mirror*; a family named Shepherd had been paid to dupli-cate the other Bratton circles. They did this by entering the field on stilts and trampling the crops underfoot. But, significantly, the hoax was quickly detected by Bob Rickard, the editor of an anom-aly magazine, the *Fortean Times*, who noted the telltale signs of human intruders, which had not been present in earlier circles, and the fact that the edges of the circles were quite rough and imprecise. The aim of the hoax was to embarrass the competing tabloid, the *Daily Express*, which had originally scooped the crop-circle story.

Over the next two years the number of circles increased, as did their complexity. There were crop circles with "rings" around them—flattened pathways several feet wide that ran around the outer edge in a neat circle. Some were even found with two or three such rings. At the same time the quintuplet formations and "singletons" also continued to appear.

It began to look as if whoever—or whatever—was creating the circles took pleasure in taunting the investigators. When believers in the whirlwind theory pointed out that the swirling had so far been clockwise, a counterclockwise circle promptly appeared. When it was suggested that a hoaxer might be making the circles with the aid of a helicopter, a crop circle was found directly beneath a power line. When an aerial photographer named Busty Taylor was flying home after photographing crop circles and mentioned that he would like to see a formation in the shape of a Celtic cross, a Celtic cross appeared the next day in the field over which he had been flying. And, as if to rule out all possibility that natural causes could be responsible, one "sextuplet" in Hampshire in 1990 had keylike objects sticking out of the sides of three circles, producing the impression of an ancient pictogram. Another crop "pattern" of 1990 (at Chilcomb) seemed to represent a kind of chemical retort with a long neck, with four rectangles neatly spaced on either side of it, making nonsense of Meaden's insistence that the circles were caused by "natural atmospheric forces."

Rickard brought together a number of eyewitness descriptions of the actual appearance of circles:

Suddenly the grass began to sway before our eyes and laid itself flat in a clockwise spiral. . . . A perfect circle was completed in less than half a minute, all the time accompanied by a high-pitched humming sound. . . . My attention was drawn to a "wave" coming through the heads of the cereal crop in a straight line. . . . The agency, though invisible, behaved like a solid object. . . . When we reached the spot where the circles had been, we were suddenly caught up in a terrific whirlwind. . . . [The dog] went wild. . . . There was a rushing sound and a rumble . . . then suddenly everything was still. . . . It was uncanny. . . . The dawn chorus stopped; the sky darkened . . .

The high-pitched humming sound may be significant. It was

noted on another occasion, on June 16, 1991, when a seventy-five-foot circle (with a "bull's-eye" in the center) appeared on Bolberry Down, near Salcombe in Devon. A local ham-radio operator named Lew Dilling was tuned into a regular frequency when strange high-pitched blips and clicks emerged. He recognized the sounds as being the same as others that had been heard in connection with crop-circle incidents. "The signals were so powerful," said Dilling, "that you could hear them in the background of Radio Moscow and Voice of America—and they would normally swamp everything."

The landlord of the local pub, Sean Hassall, learned of the crop circle indirectly when his spaniel went berserk and began tearing up the carpet, doing considerable damage.

The owner of the field, Dudley Stidson, was alerted to the circle by two walkers. He went to the six-acre hayfield and found a giant circle in the center. But this one differed from many such circles in that the hay was burned, as if someone had put a huge hot-plate on it. Stidson emphasized that there was no sign of intrusion in the field, such as trampled wheat.

Another local farmer, Peter Goodall, found a sixty-foot circle in his winter wheat (at Matford Barton) at the same time.

A few days before these incidents occurred, a Japanese professor announced that he had solved the crop-circle mystery. Professor Yoshihiko Ohtsuki, of Tokyo's Waseda University, had created an "elastic plasma" fireball—a very strong form of ionized air—in the laboratory. When the fireball touched a plate covered with aluminum powder, it created beautiful circles and rings in the powder. Ohtsuki suggested that plasma fireballs were created by atmospheric conditions and that they would flatten crops as they descended toward the ground. This certainly sounded as if it could be the solution of the mystery—until it was recalled that some of the crop circles had rectangles or keylike objects sticking out of their sides. Another objection was that fireballs are usually about the size of footballs and are clearly visible. Surely a fireball with a seventy-five-foot diameter would be visible for many miles? And why were no fireballs seen by the eyewitnesses cited by Rickard, who simply saw the corn being flattened in a clockwise circle?

Another recent suggestion is that an excess of fertilizer will cause the corn on which it is used to shoot up much faster than that which surrounds it, after which it will collapse and lie flat. There are two objections to this theory: Why would a farmer spray an excess of fertilizer in a circle—or some even more complicated design? And why would the corn collapse in a clockwise direction?

In a symposium entitled "The Crop Circle Enigma" (1990), John Michell made the important suggestion that the crop circles have a meaning and that "the meaning . . . is to be found in the way people are affected by them." In conjunction with this idea, Michell noted that "Jung discerned the meaning of UFOs as agents and portents of changes in human thought patterns, and that function has been clearly inherited by crop circles."

In order to understand this fully, we have to bear in mind Jung's concept of "synchronicity" or "meaningful coincidence." His view is basically that "meaningful coincidences" are somehow *created* by the unconscious mind—probably with the intention of jarring the conscious mind into a keener state of perception. Preposterous synchronicities imbue us with a powerful sense that there *is* a hidden meaning behind everyday reality. Certain pessimistically inclined writers—such as Shakespeare and Thomas Hardy—have taken the view that accidents and disasters indicate a kind of malevolent intelligence behind life. Jung's view is that synchronicities produce a sense of a *benevolent* intelligence behind life. He once suggested that the UFO phenomenon was an example of what he called "projection"—that is, of a physical effect somehow produced by the unconscious mind, in fact, by the "collective unconscious."

Michell was, in effect, suggesting that the crop-circle phenomenon serves the same purpose. Yet to say, as he did, that the crop circles have a "meaning" could also imply that some "other intelligence" is trying to influence human thought patterns. This is an idea that has been current since the earliest UFO sightings in the late 1940s and was popularized by Arthur C. Clarke in the screenplay of the film *2001: A Space Odyssey*: specifically, the notion that "higher intelligences" have been involved in the evolution of the human brain.

The logical objection to this theory is that to "make" man evolve is a contradiction in terms; evolution is the result of an *inner* drive. Presumably, a higher intelligence would recognize this better than we do. Yet it is also true that intelligence evolves through a sense of curiosity, of mystery, and that such apparent absurdities as flying saucers and crop circles certainly qualify as mysteries.

Michell concluded by quoting Jung's words that UFOs are "signs of great changes to come which are compatible with the end of an era." And whether or not Jung was correct, there can be no doubt that the UFO phenomenon has played an enormous part in the transformation of human consciousness from the narrow scientific materialism of the first half of the twentieth century to the much more open-minded attitude of its second half. Whether or not the crop circles prove to have a "natural" explanation, this may be their ultimate significance in the history of the late twentieth century.

Postscript: In early September 1991, a number of self-proclaimed hoaxers made simultaneous confessions to fabricating crop circles. Two of them, Dave Chorley and Doug Bower, claimed to have been making crop circles for thirteen years. Fred Day declared that he had been making them "all his life." Chorley and Bower demonstrated their technique by flattening corn in a field with a plank in front of TV cameras and crop-circle investigators. As in the case of the earlier *Daily Mirror* hoax, the investigators pointed out that the Chorley-Bower circle was visibly amateurish.

At the time of writing, the position taken by "cereologists" is that while some of the circles may be hoaxes, the majority show signs of being genuine, such as geometric perfection and an obvious lack of trampling of surrounding crops by human feet. The ultimate test, of course, will be whether crop circles now simply cease to appear—the silliest hoaxer gets tired of repetition—or whether, like "flying saucer" sightings, they continue to be as numerous as ever. Readers who pick up this book in the year 2000 will be in a better position to assess the possibilities than the authors are in 1992.

7

Was Philip K. Dick
Possessed by an Angel?

By the time of his death in March 1982, Philip K. Dick had become perhaps the most respected of modern science-fiction writers. The reason for this was expressed in an essay on Dick by Brian Stableford: "He has done more than anyone else to open up metaphysical questions to science fictional analysis."*

He was also, with the possible exception of H. P. Lovecraft, the most neurotic of major science-fiction writers, obsessed by the notion that human beings are trapped in a web of unreality. His persecution mania developed to a point where he could undoubtedly have been described as a paranoid schizophrenic. Yet, toward the end of his life, Dick became convinced that he had been "taken over" by a kind of superalien, who went on to reorganize his life. And although Lawrence Sutin, in his full-length biography of Dick, *Divine Invasions* (1991), casts doubts on some of Dick's claims, the case is too complex to be dismissed as simple self-delusion.

Philip Kindred Dick was an oversensitive little boy whose child-

---

*In E. F. Bleiler, ed., *Science Fiction Writers* (New York: Scribner), 1982.

hood was not designed to make him buoyant and optimistic. His twin sister died soon after his birth—as a result, he was later convinced, of his mother's neglect. He was a lonely child; his mother was cold and, in Sutin's words, "emotionally constrained." She was often in pain and spent long periods bedridden—she suffered from Bright's disease. Dick himself suffered from asthma and had eating and swallowing phobias. He was an introverted child who liked to retreat into daydreams of cowboys; he resisted all of his father's attempts to interest him in sports. His parents divorced when he was five. When he was nine, he and his mother moved to Berkeley, California, and Dick attended high school there. His relationship with his mother, who was slim and pretty, had classic Freudian overtones; when he was a teenager he even had a dream that he was sleeping with her. He finally left home at nineteen—he claimed his mother threatened to call the police to stop him—and moved into a bohemian rooming house populated by gay artists. From the age of fifteen he had worked in a local TV and record store and so was able to support himself.

At nineteen Dick was still a virgin who had never even kissed a girl. Then one of his customers—a short, overweight woman named Jeanette, who was ten years his senior—remedied the situation in a storeroom in the basement, and Dick decided to marry her; she was the first of five wives. When they had been married two months, Jeanette told him that she had a right to see other men; he dumped her possessions outside their apartment and changed the locks. His love life became sporadic and not particularly satisfying; one woman he fell in love with preferred his partner in the store; another went off with a lesbian. Another beautiful woman with whom he had an affair dropped him because he was so socially inept. A nervous breakdown—accompanied by agoraphobia—led him to leave the University of California a year later. "I managed to become universally despised wherever I went," he later told an interviewer. This led him, he said, to identify with the weak and to make the heroes in his stories weak.

From an early age Dick was obsessed by pain and misery. He records that when he was four his father, who had fought on the Marne in World War I, told him about gas attacks and men with their guts blown out. And during World War II, when he was still a child, he saw a newsreel showing a Japanese soldier who had been hit by a flamethrower and was "burning and running, and burning and running," while the audience cheered and laughed. Dick wrote of the incident: "I was dazed with horror . . . and I thought *something is terribly wrong.*" And in an autobiographical essay he wrote: "Human and animal suffering makes me mad; whenever one of my cats dies I curse God and I mean it; I feel fury at him. I'd like to get him where I could interrogate him, tell him I think the world is screwed up, that man didn't sin and fall but was pushed." Forced to kill a rat that had been caught in a trap in his children's bedroom, he was haunted for the rest of his life by its screams. As a youngster, Dick had had an urge to cruelty, but after an incident in his childhood that involved tormenting a beetle, the urge suddenly vanished and was replaced by a sense of the oneness of life—what he called satori: "I was never the same again."

Dick's obsession with the problem of cruelty resembled that of the Russian writer Dostoyevsky, whose Ivan Karamazov confesses that the cruelty and brutality of the world makes him want to "give God back his entrance ticket." It is unsurprising, therefore, that Dick's first science-fiction story, "Beyond Lies the Wub," concerned space explorers on an alien planet who buy a piglike creature called a wub, which is delighted to discuss philosophy with them—while their only desire is to eat it. A later wub story describes how wub fur is used to bind books because it is self-repairing, though the fur causes the texts to alter. Thomas Paine's *Age of Reason* vanishes completely—an expression of Dick's feeling that it is an absurd form of hubris for human beings to believe they are rational creatures.

From then on most of Dick's work had a morbid, not to say paranoid, streak. In "Second Variety," machines get out of hand and create duplicate humans to trap real people. "The Imposter" is about a man who finds himself subjected to the nightmarish experience of being suspected of being a robot bomb; the final twist of the story is that it turns out to be true. (Dick's early stories were heavily influenced by the work of the older science-

fiction writer, A. E. Van Vogt, who often chooses such themes—
e.g., a hero caught in a nightmare world of apparently insane
misunderstandings—although his basic outlook is optimistic.)

There is a Kafkaesque quality to Dick's work, which often features individuals beset by endless complications that frustrate all
attempts at purposeful action. Like so many modern writers—
notably Arthur C. Clarke—Dick likes to play with the idea of
computers developing their own intelligence and taking over from
human beings. He is also inclined to experiment with the idea that
the word "reality" is meaningless—that, instead, there are as
many "realities" as there are living creatures and that the notion
of "reality" is therefore purely subjective. This view, of course,
leads easily to solipsism, the belief that you are the only person in
the universe. After all, if the reality around us is "relative" and
self-created, then perhaps other people are illusions we create to
defend us from the recognition of our loneliness.

One of Dick's early novels, *Eye in the Sky* (1957), encapsulates
his views about "reality"; a group of people find themselves in an
"alternative reality" where other people's beliefs can become
"reality"; a religious cult imposes its own views on everyone's
mind. They then realize that they are trapped in the insane
reality of one of their own number. When they escape this illusion, they immediately find themselves entrapped in yet another.
Their return to "reality" is a painful process in which they have to
escape the "individual reality" of every member of the group. But
in this early work Dick at least believes that a "return to reality"
is possible. His later work becomes more darkly pessimistic,
infused with the underlying conviction that there is no overall
"reality," only our individual illusions. This could be regarded as
a dramatized version of the pessimistic philosophy of Schopen-
hauer and possibly that of Buddha.

In 1963 Dick finally achieved relatively wide recognition with a
novel entitled *Man in the High Castle*, which won the Hugo Award
for best science-fiction novel of the year. It is another "alternative
reality" novel, about a world in which the Allies lost the Second
World War, with the result that America is divided into a German
zone and a Japanese zone. A character named Tagomi has flashes

of an alternative reality in which the Allies won the war, but they seem absurd. Dick apparently plotted this novel with the aid of the *I Ching*, the Chinese book of oracles; the result is a certain arbitrary quality. A later novel, *Do Androids Dream of Electric Sheep?*, concerns an attempt by "real people" to root out the robots that are trying to take over the earth and that are virtually indistinguishable from humans. (It was made into a successful film, *Blade Runner*.) All of Dick's work seems to express his own sense of having an extremely insecure foundation in reality and his inability to cope with life. He wrote, "For us . . . there can be no system. Maybe *all* systems . . . are manifestations of paranoia. We should be content with the meaningless, the contradictory, the hostile."

Meanwhile, Dick's life lurched from crisis to crisis: nervous breakdowns, suicide attempts, divorces, novels written at top speed to stave off debt, paranoid delusions—at one point he saw a great metal face, with slots for eyes, looking down at him from the sky. His sexual relationships were reminiscent of those of the Swedish playwright Strindberg; again and again it looked as if the lonely, fear-ridden writer had found peace when some attractive woman thought that she could give him the security he needed. But his fundamental instability wrecked every relationship. And his loneliness and paranoia brought about writer's blocks. His biographer remarks, "If there is a dominant mood to his novels of the late sixties, it is that of a dark night of the soul." The novels themselves usually have a stifling, airless atmosphere that contrasts strongly with the wind of reality that seems to blow through the best of Tolstoy or Hemingway.

A quarrel he had with the science-fiction writer Harlan Ellison seems to embody everything that was wrong with Dick. At a science-fiction conference in Metz, France, Dick bewildered and bored his audience with a typically rambling speech entitled "If You Find This World Bad, You Should See Some of the Others." Audience members suspected he was drunk or on drugs. (He was, in fact, addicted to numerous prescription drugs.) Dick and Ellison had parted company before because Ellison felt Dick was unreliable and "possibly loony." When they met in the bar they engaged in a bitter philosophical debate that was basically a quarrel. Dick's girlfriend at the time gives a memorable word-portrait of the encounter:

> Phil was very antithetical to Harlan. Harlan is very cocky, glib, cool, and here is Phil going clunk clunk clunk. Phil was not a very debonair or self-assured man. Snuff falling out of his nose, ninety-two spots on his tie—you know. And Harlan thought Phil treated people very badly because he wandered away, got lost, had people support him rather than be master of his own ship.
>
> Anyway, they got into this huge debate. Phil does very well in these kinds of situations. Here is Harlan banging his chest, and Phil was more a philosopher. Phil was just great—more dynamic and sexy than I'd ever seen him.

Clearly, Dick *could* pull himself together and organize his ideas. Yet, as Ellison realized, he preferred to "have people support him rather than be master of his own ship."

But on March 2, 1974, Dick experienced a "vision" that transformed his life. He later told an interviewer, Charles Platt, "My mental anguish was simply removed from me as if by a divine fiat. . . . Some transcendent divine power, which was not evil, but benign, intervened to restore my mind and heal my body and give me a sense of the beauty, the joy, the sanity of the world."

In February 1974 Dick was convinced that he was being persecuted by both American and Soviet authorities; he was also convinced that he was destined to die the following month.

One night, lying awake and wrestling with "dread and melancholy," he began to see whirling lights. A week later he again had visions but this time of "perfectly formed modern abstract paintings"—hundreds of thousands of them replacing each other at dazzling speed. Then he experienced the "Bardo Thodol journey" (an after-death journey, as described in the *Tibetan Book of the Dead*) and found himself face to face with the goddess Aphrodite. After this he began hearing female voices as he hovered in hypnagogic states on the edge of sleep. On March 16 "it appeared—in vivid fire, with shining colors and balanced patterns—and released me from every thrall, inner and outer." Two days later "it, from inside me, looked out." In other words, Dick now felt another being inside himself; he was "possessed." But the entity seemed benevolent: "It denied the reality, the power, the authenticity, of the world, saying, 'This cannot exist; it cannot exist.' " Two days later: "It seized me entirely, lifting me from the limitations of the space-time matrix; it mastered me as, at the same instant, I knew that the world around me was cardboard, a fake. Through its power I suddenly saw the universe as it was; through its perception I saw what really existed, and through its power of no-thought decision, I acted to *free myself.*"

All this sounds like the typical rambling of a psychotic. Yet what actually took place was by no means entirely in the realm of fantasy. Dick had a conviction that he would receive a letter that would kill him. His wife, Tessa, confirms that one morning he selected a letter from a large batch of mail, handed it to her unopened, and told her that this was what he had been expecting. In fact, it was a photocopy of a book review about the decline of American capitalism, and every negative word, such as *die, decline, decay,* and *decomposition,* had been underlined. Paranoid or not, Dick seemed to have a sixth sense that enabled him to detect the strange letter unopened.

Now, says Dick, he was taken over by the "intelligence." "On Thursdays and Saturdays I would think it was God, on Tuesdays and Wednesdays I would think it was extraterrestrial. . . . It set about healing me physically, [as well as] my four-year-old boy, who had an undiagnosed life-threatening birth defect that no one had been aware of."

The "intelligence," which Dick called Valis (*Vast Active Living Intelligence System*), fired information into his brain by means of pink light beams. It told him that his son, Christopher, suffered from a potentially fatal inguinal hernia. The Dicks checked with the doctor and found that the information was correct; the hernia was remedied by an operation.

Dick told Charles Platt:

This mind was equipped with tremendous technical knowledge—engineering, medical, cosmological, philosophical knowledge. It had memories dating back over two thousand years, it spoke Greek, Hebrew, Sanskrit, there wasn't anything that it didn't seem to know.

It immediately set about putting my affairs in order. It fired my agent and my publisher. It remargined my typewriter. It was very practical; it decided that the apartment had not been vacuumed recently enough; it decided that I should stop drinking wine because of the sediment—it turned out I had an abundance of uric acid in my system—and it switched me to beer. It made elementary mistakes, such as calling the dog "he" and the cat "she"—which annoyed my wife; and it kept calling her "ma'am."

His wife, Tessa, told Dick's biographer, Lawrence Sutin, that she had no doubt of the genuineness of these "mystical" experiences. But she herself also had reason to believe that there was some basis for her husband's paranoia. Dick thought that the radio was transmitting programs in which a popular singer called him names, told him he was worthless, and advised him to die. This sounds like a typical schizophrenic delusion. But Tessa herself verified that the radio would go on at two in the morning and play music (she did not hear the voice); the odd thing was that the radio was unplugged.

Dick goes on:

My wife was impressed by the fact that, because of the tremendous pressure this mind put on people in my business, I made quite a lot of money very rapidly. We began to get checks for thousands of dollars—money that was owed me, which the mind was conscious existed in New York but had never been coughed up. And it got me to the doctor who confirmed its diagnoses of the various ailments I had . . . it did everything but paper the walls of the apartment. It also said it would stay on as my tutelary spirit. I had to look up "tutelary" to see what it meant.

Sutin verifies that Dick galvanized his agent—the one he had fired for a time—into pursuing back royalties from Ace Books and that the agent was able to send him a check for $3,000.

Tessa also confirmed that Dick normally refused to go to the doctor but that the "spirit" insisted and that the doctor immediately had Dick check into a hospital for treatment of high blood pressure. He came out physically much improved. His wife wrote, "It made Phil more fun to be with. Every day brought an adventure." And his experiences culminated in this insight: "This is not an evil world. . . . There is a good world under the evil. The evil is somehow superimposed over it . . . and when stripped away, pristine, glowing creation is visible."

Dick's life began to improve. He had always been poor. In 1974 he made $19,000, and in the following year, $35,000. As his reputation increased, so did demands for interviews, and an increasing number of his novels were translated into foreign languages. Several books were optioned by Hollywood, and one of them, as mentioned earlier, became a classic movie, *Blade Runner*. When Dick died—of a stroke and heart failure—in 1982, he had achieved cult status among thousands of science-fiction fans and had become something of a legend.

How far can we accept Dick's own estimate of his "possession" experience? His biographer, Lawrence Sutin, is obviously ambivalent about the subject. Yet the title of his book, *Divine Invasions*, indicates that he feels the experience to be the most important in Dick's life. His ambivalence is understandable. Dick sounds like a paranoid schizophrenic, and paranoid schizophrenics have "visions." Yet there is enough factual evidence to suggest that Dick may not have been suffering from delusions after all.

The problem, of course, is that a rational human being finds it practically impossible to believe in "possession"—except as a psychiatric label. Chapter 26 in this book argues that such an attitude may not be as reasonable as it sounds. It depends upon the assumption that disembodied "spirits" cannot exist, and while no one will disagree that this is a perfectly sensible *assumption* for a rational and practical human being, we cannot assume that it is *true* for that reason. And if we are willing even to admit the logical possibility of spirits, then we have also admitted the logical possibility of "possession."

An American psychiatrist, Wilson Van Dusen, found himself in this position, simply as a result of his work with mental patients at Mendocino State Hospital in California. In a book entitled *The Natural Depth in Man* (1972), Van Dusen defined madness as "a turning in on one's self that makes one a constricted uselessness that misses one's highest potentials." In other words, madness is a *limitation* of our natural potential—which inevitably raises the question: What *is* our natural potential? Van Dusen's conclusion was that all human beings have the potential to undergo "mystical" experiences, in which consciousness seems to expand far beyond its normal limitations, and that therefore, in a certain sense, we are all "mad."

He went on to describe how he managed to establish contact with one of his patient's hallucinations. The girl had a phantom lover, and "just for the heck of it," Van Dusen asked her to "report faithfully what [the lover] said and did." Van Dusen was thus able to hold "conversations" with the hallucination, using the patient as a go-between. He then found, to his surprise, that he was able to give psychological tests to his patients *and* to their hallucinations, separately. He next made a startling and disturbing discovery: the hallucinations were sicker than the patients. That should have been quite impossible, since the hallucinations *were* the patients. Yet "what was revealed of the hallucinations looked remarkably like ancient accounts of spirit possession." There could be no doubt in Van Dusen's mind that the hallucinations behaved like real people, and really replied to his remarks; for example, the patient's eyes would sometimes flash sideways as Van Dusen was talking and the hallucination interposed some remark.

Patients often told stories of how they had come to "meet" their hallucinations: "One woman was just working in her garden and a kindly man started talking to her when no one else was around. One alcoholic heard voices coming up a hotel light well. Another man saw a spaceship land and green men getting out." (This experience is worth bearing in mind, when one considers so-called contactees of flying saucers; if Van Dusen is correct, these may not always be hallucinations.) "It takes a while for the patient to figure out that he is having private experiences that are consequently not shared by others."

There was evidence that the "hallucinations" were not entirely subjective and unreal. One of the patients was a woman who had "murdered a rather useless husband." The Virgin Mary had come to her in the hospital and advised her to drive to the southern part of the state and stand trial for murder. The Virgin told her there would be an earthquake on the day she left for the south and another on the day she arrived. In fact, both earthquakes took place on cue.

Van Dusen soon noted that there seemed to be two types of hallucinations, which he termed "higher order" and "lower order." The lower order were stupider than the patient. They would lie, cheat, deceive, and threaten. They might repeat the same word over and over again for days on end; they might tell the patient he was useless and stupid and that they were going to kill him. They behaved, says Van Dusen, like "drunken bums in a bar."

The "higher order," on the other hand, were more intelligent and talented than the patient, and far from attacking him, they respected his freedom. They were "helpers." In one case, Van Dusen was introduced by his patient—a "not very gifted gas fitter"—to a "beautiful lady" who referred to herself as the Emanation of the Feminine Aspect of the Divine and who seemed to have an incredible knowledge of religious symbols: "When I or the patient said something very right, she would come over to us and hand us her panties." One day Van Dusen went home and spent the evening studying Greek myths. The next day he asked the "hallucination" about some of the obscurer parts. "She not only understood the myth, she saw into its human implications better than I did. When asked, she playfully wrote the Greek alphabet all over the place. The patient couldn't even recognize the letters, but he could copy hers for me." As the gas fitter was leaving the room, he turned to Van Dusen and asked him to give him a clue as to what the conversation had been about.

The detail of handing over the panties makes it sound as if, whatever Van Dusen thought, this hallucination was conjured up by the gas fitter—who admitted that he had made "immoral" proposals to the woman and had been rejected. Yet her description of herself as the "Emanation of the Feminine Aspect of the Divine" offers an important clue. She was describing herself as the archetypal symbolic woman, Goethe's "eternal womanly." For a male, the incredible essence of the female is that she is willing to give herself; the handing over of her panties may be regarded as a singularly apt symbol for this essence.

Van Dusen was fascinated to discover that the Swedish mystic Emanuel Swedenborg (1688–1772) had described the lower and higher orders with considerable accuracy. They were, according to Swedenborg, "spirits," and the lower order were earthbound spirits who were driven by malice or boredom. These tended to outnumber the higher spirits by about four to one. Like Kardec (see chapter 26), Swedenborg commented that spirits could only "invade" people with whom they had some affinity—which probably explained why the low spirits outnumbered the high ones. Swedenborg referred to "high spirits" as angels and said that their purpose was to help; low spirits might be regarded as devils, yet their function was often—in spite of themselves—a helpful one, for they pointed out the patient's sins and shortcomings.

Could Swedenborg have been mad? asks Van Dusen, and replies that there is no evidence for it whatever. What *is* odd is that his high and low spirits are not confined to Christian mental homes; they transcend cultural barriers and can be found just as frequently among Muslim or Hindu lunatics.

Van Dusen reaches the interesting conclusion that "the spiritual world is much as Swedenborg described it, and is the unconscious."

If he is correct, and the "spirit world" lies *inside* us—as another remarkable mystic, Rudolf Steiner, asserted—then we can begin to see why mental patients might experience hallucinations. They might have "opened" themselves to their own depths, to the curious denizens of those regions.

When Philip K. Dick's strange experiences are considered in the light of these comments, it becomes clear that it is impossible to dismiss him as a paranoid schizophrenic. We must at least be willing to leave open the possibility that he was aware—as expressed in the title of Wilson Van Dusen's second book—of "the presence of other worlds."

8

The Dogon and the Ancient Astronauts: Evidence of Visitors from Space?

The theory that the earth has been visited, perhaps even colonized, by beings from outer space has been a part of popular mythology since Stanley Kubrick's cult movie *2001: A Space Odyssey* (written by Arthur C. Clarke), came out in 1968. But it had already been "in the air" for many years—in fact, since 1947, when a businessman named Kenneth Arnold, who was flying his private plane near Mount Rainier, in Washington, reported seeing nine shining disks traveling at an estimated speed of one thousand miles an hour. Soon "UFO" sightings were being reported from all over the world—far too many and too precise to be dismissed as pure fantasy.

In 1958, in a book entitled *The Secret Places of the Lion*, a "contactee" named George Hunt Williamson advanced the theory that visitors from space had arrived on earth 18 million years ago and had since been devoting themselves to helping mankind evolve. It was they who built the Great Pyramid. Perhaps because it is so full of references to the Bible, Williamson's book made little impact.

In 1960 there appeared in France a book entitled *The Morning of the Magicians* (*Le Matin des Magiciens*) by Louis Pauwels and Jacques Bergier, which became an instant bestseller and which may claim the dubious credit of having initiated the "occult boom" of the 1960s. (Before that the fashion was for political rebellion with a strong Marxist flavor.) Its success was largely due to its suggestion that Hitler may have been involved in black magic, but it also included speculations about the Great Pyramid, the statues of Easter Island, Hans Hoerbiger's theory that the moon is covered with ice (soon to be disproved by the moon landings), and the reality of alchemical transformation. Fiction writers like Arthur Machen, H. P. Lovecraft, and John Buchan are discussed alongside Einstein and Jung. And there is, inevitably, a section on the famous Piri Re'is map (see chapter 28), in which the authors succeed in mixing up the sixteenth-century pirate Piri Re'is with a Turkish naval officer who presented a copy of the map to the Library of Congress in 1959. They conclude the discussion: "Were these copies of still earlier maps? Had they been traced from observations made on board a flying machine or space vessel of some kind? Notes taken by visitors from Beyond?"

These speculations caused excitement because the world was in the grip of flying-saucer mania. Books by people who claimed to be "contactees"—like George Adamski—became best-sellers. And while many "sightings" could be dismissed as hysteria—or as what Jung called "projections" (meaning religious delusions)—a few were too well authenticated to fit that simplistic theory.

In 1967 a Swiss writer named Erich von Däniken eclipsed *The Morning of the Magicians* with a book entitled *Memories of the Future*. Translated into English as *Chariots of the Gods?*, it soon sold more than a million copies. This work was also devoted to the thesis that visitors from space had landed on earth when men were still living in caves and had been responsible for many ancient monuments, such as the Great Pyramid, the Easter Island statues, the Nazca lines drawn in the sand of southern Peru (he suggested they were runways for spaceships), and the step pyramids of South America.

But von Däniken's almost willful carelessness quickly led to his being soon discredited. Perhaps the most obvious example of this carelessness was his treatment of Easter Island. Von Däniken alleged that the island's gigantic stone statues—some of them twenty feet high—could only have been carved and erected with the aid of sophisticated technology, which would have been far beyond the resources of primitive savages. In fact, the Norwegian explorer Thor Heyerdahl persuaded modern Easter Islanders to carve and erect statues with their own "primitive technology." Von Däniken had also pointed out that Easter Island has no wood for rollers—unaware that only a few centuries ago, the island was covered with woodland and that the Easter Islanders had been responsible for the destruction of their own environment.

Most of von Däniken's other arguments proved equally vulnerable. He had insisted that a stone tablet—known as the Palenque tablet—from Chiapas, Mexico, depicted a "spaceman" about to blast off. Archaeologists who had studied the religion of ancient Mexico demonstrated that what von Däniken mistook for instruments of space technology were traditional Mexican religious symbols. Von Däniken's assertions about the pyramids proved equally fanciful and uninformed. He asked how such monuments could have been constructed without the aid of ropes and managed to overstate the weight of the Great Pyramid by a multiple of five. Experts on the pyramids pointed out that ancient paintings show the Egyptians using ropes and were able to prove that ancient Egyptian engineers were more knowledgeable than von Däniken realized. As to the famous Nazca lines, it required no expert to see that lines drawn in the sand—even if made of small pebbles—would soon be blasted away by any kind of spacecraft coming in to land. In fact, the purpose of the Nazca lines—like that of all ancient fertility ceremonies—seems to have been to control the weather.

Much of von Däniken's literary evidence is equally dubious. He discusses the Assyrian *Epic of Gilgamesh* (getting the date of its discovery wrong) and describes how the sun-god Enkidu bore the hero Gilgamesh upward in his claws "so that his body felt as heavy as lead"—which to von Däniken suggests an ascent in a space rocket. The tower of the goddess Ishtar—visited by the hero—is also, according to von Däniken, a space rocket. A door "that spoke like a living person" is obviously a loudspeaker. And so on. Anyone who takes the trouble to check the *Epic of Gilgamesh*— readily available in a paperback translation—will discover that none of these episodes actually occurs.

But the von Däniken bubble finally burst in 1972 when, in *Gold of the Gods*, the author claimed to have visited a vast underground cave system in Ecuador, with elaborately engineered walls, and examined an ancient library engraved on metal sheets. When his fellow explorer, Juan Moricz, denied that von Däniken had even ventured into the caves, von Däniken admitted that his account was fictional, but argued that his book was not intended to be a scientific treatise; since it was designed for popular consumption, he had allowed himself a certain degree of poetic license. Yet in a biography of von Däniken, Peter Krassa ignores this admission, insisting that the case is still open and that von Däniken may have been telling the truth after all. But Krassa has a skillful technique of making an admission and then quickly taking it back again. He concludes: "Of course his report was mad, and untrue; this story about underground caverns; his description of the golden treasure to be found there was a lie. This was the judgment of many scientists and journalists."

In fact, a British expedition to the caves found them to be natural, with evidence of habitation by primitive man but no signs of von Däniken's ancient library or perfectly engineered walls. A two-hour TV exposé of von Däniken subsequently punctured every one of his major claims.

Having said which, it must be admitted that von Däniken and other "ancient astronaut" theorists have at least one extremely powerful piece of evidence on their side. Members of an African tribe called the Dogon, who live in the Republic of Mali, some 300 miles south of Timbuktu, insist that they possess knowledge that was transmitted to them by "spacemen" from the star Sirius, which is 8.7 light-years away. Dogon mythology insists that the "Dog Star" Sirius (so called because it is in the constellation Canis) has a dark companion that is invisible to the naked eye and that is dense and very heavy. This is correct; Sirius does indeed have a dark companion known as Sirius B.

The existence of Sirius B had been suspected by astronomers since the mid-nineteenth century, and it was first observed in 1862—although it was not described in detail until the 1920s. Is it possible that some white traveler took the knowledge of Sirius B to Africa sometime since the 1850s? It is possible but unlikely.

Two French anthropologists, Marcel Griaule and Germaine Dieterlen, first revealed the "secret of the Dogon" in an obscure paper in 1950; it was entitled "A Sudanese Sirius System" and was published in the *Journal de la Société des Africainistes*.

The two anthropologists had lived among the Dogon since 1931, and in 1946 Griaule was initiated into the religious secrets of the tribe. He was told that fishlike creatures called the Nommo had come to Earth from Sirius to civilize its people. Sirius B, which the Dogon call *po tolo* (naming it after the seed that forms the staple part of their diet, and whose botanical name is *Digitaria*), is made of matter heavier than any on earth and moves in an elliptical orbit, taking fifty years to do so. It was not until 1928 that Sir Arthur Eddington postulated the theory of "white dwarfs"—stars whose atoms have collapsed inward, so that a piece the size of a pea could weigh half a ton. (Sirius B is the size of the earth yet weighs as much as the sun.) Griaule and Dieterlen went to live among the Dogon three years later. Is it likely that some traveler carried a new and complex scientific theory to a remote African tribe in the three years between 1928 and 1931?

An oriental scholar named Robert Temple went to Paris to study the Dogon with Germaine Dieterlen. He soon concluded that the knowledge shown by the Dogon could not be explained away as coincidence or "diffusion" (knowledge passed on through contact with other peoples). The Dogon appeared to have an extraordinarily detailed knowledge of our solar system. They said that the moon was "dry and dead," and they drew Saturn with a ring around it (which, of course, is only visible through a telescope). They knew that the planets revolved around the sun. They knew about the moons of Jupiter (first seen through a telescope by Galileo). They had recorded the movements of Venus in their temples. They knew that the earth rotates and that the number of stars is infinite. And when they drew the elliptical orbit of Sirius, they showed the star off-center, not in the middle of the orbit—as someone without knowledge of astronomy would naturally conclude.

The Dogon insist that their knowledge was brought to them by the amphibious Nommo from a "star" (presumably they mean a planet) which, like Sirius B, rotates around Sirius and whose weight is only a quarter of Sirius B's. They worshiped the Nommo as gods. They drew diagrams to portray the spinning of the craft in which these creatures landed and were precise about the landing location—the place to the northwest of present Dogon country, where the Dogon originated. They mention that the "ark" in which the Nommo arrived caused a whirling dust storm and that it "skidded." They speak of "a flame that went out as they touched the earth," which implies that they landed in a small space capsule. Dogon mythology also mentions a glowing object in the sky like a star, presumably the mother ship.

Our telescopes have not yet revealed the "planet" of the Nommo, but that is hardly surprising. Sirius B was only discovered because its weight caused perturbations in the orbit of Sirius. The Dog Star is 35.5 times as bright (and hot) as our sun, so any planet capable of supporting life would have to be in the far reaches of its solar system and would almost certainly be invisible to telescopes. Temple surmises that the planet of the Nommo would be hot and steamy and that this probably explains why intelligent life evolved in its seas, which would be cooler. These fish-people would spend much of their time on land but close to the water; they would need a layer of water on their skins to be comfortable, and if their skins dried, it would be as agonizing as severe sunburn. Temple sees them as a kind of dolphin.

But what were such creatures doing in the middle of the desert, near Timbuktu? In fact, the idea is obviously absurd. Temple points out that to the northwest of Mali lies Egypt, and for many reasons, he is inclined to believe that the landing of the Nommo took place there.

Temple also points out that a Babylonian historian named Berossus—a contemporary and apparently an acquaintance of Aristotle (fourth century B.C.)—claims in his history, of which only fragments survive, that Babylonian civilization was founded by alien amphibians, the chief of whom is called Oannes—the Philistines knew him as Dagon (and the science-fiction writer H. P. Lovecraft borrowed him for his own mythology). The Greek grammarian Apollodorus (about 140 B.C.) had apparently read more of Berossus, for he criticizes another Greek writer, Abydenus, for failing to mention that Oannes was only one of the "fish people"; he calls these aliens "Annedoti" ("repulsive ones") and says they are "semi-demons" from the sea.

But why should the Dogon pay any particular attention to Sirius, even though it was one of the brightest stars in the sky? After all, it was merely one among thousands of stars. There, at least, the skeptics can produce a convincing answer. Presumably, the Dogon learned from the Egyptians, and for the ancient Egyptians, Sothis (as they called Sirius) was the most important star in the heavens—at least, after 3200 B.C., when it began to rise just before the dawn, at the beginning of the Egyptian New Year, and signaled that the Nile was about to rise.

So the Dog Star became the god of rising waters. The goddess Sothis was identified with Isis; and Temple points out that in Egyptian tomb paintings, Isis is usually to be found in a boat with two fellow goddesses, Anukis and Satis. Temple argues convincingly that this indicates that the Egyptians knew Sirius to be a three-star system—the unknown "Sirius C" being the home of the Nommo. An ancient Arabic name for one of the stars in the Sirius constellation (not Sirius itself) is Al Wazn, meaning "weight," and one text says that it is almost too heavy to rise over the horizon.

Temple suggests that the ancients may have looked toward the Canis constellation for Sirius B and mistaken it for Al Wazn. He also suggests that Homer's Sirens—mermaidlike creatures who are all-knowing and who try to lure men away from their everyday responsibilities—are actually "Sirians," amphibious goddesses. He also points out that Jason's boat, the Argo, is associated with the goddess Isis and that it has fifty rowers—fifty being the number of years it takes Sirius B to circle Sirius A. There are many other fish-bodied aliens in Greek mythology, including the Telchines of Rhodes, who were supposed to have come from the sea and to have introduced men to various arts, including metalwork. Significantly, they had dogs' heads.

But if the Egyptians knew about Sirius B and the Nommo, then why do we not have Egyptian texts that tell us about aliens from the Dog Star system? Here the answer is obvious: Marcel Griaule had to be "initiated" by Dogon priests before he was permitted to learn about the visitors from Sirius. If the Egyptians knew about Sirius B, the knowledge was revealed only to initiates. But it would have left its mark in Egyptian mythology—for example, in the boat of Isis.

Temple's book *The Sirius Mystery* (1976) is full of such mythological "evidence," and much of it has been attacked for stretching interpretation too far. Yet what remains when all the arguments have been considered is the curious fact that a remote African tribe has some precise knowledge of an entire star system not visible to the human eye alone and that they attribute this knowledge to aliens from that star system. That single fact suggests that in spite of von Däniken's absurdities, we should remain open-minded about the possibility that alien visitors once landed on our planet.

9

Fairies:
Are the "Little People"
Just a Fairy Tale?

In the summer of 1897 the poet W. B. Yeats went to stay at Coole Park, in Galway, with Lady Augusta Gregory, who was to become his close friend and patroness, and the two of them began collecting fairy stories from the local peasantry. Yeats had already compiled two collections of Irish myths and fairy tales by interviewing peasants in his home county of Sligo. But he now came to recognize that the majority of Irish country folk accepted the existence of fairies, not as some kind of half-believed superstition—like touching wood—but as a concrete fact of life.

Yeats's father was a total skeptic, and Yeats himself had been inclined to toy with a belief in fairies as a kind of reaction to the materialism of the modern world—in short, as a kind of wishful thinking. His collaboration with Lady Gregory made him aware that belief in fairies could hardly be dismissed as wishful thinking. G. K. Chesterton, who met him several years later, was impressed by his insistence on the factual reality of fairies and wrote of Yeats in his autobiography:

He was the real original rationalist who said that the fairies stand to reason. He staggered the materialists by attacking their abstract materialism with a completely concrete mysticism; "Imagination!"

he would say with withering contempt; "There wasn't much imagination when Farmer Hogan was dragged out of bed and thrashed
like a sack of potatoes—that they did, they had 'um out;" the Irish
accent warming with scorn; "they had 'um out and thumped 'um;
and that's not the sort of thing that a man wants to imagine."

Chesterton goes on to make a very important point:

It is the fact that it is not abnormal men like artists, but normal
men like peasants, who have borne witness a thousand times to
such things; it is the farmers who see the fairies. It is the agricultural labourer who calls a spade a spade who also calls a spirit a
spirit; it is the woodcutter with no axe to grind . . . who will say he
saw a man hang on the gallows, and afterwards hang round it was
a ghost.

A few years later Yeats was to encourage the orientalist W. Y.
Evans Wentz—best known for his translation of the *Tibetan Book
of the Dead*—to study the folklore of the fairies; the result was
Wentz's first book, *The Fairy Faith in Celtic Countries* (1911), a
bulky and scholarly volume based upon his own extensive field-
work. Yeats's friend, the poet AE (George Russell), contributed an
anonymous piece to the book (under the title "An Irish Mystic's
Testimony") in which he described his own fairy sightings with the
factual accuracy and precision of an anthropologist describing
primitive tribes: shining beings, opalescent beings, water beings,
wood beings, lower elementals:

The first of [the fairies] I saw I remember very clearly . . . . : there
was first a dazzle of light, and then I saw that this came from the
heart of a tall figure with a body apparently shaped out of half-
transparent or opalescent air, and throughout the body ran a
radiant electrical fire, to which the heart seemed the centre.
Around the head of this being and through its waving luminous
hair, which was blown all about the body like living strands of gold,
there appeared flaming wing-like auras. From the being itself light
seemed to stream outwards in every direction; and the effect left
on me after the vision was one of extraordinary lightness, joyous-
ness or ecstasy.

Wentz concludes that the factual and scientific evidence for the existence of fairies is overwhelming, that in fact, "there are hundreds of proven cases of phenomena."

But AE's fairies were essentially "visions" and could therefore be classified with unicorns or centaurs. In 1920, nine years after Wentz's book appeared, the British public was intrigued to learn of new scientific evidence that seemed to place belief in "the little people" on an altogether more solid foundation. The front cover of the Christmas issue of the *Strand* magazine announced: "An Epoch-Making Event . . . Described by Conan Doyle." Facing the opening page of the article was a photograph of a teenage girl in a white cotton dress, sitting in a grassy field and holding out her hand to a dancing gnome. Another photograph showed a younger girl gazing mildly into the camera over a group of four cavorting fairies, complete with gossamer wings. The caption under the first photograph stated: "This picture and the even more extraordinary one of fairies on page 465 are the two most astounding photographs ever published. How they were taken is fully described in Sir A. Conan Doyle's article."

It was not a seasonal joke. Doyle and his fellow investigators were convinced that the two photographs virtually proved the existence of "the little people." The resulting controversy was to remain unsettled for the next sixty years.

The girls in the photograph were Elsie Wright and Frances Griffiths, and they lived in the village of Cottingley, in Yorkshire. They had taken the photographs three and a half years earlier, in the summer of 1917, and had consistently claimed, often in the face of extremely skeptical cross-examination, that the photographs were of real fairies.

The village of Cottingley is situated near Bradford, although it has today been swallowed up by suburbs. In 1917 it was surrounded by green English countryside. It was in April of that year that ten-year-old Frances Griffiths had moved to the village with her mother, Annie, from South Africa; her father was fighting in France. She later claimed that she soon realized there were fairies in the fields around her home, especially near the local beck (stream), which ran down a steep-sided dell at the bottom of her garden. She later described the first time she said she had seen a fairy down by the stream.

> One evening after school I went down to the beck to a favourite place—the willow overhanging the stream . . . then a willow leaf started shaking violently—just one. I'd seen it happen before—there was no wind, and it was odd that one leaf should shake . . . as I watched, a small man, all dressed in green, stood on the branch with the stem of the leaf in his hand, which he seemed to be shaking at something he was looking at. I daren't move for fear of frightening him. He looked straight at me and disappeared.

But she had decided not to tell anyone for fear of being laughed at.

She explained how, as the summer wore on, she had become increasingly fascinated by the stream and how she would spend hours "fairy-watching" in the dell. She occasionally missed her footing on the slippery bank and landed up to her waist in the water. When she returned home her mother would slap her and make her promise not to go near the stream, but Frances never kept her promise—she could not resist the urge to see the fairies.

One day, when she arrived home soaked yet again, her mother and her Aunt Polly pressed hard for an explanation. What they heard left them both slightly breathless: "I go to see the fairies! That's why—to see the fairies!"

At this point, to the surprise of the two women, Frances's cousin, seventeen-year-old Elsie Wright, came to her defense and insisted that she, too, had seen fairies. No amount of questioning could shake the girls' story. According to Doyle's article, it was this confrontation that convinced the two cousins that they must produce some indisputable evidence to make the grown-ups eat their words.

That is why, on a Saturday afternoon in July 1917, Elsie asked her father, Arthur Wright, if she could borrow his plate camera. He was understandably reluctant, since the camera was new and the plates expensive, but he eventually gave way. The girls hurried off to the stream and were back in half an hour. After tea Arthur was coaxed into developing the plate.

As the plate started to develop, he realized that it was a picture of Frances leaning on a bank that seemed to be scattered with sandwich papers. Then, to his amazement, he saw that the "papers" were tiny human forms with wings growing from their backs; they were apparently four dancing fairies.

The girls' mothers didn't know what to think. Both had recently become interested in Theosophy—the movement founded by Madame Blavatsky, who taught that behind the solid world of everyday reality there was an invisible world peopled with spiritual beings, including nature spirits or fairies. In theory, at any rate, they agreed.

Arthur Wright, on the other hand, was skeptical:

"You've been up to summat."

"No we haven't," Elsie insisted.

He knew that Elsie was a gifted artist and was convinced that the fairies were paper cutouts—although a search of the girls' room and the wastebaskets failed to turn up any snippets of paper left over from manufactured fairies. And in spite of all their protestations, he remained unconvinced. Eventually, the matter was dropped. But in August the girls borrowed the camera again; this time they returned with a picture of Elsie sitting in a field watching a dancing gnome. They explained that they often saw gnomes in the field just above the stream. After this, in the interest of peace and quiet, Arthur Wright refused further loans of his camera. But several prints were made of each plate.

The whole affair might have been forgotten if it had not been for the Theosophical Society. After the war, with its appalling casualties, Spiritualism and Theosophy had made thousands of new converts, and the Bradford Unity Hall, where the Society held its meetings, was always packed.

After a meeting in which fairies had been mentioned, Polly Wright approached the speaker and told him about the photographs. He asked to see them, and copies were soon circulating among the Bradford Theosophists.

Shortly afterward Polly Wright received a letter from Edward L. Gardner, head of the Theosophist Lodge in London; he was excited about the photographs and asked to see the original prints and negatives. Upon receiving the negatives, Gardner had them copied and the copies then retouched. He was quite open about this; in a letter to Doyle he wrote:

> I begged the loan of the actual negatives—and two quarter plates came by post a few days after. One was a fairly clear one, the other much under exposed . . . the immediate upshot was that a positive was taken from each negative, that the originals might be preserved untouched, and then new negatives were prepared and intensified to service as better printing mediums.

He then took the original prints and negatives to a professional photographer, Harold Snelling. Snelling's previous employer had assured Gardner that "what Snelling doesn't know about faked photography isn't worth knowing."

It was Snelling who examined the four-dancing-fairies negative (the better-exposed plate). He reported to Gardner:

> This plate is a single exposure. . . . These dancing fairies are not made of paper nor of any fabric; they are not painted on a photo-graphed background—but what gets me most is that all these figures have *moved* during exposure.

Gardner, delighted with this verdict, began showing lantern slides of the photographs at Theosophy meetings around the country. And in the summer of 1920 he was flattered to receive a letter from the creator of Sherlock Holmes.

The sixty-year-old Doyle was not a Theosophist, but in recent years he had become convinced of the truth of Spiritualism. He had already been commissioned by the *Strand* to write an article on fairies, and the news of the Cottingley photographs must have sounded like a gift from the beyond. When he saw the photographs, Doyle was at first skeptical about them. But a meeting with Gardner convinced him that they could be genuine. The next step, obviously, was to try to obtain more of them.

Toward the end of July 1920 Edward Gardner went to visit the Wrights for the first time—Frances was then in Scarborough with her father and so was not present. Elsie's father made no attempt to conceal the fact that he was unhappy about the whole situation. He still felt that the photographs were fakes, and the high esteem in which he held Doyle had declined sharply when he heard that Doyle was now convinced "by our Elsie, and her at the bottom of her class!"

But his wife had a long and thoughtful talk with Gardner, and Elsie later showed him the field, and the spot by the stream where the photographs had been taken. Some people had felt that the stream photograph looked a little too "magical" to be true, with its little toadstools and waterfall; Gardner was delighted to find that it looked exactly as in the photograph. He reported to Doyle that he was convinced that the girls were genuine. Doyle still felt that more photographs were needed to prove the case. So, as Doyle embarked on a steamship south to Australia to lecture on Spiritualism, Gardner went north again, this time armed with new cameras and two dozen carefully numbered plates. (Oddly enough, nobody bothered to note how many plates were eventually used by the girls, so the numbering was wasted.)

On this occasion Gardner also met Frances, then fourteen, who had returned from Scarborough for the summer holidays. He soon formed the conviction that both girls were psychic. Since the weather was rainy and dull—bad visibility for fairy-spotting, according to the girls—he left the cameras behind and returned to London. The rain continued for the next two weeks.

The morning of August 19 was dull and misty, but when it brightened up later, the girls decided to try out the cameras. They returned with two more photographs, which were promptly developed by the unbelieving Arthur Wright. One was of a winged fairy, with stylish-looking bobbed hair, standing placidly on a branch, offering Elsie a tiny bunch of harebells. The other was of a slightly blurred Frances jerking her head back as another winged fairy leapt toward her. It was clear that it was leaping rather than flying because the wings were unblurred by movement. Gardner later had these photographs examined by an expert, who again reported that they showed no signs of fraud.

The last photograph was taken on a drizzly day, August 21, 1920. Later referred to by Frances as a "fairy sunbath," it seems to show two fairies hanging a gossamerlike material over a tuft of grass, to make a shelter or suntrap. Frances said she often saw the little people doing this on dull days, as if to keep themselves warm. Oddly enough, this phenomenon has been reported in various unconnected fairy sightings before and after the Cottingley photographs. The fairies in this last photograph have a semi-transparent quality, which detractors claimed was a sign of double exposure but which believers ascribed to the effect of cold on the fairy constitution.

Since Doyle had written the *Strand* article before he left for Australia, it made no reference to these last three photographs. Even so, when the magazine was published that Christmas—with retouched, much sharper prints—it caused a sensation. The Cottingley fairies became the talk of every London dinner table. But skeptics were outraged at what they regarded as the public's infantile gullibility. Their basic argument was summed up in the January 5 issue of *Truth*: "For the true explanation of these fairy photographs what is wanted is not a knowledge of occult phenomena but a knowledge of children."

One detractor, a doctor by the name of Major Hall-Edwards, even went so far as to say:

> I criticize the attitude of those who declared there is something supernatural in the circumstances attending to the taking of these pictures because, as a medical man, I believe that the inculcation of such absurd ideas into the minds of children will result in later life in manifestations of nervous disorder and mental disturbances.

(One wonders how he felt about parents telling their children that Santa Claus was a real person.)

On the other hand, the Cottingley fairies had their supporters in the media. The *South Wales Argus* commented: "The day we kill our Santa Claus with our statistics we shall have plunged a glorious world into deepest darkness." The *City News* said more pragmatically: "It seems at this point that we must either believe in the almost incredible mystery of the fairy or in the almost incredible wonders of faked photographs."

Doyle himself, still in Australia, was delighted by the new pictures. He wrote to Gardner:

My heart gladdened when out here in far Australia I had your note and the photographs, which are confirmatory of our published results. When our fairies are admitted other psychic phenomena will find a more ready acceptance . . . we have had continued messages at séances for some time that a visible sign was coming through.

In March 1921, three months after the first article, the *Strand* published Doyle's second, illustrated with the new photographs. The reaction was much as before—one major criticism being that the dresses and hairstyles looked too contemporary. Other critics objected that the fairies looked *too* much like typical "storybook" fairies. Defenders suggested that the physical appearance of the fairies might be an ectoplasmic projection based on what the spirits thought was expected of them. And since Elsie and Frances were interested in contemporary fashions, their fairies might well look like a strange hybrid of the two elements.

As the photographs were reproduced in foreign publications, and the debate spread overseas, it became more heated. But the second set of photographs failed to tip the balance. Few people felt that they made any real difference.

One basic problem was that both girls were minors, and as such their testimony was legally inadmissible; their parents were also unable to offer proof since they had never claimed to have seen any "little people." A photograph taken by an adult who could swear under oath that no trickery had been used might have been enough to swing the debate.

A friend of Doyle's the psychic Geoffrey Hodson—who also claimed to have seen fairies—went to Cottingley to see what he could find out. Hodson arrived in Cottingley with his wife and Edward Gardner in August 1921. Gardner stayed for just over a week, during which the weather was generally poor and no fairies were seen. On the day before he left both Hodson and the girls claimed to have sighted many "nature spirits" (as Hodson called them in his notebook) but failed to get any pictures. Hodson and his wife stayed on, and the fairy sightings became more frequent; but he still failed to capture any of them with a camera. In the end he admitted defeat and left.

At this point the debate ran out of steam; there seemed to be too little evidence to prove the case either way. In 1922 Doyle published a book entitled *The Coming of the Fairies*, but although it contained many photographs and reported fairy sightings, it failed to convince the skeptics. For the next forty years or so Elsie and Frances were forgotten.

In 1965 Elsie, then in her sixties, was tracked down in the Midlands by a *Daily Express* reporter, Peter Chambers. He believed that the pictures were faked, and Elsie's comment that people should be left to make up their own minds on the subject only deepened his skepticism. Elsie made the curious remark: "As for the photographs, let's say they are pictures of figments of our imagination, Frances's and mine, and leave it at that."

This might be taken in one of two ways: either she was making an oblique reference to the ectoplasm theory; or she was admitting that the fairies never existed outside her imagination. Now that the subject had been revived, there were many more interviews with both Frances and Elsie. Much was made of a new admission that they had seen *no* fairies during the visit of Geoffrey Hodson; they explained that they were thoroughly bored by the whole subject and felt him to be a fraud, so they amused themselves by pretending to see fairies and were maliciously amused when he said he could see them too. (In his own book on fairies Hodson insists that he *did* see "little people" at Cottingley.)

In 1971 Elsie was asked by the BBC's "Nationwide" program if her father had had a hand in the taking of the photographs. She replied, "I would swear on the Bible that father didn't know what was going on." But when asked if she would swear on the Bible that the photographs were not tricks, she replied after a pause, "I'd rather leave that open if you don't mind . . . but my father had nothing to do with it, I can promise you that." Again she seemed to be close to admitting that there was some kind of fraud.

On the other hand, when Frances was asked by Yorkshire Television if the photographs were fabricated, she replied, "Of course not. You tell us how she could do it—remember she was sixteen and I was ten. Now then, as a child of ten, can you go through life and keep a secret?"

This, it seemed, was the chief argument in favor of the fairy photographs—that it seemed unlikely that Frances and Elsie would and could keep such a secret for so long.

Frances made this comment in 1976; the occasion was a television program about Frances and Elsie, which had been suggested by the Yorkshire psychical investigator Joe Cooper. That is why, on September 10, 1976, the two women turned up at a house on Main Street, Cottingley, opposite the house where the Wright family had lived half a century earlier. In the intervening years, Elsie had lived in India with her husband, Frank Hill, a Scottish engineer; Frances had married a soldier, Frank Way, and had spent much time with him abroad.

Cooper describes Frances as "a bespectacled woman of middle class and height wearing fashionable denim clothes but with a dash of red and black about the scarf and blouse." Elsie, when she arrived, looked a good ten years younger than her seventy-five summers, dressed in fashionable slacks and "mod" gear, including a black derby hat. During the day Cooper became friendly with the two women, even carrying Elsie over a stile. The camera team interviewed locals—who all expressed extreme skepticism about the photographs—and filmed the women down by the stream. Interviewer Austin Mitchell made no secret of believing that the case of the Cottingley fairies had started as a joke, but had gotten out of hand. Cooper was inclined to believe Frances and Elsie. On camera, Elsie and Frances identified the place where they had seen a gnome and flatly denied that they had fabricated the photographs. When interviewed by Mitchell, Cooper stated his view that the girls had seen an "elemental form of fairy life"—that is to say, nature spirits. After all, he noted, W. B. Yeats and thousands of his fellow countrymen were quite certain about the existence of fairies.

In 1977 there was an interesting development. A researcher named Fred Gettings, working on nineteenth-century fairy illustrations, came upon *Princess Mary's Gift Book*, published during the First World War to make money for the Work for Women fund. It contained a poem entitled "A Spell for a Fairy" by Alfred Noyes, illustrated by Claude Shepperson. Two of the fairies in the illustration were virtually identical to the fairies in the first Cottingley photograph, which showed Frances gazing over the heads of five prancing sprites. Their positions had merely been reversed.

In August 1978 *The New Scientist* reported that the magician James Randi ("the Amazing Randi") and the Committee for the Scientific Investigation of Claims of the Paranormal (CSICOP) had put the photographs through an image-enhancement process and found that this revealed strings holding up the fairies. When Cooper told Elsie about the article she merely laughed and pointed out that there was nowhere in the region of the stream where string could have been tied. After a TV play about the fairies had been broadcast in October 1978, Randi expressed indignation that the BBC had failed to state clearly that the photographs had been proved to be fakes.

In 1981 Cooper was writing a book on telepathy and had some correspondence with Frances—who now lived in Ramsgate— about the subject. In September 1981 she asked him to come see her, telling him that there were "some things he should know." When he arrived she was still not ready to specify what these were. But the following day she asked him to drive her to Canterbury; once there, she asked him to wait for her while she went into the cathedral. When she returned they sat in a coffee shop, and she asked him what he thought of the first fairy photograph. He commented that it had been greatly touched up. Then Frances dropped her bombshell:

"From where I was, I could see the hatpins holding up the figures. I've always marveled that anybody ever took it seriously."

"Why are you telling me?" asked the flabbergasted investigator.

"Because Elsie has already told Glenn" [Elsie's son].

"What about the other four? Are they fakes?"

Her answer was, in its way, as astonishing as the original admission: "Three of them. The last one's genuine."

Cooper and Frances now discussed writing a book together and giving Elsie a share of the proceeds; Frances was adamant that Elsie should play no part in writing the book. Cooper went to London to talk to his publisher. Unfortunately, the publisher was not particularly interested in a sixty-year-old story about fairies, especially since it ended so anticlimactically.

By this time, the present writer (CW) had also gotten involved. I had met Joe Cooper at a weekend conference on parapsychology (at the Swanwick Conference Centre in Derbyshire) in 1980, and he had told me he had written a book on the Cottingley fairies—this, of course, was a year before Frances told him the true story. He sent me the manuscript, and I found it fascinating. I had also come across people—one of them a hardheaded Scottish TV interviewer—who claimed to have seen fairies, and I was simply not willing to rule out the possibility that "nature spirits" might exist. Joe's own research into the paranormal had convinced him that "elementals" could not merely be ruled out as an absurdity.

In fact, I was on my way to Yorkshire to research a poltergeist haunting in Pontefract, and that weekend was something of a turning point in my life, for just before I left the conference center I met Guy Lyon Playfair, a psychical researcher with whom I had been in correspondence for some time. At this time I accepted the view of most people involved in psychical research—that poltergeists were a strange manifestation of the unconscious mind of a psychologically disturbed teenager. What Playfair suggested left me rather bewildered. He felt that while some poltergeists may be "spontaneous psychokinesis," mind over matter, the majority are genuine spirits who draw their energy from human beings, particularly children on the verge of puberty.

I have described in my book *Poltergeist* how my visit to the Pritchard household in Pontefract soon convinced me that Guy Playfair knew what he was talking about. When Diane Pritchard, who had been the focus of the disturbances (i.e., the person whose energy was "stolen" by the poltergeist), described how she was dragged up the stairs by some unknown force, I suddenly knew beyond all doubt that the poltergeist was *not* some manifestation of her own unconscious mind. It was a spirit. This meant that as a writer on the paranormal, I had to get off the fence and stop keeping an "open mind" about whether such things as spirits can exist.

It seemed clear to me that the spirits involved in most poltergeist cases are those of the dead—in the Pontefract case, possibly that of a Cluniac monk who had been hanged for rape in the time of Henry VIII. (The gallows had been on the site of the Pritchard house.) But that did not necessarily mean that no other kinds of spirits can exist. The travel writer Laurens Van der Post, for example, had no doubt whatsoever that the nature spirits or gods of the Kalahari bushmen are real and can cause all kinds of problems. In *The Lost World of the Kalahari* he describes how "the spirits of the Slippery Hills" became offended when one of his team killed a warthog on their territory and caused endless mishaps until they received a proper apology. In *Poltergeist* I cited many similar stories. So it was hardly logical for me to deny the existence of nature spirits on the grounds that only a child could believe in them.

But the problem with Joe Cooper's book, even in its original version, was that the story was too slight—it could be told in fifty pages, which seemed to mean that the rest had to be some kind of "padding." And since, at that point, both Frances and Elsie were still insisting that the photographs were genuine, the story had no real conclusion. I tried to find a publisher for the book but was unsuccessful. And at this point Joe said he wanted to rewrite it anyway; and there the matter rested.

It was in the following year that Frances finally "came clean." Oddly enough, Joe was excited that the case had finally reached a definite conclusion. When he told me about Frances's confession, I was less optimistic. If the book ended with an admission of fraud, it would be an anticlimax.

Joe Cooper came to the same conclusion. Late in 1982 an anthology called *The Unexplained*, of which I was a consulting editor, published his article "Cottingley: At Last the Truth," in which he revealed that the fairies in the first four photographs were cutouts stuck to the branches with hatpins. Understandably, this upset both Frances and Elsie. When Frances called Joe's wife on New Year's Day, 1983, and Joe answered the phone, she called him a traitor and hung up. She died in 1986. Elsie died in 1988, maintaining to the end that she did not believe in fairies.

Which seems to be the end of the story . . .

Or is it? Certainly the skeptics are justified in regarding the case as closed. Possibly they are correct. Yet before we make up our minds, there are a few interesting points to be made.

What Frances is asking us to believe is this: She came to England from South Africa in 1917, when she was ten, and went to stay with her sixteen-year-old cousin, Elsie, in Cottingley. Elsie claimed to have had some odd ghostly experiences. For example, she insisted that when she was four she was regularly visited in bed by a woman who wore a tight dress buttoned up to her neck. And when she was six she woke up one night and called for a drink; when no one replied, she went downstairs and found a strange man and woman in the house. She asked where her parents were and was told they had gone out to play cards with the neighbors. Elsie said she wanted to go and find them, and the man opened the front door and let her out. Her parents—who were, in fact, playing cards with the neighbors—were startled to see her and even more startled to hear about the man and woman, for they had left the house empty. But when they went to investigate, the house *was* empty.

Frances had had no "psychic" experiences. But in the spring of 1918 she saw her first gnome. She had gone down to the stream after school and observed a phenomenon she had often observed before: a single willow leaf began to shake on the tree by the stream. Then a small man, all dressed in green, was standing on the branch. Frances watched, breathless, terrified of disturbing him. The little man looked straight at her, then disappeared. After that, she claimed, she often saw little men wearing coats of grayish green and matching caps by the stream. She gradually reached the conclusion that the little men were engaged in some kind of purposeful activity, perhaps associated with helping plants to grow. Later, she began to see fairies, with and without wings. These were smaller than the elves; they had white faces and arms and often seemed to be holding some kind of meeting. Elsie, she insists, never saw the fairies or little men.

It was after falling into the stream yet again that Frances admitted that she went there to see fairies. And it was the total skepticism of the adults that led Elsie to decide to take some fairy photographs. This was not simply a desire to deceive. Elsie believed Frances when she said she saw fairies; her own psychic experiences made it seem quite plausible. She wanted to shake the credulity of the grown-ups. So the photographs were taken with cutouts propped up by hatpins.

When the world suddenly became interested in the fairies, the girls were in a difficult position. The photographs were fakes, yet—according to the girls—the fairies really existed. If the whole thing had been a hoax, it would have been easier to confess. But it was not a hoax—not totally, anyway. They were in an embarrassing and anomalous position. If they admitted that the photographs were fakes, they would be implying that the whole affair was a deception. And that would be as untrue as continuing to maintain that the photographs were genuine. So they decided to keep silent.

When the whole affair blew up again in 1965, the situation was unchanged. It is true that Elsie, now a hardheaded woman in her sixties, was no longer convinced that Frances had seen fairies; yet she was absolutely certain that *she* had had "psychic" experiences and was therefore prepared to be open-minded. As to Frances, she *had* seen fairies and had nothing to retract. In a letter to Leslie Gardner, the son of Edward Gardner, Elsie remarked that after her interview with Peter Chambers (in 1965), in which she had declared that people must judge for themselves and that the pictures were "figments of our imaginations," Frances had said indignantly, "What did you say that for? You know very well that they were real."

In fact, Frances had always maintained that the fairies were real. In November 1918 she sent the first fairy photograph to a friend in South Africa and scrawled on the back: "Elsie and I are very friendly with the beck Fairies. It's funny I never used to see them in Africa. It must be too hot for them there."

In his original manuscript of the Cottingley book, Joe Cooper had included a chapter entitled "Other Sightings," consisting of accounts of fairies related to him by various witnesses, and it makes clear why he believed Frances. One man, a healer, told how he was sitting with a girl in Gibraltar, eating a sandwich, when it was snatched from him by "a little man about eighteen inches high." An eighty-year-old official of the Theosophical Society insisted that when he was a small boy he was often visited in bed by a green-clad gnome. Another old man described seeing a green-clad gnome, about two feet high, walking along a path in a cornfield. Some young male students told how, when walking in a wood near Bradford, they saw fairies who were "circling and dancing" but who were invisible to the direct gaze; they could only be seen "out of the corner of the eye." An elderly woman showed Cooper a photograph of a gnome seen through a frosty window; she claimed that she had come down one morning, seen the gnome, and rushed upstairs to get her camera. The photograph also shows diminutive white rabbits.

Joe Cooper finally published most of these accounts in his book *Modern Psychic Experiences*, together with many more. A New Zealand medium named Dorothy described how she used to play with a "spirit" girl named Mabel as a child and how she had first seen fairies, who came from under plants. One day she came home to find her father unconscious on the floor—a gastric ulcer had perforated—and the fairies took charge and escorted her to the doctor's house. Joe Cooper's own niece, Jo, who was in her thirties, described how, at the age of sixteen, she had seen three little men crouching on top of a wall.

When I wrote about the Cottingley fairies in *Poltergeist* (before Frances had "confessed"), I also went to some trouble to find accounts of "real" fairies. I described being interviewed on television at the 1978 Edinburgh Festival by a man named Bobbie (whose surname I forgot to note in my journal); in the pub next door he told me casually that he had once seen a gnome standing on the pavement outside a convent gate and that it had "scared the hell out of him."

My friend Marc Alexander, author of many books on the paranormal, told me a story of a friend in New Zealand named Pat Andrew, who claimed to have seen a pixie when he was six. Years later, after seeing a stage hypnotist, Marc and Andrew began experimenting with hypnosis on each other. Marc had no doubt that Andrew was genuinely hypnotized, and one day he decided to try and "regress" him to the age at which he saw the pixie. The result was an amazing one-sided conversation that left Marc in no doubt whatever that, whether Andrew had really seen a pixie or not, he undoubtedly *believed* he had.

One of the most convincing accounts I know of is an encounter with a pixie as recounted by another friend, Lois Bourne, in her book *Witch Among Us*. Lois is a "witch" in the sense that she possesses odd psychic powers, of whose reality I have not the slightest doubt. She is an extremely sensible and down-to-earth woman. And in her book, among many stories that psychical researchers will find credible enough, she tells a story that will obviously cause most readers to doubt her truthfulness or her sanity. While on holiday at a cottage at Crantock, in Cornwall, she met a member of a "wicca" coven and spent an evening at her home. The woman's husband, Rob, asked her if she would like to see a goblin, explaining that one appeared among the rushes of the millstream at Treago Mill, Cuberts Heath, every morning at sunrise; if she wanted to see him, she had to be up early. The next morning Lois and her husband, Wilfred, joined Rob at the mill gate, and they crept up to the stream. Bourne writes:

> I have never been able to decide, and still cannot decide, whether I really saw that goblin, or if Rob made me see it. . . . Whatever it was, there, sitting on a stone calmly washing his socks, was an elfin creature with a red hat, green coat and trews, one yellow sock on, and one in his tiny hands in the process of being washed. I remember thinking at the time, in my sleepy, befuddled, but practical way, "What an atrocious colour combination." Suddenly he saw us and he disappeared. . . . "Now do you believe me?" asked Rob.

I have known Lois for years. I may be gullible and she may be a liar, but I believe her. She is not the type to invent such a silly story. And her husband, Wilfred—who also saw it—is not the type to support a downright lie.

As already mentioned, the poet W. B. Yeats had been convinced of the existence of fairies ever since he and Lady Gregory went door to door collecting information from the local peasants. They recorded these interviews in a 1920 book entitled *Visions and Beliefs*. Evans Wentz concludes his *Fairy Faith in Celtic Countries* by acknowledging: "We seem to have arrived at a point . . . where we can postulate scientifically . . . the existence of such invisible intelligences as gods, genii, daemons, all kinds of true fairies, and disembodied men." (By the latter he means ghosts.) And he goes on to cite the very sound evidence for the existence of the poltergeist. George Russell (AE) and Evans Wentz emphasize that these entities are seen only by "psychics," and Russell believes that such beings are not "individuals" in the human sense: "Theirs is a collective life, so unindividualised and so calm that I might have more varied thoughts in five hours than they would have in five years."

When all of this is taken into account, we may feel that the notion that Frances really saw fairies by the stream in Cottingley no longer seems quite so absurd.

10

The Forgotten Children:
The Strange Story of
the Railway Children

The little village of Charfield, not far from Wotton under Edge
in Gloucestershire, has only a few hundred inhabitants, and
according to the gazetteer of the British Isles, its only claim to
distinction is its railway station. But it has one other: it is associated with one of the most curious puzzles in the history of
railway accidents.

At 5:20, in the morning darkness of Saturday, October 13,
1928, a signaling fault caused the Leeds-to-Bristol express to run
into a cargo train standing in Charfield Station. The express burst
into flames and was then further damaged by another cargo train
that plowed into it. Rescuers who rushed to the scene were driven
back by the intense heat—in those days, most railway carriages
were made of wood. Firemen did their best, but it was not until
about midday that it was possible to remove the bodies from the
charred carriages. There were sixteen of these, and fourteen of
them were soon identified by grieving relatives. But no one came
forward to identify the bodies of two children who were found in
a third-class carriage, clinging together for protection.

The ticket collector, Harry Haines, was one of those who survived the crash. He said that he had seen the two children get on

the train at Gloucester. He recalled them as a boy of about twelve and a girl of about six. They were both wearing school hats and were traveling alone.

The inquest was not held until December, two months later. There, Dr. Walshingham Ward gave evidence that the two charred corpses appeared to be those of a child between twelve and fourteen and a child of about six. The fire had burned them so badly that the sexes could not be determined. But part of a breast pocket of a school blazer was found, with a school motto, *Luce Magistra*, as well as two new nine-inch-long shoes—obviously the boy's—and part of a sock with the initials *C.S.S.S.*

Many theories have been put forward to explain why no one ever claimed the "railway children." One was that the remains were *not* those of two children but of a missing engineer named Philip Jenkins, who boarded the train at Derby and whose body was never found. This seems unlikely. Archie Ayres, the village carpenter who made the coffins, was certain that the remains were those of two children. And an engineer would hardly be wearing a school blazer or shoes that were the correct size for a boy of twelve. It is far more likely that the engineer's body was totally incinerated in the blaze.

Another theory is that the childrens' guardian was relieved to hear the last of them. If their parents were dead, then presumably the guardian would have been left in charge of enough money for their schooling and upbringing, and perhaps the bulk of their parents' fortune, until they came of age. Yet the "wicked guardian" theory fails to explain why the school—or schools—for which they were bound made no inquiries about their nonarrival. Or had the "wicked guardian" thought of that and told the headmaster that they were being transferred to another school, perhaps abroad?

In his account of the case in *The World's Most Intriguing Mysteries*, Rupert Furneaux has pointed out that it seems strange that two young children should have been traveling alone at that hour of the morning. Perhaps they *were* accompanied by a parent or guardian who was totally consumed in the fire. But would the ticket collector not have noticed if they had been accompanied by an adult? He stated specifically that they were alone. Furneaux suggests that the children existed only in Harry Haines's imagination, but it is hard to understand why a train guard should imagine two children.

A local newspaper reported that in the years following the crash, the grave of the unknown children was visited on a number of occasions by a man and a woman who arrived in a car of German make, driven by a chauffeur; the woman was nevertheless described as "shabbily dressed" and as weeping. This suggests another possibility: that the parents of the children were in Germany when the crash happened and did not hear about it until later, when the children failed to write from school. The headmaster may have assumed that the children had simply accompanied their parents abroad.

Again, the fact that the woman was shabbily dressed seems to suggest the possibility that she was *not* the wife of the man in the chauffeur-driven car. If so, then perhaps she had lived alone with the children and been too shattered by the news of the crash to face the complications of identifying two charred bodies and the ensuing publicity when the newspapers learned that the mystery of the "railway children" had been solved. Certainly, a feeling of guilt seems to be the likeliest explanation of why no one came forward.

Or were the children simply two orphans whom nobody cared about and nobody wanted to claim? According to the villagers of Charfield, the intervening years have never offered the slightest clue.

11

The Glozel Mystery:
Archaeological Riddle or Fraud?

One day in 1869 a band of hunters from the castle of San-
tillana del Mar, at the foot of the Cantabrian Hills of northern Spain, realized that they had lost a dog. They whistled and
searched and eventually heard the animal yelping from a crack in
the ground. Cold air blew up from the crack. They made their way
down the crack, and their torches revealed a large cave. They
rescued the dog and returned to tell their master, Don Marcelino
de Sautuola, of their discovery. The Don made his way down the
crack, determined that the cave was just a hole in the ground of
no particular interest, and decided to seal it up to prevent village
boys from playing in it. For the next nine years he forgot about it.

But in 1878 he visited the Paris Exhibition and was fascinated
by glass cabinets full of Ice Age tools and engravings. (The last Ice
Age ended about 12,000 years ago.) On his return home, Don
Marcelino consulted an expert on the correct procedure for
searching for Ice Age artifacts, then set out for the cave armed
with a spade and a torch.

His early excavations were disappointing; he found nothing.
Finally, nearly a year later, he was rewarded by the discovery of a
hand axe and some stone arrowheads. He began to dig with
renewed vigor. And one day, when his five-year-old daughter,

Maria, was in the cave with him, he heard her call out with astonishment. She was in a recess that the Don had ignored because it was too low for him. But the child had seen pictures of charging bulls on the walls. At first the Don was unable to see anything; then, as he moved his candle closer to the wall, he recognized the eye of a bison. A closer examination revealed that the wall was covered with pictures of bison—bulls, cows, and calves—in all sorts of postures. The one he had first seen was lying on its side, in the process of dying. The ceiling and the other walls were covered with even more extraordinary paintings. When he touched them he realized that the pigment was still wet.

Together with his friend Professor Vilanova, Marcelino announced his discovery to the world; visitors—including the king of Spain—flocked to the cave (today known as Altamira). But when he went to a congress of prehistorians in Lisbon, Marcelino was stunned to discover that they regarded his cave paintings as a fraud. Indeed, all the learned men of Europe denounced them. Marcelino had them reproduced in a book; it was ignored. Ancient cavemen could not possibly paint like that, said the experts; it had to be a confidence trick. His chief enemy, a prehistorian named Cartailhac, even refused him admission to a congress in Algiers.

Years later Cartailhac went to look at newly discovered caves at Les Eyzies, in the Vézère Valley, and found them full of paintings like those at Altamira. Too late, he returned to Altamira to apologize for his mistake; the child Maria, now a grown woman, could only take him to see her father's grave.

This story, not untypical of the behavior of "experts," may serve as a prelude to another tale of discovery that began in 1924, when a cow stumbled into a hole in southern France. This happened on a farm owned by the Fradin family, near Glozel, not far from Vichy. The family had turned up a few pottery fragments during the First World War; now, investigating the hole into which the cow had stumbled, they found "a kind of tomb," containing various pots and inscribed tablets. There was an oval paving of bricks, some of which had melted glass on them, and other lumps of glass lay around. A local schoolmistress told the Fradins that they had found a cremation grave and that this explained the melted glass. But another visitor to the site thought it more likely that they had stumbled upon a Roman or medieval glass kiln.

In the following year a Vichy doctor named Morlet, who was also an amateur archaeologist, came to the farm. He had recently found a skeleton in his own garden. When the Fradins told him that they had been trying to persuade the local historical society to defray the cost of their digging, Morlet made the mistake of offering to buy their finds—and any more they might stumble upon—and told them to fence off the site. It was a mistake because it later led to the accusation that the Fradins had devised a hoax for the sake of money. Yet it seems clear that they had made no attempt to profit from their discovery before Morlet came on the scene.

The Fradins and Morlet now began to excavate the site—which became known as "the Field of the Dead"—together. They soon uncovered an astonishing variety of objects. These included bone carvings of animals and pictures of reindeer on stones, as well as marks that seemed to be writing. In fact, they unearthed many inscribed tablets. They also found carved faces—each about an inch high—and a figure of a human being standing on an animal. One French writer, Robert Charroux, whose books on ancient mysteries have been credited with inspiring Erich von Däniken (see chapter 8), declared confidently in 1969: "Little is known about the Glozel civilization, except that it must have existed before the Flood, the great cataclysm which blocked the caves at Lascaux and swallowed up the necropolis or religious centre at Glozel, all the inhabitants having died in the disaster." He estimated that Glozel flourished about 15,000 years ago, toward the end of the last great ice age.

This was the period of the Magdalenian culture, to which the paintings of Altamira and Lascaux (discovered in 1940) belong. Because the hunters and fishers of this period were surrounded by an abundance of food, a population explosion occurred, and large numbers of people began to live in lakeside dwellings. If, as Charroux believes, Glozel belongs to this period, then the tablets with writing on them certainly support his thesis that civilization is far older than we believe—which in turn provides an argument for the "ancient astronaut" theory discussed in chapter 8.

The Glozel pottery makes this thesis unlikely, however, for the earliest known pottery dates from many thousands of years later—9,000 years ago in Japan and much later in Europe. Some of the Glozel pottery has owl-like faces on it, like French Bronze Age pottery (from around 2000 B.C.). On the other hand, Morlet dated certain polished axe heads to the Neolithic (New Stone Age) period, after 9000 B.C. If he was correct, then writing was not invented in the Middle East (Sumer) around 3500 B.C. but in France five thousand years earlier.

One noted French authority on the subject was Professor Salomon Reinach, the author of a best-selling book on the history of religion entitled *Orpheus*. His first reaction to the Glozel finds was that they might be forgeries. But when he went to Glozel he became convinced that they were in fact genuine. The skeptics were later to point out that Glozel seemed to support some of Reinach's pet theories, such as that reindeer lived on in France much later than archaeologists believed, and that France was the cradle of civilization. In any event, he announced his conviction that the finds were genuine, and the result was a great deal of publicity, which made Glozel a tourist attraction.

Other archaeologists reacted by declaring their conviction that Glozel was a fraud and that the Fradins were busily manufacturing "ancient" artifacts and burying them. When roughly built tombs were discovered, the anti-Glozelians pointed out that no earth had found its way between the cracks in thousands of years and that this seemed unlikely. The curator of the museum at Villeneuve-sur-Lot announced that he had taken shelter in a barn in Glozel in September 1927 and had seen some half-finished artifacts and some unbaked clay tablets. If true, this evidence was damning. On the other hand, as the Glozelians pointed out, the curator of a rival museum might have his own reasons for raising doubts about Glozel.

A commission sent to Glozel by the International Anthropological Congress of 1927 came up with an unfavorable report, declaring that the finds were "of no great age." Police now descended on Glozel and seized various artifacts, which were sent off to the police laboratory in Paris. Reinach countered by getting a Swedish policeman named Soderman to have the bone objects tested in a Stockholm laboratory. The lab reported that the bone had a lower organic content than modern bone. The Paris police report, on the other hand, declared that the artifacts seemed to be modern and that one Neolithic axe head looked as if it had been worked with a file. But the Glozelians declined to be convinced. When accused of fraud, Emile Fradin sued and won his case—although he was awarded only one franc.

The controversy dragged on, but—as in the case of Altamira—skepticism prevailed, and it became generally accepted that the Glozel finds were fraudulent. And when, in 1953, the famous "Piltdown skull" was shown to be a hoax (see chapter 23), it became the fashion to classify Glozel and Piltdown together. Glozel had also been hailed as a kind of missing link—in this case, the missing link between Old Stone Age hunters and Neolithic farmers—a gap archaeologists referred to as "the ancient hiatus." Old Stone Age hunters were supposed to have followed the retreating reindeer north and the New Stone Age farmers to have come in from elsewhere, possibly Asia. Reinach was convinced—rightly, as it turned out—that this never happened and that the New Stone Age farmers were the descendants of the Old Stone Age hunters. So Glozel filled the hiatus. Eventually, the hiatus dissolved, like the missing link. And Glozel became not merely suspect but irrelevant.

Then, in 1974, Emile Fradin—who had been seventeen at the time of the first finds—announced that scientific examination of Glozel artifacts in Denmark had proved their authenticity. The technique used was called *thermoluminescence*. When pottery is fired, it gives off trapped electrons that originate in radioactive traces in the clay. Then the pot gradually reaccumulates trapped electrons from radioactivity. If the pot is heated to between 300 and 500° C, it gives off a glow, which results from the release of trapped electrons. The greater the glow, the older the pot. Samples of Glozel pottery had been given to Dr. Hugh McKerrel of the National Museum of Antiquities of Scotland, and Dr. Vagn Mejdahl of the Danish Atomic Energy Commission. They measured the thermoluminescence of the Glozel pottery and concluded that it had been fired about the time of Christ, some of it possibly eight hundred years earlier.

This, of course, contradicted Reinach's thesis that the pottery was Neolithic. But it also contradicted the notion that the pottery finds at Glozel had been fired in a kiln on the farm. Some of the tablets with writing were also dated to the same period.

Archaeologists were outraged and accused the physicists of bungling. The BBC "Chronicle" program promptly invited a team of experts to go and have another look at Glozel. Their conclusion was that the new evidence was still at variance with the facts. If the Glozel pottery dated from between 2,000 and 2,800 years ago, then the later examples should have been like other pottery of the period when France (Gaul) was occupied by the Romans. It wasn't. It was *sui generis*—of its own unique type.

And so the mystery remains. Is Glozel another Piltdown hoax? That is a tempting conclusion, but if we accept it, we have to ignore some facts to the contrary. Charles Dawson, the man who found the Piltdown skull, was an amateur archaeologist, so he may have had a motive for the forgery (although it is still not clear what this was). But when Emile Fradin and his grandfather found the first "tomb" (or glass kiln), they had no reason for deception. And if it is true that earlier finds had turned up during the First World War, then this point is underlined. They made no attempt to cash in on the find, and it was not until a year later that Dr. Morlet arrived on the scene and the Fradins finally began to make a profit from their finds.

Did this tempt them to begin faking artifacts? That is certainly possible. But would an uneducated French farmer have the kind of knowledge to fake pottery, axe heads, bone figurines, and engraved clay tablets? Besides, one of the earliest finds was a brick with "writing" on it. If this was genuine, then the later finds may have been genuine too. And the conclusion would have to be that, at the time of Socrates, Glozel housed a small and flourishing community with its own special culture.

Reinach was undoubtedly wrong: Glozel does not prove that writing originated in France in the New Stone Age. But the (admittedly confusing) evidence seems to indicate that the experts may also be wrong and that—like Don Marcelino—the Fradins may one day be due for a belated apology.

12

Victor Grayson:
The Strange Case of the
Disappearing Member of Parliament

On a pleasant evening in September 1920, a good-looking man in his late thirties was standing at the bar of a London restaurant—the Georgian, at 43 Chandos Street, north of the Strand—talking to an acquaintance named E. K. Donovan. He was describing his research into what later became known as the "Honor's Scandal"—the sale of knighthoods and peerages by the Prime Minister, David Lloyd George. Victor Grayson had once been famous as a fire-eating Socialist Member of Parliament who had actually been ejected from the House of Commons for defying the Speaker. Now, he told Donovan, he had information that would shake the country and cause the downfall of the coalition government.

Their conversation was interrupted by the receptionist, who told Grayson that she had just had a phone call from the Queen's Hotel in Leicester Square. It seemed that some luggage belonging to Grayson had been sent there in error. (Grayson had just returned from Liverpool.) Leicester Square was only a five-minute walk away; Grayson told Donovan to keep an eye on his Scotch—which he had just ordered—and hurried off to sort out the problem.

He was never seen again. When Donovan grew tired of waiting

he rang the Queen's Hotel to ask if Grayson was still there. (Donovan knew the convivial Grayson well enough to know that he might have seen a friend and wandered into the bar.) The reception desk said that Grayson had not been there and denied knowing anything about a phone call concerning luggage. It looked as if someone had deliberately lured Grayson out of the restaurant.

Oddly enough, no one paid much attention to Grayson's disappearance. His background was working class, and his family in Liverpool was accustomed to not hearing from him for months at a time. The general public did not learn about his disappearance until seven years later, in March 1927, when the *Yorkshire Post* ran a headline: "Is Mr. Victor Grayson Dead?"

If it had happened ten years earlier, it would have caused a sensation. At that time Victor Grayson had been one of the rising stars of British politics, and his charisma was so great that many believed he would one day be the first Labour Prime Minister. Admittedly, his views were so extreme that he alienated many in his own party. But no one doubted that he had a brilliant future in politics. In fact, he wasted his opportunities in a manner that now seems baffling. One of his chief problems was alcohol—he frequently drank himself into a state of incoherence. We now also know that his most closely guarded secret was that he was bisexual. Yet even this fails to explain the curious self-destructive tendency that plunged him from celebrity to oblivion in four years.

Albert Victor Grayson was born in Liverpool on September 5, 1881, the seventh son of a carpenter. This seems amusingly—if blasphemously—appropriate, for later rumors suggested that the carpenter was not his real father and that his mother may have had some kind of affair with an aristocrat; even the names given to him—Albert Victor—were those of the Prince Consort. As a child he set out to run away to the Wild West, armed with a revolver, but changed his mind and returned home. An attempt to run away to sea at the age of fourteen was equally unsuccessful; he was returned home after a week as a stowaway. After six years as an engineering apprentice he was caught up in the newly formed Labour movement and discovered an unexpected talent for oratory. At a fairly early stage Grayson lost his working-class accent and acquired that of a "gentleman." The craving to escape his working-class background led him to become a Sunday school teacher and lay preacher; this, in turn, led to a decision to become a minister and to a church scholarship to a theological college in Manchester and a course in political economy at Manchester University. It took him three years to decide that he preferred politics to religion. In 1905, at the age of twenty-three, he launched himself on a career of public speaking by traveling around in a horse-drawn van, sponsored by Robert Blatchford's Socialist newspaper, the *Clarion*, and preaching the gospel of revolution in remote villages.

His rise to fame sounds like a cliché out of a Hollywood musical. In Huddersfield, on the other side of the Pennines, he was asked to step in at the last moment when a trade union leader had to cancel his engagement to speak at the town hall in support of the local Labour candidate. Grayson's speech—on December 16, 1905—was so brilliant that he became the *Clarion*'s star orator and suddenly found himself famous—at least among his Socialist colleagues—at the age of twenty-four. In the audience that evening were members of the Colne Valley Labour League, Colne Valley being a grim, millworking area of Yorkshire that looked as if it had come out of Dickens's *Hard Times*. Grayson began to receive many invitations to speak there, and since it stretched within ten miles of Manchester, it was conveniently close.

The millworkers liked his combination of revolutionary socialism and religion. The Labour League had failed to contest the Parliamentary seat in 1900, and again in 1905, but was determined to make up for it at the next election. Grayson's passionate oratory, and his amusing way of dealing with hecklers, made him such a favorite that his name was soon on the short list of Labour candidates for the 1907 by-election, which resulted from the elevation of the Liberal MP to the House of Lords. At the crucial council meeting Grayson lost to a trade unionist, but his rival subsequently withdrew for obscure political reasons, and Grayson took his place. The Liberals put up Philip Bright, son of the famous Liberal John Bright, and they had not the slightest doubt that he would win. They had good reason to be confident, for the

British Labour Party believed in working with the Liberals, not against them, and they withheld their support from the young revolutionary. And even at this early stage, many respectable Socialists detested Grayson. The politician Philip Snowdon, for example, regarded him as a "flamboyant windbag."

Grayson fought brilliantly. His wit and his invective guaranteed that every meeting would be packed. On one occasion he burned a hole in the seat of his trousers by sitting on a lit cigarette. He turned it into a joke, telling a bunch of hecklers, "It's not that I'm afraid to turn my back on you. I simply don't want to shock your puritan susceptibilities by showing you what I think of you."

With audiences of mill girls he shamelessly used his sex appeal. More than half a century later one of them recalled how Grayson had brushed back his flowing hair with both hands and asked, "Do you like my hair, ladies?" The answer was gasps of adoration.

Grayson was also helped by his rival's lack of platform gifts— Bright had everything but a ready wit. Nevertheless, Grayson's victory in July 1907 was a narrow one—he beat Bright by only 253 votes, and even the Conservative, Granville Wheler, was within 421 votes of the young Socialist. But it was enough. The exultant Grayson told his audience that it was a victory for revolutionary socialism and that he had every intention of carrying revolution into the House of Commons. His victory made him a national figure and a hero of the workingman.

Grayson found life as an MP an intoxicating experience. An old friend, Socialist MP Sam Hobson, put him up in his tiny flat. Hobson was a quiet man who seldom drank. Grayson came in later and later each night, full of apologies and euphoria; he was enjoying life (though at this stage he seldom drank anything stronger than lemonade in pubs). At last he was a member of the ruling class. He made a habit of dressing immaculately—his enemies never tired of sneering about his dandyism. Unfortunately, Grayson found Parliament boring and exasperating. He had not ceased to resent the Labour Party for failing to support him in Colne Valley, and he soon formed the conviction that in the House of Commons they were betraying the people.

His maiden speech made it clear that he saw himself as a rebel. It concerned a grant of £50,000 to Lord Cromer for his services in Egypt. Grayson asked why the money was not being used to alleviate poverty instead of swelling the bank balance of a man who already had plenty. But he had not lost his spontaneous wit. When he made the mistake of addressing the House as "gentlemen" and someone corrected him—pointing out that it should have been "honorable members"—Grayson remarked, "It reminds me of the curate who began his address: 'Dear friends—I will not call you ladies and gentlemen, I know you too well,' " and the house roared with laughter.

Yet in retrospect, it seems clear that Philip Snowdon was not far from the truth when he described Grayson as a flamboyant windbag. Grayson was a fire-eating young rebel—like his Socialist comrade Jack London, who was then causing a sensation in American universities with his demands for immediate revolution. Grayson was also fond of addressing strikers with demands for bloody insurrection and describing their rulers as murderers. He made no attempt to be fair; he was concerned only with making the maximum impact. And his attempts often misfired. In a speech about Belfast strikers Grayson declared, "If they have no shrapnel, they can use broken bottles." But by the time the speech was reported the next morning, the strikers *had* used broken bottles, and infuriated crowds had charged the police and soldiers, injuring more than a hundred people. Grayson had nothing to do with the incident, but he received his share of the blame. Blatchford described him in an indulgent editorial as "mad, foolish Grayson," while the Conservative press denounced him as a murderous hothead.

Grayson had little to say in Parliament—he evidently regarded it as an assembly of time-servers and hypocrites; instead, he toured the country, stirring workers to anger with crude mob oratory. On one occasion he told them that he had nothing but contempt for a man who would allow his wife and children to starve rather than turn to crime. He became the man the Conservatives and Liberals loved to hate; even Labour MPs felt closer to the Conservatives than to Victor Grayson.

On October 31, 1908, Grayson stood up in Parliament and requested that the House be adjourned to discuss unemployment; the Speaker explained courteously that it could not be done that

day because other business was already scheduled. Grayson continued to demand a debate and refused to sit down, claiming,
"People are starving in the streets." When the Speaker ordered
the Sergeant at Arms to eject the troublemaker, Grayson turned
to the Labour benches and called them traitors to their class.
Then he left amid uproar. Outside, he told the press that the
Parliamentary game was played out. Then he slipped back into the
chamber and interrupted yet again. Refusing to give way to the
Speaker, refusing to withdraw, he was finally suspended from the
House. He withdrew to jeers and derisive laughter.

His action was not as self-destructive as it sounds; it filled the
front pages, divided the country, and made Grayson a workers'
hero. At last he was even praised by the Socialist newspapers. His
meetings were fuller than ever; a tour around the country became
a triumphal procession. And, as usual, he gave his audiences what
they wanted: denunciations of the rich as thieves and murderers.
He told them that they were living in a land that was stolen from
them before they were born. The rich claimed that they had
simply "enclosed" it. "Bill Sikes was locked up last night for
'enclosing' a watch—wouldn't that sound beautiful?" He made it
clear that he was on the side of Bill Sikes.

Grayson's real political weakness was his neglect of his duties in
the House. Philip Snowdon attacked him on the grounds that he
had come to Parliament only once that year, to collect his salary,
which he then spent on entertaining his friends at a sumptuous
dinner in the House restaurant, with its subsidized prices. Grayson insisted this was untrue, but the mud stuck. It seems to have
been at this period, when he was driving himself to exhaustion as
a public speaker, that he first began to drink. Labour colleagues,
who were mostly teetotalers, were shocked when Grayson took a
glass of wine at a public dinner. But his real taste was for whisky.
At first, his drinking was sparing and highly controlled, but—
given his emotional temperament—it was bound to get out of
control.

Grayson was playing a dangerous game. When he told his
audiences that the Liberals were as much an enemy of the working class as the Tories, he alienated not only the Liberals and
Tories but his own party, which had no wish to quarrel with the

Liberals. Grayson was relying on his appeal as a demogogue to win the Colne Valley seat in the next election; in fact, on January 21, 1910, he came in last in the poll. And when he fought a seat in the London borough of Kennington a few months later, he again came in at the bottom of the poll with a humiliatingly small vote.

Grayson continued to work as the political editor of Blatchford's *Clarion*. In 1911 Colne Valley again invited him to stand as Labour candidate, and he agreed. Yet it was soon obvious that something was wrong. Grayson had lost his fire. He failed to "nurse" his constituency and had the look of a man who is tired and defeated. In fact, he had begun to suffer from epileptic fits and was drinking a bottle of whisky a day. Since no one could ever be certain if he would arrive at meetings, his supporters became increasingly disillusioned.

In November 1912 Grayson married a young actress, Ruth Nightingale, the daughter of a Yorkshire banker. They spent the evening of the wedding in a meeting at Walthamstow, where he made a characteristically brilliant speech. But his health was poor, and when a Socialist colleague called on them in their Stockwell lodging the following February, he was shocked to find them living in a bare room, with mattresses on the floor and a sugar box for a table. An appeal to the comrades raised enough money to allow the couple to sail for America. But another Socialist who visited Grayson in his Manhattan apartment again found the couple in a bare room, and Grayson sitting with a bottle of whisky in front of him, while his pretty wife looked depressed and frightened.

Back in England in January 1914, Grayson set out on another speaking tour, and at first he seemed to be the old brilliant orator; but in Bradford he was so drunk that he could not climb up to the platform. In March 1914 he avoided bankruptcy only by agreeing to pay 7 shillings and 6 pence for every pound he owed. In the following month his daughter, Elaine, was born, and Grayson made another determined attempt to revive his political fortunes; in May the Colne Valley party released him from his obligation to stand as their candidate.

His career now seemed virtually finished. But the war provided

him with a new lease on life. To the astonishment of his old
comrades, he now revealed himself to be a patriot, and even wrote
an article praising the "one hundred and seventy-eight peers" who
were fighting at the front. Then his wife succeeded in obtaining an
engagement as an actress in Australia and New Zealand; Grayson
sailed with the theatrical company in 1916. He was welcomed in
Australia by the Labour Party, and for a while it looked as if he
would rebuild his life as a politician there. But the Australian
Socialist Party split on the issue of conscription, and Grayson
sided with the defeated war party. A few days later he and Ruth
sailed for New Zealand, where he was soon embroiled in more
bitter controversy about conscription. Sarcastic opponents asked
why he did not join the army himself; to everyone's astonishment,
he did precisely that, in November 1916. In July of the following
year he was posted back to England, and then to France.

Grayson proved an unexpectedly good soldier, and the unavail-
ability of whisky improved his health. In October 1917 his regiment was ordered to go "over the top"; he was struck by shrapnel
and knocked unconscious. Back in England, an operation removed the shrapnel from his hip. In March 1918 he was given a
medical discharge from the army.

By that time he was a widower. Ruth, who was living with her
parents in Bolton, had given birth prematurely to a second child
in February; both she and the baby died. Two weeks later Grayson
was speaking on a pro-war platform in Glasgow and hinted at his
intention of returning to politics. Yet nothing of the sort happened. Instead, Grayson moved into a block of service flats,
Georgian House, in Bury Street, near St. James' Palace, and
began a strange existence that involved a number of old Socialist
comrades—like Blatchford—and some dubious allies like the amiable con man Maundy Gregory and the swindling company pro-
moter Horatio Bottomley. If we knew what Grayson was doing in
such unsavory company, we might have some clue to what happened to him two years later. But at this point in his life, Grayson
seems to have preferred remaining in the shadows.

What we *do* know is that Maundy Gregory, a homosexual who
had been an unsuccessful actor's manager and who was an early
recruit to British Intelligence, had lent his services to Prime

Minister David Lloyd George, who led a coalition government. Lloyd George urgently needed cash to fund the Liberal Party—around £4 million—and he decided to raise it by selling honors—knighthoods at £10,000 each and baronetcies, which were inheritable, at £40,000 each. He even created a new honor, the OBE (Order of the British Empire), which could be bought for a mere £100. Gregory had the task of approaching likely prospects—a master of foxhounds or a justice of the peace, for example—who would like to become knights or even peers; he probably received a 10 percent cut. As a cover for his activities, he launched a magazine, *The Whitehall Gazette*, which was devoted to attacking Bolshevism.

Horatio Bottomley, fifty-eight years old in 1918, was a journalist and orator who had made a fortune from promoting Australian gold-mining companies and succeeded in avoiding prosecution by going bankrupt with incredible frequency—269 times in all. He owned a large country house and a racing stable, but he was a far from lucky gambler. On one occasion he decided to cheat the bookies on the Blankenberg racecourse in Belgium by entering six of his own horses and instructing the jockeys in what order they were to pass the winning post. Unfortunately, a heavy sea mist rolled over the course during the race; the jockeys lost sight of one another and Bottomley lost a fortune. During the First World War he justified Dr. Johnson's assertion that patriotism is the last refuge of a scoundrel by becoming famous for his pro-conscription speeches. This much he had in common with Grayson. As a highly paid journalist, he often hired others to write his articles, and it is possible that this is why he became a regular caller at Grayson's flat.

But it is hard to imagine that Grayson would have been involved in the sale of honors. He may have abandoned many of his Socialist principles, but there is no evidence that he had become totally unscrupulous. It is just possible that Gregory and Grayson had some homosexual involvement—letters discovered in 1983 revealed that Grayson had had a homosexual affair with a young Socialist, Harry Dawson, in the first decade of the century. But the letters reveal that Grayson played a protective role—one begins "My Stricken Darling"—and it seems unlikely that he would become sexually involved with a dominant character like Gregory—who was, moreover, twelve years his senior.

What we *do* know is that Grayson's rent was paid regularly by check delivered by liveried messengers and that Gregory employed him in some capacity. There is also a curious story to the effect that in 1919 a New Zealand soldier named Walter Adams went to renew his acquaintance with Grayson in London and that one day, Grayson paused on the corner of Parliament Street and pointed to a window above them. After a while, red and green lights flashed, and Grayson told Adams that they were signals to a taxi across the road—which, in fact, moved off at that moment. "The man behind those signals is one of the evilist men in London," said Grayson. "He sells honors for money. He has spied on me, and now I am turning the tables and spying on him."

So it would seem that Maundy Gregory had a motive for wanting to see Grayson disappear. But why should he have been spying on Grayson? According to Grayson, Gregory thought he was a Bolshevik agent and that he was working for Ireland's Sinn Feiners. Again, this is conceivable—Grayson was an ex-revolutionary and was known to sympathize with the Irish struggle for freedom.

Toward the end of September 1920, Grayson went to Liverpool to stay with his mother, and he told her (and his sister) that he would be in touch with them the following day, presumably by telephone. His mother, Elizabeth Grayson, stated seven years later that he had contacted them, as promised, and then vanished. She was told soon afterward that he had had an accident and injured his head and his arm. One writer on the case, Donald McCormick, says that Grayson was attacked in the Strand, and another biographer, Reg Groves, says this happened immediately before he disappeared—that is, after he had left the Georgian Restaurant. Groves says that he learned of the attack from a police inspector in 1942, when he was interviewed about Grayson's disappearance, but that the inspector refused to give more details.

What we *do* know is that soon after his disappearance—possibly the same or the next day—an artist named George Flemwell was painting a watercolor on the banks of the Thames, near

Ditton Island, when he saw an "electric canoe" crossing the river with two men in it; one of them he recognized as Grayson. The "canoe" stopped at Ditton Island, and the men entered a bungalow. What Flemwell did not know at the time was that this was Maundy Gregory's bungalow. Flemwell, who had known Grayson since before the war—and had entertained him in Switzerland in 1919—took a ferry to the island and knocked on the door of the bungalow, which was called Vanity Fair. It was answered by a handsome middle-aged woman who irritably denied all knowledge of Grayson. Puzzled, but not alarmed, Flemwell shrugged and left. Soon after this he returned to his home in Switzerland, where he died in 1928. His story about Grayson was told in a letter to a friend, whose wife later married the journalist Donald McCormick and showed him the letter. The result was that McCormick wrote a book called *Murder by Perfection*, in which he accused Maundy Gregory of murdering Grayson.

McCormick also accused Gregory of murdering the woman who answered the door to Flemwell. It was Gregory's housekeeper, Mrs. Edith Marion Rosse, who shared Vanity Fair with Gregory and her husband. In 1923 the Rosses separated, but Mrs. Rosse stayed on as Gregory's housekeeper. Thirteen years after Flemwell's visit, Mrs. Rosse died after exhibiting symptoms of nausea, vomiting, and diarrhea; her doctor diagnosed Bright's disease. Two days earlier, when feeling unwell, she had scrawled her will on the back of a menu, leaving all her money and possessions to Gregory.

Gregory had long since ceased to prosper, and Mrs. Rosse left a fortune of £18,000. (Not long before her death, they had quarreled because she refused to lend him some of it.) Now Gregory behaved rather oddly. Alleging that Mrs. Rosse had asked to be buried "near her beloved Thames," he went to some trouble to secure a grave at Bisham, some distance away. He also instructed the undertaker not to solder the coffin. It was buried a mere eighteen inches below the surface—as if Gregory *wanted* water to get into the coffin.

Other problems were already upon him. In January 1933 Lieutenant-Commander Edward Leake was approached by Gregory's "scout" and offered a knighthood for £12,000. He declined, and the scout pressed him to meet Gregory. Leake agreed to the meeting but again declined the offer. Gregory asked for £2,000 "to keep the pot boiling" (presumably to keep the offer open). Leake reported the incident to Scotland Yard. And on February 16, 1933, Gregory appeared at Bow Street Crown Court, accused of selling honors. He was able to raise ample funds for his defense—almost certainly from recipients of honors who wanted their names to be kept out of the case. Gregory was sentenced to two months in prison and fined a mere £50.

While he was in jail, Mrs. Rosse's nephew went to the police and told them he thought his aunt's death was suspicious. In late April 1933 Mrs. Rosse's body was exhumed but proved to be badly decomposed with water. The pathologist admitted that it would be impossible to decide whether she had been poisoned, as the nephew suspected.

In the company of a young waiter with whom he had been having a long-standing affair, Gregory had already fled to Paris, where he lived in comfort for another eight years, never short of money. He was interned by the Germans at the beginning of the Second World War and died in a camp at Drancy in 1941, at the age of seventy-four.

But where did he obtain the cash to live so comfortably? The answer is: from the British government. Lord Davidson, Treasurer of the Conservative Party, mentions in his memoirs that Gregory was paid a pension of £2,000 a year. Gregory knew too much to be allowed to stay in England, so he was pensioned off and sent to France.

Clearly, then, there is a certain plausibility in McCormick's theory that Grayson was lured to Gregory's home on Ditton Island and murdered. He had a ready means of disposal at his front door—it would only have been necessary to weight the body heavily, then push it into the river. If the Thames was not deep enough near Gregory's bungalow, he had a boat to take it wherever he liked. The dandyish Gregory would not have been capable of committing a murder—let alone disposing of a corpse—but he had a possible accomplice in Mrs. Rosse's husband, Fred. (The couple did not separate until 1923.) It would have been necessary only to get Grayson thoroughly drunk—or perhaps introduce a drug into his whisky—and then suffocate him.

But there is a certain amount of puzzling and ambiguous evidence that Grayson did not die in 1920. Sidney Campion, a writer and Parliamentary reporter, reported seeing Grayson on the subway in 1949. I knew Campion well and knew him to be a truthful man and an accurate observer. He claimed that on his way to the House of Commons from his home in Wimbledon, he saw Grayson—in the company of a pretty woman—get on the train at Sloane Square. As they passed the Westminster station, Campion heard him remark, "Here's the old firm." Campion was only ten years younger than Grayson and had followed his career with admiration. The sighting was reported in the press. A year later Campion was offered a job as public relations officer for the GPO—a job he did not apply for. It was apparently offered to him by Winston Churchill. Campion was subsequently awarded an OBE for his services. Grayson's biographer, David Clark, MP, feels that there was something very odd about Churchill taking an interest in such a minor post in the first year of the war, when he had so many other things to think about.

There are other oddities. Grayson's former Unitarian college listed him as dead in 1921, reporting that he had died in the previous year. But at that time no one—except close relatives— was aware of his disappearance. It seems that someone had notified the college of his death. In 1924 Seymour Cocks, who later became a Member of Parliament, was congratulated on his oratory after a public meeting at Maidstone by a man who introduced himself as Grayson, and went to have a drink with him in a nearby pub. An old acquaintance named A. C. Murray saw Grayson from the top of a bus in 1925 and rushed off to try to catch him—only to lose him among the crowds at Charing Cross Station.

Another MP who knew Grayson well, Ernest Marklew, reported not long before he died in 1939 that he had traced Grayson to a furniture shop in London, which Grayson owned, and that Grayson told him he wanted to live in anonymity; Marklew said he felt he had to respect this wish.

In 1942, when Grayson's sister Auguste, who had returned from Canada, instituted a new search for her brother, the London *Star* ran a story to the effect that a young man named Blatchford had been approached by a middle-aged stranger in a pub in Herne Bay, Kent, after he had been engaged in a noisy political discussion. When Blatchford introduced himself, the stranger asked if he was related to the Socialist Robert Blatchford. The young man said no; the stranger then introduced himself as Victor Grayson and said he had once been an MP. It was not until the later publicity about the search for Grayson that Blatchford contacted the *Star*, and by that time the trail had gone cold.

After publishing *Murder by Perfection* in 1970, Donald McCormick received a letter from a man named Harold Smallwood, who described how, in 1948, he became acquainted with a man named Victor Garston, who was living in Rowton House, King's Cross, a hostel for down-and-outs. Garston told Smallwood many things about himself: that he was from Liverpool; that he had been an engineering apprentice; that his wife had been an actress who had died in childbirth; that he had served with Australian forces in France during the First World War; and that he had talked on platforms with Horatio Bottomley—he even had a newspaper photograph of himself with Bottomley. Garston claimed to have worked as a schoolmaster in Ireland and Austria after the war and admitted that his drinking had usually led to his dismissal.

All this certainly sounds like Grayson (and Garston also happens to be the name of a Liverpool suburb). So many coincidences would be virtually impossible. But when Grayson's biographer, David Clark, checked with Rowton House and with a bank that Smallwood had mentioned, he was unable to find any trace of a Victor Garston; neither was he able to trace Smallwood, who claimed to have spent twenty years as a Criminal Investigation Department (CID) officer. So the Garston story must be regarded as "not proven."

But if *any* of these sightings was genuine, then how do we explain why Grayson chose to vanish? On this topic, his two biographers, Reg Groves and David Clark, are in agreement; Grayson, like Maundy Gregory, was offered a government pension in exchange for disappearing and forgetting about the honors scandal. But was he working for or against Gregory? His landlady, Hilda Porter, insists that he hated Gregory. But we know that his rent was paid by a regular check, delivered by uniformed messengers such as Gregory employed. (Unfortunately, the checks were handled by Hilda Porter's secretary, and she had no idea who signed them.) It is possible that he was working for Gregory in some other capacity, perhaps for the sake of his contacts from former times, and found out about the honors scandal by accident. If he threatened to "blow the honors scandal sky high"—as McCormick quotes him as saying—then Lloyd George would have found it cheap to buy him off with a pension of £2,000 a year.

In the 1960s I began to research the Grayson story when I was contacted by his daughter, Elaine. Elaine had been brought up by her maternal grandparents in Bolton and recalled her father visiting them regularly between 1918 and the time of his disappearance. She was engaged in writing a book about her father, which she hoped might stimulate someone to produce evidence that would reveal what had happened to him; I read her manuscript and gave her some advice.

Elaine had no doubt that her father had survived his disappearance, and she believed that her grandmother, Georgina Nightingale, knew the secret. In 1932, when she was eighteen, Elaine was made a ward of the court by her grandparents; they wanted her to stop seeing a musician. But Elaine suspected that there was more to it than that—that it was a form of insurance in case her father tried to take her away. When Elaine became engaged to Raymond Watkins in 1934, Mrs. Nightingale warned him not to have anything to do with Grayson if he turned up. Soon after the two were married in 1936, they went to look at the grave of Elaine's mother, Ruth, in Kensal Green cemetery and were surprised to find that it was well tended and that there were fresh flowers on it. The grandmother denied all knowledge of who was tending it. In 1941 Elaine arrived at her grandmother's house just as she was burning the contents of a deed box. After that Mrs. Nightingale talked far more openly about Grayson—her earlier attitude had been tight-lipped.

Elaine's oddest story was that when her grandmother was dying, she kept talking ramblingly about the Marlborough family, the distinguished military family that included Winston Churchill. After the funeral Elaine asked the longtime maidservant, Jane, what her grandmother had meant. Jane replied, "Don't you realize she was telling you who your father really was?" What is being suggested, then, is that Grayson was the result of a liaison by some member of the Marlborough family. It seems unlikely that his mother (who died in 1929) engaged in a clandestine affair after she had given birth to six children; the alternative would be that Victor was "farmed out." Family records seem to support this notion, in that they show that the Grayson family became steadily more prosperous after Victor's birth, moving into a number of houses, each one better than the last. Elaine also speculated that an aristocratic background could explain her father's natural taste for high life and pointed out that he bore a distinct resemblance to Winston Churchill (who could not have been the culprit—he was only seven at the time of Grayson's birth). If Grayson knew he was not the child of William and Elizabeth Grayson (and he is the only one who could have told Mrs. Nightingale the secret), this could explain why he never attempted to contact his mother after 1920—because he knew she was only his stepmother.

But it requires only ordinary common sense to see why, if Grayson lived on after 1920, he decided to disappear. Whether or not he was the illegitimate son of the aristocracy, it is clear that he was brought up in a working-class environment that seemed to offer him no opportunity to better himself. He was apparently tongue-tied as a boy and had to have a minor operation, followed by elocution lessons. He was a romantic child who read a great deal and tried to run away to sea at fourteen. Soon after this he was apprenticed to an engineering works, where he led a strike of apprentices. Membership in a dockside debating society led to contacts with the Unitarian church and to his first opportunity to escape the treadmill and gain a foothold in life. In later years he held the Marxian view that religion is an opium of the people; there is not the slightest evidence that he was ever religious. Yet he decided to become a minister, simply because it offered a way out. Then, as quickly as possible, he slipped into left-wing politics. A friend named Redfern recalls a waitress who was attracted to Grayson, as he was to her. But when Redfern asked him if he meant to become involved with the girl, "a meaner expression hid his familiar openness. 'No,' he replied, 'I am not going to spoil my career.' " Grayson was a young man who was determined to "get on."

And when he became a speaker on the Socialist Party platform, he recognized that the best way of getting on was to be more downright, more extreme, than anyone else—hence his denunciations of the rich as robbers and murderers and his recommendations that in such a society honesty was not the best policy. The method succeeded, and he found himself in Westminster. But here he must quickly have realized that his violent rhetoric was not entirely logical. Conservative and Liberal MPs were obviously *not* crooks and murderers. He was too intelligent not to see this and to see that, in a sense, he was in Parliament on false pretenses. He had two alternatives: to settle down and try to become a good MP, doing his best for his constituents, or to continue to try to rise to the top by pursuing the old methods of violent denunciation. He was too ambitious to settle down and become just another parliamentarian. And the unemployment problem gave him the opportunity he wanted to get himself noticed and admired—at least by workingmen. At this stage, it would not be unreasonable to compare him to the young Hitler or Mussolini or Lenin. But the election of 1910 showed him that he had miscalculated; instead of becoming a popular demagogue, he found himself without a seat.

It was in the following year that his alcoholism began to develop. This could have been due to frustrated ambition, or it could have been the reaction of an intelligent man who realizes that he has landed himself in a cul-de-sac. Demagoguery had failed; yet in a sense, it was all he had to offer. Grayson's beginnings were not unlike those of his fellow Socialist, George Bernard Shaw. But Shaw had lived quietly with his mother for twenty years before acquiring a reputation as a journalist, and in that time he had taught himself to write as well as speak. Grayson had only one string to his bow. And, what was worse, he was ceasing to believe in his own denunciations of the ruling class. Something very similar was happening in America to Jack London, who had also begun as a fiery socialist and had used his early fame as a writer to preach revolution on America's campuses; after ten years of preaching, London was beginning to feel that there might be something to be said, after all, for men who acquired a fortune by intelligence and hard work. He also became an alcoholic as he became more of a realist; his early death seemed due to a kind of moral collapse.

When, at the beginning of World War I, Grayson praised the members of the aristocracy who were fighting for England, he had effectively ceased to be a Socialist. As he witnessed his wife's misery in their bare apartments in London and New York, he must have recognized clearly that this was his own fault, not that of the ruling class. Yet the only way he could support his wife was by taking up his old career as a demagogue and denouncer of capitalism. He tried in 1914 and realized he could not go through with it; the drunken evening at Bradford must have been a moment of truth. From then on he made no attempt to live up to his promise to stand again for Colne Valley; he knew it was out of the question.

The war offered him an opportunity to delay his decision. But when it was over, he knew that there could be no return to politics. He had simply outgrown it. If he went back now, it would have to be as a Liberal, perhaps even a Tory, and this would have been unthinkable; he would have had no supporters. But he mixed with "patriots" like Bottomley and no doubt wondered if there might be an opportunity to find himself a more modest position as a government employee. He seems to have done this, if we are to judge by the checks that paid his rent. One suggestion is that he was recruited by British Intelligence, but unless some old government records can be unearthed, we may never know. All that is clear is that, by 1920, Grayson wanted out. And if Reg Groves and David Clark are correct, he succeeded. Clark is convinced that Grayson returned to Australia for a while, and then came back to live quietly in the south of England. There is one interesting piece of evidence in support of this theory. In 1939 someone collected Grayson's war medals in London. The only persons who were entitled to collect them were Grayson himself or a member of his family. But his family knew nothing about them (his sisters were in Canada), and Elaine Watkins denies collecting them.

A few mysteries still remain to be cleared up. If Grayson

vanished from the Georgian restaurant after a mysterious phone call, and was attacked in the Strand, what was he doing in a boat on the Thames with Maundy Gregory, presumably the man responsible? This problem seems to evaporate when we examine the evidence more closely. The origin of the Georgian restaurant story is unknown, but it was certainly not current at the time of the first search for Grayson in 1927. It is quoted by Donald McCormick in *Murder by Perfection*, who claims to have gotten it from E. K. Donovan, who was supposedly there. Donovan, in fact, is quoted as mentioning the Georgian *Hotel*, but McCormick was unable to locate such a hotel in London in 1920—only the restaurant.

Years later Hilda Porter, the landlady of Georgian House, told her story of how Grayson spent most of the day in his flat with two men, "not gentlemen," and how he came down with two large suitcases, telling her that he would be in touch. When she checked his room, she realized that he had taken all his personal possessions. Evidently, then, he intended to go away and wanted to do so without leaving a forwarding address. In a sense, therefore, the Georgian Hotel (or restaurant) story becomes superfluous; it seems highly unlikely that he then went there and received the phone call "luring" him to the Queens Hotel. Besides, how could he be kidnapped in central London? It seems too much of a coincidence that he left a block of flats called Georgian House, and then went on to a Georgian Hotel. It seems far more likely that the Georgian Hotel is a garbled version of the Georgian House and that the famous abduction originated in someone's imagination. Grayson left Georgian House with two men, probably employees of Maundy Gregory, and went to Ditton Island with Gregory—perhaps to receive new identity papers—then left the country. He had found the oblivion that he had been seeking for the past ten years.

13

Rudolf Hess:
Was It Hitler's Deputy
Who Died in Spandau Prison?

On August 17, 1987, the man referred to as Prisoner Number 7 committed suicide by hanging in Berlin's Spandau Prison. The prison records gave his real name as Rudolf Walter Richard Hess, aged ninety-three years—the last member of the Nazi high command to be held in that prison.

Hess had been Hitler's deputy and personal secretary and was third in line to the Führership. Then, in 1941, only a few weeks before the launch of the German attack on the Soviet Union, he vanished from Berlin and flew to Scotland as a self-appointed peace ambassador. The result of that well-meant mission was a lifetime of imprisonment. At the time of his death he had been incarcerated for almost forty-six years, had been convicted of preparing and waging aggressive war, and had attempted suicide several times. Ignoring complaints by human-rights groups, the Soviet Union insisted that Hess be held in prison until he died— the real motive being to maintain that nation's access to West Berlin, where Spandau Prison was situated.

For more than ten years before his suicide, there had been odd rumors that Prisoner Number 7 was not Hess at all but a double, planted on the British for reasons unknown. The findings of a prison doctor in 1973, in fact, seem to prove that the prisoner was not Hess. But why, if that were true, would he have kept the secret so long and at such cost? Why would the authorities have imprisoned an innocent man for nearly half a century? Close scrutiny of the facts throws up a number of bizarre anomalies that suggest that, as absurd as it sounds, Number 7 may not, after all, have been Hitler's deputy.

Shortly before eleven o'clock on the night of Saturday, May 10, 1941, David MaClean, the head plowman at Floor's Farm, outside Eaglesham near Glasgow, was startled by a tremendous roar that shook the whole cottage. Rushing outside, he saw that an aircraft had crashed in a nearby field; he also saw a lone parachute descending in the moonlight. Unarmed, MaClean ran across the field and found the parachutist disentangling himself from his harness—hampered somewhat by a twisted ankle. MaClean, keeping his distance, called, "Who are you? Are you German?" The pilot, a big man, pulled himself upright with some difficulty and replied, "Yes, I am German. My name is Hauptmann Alfred Horn. I want to go to Dungavel House. I have an important message for the Duke of Hamilton."

The "Hauptmann" gave no trouble and waited quietly until a constable arrived and took him into custody. He was held at the local home guard headquarters for a few hours, then was transferred to the Mayhill Barracks in Glasgow. When questioned, he simply repeated his name and insisted that he must see the Duke of Hamilton on a matter of urgency.

The next morning this information was passed on to the Duke, who was then a wing-commander with the city of Glasgow (bomber) squadron. Together with an RAF intelligence officer, he hurried immediately to interview the captured pilot—who was by then laid up in bed with a painfully swollen ankle. After the introductions the prisoner insisted on speaking to the Duke alone. The intelligence officer obligingly went outside; as soon as they were alone, the prisoner greeted the Duke of Hamilton as an acquaintance. He explained that they had met in Germany during the 1936 Olympics and that the Duke had even attended a luncheon party at his house. When Hamilton continued to look puzzled, the "Hauptmann" said, "I do not know if you recognize me, but I am Rudolf Hess."

Hamilton was staggered. If the man before him was indeed Hess—and the resemblance was striking—it meant that they had captured the deputy Führer of the Nazi Party—one of the top men in the Nazi high command and third in line to Hitler himself. Yet why would one of the most powerful men in Europe risk his life by flying into an enemy country at night and then hand himself over as if he were a common criminal hoping for amnesty?

Hess went on to explain that he was on a "mission of humanity," a diplomatic errand of the highest importance, carrying a message that could save thousands, perhaps millions of lives. He was here, he told the astonished duke, to try to negotiate peace between Britain and Germany.

Rudolf Hess had the reputation of being the most intellectual member of Hitler's inner circle. Born in 1894 in Egypt, he had been schooled in Germany and had immediately volunteered for active service at the outbreak of war in 1914. Shot through the left lung on the Rumanian front in 1917, he was given a medical discharge from the army, but after a six-month recovery period he joined the Imperial Flying Corps. He successfully completed pilot training in time to serve only ten days before the armistice.

The National Socialist Workers Party, led by a spellbinding orator named Adolf Hitler, consisted mainly of ex-servicemen who felt that the peace had betrayed them. Hess joined in 1920, the year Hitler took over the leadership. He quickly achieved prominence and in 1923 helped Hitler plan the attempted overthrow of the Bavarian government—later known as the "Beerhall Putsch." When this failed, and Hitler was arrested, Hess fled the country. After a spectacular self-defense that was virtually a condemnation of his judges, Hitler was sentenced by a sympathetic court to five years' imprisonment but was offered a considerably reduced sentence if he remained on good behavior. When he heard the news, Hess returned of his own free will and gave himself up. He was sentenced to an eighteen-month term and sent to serve his time with Hitler in the Landsberg fortress.

During their imprisonment Hitler and Hess kept busy, Hitler writing a book and Hess acting as his secretary. It is certain that Hess had an important influence on the development of ideas in *Mein Kampf*; he had a better intellectual and academic training than Hitler and had already developed his own strong views on German racial purity and the need for territorial expansion. The two worked well together, and the foundations of Hess's future influence in the Nazi Party were laid.

When Hitler won an election and became Reichschancellor in 1933, Hess was appointed his deputy, and during the establishment of the totalitarian dictatorship he was never far from Hitler's side. But when Hess announced plans to make the first east-west trans-Atlantic flight, Hitler turned down the scheme, insisting that Hess was too valuable to the Reich to risk his life.

In February 1938 Hess was appointed head of a department whose purpose was to make secret plans for the war of German expansion, which broke out a year later. Hess is known to have advocated expansion eastward, into Poland and then into the Soviet Union, but he was strongly against war on two fronts. And when France capitulated in 1940, he seems to have decided that Germany's new western frontier was reasonably secure and that therefore the war with Great Britain was dangerous and unnecessary. The question was, would Hess have felt strongly enough about the subject to risk his own life to make peace, and would such a madcap scheme have had Hitler's backing?

Although stating that he was acting on his own initiative, the man who claimed to be Hess insisted to Hamilton that he was speaking for Hitler in all but name. The Führer had never wanted to go to war with the British Empire, he said. Britain's impending total defeat—and in 1941 many people thought this increasingly likely—was something Hitler truly wished to avoid. There was a chance now for the nations to come to peace and perhaps even to join forces to smash the threat from Communist Russia. He was there to try to put an immediate stop to the war.

Hamilton asked him why he had specifically asked to see him, and the prisoner replied that a mutual friend, Dr. Albrecht Haushofer, had recommended the duke as a man who would support his peace initiative. To back this he pointed out that among his confiscated belongings were the visiting cards of Haushofer and his father, Professor Karl Haushofer. He also mentioned a letter that Albrecht Haushofer had sent to the Duke, inviting him to a secret diplomatic meeting in neutral Portugal.

The Duke had indeed received this letter, after it had been intercepted and investigated by MI5, but he was still dubious about the identity of the prisoner. For one thing, he was carrying no identification other than the visiting cards and some photographs of Rudolf Hess as a small child—a very odd choice of material to back such an incredible story.

It all seemed beyond belief. Capturing Rudolf Hess—under any circumstances—was almost too good to be true, and it occurred to Hamilton that it might be a trick using a look-alike, in order to sound out the British government's willingness to continue fighting. Even so, he found himself more than half believing that the prisoner was indeed Hess, but he was careful not to give this away during the interview.

The Duke, wary of using the telephone system, flew to inform Churchill in person. Ushered in to see the Prime Minister a few hours later, he told his strange story. Churchill exclaimed, "Do you mean to tell me that the Deputy Führer of Germany is in our hands? . . . Well, Hess or no Hess, I'm going to see the Marx Brothers!" Which in fact he did—*The Marx Brothers Go West*—at a local cinema.

On his return he interrogated Hamilton more thoroughly. The Duke said that the more he thought about the secret letter from Dr. Haushofer, the more certain he was that only the real Hess could have known about it. Hess was known to be a close associate of Haushofer, and it was quite possible that the letter had been sent on his orders. If this was the case, or even if Hess had simply condoned the letter, it was highly unlikely that he would broadcast the fact to his colleagues, many of whom would have argued that it was treason. After a three-hour session, Churchill sat deep in thought and was heard to mutter, "The worm is in the bud."

The next day Hamilton, who admitted that his memory of meeting Hess in 1936 was a dim one, was sent back to Glasgow with Ivone Kirkpatrick, a man who had served as First Secretary to the embassy in Berlin from 1933 to 1938 and had met Hess on many occasions. When they landed they were greeted by a call from the Foreign Secretary, Anthony Eden. The following broadcast had just been sent out on German public radio:

On Saturday 10th May Rudolf Hess set out at 18:00 hours on a flight from Augsburg from which he has so far not returned. A letter that he left behind unfortunately shows by its distraction traces of a mental disorder, and it is feared that he was a victim of hallucinations. . . . In the circumstances it must be considered that party member Hess either crashed or met with an accident.

Hamilton and Kirkpatrick were told that the Ministry of Information was shortly going to release a statement headed "Rudolf Hess in England." The British government was committing itself.

If this was indeed some cunning Nazi trick, then Hitler was playing for high stakes. The real Hess might have dropped out of sight for a while to give an impostor a chance to convince the British, but Hess's public credibility would be destroyed in Germany if the "mission" came to nothing. And if this were to happen, the Nazi high command would have to admit that they had been attempting a confidence trick on the highest diplomatic level; the loss of face to the party as a whole would be enormous. Since nobody could imagine what such a plot might achieve that would be worth such a risk, it seemed logical that the simple explanation—that Hess had flown to England without Hitler's knowledge—was the only possible one.

The prisoner did not recognize Kirkpatrick when they were first introduced, but as they talked he seemed to remember him and mentioned several incidents they had witnessed together in Germany. This convinced Kirkpatrick and Hamilton that they were talking to Hess. Then, just as the interview was becoming more relaxed, the prisoner drew out a large packet of manuscript notes and launched into a four-hour diatribe on the subject of Anglo-German historical relations and the unfairness of Britain's declaration of war on Germany.

The exhausted Kirkpatrick later telephoned the Foreign Office, to be told that Churchill had definitely ruled out any possibility of negotiating with the Deputy Führer. To do so might be interpreted, by friend and foe alike, as unwillingness to fight—perhaps just the result the Nazis were hoping for. Hess, said Churchill, was to be treated as a prisoner of war and nothing else. He was to be told that if, after the war, he was found guilty of war crimes, his repentance would stand in his favor; other than that the British government had no interest in him.

After eighteen months of imprisonment, Hess began to show signs of mental illness; he complained that his food was being poisoned and made a number of suicide attempts. He was moved to a mental hospital and held there for the rest of the war.

It was now generally accepted that the prisoner was Rudolf Hess—even his mental illness seemed to support the Nazi statement that he had been suffering from a breakdown at the time of his flight. Yet an observant doctor might have noted reasons for doubt. To begin with, Hess insisted that he was suffering from periodic bouts of amnesia, which made it impossible for him to answer questions about himself. But he also seemed to have undergone a personality change. The Deputy Führer had been known to be obsessed with his health. Like Hitler, he had been a strict vegetarian, who refused even to eat eggs, fried foods, or any products grown with artificial fertilizer, considering them "impure." He was known to have eaten with fastidious care and to have been punctiliously neat and tidy. In confinement in England, he ate anything set before him voraciously and messily and seemed to have lost all interest in his appearance.

While held in Britain he was allowed to write to his wife, Ilsa Hess, via neutral Switzerland. She later said that the handwriting seemed to be that of her husband and that she never had any doubts that that was who he was. What did bother her occasionally was that her husband seemed to be desperately trying to prove to her that he *was* Rudolf Hess.

The war ended; in October 1945 the prisoner was transferred to Nuremberg, Germany, to face the War Crimes Tribunal. On his arrival he seemed to suffer a total memory breakdown and was judged incapable of standing trial. The doctors tried to jog his memory by introducing him to old colleagues; but although he showed some sign of recognition when confronted by his two secretaries, he failed to recognize Hermann Göring or Karl Haushofer, the father of the man who had recommended that he seek out the Duke of Hamilton.

Perhaps understandably, the prisoner was also in poor physical shape. Hess had once been a large, well-built man in excellent health. He was now gaunt and sickly; although in defense of his jailers it should be noted that he had already been in poor physical condition when captured.

As the authorities wrangled over his mental competence, the prisoner suddenly issued the following statement:

> Henceforth my memory will again respond to the outside world. The reasons why I simulated loss of memory were tactical. The fact is that it is only my ability to concentrate that is somewhat reduced. However, my capacity to follow the trial, to defend myself, to put questions to witnesses, or even to answer questions is not being affected thereby.

He subsequently stood trial, and though clearly tired and less than fully alert, gave a reasonable account of himself. On September 2, 1946, he was found guilty of conspiracy and crimes against peace. Since it could not be proved that he had known about the death camps, he was acquitted of the charge of war crimes. Together with Walter Funk, Admiral Donitz, Admiral Raeder, Baldur von Schirach, Constantin von Naurath, and Albert Speer, Rudolf Hess was sentenced to life imprisonment in Spandau Prison in West Berlin. There he was simply referred to as Prisoner Number 7.

Throughout the trial and for the next twenty-three years, the prisoner declined to see his wife or his only son. When he finally agreed to allow Ilsa Hess to visit him, she expressed surprise that his voice had deepened—it might have been expected to become higher with increasing age.

Spandau Prison was an oddly anomalous product of the cold war. Situated in the British-occupied section of West Berlin, it was administered by the four major victorious powers: the United States, Britain, France, and the Soviet Union. Under a special convention drawn up for the prison, control of the prison alternated between these four nations every month; this included a total change of guard.

In the course of time the other six prisoners were released, the last two being von Schirach and Speer in 1966. But Prisoner Number 7 was offered no hope of release. The Soviets made it clear that they would block any such move and that Hess was to remain imprisoned until he died.

There were two reasons for this. First, the Soviet people felt particularly bitter toward Hess, who had collaborated with Hitler on the plan to conquer and enslave them. But the main reason was undoubtedly that Hess's release would involve the Soviets losing their foothold in West Berlin, and with it, presumably, all kinds of opportunities for spying.

And so, on August 17, 1987, the last Spandau prisoner committed suicide by hanging at the age of ninety-three. But for at least fourteen years before that, there were very real doubts about his identity. In 1972 Dr. Hugh Thomas was appointed consultant in general surgery at the British Military Hospital in Berlin. Three years earlier, in 1969, Hess had almost died when a duodenal ulcer perforated, and his Russian captors allowed several days to pass before sending for a doctor; now Thomas insisted on giving him a complete medical checkup—although it was not until the following year, 1973, that he was finally allowed to examine Hess in the presence of representatives of all four powers. Thomas was revolted by the inhumanity toward Hess shown by Voitov, the Soviet commandant; any attempt to show sympathy was immediately met by a command of "Stop that! It is contrary to the Nuremberg convention."

What Thomas now discovered puzzled him deeply. Hess had been wounded in the chest in the First World War, and the resultant lung injury had caused him much bronchial trouble in the days when he was Hitler's deputy. Now there was no sign of a war wound and no bronchial trouble. Examination of Hess's medical records made it clear that there should have been many scars from war wounds, none of which was visible on the body of the Spandau prisoner. When, at a second examination, Thomas asked him, "What happened to your war wounds?," Hess blanched, began to tremble, then muttered, "Too late, too late." What did that mean? That there would now be no point in admitting that he was not Rudolf Hess?

Thomas concluded that it was impossible that this prisoner— who had been code-named "Jonathan" when in England—could be Hess. X-rays should at least have shown signs of tissue scarring, but there were none.

Thomas went on to study the documents concerning Hess's flight to Scotland and concluded that it should have been impossible for a Messerschmitt 110D to carry enough fuel to make the 850-mile journey if it had included as many detours as Hess claimed. The range of the aircraft—on full tanks—was only a little more than 850 miles. It could possibly have been carrying spare tanks under the wings, but Hess's adjutant, Pintsch, had taken a photograph of the plane as it took off, and it showed no spare fuel tanks.

In his book *The Murder of Rudolf Hess*, Dr. Thomas suggests that Hess never left Germany; rather, he died there and was replaced by a double. The commander of fighter squadrons along the Dutch coast, Adolf Galland, tells in his book *The First and Last* how, on the night of Hess's flight, Hermann Göring—who loathed Hess—rang him and ordered him to intercept an aircraft flying out of Germany, claiming, "The Deputy Führer has gone mad and is flying to England. . . . He must be brought down." But Galland's planes were unable to locate Hess's Messerschmitt.

What do we know to support the notion that Hess flew to Britain on a peace mission? To begin with, it is clear that Hitler wanted peace. He was known to admire the British and would have preferred them as allies rather than enemies; Russia was his real target. On June 25, 1940, Hitler made a speech in which he appealed to England from a position of strength ("since I am not the vanquished") for peace "in the name of reason." Churchill rejected this offer.

But Hess is known to have favored a direct appeal to the British. One of his closest friends was the aforementioned Albrecht Haushofer, whose father, Karl, had been Hess's personal adviser in the mid-1930s and was sent on a number of diplomatic missions. It seems certain that he knew about Hess's plans to appeal directly to the British. On the day after Hess's adjutant Pintsch delivered Hess's "farewell" letter to Hitler at Berchtesgaden, describing his peace mission, Albrecht Haushofer was summoned to write an account of his own attempts to make contact with the British to make peace. Unfortunately, Albrecht was murdered by the S.S. in the last days of the war, so the one witness who might have been able to tell the truth about the prisoner in Spandau was silenced.

But if we know that Hess wanted to make peace, and even that he went to talk to the Duke of Windsor in Lisbon in July 1940, why should we doubt that it was Hess who landed in Scotland on May 10, 1941? Because, as we have seen, the medical evidence suggests that the prisoner code-named "Jonathan" was not the man who received so many wounds in World War I. If "Hauptmann" Horn was Hess, why was he carrying so little documentation, so few papers to establish his identity? Why did he refuse to see his wife and son for twenty-three years after being incarcerated in Spandau?

Thomas's theory, briefly, is this: Göring detested Hess and would have been glad to see him dead. And Heinrich Himmler, head of the S.S., is known to have nurtured plans to replace Hitler. For either of them, Hess's death would have been a bonus. But if Hess was murdered on his peace flight—or intercepted and shot down—Hitler would have been unforgiving. It was important that "Hess" should arrive. So when Hess's planned flight became known to Göring, a double was found and carefully schooled. And when Hess had been eliminated—sometime on that night of May 9–10, 1941—the double was hastily sent off, probably from a Danish airfield. This is why the Duke of Hamilton did not recognize him. This is why he began feigning loss of memory at the earliest opportunity.

But British intelligence must have found out very soon that he was not Rudolf Hess. This could explain why the British made no attempts to use their prisoner for propaganda purposes.

Then, why did Hess's double not reveal his secret after the war? Thomas speaks of Himmler's known habit of eliminating whole families of "traitors" to the Reich. This would have explained the double's silence before Himmler's death—before the Nuremberg trials began. And after that, he may either have continued to believe his family to be in danger from ex-Nazis or simply have assumed that he stood no chance of being believed. If, in fact, he had been virtually brainwashed during a series of breakdowns and suicide attempts, and mental exhaustion, he may simply have settled into the state of blank indifference that is sometimes seen in the very old.

Whatever the reason, it seems clear that Prisoner Number 7 recognized that it was "too late, too late" when Dr. Thomas finally began asking the right questions.

14

The Disappearance of Harold Holt: Was the Australian Prime Minister a Chinese Spy?

As the Australian Prime Minister, Harold Holt, flew out from Canberra to his weekend retreat on Friday, December 15, 1967, attendant journalists noted that the usually jovial, energetic politician looked tired and sullen. This in itself was not surprising; Holt had just gone through an exhausting week of political wrangling in an attempt to hold his shaky coalition government together. Certainly, few journalists thought it worth more than a passing comment in their reports; the premier was well known for his rapid recuperative powers. Thus, they must have been staggered when, two days later, the wires brought in the news that the Prime Minister was missing, presumed dead, with suicide a distinct possibility.

He had spent the weekend at his house in Portsea, sixty miles down the coast from Melbourne, and once there he had seemed to recover his usual good spirits. On Saturday December 16 he had played tennis and hosted a dinner party for fourteen, during which he talked cheerfully about spear-gun fishing, his favorite sport. Although close to sixty, Holt spent much of his leisure time engaged in this strenuous activity and was proud of his record catches.

The next morning he and a group of friends drove to Cheviot

Beach, a strip of coast that was out of bounds to the general public because it was attached to the local Officer Cadet Training School; it was known to be an excellent spot for spear-gun fishing. It also had the reputation for being one of the most dangerous beaches on the Victoria Coast, with unpredictably treacherous currents.

Most of the Prime Minister's friends decided against swimming, but Holt waded in and swam out to sea without hesitation. A young businessman, Alan Stewart, decided to follow suit. After swimming out diagonally about thirty-five yards, Stewart felt a strong undertow pulling at his legs and saw that the bottom had dropped away sharply. He decided to turn back, and as he did so he was disturbed to see that the Prime Minister was still ahead of him and swimming strongly out to sea.

Stewart swam back to shallower water and called to Marjorie Gillespie, a neighbor of Holt's who was with the party on the beach, "Does he usually swim this long?" She became alarmed when she saw how far out Holt was and ran down to the surf to see better. She later told the police, "I saw that Harold was still swimming. But he seemed to be getting further away all the time, and I felt very strongly that all was not well. I watched Harold continuously, and the water became turbulent around him very suddenly. It seemed to boil and these conditions seemed to swamp him." That was the last time Harold Holt was seen.

Within hours, dozens of scuba divers were searching the sea, while helicopters flew as low as they dared. The search continued for six days, but no body was ever found. Many distinguished statesmen attended Holt's memorial service, including Lyndon Johnson, Harold Wilson, Edward Heath, and Prince Charles.

Inevitably, there was speculation that Holt might have committed suicide. He had been Prime Minister for two years and had been in trouble from the beginning. Young Australians demonstrated vigorously against his commitment to the war in Vietnam—Holt had trebled the Australian contingent, to 8,500 troops. He had been accused in Parliament of using air force planes as a personal taxi service for himself and his family. His party lost two by-elections under his leadership and also suffered in elections for the Senate. Also, there were persistent rumors that his own Liberal Party wanted to get rid of him, and nothing would have humiliated Holt more deeply—he was a man who was very sensitive to snubs and setbacks. His opponents in Parliament felt he showed signs of cracking under the strain.

However, those who had seen him that weekend scoffed at the idea of suicide. Harold Holt had a remarkable capacity for relaxing and forgetting his worries, and to his housekeeper, his stepson, and his various friends, he had seemed to be a man without any serious problems. At fifty-nine, after more than thirty years in politics, Holt had become accustomed to the ups and downs of the life of a statesman.

Fifteen years after his disappearance, Harold Holt became the center of a scandal that eclipsed anything that had happened during his lifetime. A book by a highly respected journalist, Anthony Grey, accused him of leading an extraordinary double life. The title tells its own story: *The Prime Minister Was a Spy.* Grey claimed to have reliable information from Chinese sources that revealed that Holt had not drowned on that December afternoon. He had swum out to a Chinese submarine and been taken to the People's Republic of China.

The story sounds incredible, and most reviews of the book were scathing. The story told by Anthony Grey, with its wealth of detail, needs to be absorbed slowly. Anyone who does this will agree that Grey has made a strong case for the notion that Australia's Prime Minister was a Chinese spy.

Harold Holt was the type of politician more often found in America than in England: the charming, flamboyant spellbinder. He once stated that if he had not been a politician, he would have been an actor—an admission that no doubt led many of his opponents to retort, "You are." He was certainly born under the right astrological sign for an actor, that of Leo, in the year 1908. Holt's background was theatrical: his father was a self-made impresario, while his mother was a member of a well-known family in the theater. When he was still a child, his parents moved to England, where his father had become the representative of J. C. Williamson, Australia's biggest theater group. Holt and his brother were educated at a private school, Wesley College, with a minimum of parental affection or interference. When he was only ten his parents divorced.

At Queen's College, Melbourne, Holt studied law. It was not that he found the subject particularly attractive, but it seemed to offer opportunities to exercise his considerable theatrical talent—at college he proved to be a brilliant orator and debater. He also played on the cricket team, acquired fashionable left-wing opinions, and showed himself to be an ardent enthusiast of the opposite sex. He lacked money to entertain his girlfriends, but at least his theatrical contacts provided him with endless complimentary tickets to the theaters and cinemas of Melbourne.

It was in July 1929, when he was twenty years old, that Holt delivered, at the college debating society, a paper advocating a closer relationship between Australia and China. China was at that time in turmoil, with Communists and Nationalists, under Chiang Kai-shek, struggling for supremacy. Young Australian Liberals had mounted a "Hands Off China" campaign. Holt went to see the Chinese consul to request information for his paper. The consul asked if he could see a copy of his paper when it was finished. Holt obliged. And, according to Anthony Grey, Holt was later asked to tea by the consul, who told him that a small publishing firm wanted to print his paper on China, and gave him £50 for it. He was urged to write more articles on China and was delighted to oblige. He needed the money, and the payments of £50, rising soon to £100, were extremely generous.

In 1931, Grey (who claims to be quoting official Chinese sources) reports, Holt was asked by his Chinese contact if he would become a member of the Chinese Intelligence Service. His assignment seems to have been vague, simply "to help China's cause." Holt promptly agreed. After all, there was no hostility between China and Australia, and he was working for Chiang Kai-shek's Nationalists, not for the Communists who might well have been regarded as enemies.

In the following year Holt established a law partnership that quickly prospered, largely because of his old theatrical contacts. His father, now back in Melbourne, also did his best to push business his son's way, in spite of the fact that Harold was refusing to speak to him. The reason for this behavior sheds an interesting light on Harold's character. When his father returned to Melbourne, he invited Harold to a dinner party, where he found himself sitting next to a beautiful young actress named Lola. Being a fast worker, the young man was soon making advances, only to be rebuffed and told that she was in love with his father. The humiliation was like a slap in the face; he walked out of the party and never spoke to his father again. When invited to the wedding of his father and Lola, he ignored the invitation. Later he went so far as to tell new acquaintances that his father was dead.

In December 1931 Harold Holt met Robert Menzies, the distinguished right-wing politician who had attended the same school. They liked one another, and the result was that in 1934 Holt was invited to contest a by-election in Melbourne. His chances seemed minimal, for his opponent was an ex–Labour Prime Minister. Nevertheless, Holt's charm and spellbinding oratory came close to gaining him the seat. In the following year, at the age of twenty-seven, he again stood for the United Australian Party (the Liberals) at Fawkner, and gained the seat. On Monday, September 23, 1935, he swore the oath of allegiance.

Holt's Socialist sympathies were widely known, but his party was liberal in spirit as well as name. A month after entering Parliament he received a dressing-down from the Prime Minister, Menzies, for attacking the Italian invasion of Abyssinia in terms that sounded distinctly Communist. The young politician learned his lesson, and subsequent speeches showed tact and restraint as well as a thorough grasp of his subject.

Grey states that Holt's activities as a "spy" did not involve the kind of betrayal of his country that we associate with the names of Kim Philby in the United Kingdom or Alger Hiss in the United States. He was merely a kind of glorified information officer. His position meant that he had access to information from all over the world. In the 1930s, when the world was seething with political turmoil, such information was worth having. Holt could openly ask questions in Parliament on matters that might affect China— such as whether Britain would sell Australia old air force planes that China urgently wanted to purchase. The answers could play an important, if indirect, part in the complicated chess game of world politics.

A few weeks after the outbreak of World War II, Holt acquired a position that made him even more valuable to the Chinese—he became Minister Without Portfolio to the Ministry of Supply and Development. He was still only thirty-one and known to his friends as something of a playboy—a keen racegoer, a friend of theater and film personalities, and a frequenter of nightclubs (where his preference for wearing a top hat earned him the nickname "Topper" Holt). His political success made him one of the most desirable bachelors in Australia. Moreover, he was appointed Minister of Air and Civil Aviation in 1940.

Then came an episode that disturbed his Chinese friends. After a snap election, the Liberal Party was returned by only one vote. Menzies had to form a coalition, and Holt (as the youngest minister) lost his post and was returned to the back benches. Most politicians would take such a demotion in their stride, but it seemed to shatter Holt. He announced that he was leaving the government to join the army as a private. His Chinese contact, who called himself Mr. Wong, tried hard to dissuade him, but when Holt insisted he told him to regard himself as temporarily "deactivated" as an agent. To report on military matters as a soldier would be far more dangerous than as a minister.

In fact, Holt was soon back in government: three ministers were killed in a plane crash, and he was subsequently offered the post of Minister of Labor and National Service. He accepted with delight and relief. But the Chinese must have felt that his fit of pique revealed a certain weakness of character.

In 1948 Holt was again "deactivated" as a result of the new political turmoil in China—with Mao Tse-tung now making an all-out effort to overthrow Chiang Kai-shek. He remained deactivated for three and a half years. At the end of that time, in 1952, his old friend Wong contacted him again and asked him to provide more information. Anthony Grey tells us that Holt did not know that Wong had now defected to the Communists (who had been in power since 1949). So, although unaware of it, Holt was working for Mao.

If Grey is correct, the rewards for spying were considerable—around £30,000. Holt's value as a spy increased during the Korean War, even more so when it became clear that Menzies was grooming him to be the next Prime Minister. When he came to England in 1953 to attend the coronation of Queen Elizabeth II, he was made a Privy Councillor.

In the following year, Holt told "Mr. Wong" that he had ceased to sympathize with the Chinese Nationalists and had decided not to spy for them any more. Three years later Wong was told to admit to Holt that he was working for the Communists and ask for his help again. Holt had, by this time, discovered that "Wong" was really a vice-consul named Y. M. Liu and summoned him to a meeting to explain himself. "Wong" took the opportunity to confess the deception. However, when he left the meeting Holt had agreed to become once more an information gatherer for the Chinese. After all, he was a Socialist, and the Chinese were preparing to break with Soviet Russia.

According to Grey, the Chinese first became seriously worried about Holt in 1964, when a series of political and personal setbacks seemed to have shaken him as deeply as had the loss of his ministerial post in 1940. Not for the first time, the Chinese prepared a contingency plan to "evacuate" Holt by submarine. But the situation stabilized, and an evacuation proved to be unnecessary.

Then, in 1966, Sir Robert Menzies unexpectedly announced his resignation, after seventeen years; Holt was appointed Prime Minister. For the first month or so he was immensely popular. Menzies had been a remote, rather aristocratic figure; Holt was a populist who could set the crowds cheering. He had taken up scuba diving, and when he was photographed on a beach with his three beautiful daughters-in-law, the press made remarks about James Bond and showed a disposition to treat him like a film star.

The honeymoon period was soon over, however, and things began to turn against him. He was accused of lying to Parliament about the use of air force planes as "taxis"; he interrupted the maiden speech of a new MP and was booed and jeered by the whole house. When he rose to his feet and stalked out, his Labour opponent, Gough Whitlam, felt that he had begun to "dig his own grave." In May 1967 he was shown a secret file on various Soviet spies in Australia and was shocked to discover his own code name, "H. K. Bors," among them. For a while he was terrified that the intelligence services knew all about him. It was then, says Anthony Grey, that he decided the time had come to make a getaway to China. The Chinese, observing the signs of nervous tension and exhaustion, were glad he had made the suggestion before it became necessary for them to step in. So, on that December day in 1967, Holt swam out to a prearranged point off Cheviot Beach, where two Chinese scuba divers were waiting. Their inverted "air bubble" almost escaped them, causing the water to boil and bubble (as Alan Stewart and Mrs. Gillespie had observed), but Holt was successfully steered into the air pocket and propelled by a small undersea vehicle to the escape hatch of the waiting submarine.

Anthony Grey believes this is the incredible story of the escape of Harold Holt. It raises the obvious question: Where did he get his information and how much of it can be cross-checked? Grey claims that in May 1983 he was approached by an Australian businessman who wanted his help to publish a book on the true story of Harold Holt. The man had been in the navy when Holt disappeared and had noted inconsistencies in confidential reports that had crossed his desk. In Baghdad in 1973 a comment by an aide to the Iraqi oil minister about a "high Australian government official" who had sought asylum abroad led him to institute inquiries among business associates in Peking.

The most baffling and unbelievable part of the story is that Peking was apparently willing to tell him the story, albeit in fragments and tantalizing hints. What is more, his own research seemed to vouch for its truth. In the archives of Melbourne University he found that original debating paper urging closer friendship between Australia and China. He saw the secret file that terrified Holt so much when he found his own code name in it—and was able to check that Holt had initiated an inquiry about the real name of Mr. Wong. The businessman also claimed that the Chinese had shown him photostats of the receipts Holt signed for various sums of money in those early days.

Altogether, it must be admitted that it all sounds very convincing. So many parts of the story can be easily checked that it is hard to see why either the businessman or Mr. Grey should lie about them. So it seems that the story of how Harold Holt slipped gradually into the role of a Chinese "spy" (or information gatherer) is highly plausible.

The question remains, however, of why the Chinese should want to tell the story. Grey suggests that it may be out of a desire to emphasize that, unlike the Soviets, they are not given to "dirty tricks" and underhanded activities. That is, indeed, in keeping with the Chinese character and could well be a part of the answer.

Grey's book itself suggests a rather more likely explanation. According to Grey, some of Holt's government colleagues had their doubts about him. Sooner or later, the story of Holt's spying activities was bound to leak out in Australia. If the Chinese themselves leaked the information and declined to supply the precise corroborative details, their story would be only half believed. In fact, the reception of Grey's book proved the point: very few reviewers took it seriously. If this was, indeed, the Chinese motive, then they have showed a psychological subtlety worthy of Machiavelli. They have allowed the truth to be told, in the certainty that no one will believe it. If Harold Holt was alive to read the book—a point on which the Chinese informant declined to comment—he must have felt totally justified in placing implicit reliance in his old allies and co-conspirators.

15

Homer and the Fall of Troy:
Are They Both a Myth?

Although Shakespeare is acknowledged to be England's great-est poet, serious doubts have been expressed about whether he wrote any of the works attributed to him. In the case of Homer—the first great poet of Western civilization—many scholars have gone even further and raised doubts as to whether he actually existed. A children's book entitled *How Much Do You Know?* carries the following entry under the question: "Who Was Homer?":

> The traditional author of the *Iliad* and the *Odyssey*. No evidence exists that such a person ever lived, though every known test has been applied to the poems, and every possible source of information scrutinized. All the *Lives* of Homer are apocryphal. The best one can say is that an authoritative text of the two poems existed at Athens between 550 and 500 B.C. According to tradition, Homer was blind, and conventional busts and pictures show him as sightless.

How could a famous poet be nonexistent? One widely held opinion is that various Greek bards (or *rhapsodes*) invented poems about the Trojan War and its aftermath and that these

145

various accounts were later stitched together into the poems we know as the *Iliad* and the *Odyssey*. We can add to this question about the existence of Homer the question of whether the Trojan War really took place or whether—as many scholars have suggested—it was a purely mythical event, like the wars of the gods. However, no one who has actually read straight through these two poems can believe that they were written by a committee.

There is one very sound reason for believing that Homer really existed. By studying the language of the *Iliad* and the *Odyssey*, scholars have dated the poems to some time between 750 and 650 B.C. Now this is a mere two or three centuries before the Golden Age of Athens, the age of Plato and Aristotle and Euripides. In other words, it was closer to the age of Plato than Shakespeare is to our own period at the time of this writing. Moreover, the Greek bards learned their poetry by heart and could recite many thousands of lines from memory—as their modern descendants still can today. So there was no question of Homer being lost in the dim mists of antiquity, in the days before there were any historical records. The memories of the bards themselves were the historical records. And it is impossible to believe that they simply invented a poet named Homer and attributed various poems to him—as unlikely as believing that Sir Isaac Newton was the invention of a group of seventeenth-century scientists, who also wrote his *Principia*.

What seems to emerge from the available evidence is that Homer was a blind poet who was born some time around 750 B.C. in Asia Minor (now Turkey) and who spent much of his life in poverty, wandering from place to place, until he found a measure of fame on the island of Chios. Many fragmentary biographies of him exist among the works of the classical writers, the longest and best of which is attributed to the historian Herodotus (known as the Father of History), who was also born in Asia Minor about two and a half centuries later.

Herodotus's story is as follows. Homer's mother was a poor orphan girl named Critheis who became pregnant out of wedlock, as a result of which she moved from Asia Minor to a place near the river Meles in Greece (Boeotia) and gave birth to a son, whom she named Melesigenes (pronounced Mellis-igenees), after the river.

He was to acquire the nickname Homer (which means "blind man"*) many years later. She then returned to Smyrna (now called Izmir) and became housekeeper to a teacher of literature and music named Phemius, who fell in love with her and married her. So Homer acquired a stepfather who knew all about poetry and music.

The young Homer distinguished himself at school. When his stepfather died—followed shortly by his mother—he took over the school with brilliant success and became something of a celebrity among his fellow citizens. He became friendly with a traveler named Mentes, from the island of Leucadia (now called Leukas) in western Greece, who persuaded Homer to accompany him on his travels and offered to pay all Homer's expenses. Unable to resist this offer to see the world, Homer set off with Mentes and traveled by land to what is now called Italy. Full of curiosity, he asked questions everywhere he went. But in the course of his travels, he picked up an eye infection, and by the time he reached Ithaca—just south of Leucadia—it had become so serious that Mentes left him behind with a doctor named Mentor. It was Mentor who taught Homer about the legends of Odysseus (whom the Romans would call Ulysses**) and the story of his epic voyage home from the Trojan War. When he came to compose the *Odyssey*, Homer gave the name Mentor to the teacher of Ulysses's son Telemachus, and the name has become synonymous with "teacher." But Mentor was unable to cure Homer's eye problems. Homer decided to try to get back home, but in Colophon, in Asia Minor, he finally became blind.

Back in Smyrna, he continued to devote himself to poetry. But now he had no school to support him, and he set out on the wanderings that would last the rest of his life. In a place called Neon Teichos (New Wall) he was befriended by an armorer named Tychias and earned his bread by reciting verse. And although

---

*Other meanings suggested by scholars are "hostage," "comrade," and "orderer," in the sense of one who gives order to thoughts.

**And I shall follow their example, as well as changing the names of other Greek gods to their more familiar Latin equivalents.

poverty drove the blind poet to move on, the inhabitants of Neon Teichos remembered him with affection and would point out the spot where he used to recite. In Cumae, his mother's birthplace (from which she had fled to conceal her pregnancy), he once again found such a sympathetic audience for his verses that he decided he would like to settle there and asked the town council if they would support him with public funds in exchange for entertainment—promising them that he would make their city famous. But one grumpy councillor declared that if they fed every Homer ("blind man") who came to Cumae, they would soon be overrun with vagabonds. Thereupon the council decided not to grant the poet's request. The name "Homer" stuck, however.

Homer moved to nearby Phocoae, on the island of Chios, where a would-be poet named Thestorides persuaded him to enter into an odd bargain. Homer would write poetry for Thestorides, in exchange for food and lodging. But his host finally broke his bargain and threw the blind man out. Homer continued as a homeless wanderer, singing for his supper. Sometime later, back on the mainland, he met some merchants from Chios who told him that their local poet, Thestorides, was singing verses that were virtually identical with Homer's. Enraged that Thestorides was passing off his (Homer's) verses as his own, Homer hastened back to Chios, where he met a kindly goatherd named Glaucus who put him up for the night in his hut. Homer's story of his travels so moved Glaucus that he went to his master and asked him to help the poet. The master was scornful, feeling that Glaucus had been taken in by a vagabond. But when he actually met Homer, he was so impressed by his learning and by his poetry that he engaged him as a tutor for his children.

Now, at last, Homer's misfortunes were over. In the town of Chios he became a celebrity, and when the truth became known about Thestorides, the imposter was driven from the island. Homer became highly successful, both as a poet and a teacher of youth, and he married and had two daughters. Chios became so proud of Homer that it claimed to be his birthplace. As his reputation spread to Greece, he decided to travel there again. On the island of Samos he was recognized and played a part in a religious festival, then was a guest in many rich houses. After this he set sail for Athens but had only reached the island of Ios when he fell ill and died, probably of a stroke. (The legend claims that his death was brought on by frustration at being unable to answer a riddle propounded by the children of fishermen.) But as his fame spread throughout Greece, and bards recited his poems, Chian bards formed a school known as the children of Homer—or Homeridae—which was still flourishing when Herodotus wrote his life of Homer.

So while scholars insist on preserving caution, it seems a commonsense assumption that a blind poet named Homer was born in Asia Minor, traveled in Greece and Italy—perhaps even as far as Spain—settled in Chios, and died on his way to Athens. The school he founded learned his words by heart; why not the events of his life? The dates of these events are altogether more doubtful. Herodotus thinks Homer lived some four hundred years before himself—around 900 B.C. A later scholar, Crates, placed him around eighty years after the Trojan War (which has generally been dated about 1180 B.C. but which modern scholars place as early as 1250—a question to which we shall return in a moment). We now know that to be virtually impossible; for example, a reference in the *Odyssey* to the Phoenicians as traders dates it later than 900 B.C.

But anyone who has read the two epics will have noticed basic differences between them. Although a great deal longer than the *Odyssey*, the *Iliad* covers only a small part of the Trojan War—a few weeks in its tenth year—and is full of slaughter and violence. (The story is a simple one: The Greek hero, Achilles, quarrels with King Agamemnon about a pretty slave girl and refuses to take any part in the battle—until his closest friend, Patroclus, is killed by the Trojan Hector; then Achilles goes out to meet Hector, chases him three times around the walls of Troy, and kills him.) The *Odyssey* is altogether softer and more lyrical in tone, describing the adventures of Ulysses as he tries to make his way back home from Troy to Ithaca. The Greek scholar Longinus, author of *On the Sublime*, takes the view that this difference is attributable to the fact that Homer wrote the *Iliad* when he was young and at the height of his powers, and the *Odyssey* in old age. But most modern scholars explain the difference by suggesting that two different poets wrote the two works. The author of the *Iliad*, they claim, was the blind poet described by Herodotus. The *Odyssey* was written by a later poet, whose identity is unknown. A widely held view is that the *Iliad* was composed about 750 B.C. and the *Odyssey* about 700.

There is one very obvious difference between the two poems. In the *Iliad*, the gods play as prominent a part as the men; they are always interfering in the battle, and the goddess of love, Aphrodite, even swoops down and carries off Paris when he is about to be defeated by Menelaus. In the *Odyssey*, the gods still interfere in the narrative, but they could be eliminated without making much difference to the story of Ulysses. One example will suffice: When Ulysses is slaying his wife's suitors, the goddess Minerva (Athena) puts in an appearance, disguised as the estate manager; but after the suitors have threatened her with violent reprisals, she turns herself into a swallow and flies up to the rafters. Such an event, one would expect, would clearly convince the suitors that something supernatural was going on and would lower their morale; in fact, they seem not to notice and proceed to attack Ulysses as if nothing had happened. The appearance of the goddess is not only pointless, it makes the scene absurd. It is almost as if the *Iliad* belongs to an earlier period of belief, while the *Odyssey* was written by someone for whom the gods were little more than a convenient plot mechanism.

But if the author of the *Odyssey* was not the blind Homer, then who was he?

The English writer Samuel Butler became aware of the puzzle in 1891. Butler is best known for his amusing satirical novel *Erewhon*, but it would be a mistake to think of him as a satirist. He was a serious thinker who devoted an important part of his life's work to attacking Darwin's theory of evolution. He objected to Darwin's view that mutations cause species to change *at random* and that evolution is due simply to the survival of the fittest. Butler objected that Darwin had "banished God from the universe" and turned the universe into a gigantic machine. He preferred the views of the earlier zoologist Lamarck, who believed that species change because they make determined *efforts* to change. (For a more detailed account of the problem, see chapter 23.)

At the age of fifty-six Butler decided to compose a cantata entitled *Ulysses*. (He was also an amateur composer who wrote in the style of Handel.) His librettist, Henry Festing Jones, was relying on Charles Lamb's *Adventures of Ulysses*, but Butler felt he should reread the *Odyssey*, of which he retained only vague memories from his schooldays. Butler found Homer's Greek simple and straightforward and decided to make his own prose translation. As he worked, he became aware of a feeling of unease, of "a riddle that I could not read." The *Iliad* is full of larger-than-life heroes. The *Odyssey*, by comparison, struck Butler as far more lifelike, in fact, as a kind of novel rather than an epic, full of real people and real observations. The latter begins by telling how Ulysses's son Telemachus, sick of the horde of suitors who surround his mother, Penelope, goes off to see if he can find news of his father; he calls on King Menelaus, who is now living happily with his errant wife, Helen of Troy, and the domestic scene has an almost tongue-in-cheek atmosphere. Here he learns that his father is a prisoner of the nymph Calypso.

The scene shifts to Calypso's island, where Ulysses has been allowed to leave (owing to the intervention of Jupiter). But the god Neptune, who disliked Ulysses, caused a storm, which wrecked the hero on the coast of a country called Scheria. Here he was found lying asleep by Nausicaa, the king's daughter, who took him back to the palace. And here, in due course, Ulysses tells the story of what happened to him after he left Troy (which was captured by means of a wooden horse). At this point, we have a long story-within-a-story, which forms the main part of the *Odyssey*.

Butler was struck by the realism of the Nausicaa episode and its many homely touches. It confirmed his feeling that the *Odyssey* was a kind of novel, based on real people. A few books later, after Ulysses has encountered the Cyclops, the god of wind (Aeolus), and the man-eating Laestrigonians, he lands on the island of the enchantress Circe, who changes his men into swine. And it was as he was reading about Circe that Butler was suddenly struck by a dazzling intuition: that Circe was not created by a man but by a

woman—and, moreover, by a young one. Closer reading convinced him of this. The males of the *Odyssey* are wooden creatures compared to the women, who have that touch of life. Butler
also concluded that while the author of the *Odyssey* shows intimate knowledge of the affairs of women, he is often oddly uncomfortable when describing things that are the province of males,
especially seamen or farmers. What male would place the rudder
in front of the ship? What seaman would believe that seasoned
timber can be cut from a growing tree? Or make the wind "whis-
tle" over the waters? (It whistles on land, because of obstacles, but
there are no obstacles at sea.) What man with any knowledge of
farming would make a herdsman milk the sheep, then give them
their lambs to feed (presumably with empty udders)? What coun-
tryman would make a hawk tear its prey *on the wing*? The author
of the *Odyssey* makes these curious errors, and many more.
Butler goes on to argue with great skill and conviction that the
author of the *Odyssey* had to be a woman, and a young one at
that.

Now if, for the sake of argument, we are willing to admit the
possibility that the *Odyssey* was written by a young woman, a
kind of Greek Jane Austen or Elizabeth Barrett Browning, then
certain things become obvious. The first is that she had a great
deal of leisure. In Jane Austen's day the daughter of a country
vicar would have had sufficient leisure to write novels; but in
ancient Greece, life was far harder. (What moderns find so hard
to grasp is that life in ancient Greece was a poverty-stricken affair,
with most people living on a diet of olive oil and vegetables, with
some boiled mutton every week or so.) For a woman to have had
leisure enough to write, she would have had to have been a
member of the aristocracy, one who had servants to look after
her. (And we note that even Princess Nausicaa goes to the beach
to do her own washing.)

Second, a Greek Jane Austen, like the English one, would have
had a fairly restricted knowledge of life (in those days, girls stayed
at home), and you would expect her to use her own background in
her poem. Butler felt that all the older women in the poem—
Helen, Penelope, Queen Arete (Nausicaa's mother)—are basically
the same person and that the same applies to the younger

women—Nausicaa, Circe, and Calypso—and to the men—
Ulysses, Nestor, Menelaus, and King Alcinous (Nausicaa's father).
And if, like any young lady novelist, the authoress of the *Odyssey*
put a portrait of herself into her book, then we have to choose
between Nausicaa, Circe, and Calypso. Nausicaa is the obvious
choice. And presumably, Queen Arete and King Alcinous are
portraits of the authoress's parents.

But if the young authoress knew only her own home, then how
did she manage to describe the travels of Ulysses so convincingly?
Presumably, by using places she actually knew and transforming
them into the lands of Polyphemus, Circe, the Laestrigonians,
and so on. In other words, if one could find out where "Nausicaa"
lived, one might recognize various features of the poem in its
geography.

Now Nausicaa, as we have said, lived in a land called Scheria—
which means "jut-land"—a peninsula jutting into the sea, which,
according to Homer, was the land of a people called the Phaecians. When the naked Ulysses approaches her on the beach—
covering himself with a bough for decency—she gives him food
and clothing and instructs him precisely how to get back to her
father's house: "You will find the town lying between two harbors,
approached by a narrow neck of land." Later in the *Odyssey*, after
the Phaecians have taken Ulysses back to his own land of Ithaca,
the angry sea-god, Neptune, turns their ship into a rock in the
mouth of the harbor. So Butler felt he had a number of clues
about Scheria: it had to have a neck of land jutting into the sea
between two harbors and a large rock that resembled a ship in the
mouth of one of the harbors. It also seems clear from the *Odyssey*
that Ulysses approaches Scheria from the east, so that the harbor
must be on the western coast. Butler went to the British Museum
and studied a map of Greece and Italy, looking for any west coast
that had two harbors on either side of a promontory. He could
find only one—the site of the town of Trapani, on the west coast
of Sicily. Butler looked at Trapani more closely and became
convinced that this had to be the home of Nausicaa. It was the
only western coast in the whole area—including Italy and
Greece—that fit the description. There was also a mountain—
Mount Eryx—above Trapani, and Neptune is also reported in the

Odyssey as threatening to bury the city of the Phaecians under a high mountain.

Two earlier Greek history scholars, Stolberg and Mure, had also been convinced that Mount Eryx fit the geography of the Cyclops episode. And the Greek historian Thucydides, writing around 403 B.C., had mentioned that Sicily was probably the home of the Cyclops and the Laestrigonians. In the *Odyssey*, of course, these episodes take place far from the home of Nausicaa. But what would be more natural than for a young authoress writing a kind of novel about Ulysses to use local scenery as its background?

The next step was to visit Trapani; this Butler did in 1892. Now he had the satisfaction of finding that everything confirmed his views. Admittedly, one of the two harbors was now silted up and contained a saltworks; but it was obvious that it had once been just such a harbor as "Homer" had described. A few miles away, on the lower slopes of Mount Eryx, was a cave that the locals still called the "grotto of Polyphemus." Near the entrance to the northern harbor was a rock that looked not unlike a ship. Local legend said it was a Turkish pirate ship turned to stone by the Blessed Virgin—obviously a Christianized form of the ancient legend.

Now Butler no longer had any doubt that he was on the right track. He noted that the description of Ithaca in the *Odyssey* is quite unlike the real Ithaca: It is described as "highest up in the sea" with a clear view to the west, whereas the real Ithaca is completely masked by the much bigger island of Samos (now Cephalonia) to the west. But if the authoress of the *Odyssey* modeled her Ithaca on the little island of Marettimo, facing the harbors of Trapani, it would correspond to the description in the *Odyssey*.

A voyage around Sicily convinced Butler that his authoress had simply taken the island she knew and used its scenery as the geographical background for the voyage of Ulysses. Ulysses himself describes how he sailed down to the island of Cythera, just south of Greece, and then was prevented from turning northward (for Ithaca) by strong winds that drove him west to the land of the lotus-eaters, which must have been on the coast of north Africa. But after this, according to Butler, he made for Sicily, to the north, hunted goats on the island of Favagnana (known to the ancients as Goat Island—Aegusa), then landed on Sicily and had his adventure with the one-eyed giant, Polyphemus, whose eye he burned out with a stake. Then he sailed north to the island of Aeolus, the god of winds, which Butler identifies as the little island of Ustica. The town of Cefalù, on the north coast, he thinks is the site of the adventure of the man-eating Laestrigonians. The site of Scylla and Charybdis is off the east coast, near present-day Messina. Finally, on his way back, he encountered Calypso's island, which Butler identifies as the island of Pantelleria. And so back to Trapani—or rather, to Marettimo, which is Homer's Ithaca.

If Butler had lived a century later, he would have taken a good photographer with him to Sicily and published a series of color photographs of the various sites of the adventures of Ulysses in a coffee-table book, together with Homer's descriptions. In fact, in his book *The Authoress of the Odyssey* (finally published in 1897), Butler includes half a dozen or so photographs, but none are as convincing as they might be. Probably the best way for a modern reader to make up his own mind would be to go to Sicily with a copy of Butler's book. It has to be admitted that Butler's own sheer excitement and enthusiasm convey a great deal of conviction. But the section of the book that describes the various places is less thorough than it could be. My own suspicion is that Butler was disheartened by the general skepticism he encountered and by the total lack of response from the various scholars to whom he sent pamphlets about his theory. The famous Professor Jowett, an Oxford scholar and translator of Plato, admitted frankly that he had not even glanced at the two pamphlets Butler sent him. A dozen publishers turned down Butler's excellent prose translation of the *Odyssey*. So on the whole, it is not surprising that he failed to summon the necessary energy to argue the topographical part of the book as thoroughly as the rest.

The achievement is nevertheless considerable. At the time Butler was writing his book, most scholars took it for granted that Homer was the author of both the *Iliad* and the *Odyssey*. Nowadays, very few take that position. Butler was admittedly wrong about the dates—he thought that at least a hundred years separated the two epics and that the *Odyssey* was composed around

1050 B.C. But then, Butler lacked the tools—and the archaeological information—that have enabled later scholars to be far more precise. As to his essential thesis—that the *Odyssey* was written by a woman—few people who follow his arguments with the *Odyssey* in the other hand will fail to admit that he could be right. George Bernard Shaw attended a Fabian Society meeting at which Butler lectured on the female authorship of the *Odyssey* and admitted that, while initially skeptical about the idea, he took up the *Odyssey* and soon found himself saying, "Of course it was written by a woman."

Robert Graves was another classical scholar who allowed himself to be convinced, and whose novel *Homer's Daughter* is inspired by the theory. The story is told by Princess Nausicaa, who describes how her brother disappeared after a quarrel with his wife and was assumed to have gone off to foreign parts. In fact, he has been murdered by a treacherous friend. Her father, King Alpheides, sails off to look for him, leaving Uncle Mentor in charge. Nausicaa's suitors then behave exactly like Penelope's suitors in the *Odyssey* and move into the palace. But when Nausicaa and her attendants are doing the laundry near the sea, they are approached by a naked man who has been shipwrecked; he is a Cretan nobleman named Aethon, and it is he who eventually slays the suitors and marries Nausicaa. Nausicaa then goes on to write the *Odyssey*, in which biography and legend freely intermingle. The merit of the book is that it enables us to grasp the sheer plausibility of Butler's theory. *Homer's Daughter* is one of Graves's most underrated books—a careful re-creation of Sicily around 800 B.C. that deserves to be as widely read as *I, Claudius*.

Another interesting footnote to the Butler theory is that James Joyce used his prose translation of the *Odyssey* as the basis of *Ulysses*.

To summarize this part of the argument: it is probably fair to say that *if* the *Odyssey* was indeed the work of one single person—and was not the collective work of many bards—then the contention that it was written by a woman is highly plausible.

But what of our second question: did the siege of Troy really take place, or was it simply a myth? After all, it is obvious that the

Odyssey, with its one-eyed giants, wandering rocks, and enchant-resses who turn men into pigs, is basically a fairy tale. And the action of the *Iliad* is even more mythical, with the gods playing as important a part in the action as the heroes.

Let us review the story again. According to Greek legend, mostly based on the works of Homer, a prince named Paris (or Alexandros), son of King Priam of Troy, was a guest of King Menelaus of Sparta when he fell in love with Menelaus's wife, Helen, who was a famous beauty. She was the daughter of the god Jove (or Zeus) and a princess named Leda, whom Jove seduced by turning himself into a swan. Many princes had sought her hand before she accepted Menelaus. So when Paris carried her off—with or without her consent—the indignant Menelaus went to ask for help from his brother, King Agamemnon, in Mycenae (he would have had to travel by sea, for roads were almost nonexis-tent), and an armada of ninety ships sailed for Troy. These included contingents led by many of Helen's rejected suitors.

Troy—or Ilion—was a town whose wealth was founded on trade (like Mycenae, which was so rich that it was known as "golden Mycenae"). Its main industry seems to have been horse breeding. It is important for us to realize that in those days, the Mediterra-nean was swarming with pirates, so that no town could afford to be on the sea unless it had mighty defenses. Troy was a mile inland, but it had mighty defenses anyway, including immense walls with defensive towers. It is also important to realize that in the ancient world, peace was a rare commodity. The first thing man seems to have done when he began to live in settlements was to wage war on his neighbors, so that in the ancient world, the words "peaceable nation" were virtually a contradiction in terms. It was not until relatively modern times—about 1700 or so—that the rules of history changed and it became such a costly and highly destructive business to go to war that long periods of peace became the norm.*

So the Greeks attacking Troy found themselves in the position of a hawk trying to attack a tortoise. This was no ordinary siege—

---

*For a longer account of all this, see my *Criminal History of Mankind* (1984).

no town could hold out for ten years, as Troy did, if it was surrounded. The plain of Troy was notoriously windy—it still is— so the Greeks camped in a sheltered spot between two headlands and built a rampart to protect themselves. The Trojans had allies in other parts of Asia Minor, who sallied out to help them periodically. So it was less a siege than a spasmodic series of engagements.

But in the tenth year of the war something happened, and Troy fell and was destroyed; all its men were massacred, and its women and children were carried off into slavery. According to Ulysses in the *Odyssey*, it was he who suggested the strategem of building a wooden horse and filling it with armed men, then pretending to sail away. But of course, this could well have been an invention of the author (or authoress) of the *Odyssey*.

The story of the search for Troy is one of the most fascinating in the history of archaeology, and its conclusions are more satisfyingly positive than those in the case of the search for Homer's identity.

One story concerning the search for Troy begins in 1829, when a seven-year-old boy named Heinrich Schliemann received a copy of Jerrer's *Universal History* for Christmas. When he saw the picture of Troy in flames, he was struck by the thought that nothing could possibly destroy such mighty walls. The young Schliemann resolved that he would one day go and investigate the matter for himself. His father was a country parson in Neu-Buckow, Germany, who was dismissed after being falsely accused of misappropriating church funds. Heinrich had to become a grocer's assistant at the age of fourteen. Tuberculosis led him to give up his job and embark for South America as a cabin boy. After a shipwreck he drifted to Amsterdam, where he became a clerk and learned English. At the age of thirty-two he learned that his brother had died in California and sailed for America to claim his estate. It was a good time to go; the gold rush made him rich, and in 1863 he was finally able to realize his ambition to search for Troy. Together with a sixteen-year-old Greek schoolgirl, whom he married, he sailed for the northern coast of Turkey to begin his search.

Most scholars accepted the notion that the remains of Troy

would be found on a mountain near Bunarbashi, about three hours from the sea. Schliemann, using the *Iliad* as a guide, disagreed—Homer's heroes rode between Troy and the coast several times a day. Schliemann concluded that a more likely site was a mound called Hissarlik in present-day Turkey, about an hour from the sea. (And in ancient times, the sea came much farther inland.)

It was an inspired guess, typical of Schliemann's incredible luck. When he had obtained permission to dig there, Schliemann began excavations—in 1871—with a large gang of workmen. They soon encountered the remains of a town, but it dated from the Roman period, and it was a mere hundred yards in diameter. Below this was another ruined town. And then another. And then another. Eager to find Homer's Troy, Schliemann ordered his men to slice a great trench through the middle of the mound and keep going until they reached bedrock. All told, there proved to be the ruins of nine cities, one on top of the other.

Twelve years later, Schliemann announced that he had found the treasures of King Priam—treasures that, for some odd reason, he had always been convinced would still be there. (He never explained why the conquerors had not simply stolen them when they destroyed Troy and massacred its inhabitants.) In his autobiography he tells a remarkable story of how he had glimpsed a copper vessel through a hole in the wall and waited until his workmen had gone to lunch—he was afraid they might be tempted to steal—before he and his wife removed a treasure of drinking vessels and jewelry. The finds were to make him world famous.

There is, in fact, a disappointing postscript to this story. When, in 1972, Professor William Calder, of the University of Colorado, decided to start checking on Schliemann's biographical information, he soon discovered that the great archaeologist was a mythomaniac of the first order. His story about being received by the president of the United States on his first visit to America was pure invention; so was his tale of being present in San Francisco on the night of the great fire in May 1851. It became clear that his fortune was founded on cheating the bankers to whom he sold gold dust and that the story of the finding of the Trojan treasure was also an invention—it had actually been found over a considerable period and concealed from the eyes of his partners in the enterprise, a Turkish pasha and an American named Frank Calvert. Calder's research proved that Schliemann was a crook. Yet there can be no doubt that, in spite of this, he was an inspired archaeologist.

In fact, Schliemann's next major venture was to excavate Mycenae, in southern Greece, the home of Agamemnon, the Bronze Age king who led the expedition to Troy; here he uncovered still more treasure and revealed again that, where archaeology was concerned, his intuition was awesome. A dig at Tiryns, the home of King Diomedes (another Homeric hero), in 1884 uncovered some of the finest remains of Bronze Age civilization to date.

In 1889 Schliemann returned to Hissarlik and renewed his search for evidence of Homer's Troy. What he found, in 1890, was at once exciting and depressing. Outside the mound, and well beyond the limits of what he had believed to be Homer's Troy, he came upon the remains of a large building that in turn contained the remains of pottery that was unmistakably Mycenaean. The conclusion was obvious: he had sliced straight through the Troy he was looking for. In the following year, Schliemann died of a stroke, collapsing in the street; his death frustrated his plans for still more ambitious excavations.

Schliemann had indeed proved that Troy existed—ancient records make it clear that there was simply no other great city in the area. But of the nine cities that had been uncovered, which one was it? Schliemann had been convinced that it was the second from the bottom—because it showed signs of having been destroyed by fire—and in order to reach it, he had ordered his workmen to slice a huge trench through the seven layers of ruins that lay above. He was to learn too late that *his* Troy was a thousand years too old and that his brutal methods had destroyed a large part of the city he was looking for. But again, which of the other eight *was* Homer's Troy?

Schliemann's collaborator, Wilhelm Dörpfeld, continued and completed Schliemann's work. The discovery of the large building containing Mycenaean pottery—probably a royal hall—had furnished him with the clue he needed. It indicated that the walls of

Homer's Troy extended well beyond the boundaries of the mound of Hissarlik. And when Dörpfeld excavated at the southern edge of the mound, he soon uncovered walls greater than any Schliemann had found. This—the sixth city from the bottom—was the city they had all been looking for. These walls had a slight inward slope, just as Homer had indicated in the *Iliad* (Patroclus had made a determined attempt to scale them), and there was a mighty tower that must have been about sixty feet high before it had been reduced by more than half. There was a gate in the east wall and the remains of another tower, built of limestone blocks. Inside the walls he uncovered the ruins of five large houses and deduced that the citadel had risen in concentric circles. And although "Troy 6" measured only two hundred yards by a hundred and fifty yards, it must have been as impressive as a medieval castle. It was obvious now why the Greeks had failed to take it by storm. It must have towered over the plain of Scamander as Mont Saint Michel still towers over the flat Britanny marshes.

The next great step forward in Mediterranean archaeology was taken by the Englishman Arthur Evans, who began to excavate near the city of Heraklion, on the island of Crete, in 1900 and uncovered the remarkable royal palace at Knossos. He announced this as the palace of the legendary King Minos. According to Greek legend, the king's wife, Pasiphae, had a taste for bestiality and became pregnant by a bull, giving birth to a monster called the Minotaur, which was half man and half bull. The legend also tells how Minos demanded a yearly tribute of seven youths and seven maidens from Athens and how these were thrown to the Minotaur, which was kept in a specially built labyrinth. The Greek hero Theseus went to Crete as part of the yearly tribute, killed the Minotaur, and escaped from the labyrinth with the help of a thread, given to him by Minos's daughter Ariadne. Evans's excavations revealed pictures of youths and maidens turning somersaults over the back of a bull, suggesting that there had been a bull cult at Knossos. And the mazelike palace was full of symbols of a double-headed axe, known as *labrys*. It began to look as if the legend of Theseus and the Minotaur was based on fact after all. If so, the same could apply to the story of the Trojan War.

One of Evans's most important discoveries at Knossos was a

quantity of clay tablets written in a form of hieroglyphics—
actually, two forms, which became known as Linear A and Linear
B. Evans was convinced that they were written in the unknown
language of the ancient Cretans, which would mean that the
Minoan civilization of Crete was not Greek. However, Linear B
was deciphered by the scholar Michael Ventris in 1952, eleven
years after Evans's death, and proved to be an early form of
Greek. (Linear A remains undeciphered.) And names found in
the Linear B tablets included many place-names that had been
mentioned in Homer.

Evans's view dominated British archaeology for many years. An
American named Carl Blegen disagreed. His excavations on mainland Greece in the 1920s convinced him that the Greeks had
dominated Mediterranean civilization for a very long time indeed—as far back as 1900 B.C. In 1932 he began a new series of
excavations at Hissarlik, whose aim was to use the latest dating
techniques (which relied heavily on pottery) to try to establish
the age of *all* the levels and to learn as much as possible about
each.

Blegen was able to establish that the bottom layer dated back as
far as the fourth millennium B.C. (Modern dating is 3600.) But
when he came to study the sixth Troy, which Dörpfeld had believed to be Homer's, he reached a conclusion that seemed to
contradict Dörpfeld: that it had been destroyed by an earthquake.
The walls had crumbled, and in one place the foundations had
even shifted. That seemed to rule it out as the Troy burned down
by Agamemnon. And Dörpfeld, who visited the site in 1935, had
to agree. Blegen dated Troy 6 about 1260 B.C., possibly ten years
earlier.

But at the next layer, which he called 7a (because he found
many subordinate layers in the course of his digging—a total of
no less than fifty), he found something that looked much more
promising. The streets of 7a were a kind of shantytown, where
there had formerly been houses of the nobility, now there were
cramped "bungalows." It looked as if all the people who normally
lived outside Troy had been crowded into its confines—which is
what you would expect in a siege. Inside the gate was a building
that Blegen called the "snack bar"—a combination of bakery and

wine shop. (Blegen imagined the Homeric heroes rushing in there after battle to refresh themselves.) Moreover, this Troy *had* been burned. He found smashed skulls, charred skeletons, and an arrowhead. It was this that led Blegen to announce triumphantly, "The sack of Troy is a historical fact."

There was one obvious objection to this shantytown being Homer's Troy: if the walls had been badly damaged by earthquake at some earlier stage, then surely the Greeks would have had no trouble in conquering the unprotected citadel? But closer examination disposed of this objection. Although the walls had been damaged, the circuit still remained complete; they would still have been a formidable obstacle. Many scholars were convinced that Blegen had found the Troy of the *Iliad*.

But other objections began to appear. There *was* evidence of burning in Troy 6—Dörpfeld had noted it at the turn of the century. What is more, the "bungalows" and the "snack bar" had been built on the sites of the noble houses. But the *Iliad* is full of noblemen and -women. Surely, the obvious scenario is that Troy 6—"earthquake Troy"—was the Troy besieged by the Greeks, and that when it fell, its noblemen were slaughtered; that is why their houses gave way to lesser structures.

It is possible, however, that an earthquake caused the downfall of Homer's Troy. It has even been suggested that the story of the wooden horse may be a "folk memory" of this event. The sea-god Neptune (Poseidon) was often worshiped in the form of a horse and was supposed to be the master of horses. He was also the god of earthquakes. Suppose a great earthquake occurred in the tenth year of the war, which shook the walls and destroyed some of the noble houses in the citadel. And suppose the Greeks seized this opportunity to scale the walls—perhaps even using a siege engine that looked not unlike a horse?

What we *do* know is that the palaces of these Greek heroes—Agamemnon and Nestor and Diomedes—were themselves destroyed half a century later (about 1200 B.C.), probably by mysterious raiders known as the "sea peoples." So the mighty Achaean civilization was brought to its knees not long after it had destroyed Troy. Writing still did not exist, except on clay tablets (and they were used only for making lists or writing letters, not for preserving poetry); but the stories of Troy and its heroes lived on in the memories of the bards. Centuries passed; the Mediterranean was plunged into a dark age. Finally, writing in its modern form—with paper and ink—was invented and at last the great epics were written down. Apart from the *Iliad* and the *Odyssey*, there were other epic poems—the *Thebais*, about the siege of Thebes and the *Cypria*, about how Paris stole Helen—and comic epics like the *Margites* (whose hero is a fool) and the unpronounceable *Batrachomyomachia*, or Battle of the Frogs and Mice. All these are attributed to Homer. Yet since scholars are inclined to date writing in Greece as late as 650 B.C., this means that Homer may have been alive six centuries after the fall of Troy.

So far, we have been obliged to admit that there is not the slightest scrap of real evidence for the siege of Troy, as described by Homer. Schliemann claimed to have found the jewels of Helen and the mask of Agamemnon, and Blegen claimed to have found the palace of King Nestor at Pylos. This may all have been wishful thinking—in fact, it undoubtedly *was* in the case of Schliemann. But confirmation of the Trojan War and its heroes was to come from a completely unexpected source.

In 1834 a young Frenchman named Charles Texier was riding through central Turkey when he heard of some ruins near the village of Boğazköy. They proved to be the gigantic remains of an earlier civilization, with tremendous walls and magnificent ruined buildings ornamented with winged demons and unknown hieroglyphs. It took half a century before it was recognized that these were the remains of a mighty empire that had once extended from Asia Minor down to Syria—the empire of the people known as the Hittites, who had once attacked Babylon. Their empire, like that of the Greeks, collapsed about 1200 B.C.; but two centuries earlier it had been one of the greatest nations of the Middle East. The period of the fall of Troy had been the period of the slow disintegration of the Hittite empire. Moreover, most of Asia Minor had been a part of that empire. So Troy was, in a sense, a Hittite town.

The ruins discovered by Texier were those of the Hittite capital, Hattusas, and in excavations undertaken between 1906 and 1908, the archaeologist Hugo Winkler found a mighty library of clay tablets, some in Hittite and some in Akkadian, the language in which diplomacy was conducted. Deciphered during the First World War, the tablets, from the Hittite equivalent of the foreign office, gave a detailed impression of the working of Hittite foreign policy.

These documents provided some fascinating glimpses into Near Eastern history. They revealed, for example, that after the death (around 1360 B.C.) of the Egyptian pharaoh Tutankhamen (he died of a blow to the head at the age of eighteen), his widow, Enhosnamon, wrote to the emperor of the Hittites, Suppiluliumas, requesting a husband. An ambassador was sent to Egypt and was there shown tablets containing details of an old treaty between Egypt and the kingdom of Hatti (the land of the Hittites); this convinced him of their good faith, and a prince named Zannanza was sent to Egypt. However, the high priest Ay wanted to marry the widow, and Zannanza was murdered—which caused a diplomatic crisis. All this was told in a document by the son of Suppiluliumas, King Mursilis II.

Was there anything about Troy or the Mycenaean civilization in these amazing records? In 1924 the Swiss historian Emile Forrer announced that he had found references to a country named *Ahhiyawa*, somewhere to the west, and he identified this as meaning "Achaia-land"—Homer always referred to the Greeks as Achaeans, or Achaiwoi. And although a philologist named Ferdinand Sommer criticized Forrer's findings in a 1932 book entitled *The Ahhiyawa Documents*, Forrer's case remains remarkably convincing.

Moreover, in 1963 an archaeological dig at Thebes (northwest of Athens) revealed more Hittite documents dating from the right period. Oddly enough, some of these were from the Hittite "foreign office" to the king of Ugarit, the great trading center in northern Syria. There were also seals from Babylon, which research has shown to have been plundered from the temple of Marduk, sacked by the Assyrians around 1225 B.C. It seems that the Assyrians, who were gaining power in the area and were therefore enemies of the Hittites, regarded the Greeks as allies. So it appears certain that the Hittites were aware of the Greeks (a fact that has been denied by some of Forrer's critics). In some Linear B tablets, Greece is called Achaiwia, which sounds very like the Hittite Ahhiyawa.

What also emerges from the Hittite records is that the Ahhiyawans controlled some territory of the coast of Asia Minor, including a city called Millawanda or Milawata. Now on the coast of Asia Minor, some two hundred miles south of Troy, there was a Greek-controlled city called Miletus, earlier known as Milatos. Geographical accounts make it clear that Miletus is Milawata. And since the Hittite records refer to the land of the Ahhiyawa as "overseas" from Miletus, this seems to suggest that it *is* "Achaiwia" or Achaea—that is, mainland Greece. Relations between the Miletan Greeks and the Hittites were basically friendly, although Miletus was sacked by the Hittites in 1315 B.C. in the course of a quarrel.

The records also show that a Greek king was in dispute with the Hittites around 1260 B.C. over a northern city called Wilusa. We know that the early Greeks called Ilios (Troy) "Wilios." And 1260 was, of course, the approximate date of the Greek expedition against the Trojans. At about this date the Hittite king Hattusilis mentions in a letter his troubles with the Greeks as well as the sack of the city of Carchemish—far to the east—by his new enemy, the Assyrians.

Some ten years later the Hittite emperor wrote to the king of the Greeks, whom he addressed as *brother*. It seems that this king's brother had been causing trouble for the Hittites. What seems to have been happening was this: the brother of the Greek king, a man named Tawagala, had joined with a rebel from Arzawa—a region northeast of Miletus—in harassing the Hittite garrison. The emperor of the Hittites marched with an army to Miletus, found that his enemies had fled, and wrote an aggrieved letter to the Greek "king" that made it clear that the Greeks were then a major power in the Mediterranean. The king to whom the Hittite emperor was writing could well have been Agamemnon. His rebellious brother Tawagala has been identified as a Greek named Eteocles, and if we knew that Agamemnon had a brother of that name, it would clinch the argument. Unfortunately, we only know of his other brother, Menelaus.

In the television series, "In Search of the Trojan War," the historian Michael Wood argues strongly that Wilusa was Troy (not just the city, but the whole area around it), using a great deal of geographical evidence from the Hittite records. Moreover, the king of Wilusa is called Alaxandus. Homer often refers to Paris—who abducted Helen—as Alexandros of Troia. Wood cites other Hittite records that show the king of the Greeks was in Asia Minor in the reign of Hattusilis III (1265–35 B.C.—which would include the date of the Trojan War). If that king was Agamemnon—as seems likely from the dates—then we have powerful evidence for Homer's story.

There is another piece of evidence for the existence of the Trojan War, unearthed by Blegen in his excavations at Pylos, the home of Homer's King Nestor. Among the Linear B tablets found at Pylos were many referring to a large number of "Asian" women who were apparently slaves, and whose main tasks were grinding corn and preparing flax. Asia is short for Asia Minor and actually refers to the kingdom of Lydia, south of Troy. But references to the places from which these captives were taken make it clear that they came from many places on the coast of Asia Minor, including Chios and Miletus. We know, of course, that the Greeks were pirates, so these women may have been captured on raids. But the sheer number—seven hundred women, four hundred girls, and three hundred boys—suggests that they were captives of war. Some of these women are referred to as *To-ro-ja*, which sounds like "people from Troy." Again, the date is right—the period of the Trojan War. No men are mentioned—and Homer tells us that the men of Troy were killed, and their women and children enslaved and taken back to Greece.

So what seems to emerge from the historical record is this: The period of the Trojan War was, in fact, a period of many wars in Asia Minor. The empire of the Hittites was weakening, and the Greeks took advantage of this to raid "Asian" settlements and to encourage rebellion. Troy (or Wilios) had always been a faithful ally of the Hittites, and records show that the Trojan prince Alaksandus had fought on the side of the Assyrian king Muwatallis (1296–1272 B.C.), the elder brother of Hattusilis. Another independent tradition from southwest Asia Minor declares that the lover of Helen is an ally of Muwatallis. So *if* this Alaksandus is indeed Prince Alexandros—Homer's Paris—then he was not a young man when he seduced Helen but a grizzled veteran.

Some ten years after fighting on the side of Muwatallis at the battle of Kadesh (in Syria) in 1274 B.C., Alexandros went to call on Menelaus, brother of Agamemnon, in Sparta. We may surmise that Menelaus was not a particularly strong character—legend represents him as unlucky in love and war—and that Helen found the battle-scarred veteran Paris much more attractive, and eloped with him.

When Menelaus went to his brother, the mighty "King of the Achaeans," to complain, Agamemnon may or may not have been indignant at the abduction of his sister-in-law. But he knew perfectly well that the west coast of Anatolia ("Asia") was highly vulnerable since the Hittites had been forced to go to war with various neighbors, including the Assyrians. It was just the kind of opportunity for plunder that the piratical Greeks loved. So off they sailed with a vast fleet. Achilles, we learn from Homer, landed by mistake in Mysia, south of Troy, but was driven back to his ships by Telephus, the king of Mysia—though not before ravaging the country.

The Greeks attacked Troy, and the Hittites were too weak to send aid. But Troy was virtually impregnable, and it was not until the tenth year of the war that an earthquake caused a certain amount of chaos and finally permitted the Greeks to take the city. The men were killed, and the women and children were taken back to Greece as slaves. Troy itself was burned and its noble houses destroyed. In its place there sprang up a city of "bungalows." The Greeks continued to make nuisances of themselves with impunity, aiding rebels against the Hittites—who had to do their best to make peace with them—and carrying off more captives from other cities of "Asia."

What happened during the next half century is still not clear to historians. All we know is that raiders who are known only as the "sea peoples" wreaked havoc throughout the Mediterranean area; some ancient records credit them with causing the downfall of the Hittite empire. They certainly fought against Egypt and caused the downfall of Agamemnon's Mycenae, Nestor's Pylos, and the new "bungalow" Troy. (Agamemnon, of course, had long been dead, murdered by his wife, Clytemnestra, and her lover, Aegisthus, who were in turn killed by Agamemnon's children, Orestes and Electra.)

The identity of the "sea peoples" used to be one of the great mysteries of ancient history: Who were they? Where did they come from? How did they succeed in overthrowing great empires? But the answer that is beginning to emerge shows that the question itself is too simple. The sea peoples were not a single racial group: they came from many countries.

We must remember that Mediterranean civilizations were not as stable as those of, say, northern Europe. To begin with, the Mediterranean is a poor region, where even today, a large proportion of farmers only scratch out a subsistence living. In the midst of this widespread poverty, a few powerful rulers became rich, usually by plundering their neighbors. Piracy was regarded as a respectable way of living. But such a situation was rather like Al Capone's Chicago; you might become very rich, but you were likely to die violently.

In this crime-ridden Mediterranean slum, empires rose and fell fairly quickly. While you were at your peak, you had plenty of allies; but as soon as you were past your peak, or your attention was distracted elsewhere, your former allies lost no time in attacking you. What happened around 1200 B.C. was that the two mighty empires—the Egyptian and the Hittite—were buckling, like the earth's tectonic plates under stress, and around 1190 B.C. there was an earthquake that caused a great collapse and released hordes of "criminal rats" all over the Mediterranean.

The ancient world virtually came to an end. The twelfth century B.C. was a period of collapse, a dark age, in which Greece was full of wandering tribes; the age of great kings and great palaces was over. Recovery came slowly. Around 800 B.C. Greeks began trading again with overseas partners; some may have settled on the west coast of Italy and founded the city of Rome. Meanwhile, the Assyrians became the new empire builders—the most bloodthirsty and cruel so far. But they did not reach Greece, which became a conglomeration of city-states and invented democracy. Out of the chaos came law giving and a sense of order. And one of the major voices of this new order was the poet we call Homer, a traveler with an immense appetite for old tales of gods and heroes. We do not know whether Homer memorized these stories or whether he was the first to write them down, in the days before his blindness. All we know is that he became a legend and that he founded a school of bards who continued his work.

If Samuel Butler is correct, Homer's greatest disciple was a young girl from Sicily, a girl of noble family who shared his passion for ancient tales, and who one day decided that she would write a sequel to the *Iliad*, a sequel that would not be a tale of bloodshed and treachery but a gentler story of the aftermath of the war, and of noble women as well as heroic men. The result was the *Odyssey*, the first novel, whose translation into rough-and-ready prose by Samuel Butler would inspire a twentieth-century novelist, James Joyce, to create his own peculiar version of the Ulysses legend.

Much of this story is speculation. All that we can say for certain is that Homer—whether one person or two—created a concept that is now almost synonymous with the human imagination: the concept of literature.

16

The Hope Diamond:
The Famous Cursed Jewel

Like the "skull of doom" (described in chapter 30), the story of the Hope diamond seems to suggest that crystals have some power to absorb human emotions.

The diamond was purchased by Louis XIV in 1668 from a French trader named Jean-Baptiste Tavernier, who is believed to have stolen it (like Milton Hayes's "Green Eye of the Little Yellow God") from the eye socket of an idol in an Indian temple. (One writer mentions the temple of Rama-sitra, near Mandalay.) Tavernier subsequently went bankrupt, sailed for India to try to recoup his fortune, and died en route.

The King had the diamond cut into the shape of a heart, and it was worn by Mme. de Montespan, the King's mistress, who was also involved in the notorious "affair of the poisons," in which a number of old crones who told fortunes provided poisons for killing off unwanted husbands. Black magic was involved, and an abbé named Guiborg took part in black masses in which babies were sacrificed; the naked body of Mme. de Montespan was used in these ceremonies as an altar. The scandal was suppressed, but Mme. de Montespan fell from favor, and the old crones were secretly tried in the *chambre ardente* ("candlelit chamber") and later burned. So after Tavernier, it would seem that Mme. de

Montespan was the next person on whom the "French blue" (as it was then known) brought misfortune.

A century later the stone was given by Louis XVI to his Queen, Marie Antoinette; her involvement in the scandal of the diamond necklace caused her to lose credit with the populace and was an indirect cause of the French Revolution in which she lost her head. The Princesse de Lamballe, to whom Marie Antoinette lent the diamond, was murdered by a mob.

The diamond reappeared in London, but now greatly reduced from its original 112.5 carats (22.5 grams) to 44.5 carats—less than half its original size. It was purchased in 1830 by the London banker Henry Thomas Hope for £18,000 and from then on was known as the Hope diamond. As far as we know, Hope suffered no ill effects from the diamond. Neither did any other member of his family until the diamond passed into the hands of singer May Yohe, who married Lord Francis Hope; they were plagued by marital problems, and the wife prophesied that the diamond would bring ill luck to all who owned it. She herself died in poverty, blaming the diamond.

Lord Francis, in severe financial trouble, sold it in the early 1900s to a French broker, Jacques Colot, who went insane and committed suicide—but not before he had sold it to a Russian, Prince Kanitovsi, who lent it to a French actress at the Folies Bergère, then shot her from his box the first night she wore it. He was stabbed by revolutionaries.

A Greek jeweler, Simon Mantharides, bought it and later fell over a precipice (or, according to another account, was thrown). The Turkish sultan Abdul Hamid, known as "Abdul the Damned," bought it in 1908 and was deposed in the following year; he went insane. Habib Bey, its next owner, drowned.

The diamond then passed, via the French jeweler Pierre Cartier, to America, to Edward Beale Maclean, proprietor of the *Washington Post*. Soon after he purchased it, his mother died, and so did two servants in the household. His son, ten-year-old Vinson, who was always heavily protected and watched over, evaded his minder one day and ran out of the front of the house, where he was knocked down and killed by a car. Maclean himself parted from his wife, Evalyn, was involved in the famous Teapot Dome scandal, and ended as an insane alcoholic. Evalyn kept the diamond and frequently wore it, dismissing stories about its malign properties. But when her daughter committed suicide in 1946—with an overdose of sleeping pills—it was recalled that she had worn the diamond at her wedding.

After Evalyn Maclean's death in 1947, all her jewels were purchased by the New York jeweler Harry Winston for a sum rumored to be a million dollars. He displayed the diamond in New York but eventually decided to present it to the Smithsonian Institution; the fact that he sent it by ordinary parcel post seems to indicate that he had no misgivings about the "curse." The packet is now exhibited together with the diamond.

When it was tested under ultraviolet light at the De Beers Laboratory in Johannesburg in 1965, it continued to glow like a red-hot coal for several minutes afterwards—a unique phenomenon among diamonds.

Skeptics regard the curse of the Hope diamond, like "the curse of Tutankhamen"* as mythical, pointing out that many of its owners suffered no misfortune. Yet while skepticism may be the correct attitude in this case, it would undoubtedly be premature to dismiss the whole notion of curses as superstition. The late T. C. Lethbridge (see chapter 32) was convinced that tragedies and unpleasant events can leave behind their "imprints" on the places where they occurred—a theory first put forward in the early twentieth century by Sir Oliver Lodge, who felt that certain so-called hauntings could be explained as a kind of "recording." Lethbridge called such recordings "ghouls"—meaning the unpleasant sensations that may be experienced in certain places. When he was eighteen he and his mother had been on a walk in the Great Wood near Wokingham when they both felt suddenly depressed. Later they learned that the body of a man who had committed suicide had been lying close to the spot where they were standing; Lethbridge believed that the man's depression had been somehow "recorded" by his surroundings. Four decades later Lethbridge and his wife, Mina, set out one afternoon to

*See "The Curse of the Pharaohs" in my book *The Encyclopedia of Unsolved Mysteries* (1988).

collect seaweed from a nearby beach—Ladram, in Devon. As they walked to the beach, Lethbridge again experienced a "blanket" of depression, as if he had walked into a fog. A few minutes later Mina said, "I can't stand this place any longer," and they left.

The following weekend they repeated the trip. Again, he experienced the same "blanket of depression." This time Mina went to the top of a cliff to make a sketch and suddenly experienced an unpleasant sensation, as if someone was urging her to jump.

Later, Lethbridge discovered that a man *had* recently committed suicide by jumping from the spot where Mina had been standing. He concluded that this was again the reason for the depression; the man's misery had somehow been "recorded" on the electrical field of water. (Both days had been warm and damp, and he had also noted that a small stream ran on to the beach at the point where the "depression" was strongest.) It was not the suicide's ghost that was urging Mina to jump; rather, she was responding to his own suggestion of jumping. This notion of "tape recording" lies behind the theory of *psychometry*, the ability of certain people to "read" the history of an object by holding it in their hands.

Clairvoyants believe that crystals possess this power of absorption to a high degree—hence the popularity of crystal balls, which are kept wrapped in black velvet to protect them from light and heat (on the same principle that recorded tapes should not be left in hot sunlight or on radiators).

There is also a great deal of documentation on "curses," which seems to indicate that certain objects can carry "bad luck." For example, a whole book has been devoted to the career of the ship called *The Great Eastern*, built by the great nineteenth-century engineer Isambard Brunel. During its construction, a riveter and his boy apprentice vanished; no one realized that they had been sealed into the hull. The ship (the largest ever built at that time) got stuck during its launching and took three months to free. Brunel then collapsed on its deck and died a week later. From then on the career of *The Great Eastern* was a long series of disasters. Five firemen died when a funnel exploded. While in port for repairs, the ship was damaged in a storm. The captain was drowned in a boat with a cabin boy. A sailor was crushed by the wheel; a man was lost overboard. The disasters and the damage continued until the ship was abandoned, a mere fifteen years after its launching. When it was broken up for scrap, the skeletons of the riveter and his apprentice were found sealed in the hull.

Many similar stories could be told of "jinxed" ships, houses, airplanes, and cars.* The car in which the Archduke Ferdinand was assassinated at Sarajevo (thus precipitating the First World War) went on to bring death or disaster to its next seven owners.

Now if Lethbridge is correct, and a curse is merely a kind of negative tape recording, it also suggests a reason why some people may be affected and others escape unscathed. Lethbridge believed that "sensitives" like himself—for example, good dowsers—would be unusually receptive to these "recordings," while other people would not even notice them.

If physical objects—like crystals—*are* sensitive to the vibrations of the human mind, it would also seem to follow that under certain circumstances, a "curse" might be deliberately imprinted on them—rather like marking one's possessions with an invisible marking pen. The ancient Egyptians certainly believed that their tombs could be "cursed" against robbers. The priests of the temple of Rama-sitra may have taken the same precaution with the Hope diamond.

---

*See my book *Mysteries* (1978), part 2, chapter 10.

17

The Mystery of Hypnosis:
Real-Life Svengalis and
the Telepathy Theory

In May 1991 a hypnotist named Nelson Nelson (his real name was Nelson Lintott) was tried in Bristol Crown Court on the charge of raping and/or otherwise sexually assaulting 113 girls under hypnosis. Nelson, fifty-seven, had apparently learned hypnosis in South Africa at a party. After a varied career as a driving instructor, swimming pool superintendent, barkeep, and restaurateur, he established the Britannia Lodge Health Centre in Appledore, Devon, where, among other things, he undertook to cure people of all kinds of complaints, from nail biting to smoking.

While the girls were in a trance, Nelson would remove their clothes and commit sexual assaults that were described in court as "perverted." Nelson also videotaped many of these assaults. His downfall came when one of his employees borrowed a videotape from his bedroom without permission and found that it contained footage of Nelson undressing girls who appeared to be in a trance and committing sexual acts with them. The employee went to the police, who raided Nelson's premises and found a video camera behind a two-way mirror in his bathroom. They also found forty-five videotapes, loaded guns, and numerous photographs that Nelson had taken over the years; the latter featured 113 different girls and women, ranging in age from ten to thirty-four.

One girl who had worked for Nelson as a barmaid from the age
of sixteen described how he had hypnotized her twice a week over
a long period to cure her of nail biting. While she was under
hypnosis, Nelson had induced her to commit various sex acts; the
girl was "distraught and horrified" when she viewed the videotapes
and realized what had been happening. Other girls—the police
succeeded in identifying 112 out of the 113—were equally astonished to learn what had happened to them.

Nelson was sentenced to eleven years' imprisonment.

The case appears to contradict one of the most basic assertions
of psychiatric medicine—that no one can be made to perform
acts under hypnosis that he or she would not perform when awake.
A mischievous student of the great nineteenth-century French
doctor—and hypnotist—Jean-Martin Charcot tried to make a
hypnotized girl remove her clothes in a medical class; she immediately woke up. As to criminal acts, the general view is stated by
Bernard Hollander in his book *Hypnosis and Self-Hypnosis*
(1928): "Criminal suggestions would be accepted only by criminal minds."

The general public became fascinated by hypnosis in the last
years of the nineteenth century, when George Du Maurier's novel
Trilby (1894) achieved tremendous success. It tells the story of an
attractive artist's model (Trilby) in the Latin Quarter of Paris, who
is one day hypnotized by a Hungarian musician named Svengali
in order to cure her headache. Three young English artists firmly
refuse to allow him to hypnotize her again. But when the Englishmen leave Paris, Svengali again approaches Trilby and hypnotizes
her into becoming a great singer. (In her normal state, she cannot
even sing in tune.) When her English friends see Trilby again, she
fails to recognize them and merely looks vague and confused—
until Svengali murmurs something in her ear, whereupon she
becomes cold and hostile. Later, when Svengali is stabbed by a
fellow musician, she becomes virtually an imbecile. And when he
dies, she loses all memory of her years as Svengali's "slave."
Without her sinister master, her vitality seems to drain away, and
she also dies.

Svengali became one of the most famous villains of the century, and his name became a synonym for an evil manipulator,

someone who takes over another's will. (The book implied, of course, that Trilby was also Svengali's "sex slave.") But since hypnosis was by that time beginning to achieve a certain medical respectability, psychiatrists lost no time in assuring the public that a real-life Svengali was an impossibility. If a person under hypnosis was ordered to do something that he would normally find repugnant, he would instantly wake up. Charcot's mischievous student might have induced the girl to undress if he had told her that she was in her own bedroom, about to go to bed; otherwise, her natural modesty would have caused her to wake up.

The hypnosis of human beings dates from the last years of the eighteenth century. Hypnosis of animals has been known in Europe since 1636, when the mathematician Daniel Schwenter observed that if a small piece of bent wood was fixed on a hen's beak, the hen would stare at it and go into a trance. The same thing would happen if a hen's head was held on the ground and a chalk line drawn in front of its beak. Ten years later a German Jesuit priest, Athanasius Kircher, described how, if a hen's head was tucked under its wing, a few gentle swings through the air would send it into a trance. French peasants still use this method at market when buying a live hen. Africans probably knew about animal hypnosis long before that; in his book *Hypnosis of Men and Animals* (1966), Ferenc Volgyesi describes how wild elephants can be tamed by tying them to a tree and waving leafy boughs in front of their eyes until they blink and become docile.

The man with whose name hypnosis is usually associated— Franz Mesmer—was, in fact, the discoverer of a completely different technique. Convinced that our health depends upon the flow of "vital currents" around the body, Mesmer came to believe that the flow could be increased by stroking with magnets. When, later, he observed that bleeding increased or decreased when he moved his hand above the bleeding, he concluded that human beings exercise "animal magnetism." He "magnetized" trees and got his patients to embrace them; he magnetized tubs of water and made his patients sit with their feet in them. All of this was supposed to increase the flow of vital energy around their bodies.

One of Mesmer's disciples, Armand Marie Jacques de Chastenet, the Marquis de Puységur, practiced "mesmerism" on his estate at Buzancy. One day he tied a young peasant named Victor Race—whom he was treating for asthma—to a tree, and was making "mesmeric" passes over him when Race's eyes closed. Yet he continued to reply to Puységur's remarks. And on Puységur's orders, he untied himself and walked off across the park. Puységur had discovered hypnosis. He also made another important discovery that has since been forgotten. He could give Race *mental* orders—for example, to repeat the words of a song that he was singing mentally—and Race would obey them. With another excellent hypnotic subject named Madeleine, Puységur would give public demonstrations of mind reading; one total skeptic was converted when he himself was able to order Madeleine—mentally—to put her hand in his pocket and take out an object he had placed there. This ability to influence hypnotized subjects *telepathically* was demonstrated again and again during the nineteenth century; but medicine has continued to dismiss it as a myth.

Mesmer's enemies drove him out of Paris and Vienna; he died, discredited and embittered, in 1815. And the medical profession made sure that hypnosis was treated as a fraud throughout the nineteenth century; any doctor who practiced it was likely to be struck off the register. It was only toward the end of the century that Charcot rediscovered it. Charcot had noticed that patients suffering from hysteria behaved as if they were hypnotized. For example, a man who was convinced that his arm was paralyzed would behave exactly as if it *was* paralyzed, although there was nothing physically wrong with his arm. But he could be cured by being told under hypnosis that his arm was not paralyzed—and the paralysis could also be reinduced by hypnosis. When Charcot announced to the medical profession that hypnosis was simply a form of hysteria, his colleagues believed that he had solved the mystery and ceased to regard hypnosis as a fraud. It took some time before it was recognized that Charcot had inverted the truth and that hysteria is, in fact, a kind of hypnosis. A hysterical patient becomes convinced that he is suffering from some disability and "suggests" himself into it. Freud was one of the many who were impressed by Charcot's theory of hypnosis; he later made it the basis of his own theory of the unconscious.

But what precisely *is* hypnosis? This is a question that no one at that time could answer—and that remains (officially, at all events) unanswered today. Bernard Hollander's book includes a chapter entitled "Explanation of Hypnosis" that has some useful suggestions. He points out that a subject under hypnosis *forgets his body*; if his attention is drawn to his body, it feels heavy and immobile. Yet the patient is not asleep. Hollander compares a hypnotized patient to someone absorbed in a play—the mind is wide-awake but totally abstracted. We have all seen a child staring at the television with his thumb in his mouth, so absorbed that he has to be prodded to gain his attention. This seems to imply that we have *two minds*, one of which deals with the world that surrounds us and copes with immediate experience, while the other can go off "inside itself," into a subjective world, a kind of cinema inside the head.

At about the time Freud was studying under Charcot in Paris, an American newspaper editor named Thomson Jay Hudson was also puzzling over the mystery of hypnosis. Hudson had attended a hypnotic performance by the eminent physiologist William B. Carpenter in Washington, D.C., and what he saw amazed him. Carpenter placed a young college graduate under hypnosis and asked him if he would like to meet Socrates. The young man objected that Socrates was dead, and Carpenter told him that he had the power to evoke the spirit of Socrates. Then he pointed to a corner of the room and exclaimed, "There he is." The young man—whom Hudson called C.—looked awestruck. Carpenter then urged C. to enter into conversation with Socrates and ask him any question he liked—mentioning that, since the audience could not hear Socrates, C. would have to repeat his replies aloud. For the next two hours the audience witnessed an incredible conversation, in which the replies of Socrates seemed so brilliant and plausible that some of the audience—who were interested in Spiritualism—were inclined to believe that Socrates was actually there.

After this Carpenter introduced C. to the spirits of various modern philosophers, and more brilliant and plausible conversations followed. These were quite different from one another and from the conversation with Socrates—although they usually had nothing whatever in common with the ideas of the philosophers under interrogation. Finally, to convince the audience that they were not listening to the words of spirits, Carpenter summoned a philosophic pig, which discoursed learnedly on Hinduism.

What impressed Hudson was that C. was obviously of fairly average intelligence, whereas the answers of the philosophers were close to genius level. Obviously, C.'s "unconscious mind"—or whatever it was—was far cleverer than *he* was. And as Hudson studied similar cases he came to the conclusion that we possess two minds—what he called the "objective mind," which copes with everyday reality, and the "subjective mind," which can become totally absorbed in an *inner* world. C. only became a man of genius under hypnosis, when the operations of his objective mind, like those of his body, were suspended. Then the subjective mind could operate freely. In other words, the objective mind serves as a kind of anchor, or ball-and-chain, on the subjective mind. But men of great genius, Hudson concluded, have an odd faculty for allowing the two to work in harmony—like children. He cited the case of an American orator, Henry Clay, who was once called upon to answer an opponent in the Senate when he was ill. He asked the friend sitting next to him to tug on his coattails when he had been speaking for ten minutes. Two hours later he sank down exhausted—then looked at the clock and asked his friend why he had failed to interrupt. The friend explained that he had not only tugged at Clay's coattails, he had pinched him repeatedly and even jabbed a pin into his leg. Clay had remained totally oblivious to all this. It would seem that Clay was in the same trancelike state as the child watching television with his thumb in his mouth, and that it was, in fact, a kind of hypnosis.

The theory that Hudson developed in his book *The Law of Psychic Phenomena* (1893) is that the "subjective mind" has virtually miraculous powers. All men of genius—particularly those whose talent seems to burst forth like a wellspring, such as Shakespeare and Mozart—are able to tune in at will to the enormous powers of the subjective mind. The miracles of Jesus, and of various saints, were simply manifestations of the same mysterious power.

Hudson himself became convinced that he could also perform

miracles of healing with the aid of the subjective mind and decided to try to cure a relative of severe rheumatism that had
almost killed him. The man lived a thousand miles away. Hudson
decided that the best time to send "healing suggestions" was on
the edge of sleep, when the "objective mind" is passive—exactly
as in hypnosis. On May 15, 1890, he told a number of friends that
he meant to start the experiment. A few months later one of the
friends met the invalid and found that he was well again; the
attacks had ceased and he was working normally. Asked when the
attacks ceased, he said, "About mid-May"—exactly when Hudson
had started his "experiments."

Hudson claimed that he went on to cure about five hundred
people in the same way. He failed in only two cases and these—
oddly enough—were patients who had been told that he intended
to try to cure them.

This, Hudson believed, underlined another peculiarity of the
subjective mind: its powers have to work *spontaneously*, without
self-consciousness. As soon as it becomes self-conscious, it freezes
up, like the hand of a schoolboy when the teacher looks over his
shoulder as he is writing. This also explains why so many "psychics" fail when they are tested by skeptics. It is like trying to
make love in a crowded public square.

Because we have two minds, our powers tend to interfere with
one another. In the 1870s a stage hypnotist named Carl Hansen
loved to demonstrate a spectacular trick; he would tell the hypnotized subject that he (the subject) was about to become as rigid as
a board. The subject was then placed across two chairs, with his
head on one and his heels on the other, and several people would
sit or stand on his stomach; he never bent in the middle. What
happened was that the objective mind had been put to sleep, and
the hypnotist then *took over the role of the objective mind*.
Normally, "you" tell your body to stand up or sit down. But "you"
are often negative or tired or unsure of yourself, so your "orders"
are given in a hesitant voice. We are undermined by self-doubt.
The hypnotist delivers his orders like a sergeant major, and this
has the effect of unlocking the powers of the subjective mind. It
obviously follows that if *you* could learn to give orders with the
same assurance, you would also be capable of "miraculous" feats.

But in that case, why aren't self-confident people capable of miraculous feats? Because they have developed the objective mind, the conscious "self" that copes with reality, rather than the subjective mind. Genius—and miracles—is about *contact* between the two minds.

Hudson was also certain that all so-called psychic phenomena are due to the powers of the subjective mind. He attended a séance at which a pencil wrote of its own accord on a slate, delivering messages that were relevant to Hudson and to the other "sitter," a general. Yet when thinking it over later, Hudson concluded that nothing was written that could not have emanated from the mind of the medium, if the medium had telepathic powers. He decided that the medium had—unconsciously—read the mind of his sitters and then used the miraculous powers of his own subjective mind to make the pencil write on the slate. And if *that* was possible, Hudson argued, then all psychical phenomena, including ghosts and poltergeists, could be explained in the same way. In fact, Hudson was ahead of his time. It would be several years before psychical researchers came to the conclusion that poltergeists are due to the unconscious minds of disturbed adolescents.

Here it could be argued that Hudson was carried away by his own brilliant insights into the powers of the subjective mind. I have argued elsewhere that the evidence for "spirits" cannot be so easily dismissed. In fact, he was quite definitely wrong when he came to deal with the curious power known as *psychometry*, the ability of certain people to "read" the history of an object they hold in their hands. Some of the most remarkable tests in the history of psychical research were carried out by a professor of geology named William Denton. He would wrap geological and archaeological specimens in thick brown paper packages, shuffle them until he no longer knew which was which, then get his "psychometrists"—his wife and sister-in-law—to describe the contents and history of packages chosen at random. Their accuracy was amazing—for example, a fragment of volcanic lava from Pompeii produced an accurate description of the eruption, while a fragment of tile from a Roman villa produced a description of Roman legions and a man who looked like a retired soldier.

However, this latter experiment worried Denton, because the tile came from the villa of the orator Cicero, who was tall and thin, and the "soldier" was described as heavily built. It was only some years later, after publishing his first account, that Denton learned that the villa had also belonged to the Roman dictator Sulla, who *did* correspond accurately to the description.

But all this leaves Hudson's central insight untouched: that man has two minds and it is because of these two minds impede each other instead of supporting each other that our powers are so limited. His basic proposition is that if we could learn to tap the powers of the subjective mind, we would develop into supermen.

Hudson's book became a bestseller and went into edition after edition between 1893 and Hudson's death in 1903. Why, then, did its remarkable new theory not make a far greater impact? The reason can be summarized in a single word: Freud. The objective and subjective minds obviously correspond roughly to Freud's ego and id—or conscious and unconscious. But there is a major difference. Freud was a pessimist who saw the unconscious mind as a *passive* force, a kind of basement full of decaying rubbish that causes disease—or neurosis. The conscious mind is the victim of these unconscious forces, which are basically sexual in nature. Hudson would have been horrified at such a gloomy and negative view of the subjective mind. But because Freud was a "scientist" and Hudson was merely a retired newspaper editor, the latter's achievement was ignored by psychologists.

Yet the "two minds" theory was to receive powerful scientific backing a few decades later. Even in the nineteenth century it had been recognized that the two halves of our brains have different functions. The speech function resides in the left half of the brain; doctors observed that people with left-brain damage became inarticulate. The right side of the brain controls recognition of shapes and patterns, so that an artist who had right-brain damage would lose all artistic talent. One man could not even draw a clover leaf; he put the three leaves of the clover side by side, on the same level.

Yet an artist with left-brain damage only became inarticulate; he was still as good an artist as ever. And an orator with right-brain damage could sound as eloquent as ever, even though he could not draw a clover leaf.

The left brain also governs logic and reason, which are involved in such tasks as adding up a laundry list or doing a crossword puzzle. The right is involved in such activities as musical appreciation or facial recognition. In short, you could say that the left is a scientist and the right is an artist.

One of the odd facts of human physiology is that the left side of the body is controlled by the right side of the brain, and vice versa. No one quite knows why this is, except that it probably makes for greater integration. If the left brain controlled the left side and the right brain the right side, there might be "frontier disputes"; as it is, each has a foot firmly in the other's territory.

If you removed the top of your head, the upper part of your brain—the cerebral hemispheres—would look like a walnut with a kind of bridge connecting the two halves. This bridge is a knot of nerves called the *corpus callosum*, or commissure. But doctors learned that there are some freaks who possess no commissure yet seem to function perfectly well. This led them to wonder if they could prevent epileptic attacks by severing the commissure. They tried it on epileptics and it seemed to work. The fits were greatly reduced, and the patients seemed to be unchanged. It led the doctors to wonder what the function of the commissure was. Someone suggested it might be to transmit epileptic seizures; another suggested it might be to keep the brain from sagging in the middle.

In the 1950s experiments in America began to shed a good deal of light on the problem. Someone noticed that if a "split-brain" patient knocked against a table with his left side, he didn't seem to notice. It began to emerge that the split-brain operation had the effect of preventing one half of the brain from learning what the other half knew. If a cat was taught a trick with one eye covered, then asked to do it with the other eye covered, it was baffled. It became clear that we literally have two brains.*

---

*For the sake of simplicity I speak here of the left eye and the right eye; in fact, both eyes are connected to both sides of the brain, so it would be more accurate to speak of the right and left *visual fields*. In visual experiments with split-brain patients, the patient is asked to keep his eyes fixed either to the left or to the right. This piece of information is unimportant for understanding what follows.

Moreover, if a split-brain patient was shown an apple with the left eye and an orange with the right, then asked what he had just seen, he would reply, "Orange." Asked to write what he had just seen with his left hand, he would write *Apple*. A split-brain patient who was shown a dirty picture with her right brain blushed; asked why she was blushing, she replied truthfully, "I don't know." The person who was doing the blushing was the one who lived in the right half of her brain. *She* lived in the left half.

This is true of all of us (except left-handed individuals, whose brain hemispheres are reversed). The person you call "you" lives in the left half—the half that "copes" with the real world. The person who lives in the right is a stranger.

You might object that you and I are not split-brain patients. That makes no difference. Mozart once remarked that tunes were always walking into his head fully fledged, and all he had to do was write them down. Where did they come *from*? Obviously, from the right half of his brain, the "artist." Where did they go *to*? To the left half of his brain, where Mozart lived. In other words, Mozart was a split-brain patient. And if Mozart was, then so are the rest of us. The person we call "I" is the scientist. The "artist" lives in the shadows, and we are scarcely aware of his existence, except in moods of deep relaxation or of "inspiration." We all become more "right brain," for example, after an alcoholic drink; it makes us more aware of our "other half." It does this, to some extent, by anesthetizing the left brain (which explains why you find it harder to do a mathematical problem when you have had a few glasses of wine). This is why alcohol is so popular. The same— unfortunately—applies to other drugs.

We can see that the left and right halves of the brain corre- spond roughly to Hudson's objective and subjective minds. And how does this help us to understand hypnosis? Well, it would seem that the hypnotist "anesthetizes" the left brain—makes it fall asleep—while the right remains wide awake. If Hudson is cor- rect—and there seems every reason to believe that he is—the right brain is then able to operate with the full powers of the subjective mind. There seem to be obvious clues here to how we could all make better use of our powers.

According to modern medicine, hypnosis merely enables you

to relax and become less self-conscious. It has no power to make you "superhuman." Yet once again, this is contradicted by the facts. We have already seen that the Marquis de Puységur was able to communicate telepathically with Victor Race when Victor was in a trance. And anyone who takes the trouble to look into the four volumes of Eric J. Dingwall's *Abnormal Hypnotic Phenomena*—which is devoted mainly to the nineteenth century—will find dozens of cases that leave no doubt whatever that "telepathy under hypnosis" has been demonstrated over and over again. One of Dingwall's most astonishing accounts concerns the brothers Alexis and Adolphe Didier, who could both perform remarkable paranormal feats under hypnosis. For example, the two would play a game of cards with cards that were turned facedown. Nevertheless, one brother would be able to tell his partner which cards the other held, as if he were looking over his shoulder.

The father of the Didiers was himself a remarkable hypnotic subject who would sometimes go into a trance at the breakfast table while reading the newspaper—and continue reading the newspaper although he had dropped it onto the table and was not looking at it. Alexis, the more talented of the two brothers, was particularly expert at "traveling clairvoyance." The person he was talking to could ask him to describe what he (the "client") had been doing that day, or to "travel" to his home and describe it. This sounds as if it could be explained by telepathy—except that Didier could tell the client things he did not know himself. On one occasion Didier described a magistrate's study with great accuracy and mentioned that there was a bell on the table; the magistrate denied this. But when he got home he found that Didier was correct; his wife had placed the bell there since he had left home.

Alfred Russel Wallace, codeveloper (with Darwin) of the theory of evolution in the mid-nineteenth century, became interested in hypnosis when he was a young schoolteacher, and he discovered that some of his pupils were excellent hypnotic subjects. One boy would actually share Wallace's perceptions when in a trance; if Wallace pinched his own arm, the boy started and rubbed his arm; if Wallace tasted sugar, the boy smiled and licked his lips; if Wallace tasted salt, the boy grimaced.

In the 1880s, the French psychologist Pierre Janet was able to place one of his patients, a woman named Leonie, in a hypnotic trance *from the other side of Le Havre* and summon her to come to him. The experiments were performed under test conditions under the auspices of the Society for Psychical Research.

Almost a century later Dr. Gustav Pagenstecher discovered that one of his patients, Maria Reyes de Zierold, was able to share his own sensations, tasting substances he put on his tongue and wincing if he held his hand over a lighted match. The first time he hypnotized her, she told him that her daughter was listening at the door; Pagenstecher opened the door and found that this was true. This sounds as if she may simply have heard the girl outside; but she was also able to describe what Pagenstecher was doing when he was in the next room. Under hypnosis, Maria also became an excellent psychometrist and could describe with great accuracy the history of objects placed in her hands.*

All of this obviously raises a fascinating possibility—that hypnosis may not merely involve placing someone in a trance through suggestion but that it might be *the direct influence of one mind upon another.* In *Over the Long High Wall*, writer J. B. Priestley tells how, at a boring literary dinner in New York, he told the person sitting next to him that he intended to try to make one of the poets wink at him. He chose a serious-looking woman, "no winker," and concentrated on her. After a while she turned and winked at him. Priestley's neighbor was inclined to doubt whether it had been a wink, but after the dinner, the woman came up to him to apologize for winking at him, remarking, "I don't know what made me do it."

This brings us back to the question raised at the beginning of this article: whether a hypnotist can influence someone to commit a criminal act against his will. The evidence suggests that it *is* possible. In 1865, in France, a vagabond named Thimotheus Castellan was tried for abducting and raping a young peasant girl named Josephine. He had knocked on the door of her father's cottage, begging shelter for the night. The next morning, when the father and brothers had gone off to work, neighbors noticed

---

*For a longer account of Pagenstecher and Maria Reyes de Zierold, see my book *The Psychic Detectives* (1985).

him making passes in the air behind Josephine's back. Over the midday meal, Castellan made a movement with his fingers, and she felt her senses leaving her; he then carried her into the next room and raped her. She said she wanted to resist but was paralyzed. Later, he left and took her with him, demonstrating his power over her at various farms where they stayed by making her walk on all fours like an animal. He was finally arrested and sentenced to twelve years in prison.

In 1934 a Heidelberg hypnotist named Franz Walter met a woman on a train and caused her to pass into a trance simply by taking her hand. After raping her, he ordered her to work for him as a prostitute. He subsequently ordered her to make several attempts on her husband's life; when these failed, he ordered her to commit suicide. She was saved by passersby on two occasions. Finally, a police surgeon guessed that she had been hypnotized and ordered to keep silent about it; he succeeded in "unlocking" her memory, and Franz Walter was sentenced to ten years in prison.

In 1985 two Portuguese criminals, both named Manuel, succeeded in parting a number of victims from their life savings through hypnosis. One woman described how she had simply been talking to one of the men when he took her hand and she felt "cold all over," then went into a stupor in which she obeyed orders to go home and withdraw her savings; she handed over more than £1,000. The two men were caught by accident when a hairdresser heard one of her clients agreeing (over the telephone) to meet them and give them money; she had heard of the earlier case and notified the police. The men were deported.*

All of this seems to suggest that there is a telepathic element in hypnosis—of one mind directly influencing another—and that legends about real-life Svengalis may have some basis in fact. Ferenc Volgyesi, whose book *Hypnosis in Men and Animals* has already been mentioned, was convinced that legends about the "hypnotic gaze" of the snake were not without foundation; he cites examples of toads, frogs, and rabbits being "transfixed by a

---

*For a longer account of all these cases, see my *Mammoth Book of the Supernatural* (1991).

snake's gaze," which involved the expansion of its pupils; but he has photographs of other creatures engaged in "battles of will" in which they simply stare at each other. In one case, a toad won a "battle of will" against a snake.

This is not, of course, to deny the validity of the generally accepted theory of hypnosis—that it is basically a matter of suggestion. Hypnosis, as we have seen, is based on a state of abstraction, and hypnotists undoubtedly create this state by suggestion—usually by suggesting that the subject is becoming sleepy, that his limbs are becoming heavy, and so on. But it is the right brain—the "other you"—that accepts these suggestions and puts "you" to sleep, while *it* remains wide awake. Its powers are then at the disposal of the hypnotist (which suggests, in turn, that a good hypnotic subject ought to be able to cure people at a distance, as Hudson did).

What seems to have happened, in the case of Nelson Nelson, the rapist described at the beginning of this chapter, is that his suggestions made his patients totally unaware of their bodies and that he committed the sexual assaults while the patients were virtually asleep, as if under anesthesia.

But it would be a mistake to assume that this supports the view that a hypnotist could not persuade an unwilling subject to submit to sexual intercourse. In his book *Open to Suggestion* (1989), a study of the abuse of hypnosis, Robert Temple devotes a whole chapter to rape under hypnosis. One assault victim describes how the hypnotist raised her bra and caressed her breasts, yet she still made a further appointment. The next time, after placing her in a light trance,

> he caressed my breast again and after a while pulled down my pants and panties, and he even put his hand in my vagina. . . . He wanted me to take his genitals in my hand. I said no. . . . After a while I held his penis. . . . I would have liked to have knocked him away, but in one way or another I couldn't do it. [When] he started to get closer with his genitals, I started to panic and cried.

Here it seems clear that she had no more desire to be raped than the victim of the two Portuguese criminals had to hand over

her life savings. This is clearly a case in which—as with Thimotheus Castellan and Franz Walter—the will of the hypnotist prevailed over the will of the victim. Temple also cites a case of a
homosexual assault on a soldier by a hypnotist—his colonel—in
which the soldier felt immobilized and unable to get up from the
bed, although he objected to the colonel's advances.

Temple himself describes a personal episode that throws an
interesting light on hypnosis. He was undergoing a course of
hypnotic treatment and one day failed to "wake up." But because
he was aware that his doctor was in a hurry to get away, he
pretended to be fully conscious. Outside, he told his wife—who
was waiting in the car—that he was still hypnotized and asked her
to blow on his face; she thought it funny and screamed with
laughter. On the way home, he saw a tree and ordered her to stop.
Then he went and embraced the tree and burst into tears, telling
it how beautiful it was. After that he lay on his back, staring at the
night sky and uttering maudlin remarks. In fact, he behaved
exactly as if drunk. Back at home, he drank down half a glass of
neat gin—a drink he disliked—and finally "came to." It is clear
that he knew that a part of his mind was still under hypnosis but
was unable to awaken it.

This raises another important point. William James has pointed
out that there are certain days on which we feel that our vital
powers are simply not at their best; "our fires are damped; our
draughts are checked." We feel curiously dull, like a car whose
engine is still cold and that keeps "cutting out." In fact, the
remarkable teacher Gurdjieff asserted that our ordinary consciousness is literally a state of sleep and that we have to make
superhuman efforts if we are to wake up. (Hypnosis comes from
the Greek hypnos—"sleep.")

Clearly, then, hypnosis is not some abnormal, freak condition
that we can ignore. It offers clues to what is wrong with human
beings and to why it is the easiest thing in the world to waste one's
life. Our basic problem is to "shake the mind awake."

Notice that when we are dull and bored, we feel "alienated"
from reality. We feel trapped in the physical world and in the
present moment; "reality" is a prison. This is the opposite of what
happens when we are happy and excited—for example, when

looking forward to some eagerly anticipated event—or when we are deeply relaxed. In these states, the world seems infinitely fascinating; reality seems to stretch around us in endless vistas, like a view from a mountaintop.

It is obvious that in such states, the right and left brains are in close communication. When you are bored, you are trapped—not only in the physical world, but in your left brain. You are, in essence, a split-brain patient. The same thing happens if you are absorbed in a daydream, except that in this case you are trapped in your inner world—your right brain. If you spend too much time in such states—what is sometimes called "escapism"—you begin to find the real world unbearable, and you alternate between being trapped inside yourself and feeling trapped in the physical world.

On the other hand, in moods of happiness or relaxation, you become, for a short time, a "whole-brain" patient. Your right brain—your intuitive self—now feels awake, and you realize that this "whole" state is far closer to what human consciousness was intended to be. One of the oddest things about these states is that, when we look back on our miseries and misfortunes, most of them seem laughably trivial, the result of the lopsided half-consciousness that we regard as "normal."

The French philosopher Sartre had a word for these states in which we feel trapped in the present moment: "nausea." And, oddly enough, he regarded "nausea" as the fundamental reality of human existence—what you might call the basic state of human consciousness—rather like seeing an attractive woman with her hair in curlers and cold cream smeared all over her face. It follows, of course, that Sartre felt that human life is meaningless and that—as he put it in a famous phrase—"man is a useless passion." His close associate Simone de Beauvoir captured the spirit of "nausea" when she wrote: "I look at myself in vain in a mirror, tell myself my own story. I can never grasp myself as an entire object. I experience in myself the emptiness that is myself. I feel that I am not." But obviously, she was simply talking about the experience of being trapped in left-brain consciousness. Yet it is quite clear that she was mistaken when she said that she could never grasp herself as an entire object and that she felt "she is not." In "whole-brain" states, we have a curious sense of our own reality *and* that of the world. We suddenly *know* that "we are."

What is so interesting here is that Sartre's whole philosophy of human existence—he is known as one of the founding figures of existentialism—is based on his mistaken notion that "nausea" is some fundamental truth about human reality—the beautiful woman in hair curlers. Moreover, it is a philosophy that is echoed by some of the most respectable figures in modern literature, from Ernest Hemingway and Albert Camus to Graham Greene and Samuel Beckett. It could be said to dominate modern philosophy and modern literature. Yet we can see that it is simply a misunderstanding. "Nausea" is not some glimpse of reality; it is as unimportant as a headache, and in some ways curiously similar. If Sartre had known about the right and left hemispheres, he would have recognized that he was greatly exaggerating the importance of "nausea." And if we could grasp, once and for all, that "alienation" in left-brain consciousness is not a glimpse of the reality of the human condition, we would experience an enormous and immediate rise in our level of optimism and vitality.

There is another important inference to be drawn from all this. Hypnosis, as we have seen, is basically suggestion. The hypnotist's suggestion ("your eyelids are feeling heavy . . .") has the effect of trapping us in left-brain consciousness. Boredom and pessimism have the same effect. But if you believe—like Sartre—that life is meaningless and "man is a useless passion," then you are in a permanent condition of negative self-suggestion, and entrapment in left-brain consciousness becomes your normal mode of awareness. So "nausea" becomes a kind of self-fulfilling prophecy. Entrapment in left-brain consciousness is bad enough, but it becomes ten times worse if you accept it as a norm. On the other hand, if you are aware that whole-brain consciousness is the norm, then states of "trapped" left-brain consciousness would be accepted as casually as a headache.

This, then, is the real importance of Puységur's discovery of hypnosis. It was the recognition of a curious anomaly that raised enormous questions about the human mind. The total eclipse of hypnosis during the nineteenth century reveals that these questions were too uncomfortable to be faced; it was easier to dismiss

them and to stick to the old commonsense view of human awareness. Now we find ourselves at an interesting crossroads when we
accept the reality of hypnosis (although there are still a few
academics who dismiss it as a delusion) yet fail to grasp its
implications. When these are finally grasped and taken for
granted by every high school student—as we now take for granted
the notion of the unconscious mind or of childhood eroticism—
man will be prepared to begin a voyage of discovery into his own
unexplored potentialities.

18

Jack the Ripper:
Shedding New Light on the World's
Most Infamous Serial Killer

In spite of the epidemic of twentieth-century serial killers with sobriquets like the Boston Strangler, the Buffalo Slasher, and the Sunset Slayer, Jack the Ripper still remains far and away the world's most famous—or infamous—serial killer. This is not due simply to the grisly picturesqueness of the nickname but to the fact that the murders took place in the fog-shrouded London of Sherlock Holmes and that—unlike the three killers mentioned above—the identity of Jack the Ripper is still a total mystery.

One other interesting fact deserves to be taken into account: Jack the Ripper was the first sex killer in the modern sense of the term. The notion that sex crimes made their first appearance as late as 1888 sounds rather strange. What about Roman emperors like Tiberius, who enjoyed deflowering altar boys? What about Gilles de Rais and Vlad the Impaler and Ivan the Terrible? The first thing we notice about these men is that they were all rulers or members of the aristocracy. They had leisure—which can also lead to boredom—and sufficient authority to be able to impose their will on their victims. But the majority of criminals throughout history have killed or robbed for purely economic reasons. *The Newgate Calendar*, a compilation of crimes published in London in the late eighteenth century, contains only half a dozen "sex crimes," and these were not violent rapes but what we would call seductions. The lower classes were too hungry to bother about "forbidden" sex, and the upper classes could obtain it so easily that rape would have been pointless.

In the early nineteenth century a significant development occurred: the rise of pornography. The man most responsible for this was the Marquis de Sade—again an aristocrat—who died in an asylum in 1816. He was very highly sexed, and since he spent most of his life in prison, he had little to do but fantasize about sex. His books, with their monstrous daydreams of rape and torture, inspired many imitators in the 1820s, not all of whom shared his taste for flogging and being flogged, but every one of whom was excited by the notion of the forbidden.

In the two decades preceding Jack the Ripper, there *were* a few crimes that we would nowadays describe as sex murders, but these were usually perpetrated by people who would today be committed to an asylum—like the Italian youth Vincent Verzeni, who graduated from killing chickens to disemboweling women and "sucking their blood," or the Boston teenager Jesse Pomeroy, who enjoyed inflicting pain on younger children and ended by killing two of them.

Compared to these, there was something utterly calculated about the Jack the Ripper murders, which took place in the Whitechapel area of East London, in the autumn of 1888, and which produced a morbid sense of shock and panic.

It was still dark on the morning of September 1 when a cart driver named George Cross walked along Bucks Row on his way to work. It was a narrow, cobbled street with the blank wall of a warehouse on one side and a row of terraced houses on the other. In the dim light Cross saw what he thought was a bundle of tarpaulin and went to investigate. It proved to be a woman lying on her back, her skirt above her waist. Cross decided she was drunk, and when another man approached, he said, "Give me a hand getting this woman on her feet." The other man, a market porter, looked down dubiously; his first impression was that she had been raped and left for dead. He bent down and touched her cheek, which was cold, and her hand. "She's dead," he said. "We'd better find a policeman." He pulled down her skirt to make her decent.

In fact, the beat of Police Constable John Neil took him through Bucks Row, and a few minutes after the men had left, the light of his bull's-eye lantern showed him the woman's body, which lay close to a stable door. It also showed him something the men had been unable to see: that the woman's throat had been cut so deeply that the vertebrae were exposed.

An hour later the body, which was that of a middle-aged woman, lay in the yard of the local mortuary, and two paupers from the workhouse next door were given the job of stripping it, while a police inspector took notes. It was when they pulled off the two petticoats that the inspector saw that the woman's abdomen had been slashed open with a jagged incision that ran from the bottom of the ribs to the pelvis.

The woman was identified through a Lambeth Workhouse mark stenciled on her petticoat. She was Mary Ann Nicholls, a prostitute who had been living at a common lodging house in Thrawl Street—one of the worst slums even in that poverty-stricken area. A few hours before her death she had staggered back to the lodging house, her speech slurred with drink, and admitted that she lacked the fourpence necessary for a bed. The keeper had turned her away. "I'll soon get the money," she had shouted as she went off down the street. "See what a jolly bonnet I've got." She went looking for a man who would give her the price of a bed in exchange for an uncomfortable act of intercourse on the pavement in a back alley. What had happened, the police surgeon inferred, was that her customer had placed his hands around her throat as she lay on the ground and strangled her into unconsciousness—there were bruises on her throat. Then he had cut her throat with two powerful slashes that had almost severed the head, raised her skirt, and stabbed and slashed at her stomach in a kind of frenzy.

Oddly enough, the murder caused little sensation. Prostitutes were often killed in the slums of London, sometimes by gangs who demanded protection money. The previous April a prostitute named Emma Smith had dragged herself into London Hospital,

reporting that she had been attacked by four men in Osborn
Street. They had rammed some object, possibly an iron bar, into
her vagina with such force that it had penetrated the uterus; she
had died of peritonitis. In July dismembered portions of a woman's body had been recovered from the Thames. And on August 7,
1888, a prostitute named Martha Tabram had been found dead
on a landing in George Yards Buildings, Whitechapel; she had
been stabbed thirty-nine times with a knife or bayonet. Two
soldiers were questioned about her murder but proved to have an
excellent alibi. Evidently some sadistic brute had a grudge against
prostitutes; it was hardly the kind of story to appeal to respectable
newspaper readers.

That attitude was to change dramatically eight days after the
murder of Mary Ann Nicholls, when another disemboweled body
was found in the backyard of a barber's shop in Hanbury Street,
Whitechapel. It was a place where prostitutes often took their
customers, and this is evidently what Annie Chapman had done at
about 5:30 on the morning of Saturday, September 8, 1888; a
neighbor had seen her talking to a dark-looking man "of foreign
appearance," dressed in shabby genteel clothes and wearing a
deerstalker hat. Half an hour later a lodger named John Davis
went downstairs and into the yard, where the lavatory was situated. He saw the body of a woman lying against the fence, her
skirt drawn up above her waist and her legs bent at the knees. The
stomach had been cut open and some of the intestines pulled out.
As in the case of Mary Ann Nicholls, the cause of death was a
deep gash in the throat. The murderer had placed the woman's
rings and some pennies at her feet and a torn envelope near her
head. Medical examination revealed that the killer had also removed the uterus and upper part of the vagina.

Now, suddenly, the press awoke to the fact that the unknown
killer was a sadistic maniac. The *Star* that afternoon carried the
headline: "Latest Horrible Murder in Whitechapel." When Mrs.
Mary Burridge, of Blackfriars Road, South London, read the
story, she collapsed and died "of a fit." Sir Melville Macnaghten,
later head of the Criminal Investigation Department (CID), would
eventually write in his memoirs: "No one who was living in London that autumn will forget the terror created by these murders.
Even now I can recall the foggy evenings, and hear again the

raucous cries of the newspaper boys: 'Another horrible murder, murder, mutilation, Whitechapel.' "

In our own age of mass violence, we find it impossible to imagine the shock created by the murders. A journalist who reported the crimes later began his account of them in a popular booklet: "In the long catalogue of crimes which has been compiled in our modern days there is nothing to be found, perhaps, which has so darkened the horizon of humanity and shadowed the vista of man's better nature as the series of mysterious murders committed in Whitechapel during the latter part of 1888." "Shadowed the vista of man's better nature"—this is what so frightened Londoners. It was as if an inhuman monster, a kind of demon, had started to hunt the streets. Hysteria swept over the whole country. There had been nothing like it since the Ratcliffe Highway murders of 1811, when two families were slaughtered in East London, and householders all over England barricaded their doors at night.

On September 29, 1888, the Central News Agency received a letter that began: "Dear Boss, I keep on hearing the police have caught me but they won't fix me just yet." It included the sentence: "I am down on whores and I shan't quit ripping them till I do get buckled" and promised: "You will soon hear of me with my funny little games." It was signed "Jack the Ripper"—the first time the name had been used. The writer requested: "Keep this letter back till I do a bit more work, then give it out straight." The Central News Agency decided to follow his advice.

That night, a Saturday, the "ripper" killed again—this time not one, but two prostitutes. At 1:00 A.M. on Sunday morning a hawker named Louis Diemschutz drove his pony and cart into the backyard of a workingman's club in Berner Street. The pony shied and Diemschutz saw something lying in front of its feet; a closer look showed him that it was a woman's body. The Ripper was either in the yard at that moment or had only just left it when he heard the approach of the horse and cart. When Diemschutz returned a few moments later with a lighted candle, he was able to see that the woman's throat had been cut. There had also been an attempt to cut off her ear. She was later identified as Elizabeth Stride, an alcoholic Swedish prostitute.

The killer had been interrupted but his nerve was unshaken. He hastened up Berner Street and along Commercial Road—this murder had been farther afield than the others—and reached the Houndsditch area just in time to meet a prostitute who had been released from Bishopsgate police station ten minutes earlier. Her name was Catherine Eddowes, and she had been held for being drunk and disorderly. He seems to have had no difficulty persuading the woman to accompany him into Mitre Square, a small square surrounded by warehouses, only a few hundred yards away. A policeman patrolled the square every fifteen minutes or so, and when he passed through at 1:30, he saw nothing unusual. At 1:45 he found the body of a woman lying in the corner of the square. She was lying on her back, with her dress pushed up around her waist, and her face had been slashed. Her body had been gashed open from the base of the ribs to the pubic region, and the throat had been cut. Later examination revealed that a kidney was missing and that half of one ear had been cut off.

The murderer had evidently heard the approach of the policeman and hurriedly left the square by a small passage that runs from its northern side. In this passage there was a communal sink, and he had paused long enough to wash the blood from his hands and probably from his knife. In Goulston Street, a ten-minute walk away, he discarded a bloodstained piece of his victim's apron. The policeman who found it also found a chalked message scrawled on a nearby wall: "The Juwes are not the men that will be blamed for nothing." The police commissioner, Sir Charles Warren, ordered the words to be rubbed out, in spite of a plea from a local CID man that they should be photographed first; he thought they might cause a riot against the Jews, thousands of whom lived in Whitechapel.

Macnaghten admitted later: "When the double murder of 30th September took place, the exasperation of the public at the non-discovery of the perpetrator knew no bounds." The "Jack the Ripper" letter was released, and the murderer immediately acquired a nickname. And early on Monday morning the Central News Agency received another missive—this time a postcard— from Jack the Ripper. It read: "I was not codding [joking] dear old boss when I gave you the tip. You'll hear about Saucy Jack's work tomorrow. Double event this time. Number one squealed a bit.

Couldn't finish straight off. Had not time to get ears for police. Thanks for keeping last letter back till I got to work again."

The public exploded in fury. Meetings were held in the streets, criticizing the police. Sir Charles Warren's resignation was demanded. Because the murderer was suspected of being a doctor, men carrying black bags found it dangerous to walk through the streets. The police decided to try bloodhounds, but the dogs promptly lost themselves on Tooting Common.

Yet as October passed with no further murders, the panic began to die down. Then, in the early hours of November 9, the Ripper staged his most spectacular crime of all. Mary Jeanette Kelly was a young Irishwoman, only twenty-four years old, who lived in a cheap room in Miller's Court, off Dorset Street. At about two o'clock that morning she was seen talking to a swarthy man with a heavy moustache; he seemed well dressed and had a gold watch chain. They entered the narrow alleyway that led to her lodging: room 13.

At 10:45 the next morning a rent collector knocked on her door but received no reply. He put his hand through a broken pane of glass in the window and pulled aside the curtain. What he saw sent him rushing for a policeman.

Jack the Ripper had surpassed himself. The body lay on the bed, and the mutilations must have taken a long time—an hour or more. One of the hands lay in the open stomach. The head had been virtually removed and was hanging on only by a piece of skin, as was the left arm. The breasts and nose had been removed and the skin from the legs stripped off. The heart lay on the pillow, and some of the intestines were draped around a picture. The remains of a fire burned in the grate, as if the Ripper had used it to provide himself with light. But this time, medical examination revealed that the Ripper had taken away none of the internal organs; his lengthy exercise in mutilation had apparently satisfied his peculiar sadistic fever.

This murder caused the greatest sensation of all. The police chief finally resigned. Public clamor became louder than ever; even Queen Victoria made suggestions on how to catch the murderer. Yet the slaughter of Mary Kelly proved to be the last of the crimes of Jack the Ripper. The police, hardly able to believe their luck as weeks and months went by without further atrocities, reached the conclusion that the Ripper had either committed suicide or been confined in a mental home. A body taken from the river early the following January was identified as that of a doctor who had committed suicide, and Scotland Yard detectives told themselves that this was almost certainly Jack the Ripper. But their claims have never been confirmed.

There have, of course, been many fascinating theories. Forty years after the murders, an Australian journalist named Leonard Matters wrote the first full-length book on Jack the Ripper. He ended by telling an extraordinary story: how a surgeon in Buenos Aires was called to the bedside of a dying Englishman, whom he recognized as the brilliant surgeon Dr. Stanley, under whom he had studied. Stanley told him a horrifying story. In 1888 his son Herbert had died of syphilis contracted from a prostitute two years before; her name had been Mary Jeanette Kelly. Dr. Stanley swore to avenge Herbert's death and prowled the East End of London looking for the woman. He would pick up prostitutes, question them about Mary Kelly, then kill them to make sure they made no attempt to warn her. Finally, he found the woman he was seeking and took his revenge. Then he left for Argentina.

Matters admitted that his own search of the records of the British Medical Association had revealed no Dr. Stanley nor anyone who even resembled him. But there are other reasons for regarding the Stanley story as fiction. If Dr. Stanley was only trying to silence his first four or five victims, why did he disembowel them? In any case, syphilis is unlikely to kill a man in two years—ten is a more likely period. But the most conclusive piece of evidence against the Dr. Stanley theory is that Mary Kelly was not suffering from syphilis.

Ten years later an artist named William Stewart published *Jack the Ripper: A New Theory*. Stewart had studied the inquest report on Mary Kelly and discovered that she was pregnant at the time of her death. He produced the remarkable theory that Jack the Ripper was a woman—a midwife who had gone to the room in Miller's Court to perform an abortion. After killing Mary Kelly in a sadistic frenzy, she had dressed up in her spare clothes and left, after burning her own bloody garments in the grate. The imme-

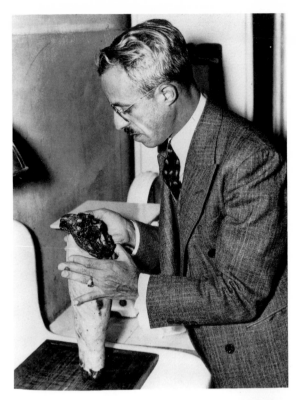

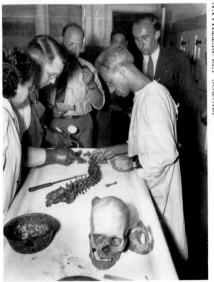

In 1938, Cleveland coroner S. R. Gerber (above) examines the grisly remains of a human leg found in the Cuyahoga River, thought to be that of the tenth victim of the "Mad Butcher of Kingsbury Run," who murdered and dissected at least a dozen Cleveland citizens during the period from 1935 to 1938. Coroner Gerber examines bones of two more victims, found in a waterfront dump (right). The victims were never identified. (See chapter 5.)

PHOTOS: UPI/BETTMANN

PHOTO: MARY EVANS/T. MEADEN

Crop circles—actually ellipses—found in the fields of Wiltshire, England, in July 1990. Note the rectangles and keylike shapes, which are associated with many of these unexplained phenomena. (See chapter 6.)

PHOTO: SYNDICATION INTERNATIONAL LTD.

Member of Parliament Victor Grayson speaking at a demonstration on Tower Hill, London, in 1909. He disappeared eleven years later. (See chapter 12.)

PHOTO: THE HULTON-DEUTSCH COLLECTION

PHOTO: TOPHAM

DAILY NEWS FINAL

HESS QUITS HITLER, FLIES TO SCOTLAND

No. 3 Nazi Lands by Chute

Pals—to
The End

Until 1941, Rudolf Hess was Hitler's deputy and personal secretary (left). The May 10, 1941, flight from Germany to Great Britain by a man claiming to be Hess made international headlines (right). Genuine doubts exist about his identity. (See chapter 13.)

PHOTO: TOPHAM

The wreckage of the plane from which "Hess" parachuted into Scotland.

PHOTOS: TOPHAM

After Harold Holt (left), the Prime Minister of Australia, disappeared while skin diving on December 17, 1967, evidence surfaced to support the theory that he had been a spy for China for decades. (See chapter 14.)

PHOTO: MARY EVANS PICTURE LIBRARY

An illustration from George Du Maurier's popular 1894 novel, *Trilby*, shows Svengali, the evil manipulator, hypnotizing Trilby into becoming his "slave." Stories of real-life Svengalis seem to have some basis in fact. (See chapter 17.)

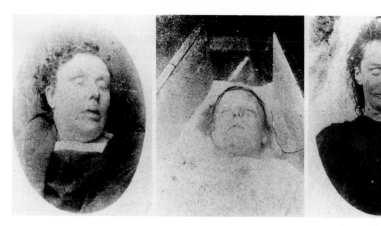

PHOTO: PRESS ASSOCIATION/TOPHAM

Scotland Yard photos of three of Jack the Ripper's East End victims: Annie Chapman, Mary Ann Nicholls, and Elizabeth Stride.

Anonymous letter (right) received by the Central News Agency on September 29, 1888, the day before the double murder of Elizabeth Stride and Catherine Eddowes. It was the first letter signed "Jack the Ripper." (See chapter 18.)

PHOTO: PRESS ASSOCIATION/TOPHAM

·25. Sept. 1888.

Dear Boss

    I keep on hearing the police have caught me but they wont fix me just yet. I have laughed when they look so clever and talk about being on the right track. That joke about Leather apron gave me real fits. I am down on whores and I shant quit ripping them till I do get buckled. Grand work the last job was I gave the lady no time to squeal. How can they catch me now. I love my work and want to start again. you will soon hear of me with my funny little games. I saved some of the proper red stuff in a ginger beer bottle over the last job to write with but it went thick like glue and I cant use it. Red ink is fit enough I hope ha. ha. The next job I do I shall clip the ladys ears off and send to the police officers just for jolly wouldnt you. Keep this letter back till I do a bit more work. then give it out straight. My knife's so nice and sharp I want to get to work right away if I get a chance. Good luck.

            yours truly

               Jack the Ripper

Dont mind me giving the trade name

PHOTO: SPRINGER/BETTMANN FILM ARCHIVE

Glenn Miller, playing with his band during a radio broadcast in the 1940s. Was he in the plane that disappeared while flying from London to Paris, or did he die in Ohio? (See chapter 22.)

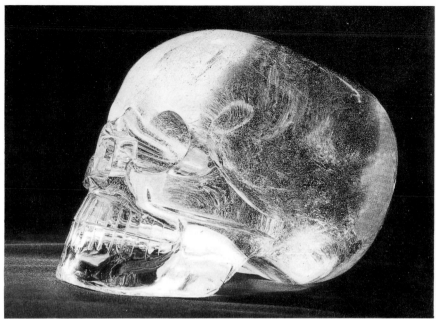

PHOTO: BRITISH MUSEUM

The "skull of doom": the life-sized human skull of rock crystal, origin unknown, is said to have mystical properties. (See chapter 30.)

PHOTO: THE BETTMANN ARCHIVE

Legend has it that one way to kill a vampire is by driving a stake into his heart. (See chapter 31.)

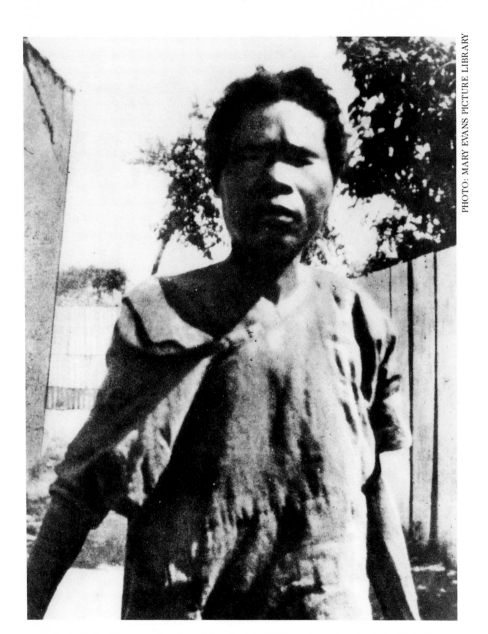

PHOTO: MARY EVANS PICTURE LIBRARY

Felicia Felix-Mentor, dead and buried in 1907, photographed in Haiti in 1937 by Zora Neale Hurston. (See chapter 33.)

diate objection to this theory is that Mary Kelly had no spare clothes—she was too poor. But the major objection is that there has never yet been a case of sadistic mutilation murder in which the killer was a woman. Stewart's "Jill the Ripper" is a psychological improbability.

In 1959 the journalist Donald McCormick revived a theory that dated to the 1920s. A journalist named William LeQueux described in a book called *Things I Know* how, after the Russian revolution, the Kerensky government had allowed him to see a manuscript written in French by the "mad monk" Rasputin and found in a safe in the basement of Rasputin's house. It was called *Great Russian Criminals*, and it declared that Jack the Ripper was a sadistic maniac named Alexander Pedachenko, who was sent to England by the Russian secret police to embarrass the British police force. Pedachenko, said LeQueux, was later arrested after he tried to kill a woman in Tver (Kalinin). In fact, LeQueux wrote three books about Rasputin, all full of cynical invention. And although they were written before *Things I Know*, they all fail to mention this extraordinary theory. But the strongest objection to the Rasputin-Pedachenko theory is that Rasputin did not speak a word of French and that he lived in a flat on the third floor, in a house with no cellar.

In the same year that McCormick's book was published, Daniel Farson investigated the Ripper murders for a television program and succeeded in securing an extraordinary scoop. Sir Melville Macnaghten had hinted strongly in his memoirs that he knew the identity of Jack the Ripper and spoke of three suspects, although he finally dismissed two of these. Farson succeeded in getting hold of Macnaghten's original notes and learned the name of this chief suspect: an unsuccessful barrister named Montague John Druitt—the man whose body was found in the Thames in early January 1889. Farson did some remarkable detective work and learned a great deal about Druitt's life and death.

Alas, when Macnaghten's comments are examined closely, it becomes very clear that he knew little or nothing about Druitt. He calls him a doctor when he was a barrister. He says he believes Druitt lived with his family, when in fact he lived in chambers, like most lawyers. He says he believes Druitt's mind snapped after his

"glut" in Miller's Court and that he committed suicide the following day. We know that Druitt killed himself three weeks later and
that he did so because he was depressed after going to see his
mother, who had become insane—he was afraid that the same
thing was happening to him. In fact, Macnaghten joined the
police force six months after the Ripper murders came to an end,
and it is obvious that his Druitt theory was pure wishful thinking,
without a shred of supporting evidence.

When, in 1960, I published a series of articles entitled "My
Search for Jack the Ripper" in the London *Evening Standard*, I
was asked to lunch by an old surgeon named Thomas Stowell,
who told me his own astonishing theory about the Ripper's identity: that it was Queen Victoria's grandson—the heir to the
throne—the Duke of Clarence, who died during the flu epidemic
in 1892. Sowell told me that he had seen the private papers of Sir
William Gull, Queen Victoria's physician, and that Gull had
dropped mysterious hints about Clarence and Jack the Ripper, as
well as mentioning that Clarence had syphilis, from which he died.
When, subsequently, I asked Stowell if I could write about his
theory, he said no. "It might upset Her Majesty." But in 1970 he
decided to publish it himself in a magazine called *The Criminologist*. Admittedly, he did not name his suspect—he called him
S—but he dropped dozens of hints that it was Clarence. Journalists took up the story and it caused a worldwide sensation. Stowell
was so shaken by all the publicity that he died a week later, trying
to repair the damage by claiming that his suspect was *not* the
Duke of Clarence.

A writer named Michael Harrison, working on a biography of
Clarence, carefully reread Stowell's article and realized that there
were many discrepancies between the career of S and that of the
Duke of Clarence. He concluded that Sir William Gull had indeed
referred to a suspect as S but that it was not the Duke of Clarence,
but someone who was closely acquainted with him. Studying
Clarence's acquaintances, he discovered the ideal suspect: James
Kenneth Stephen, a poet, lawyer, and man-about-town who had
become distinctly odd after being struck on the head by the vane
of a windmill and who, like Clarence, had died—in a mental
home—in 1892. Harrison had no trouble in disposing of Clarence

as a suspect, pointing out that at the time of the Miller's Court murder, Clarence was celebrating his father's birthday at San- dringham. But he was far less successful in finding even a grain of evidence to connect Stephen with the crimes. It is almost impos- sible to imagine the intellectual young aesthete, author of a great deal of published verse, stalking prostitutes with a knife.

The next major book on Jack the Ripper was optimistically entitled *Jack the Ripper: The Final Solution* (1976) and was written by a young journalist named Stephen Knight; he was following up a story propounded in a BBC television series called "The Ripper File," which in turn was based on an astounding story told by Joseph "Hobo" Sickert, son of the famous Victorian painter Walter Sickert. This story also involved the Duke of Clar- ence—although not, this time, as the murderer.

According to Hobo Sickert, his father and the heir to the throne were close friends, and the Duke often went slumming with the bohemian painter. In Sickert's studio in Cleveland Street, Soho, Clarence met an attractive young artist's model named Annie Crook. She became his mistress and in 1885 gave birth to a baby girl they named Alice Margaret. Then, according to Sickert, Clarence and his mistress got married in a private ceremony.

The story becomes more preposterous. When the secret mar- riage reached the ear of Queen Victoria, she was horrified. Annie was not only a commoner but a Catholic. The Prime Minister, Lord Salisbury, gave orders that Annie and the baby were to be kidnapped. A carriage drove up to the house at 6 Cleveland Street, and Annie and her baby daughter were hustled into a carriage and taken off to a mental home; there Sir William Gull performed a sinister brain operation on Annie to make her lose her memory. (This, incidentally, is virtually impossible; even nowadays scientists are uncertain where the source of memory lies, and in 1888 ignorance was total.)

The child, Alice, was handed over to a nanny in the East End of London—one Mary Kelly. Eventually, Alice found her way back to Walter Sickert and became his mistress. Joseph "Hobo" Sickert was the outcome of this union.

But Mary Kelly made the mistake of deciding to blackmail the royal family. She had taken a number of fellow prostitutes into her confidence, and the Prime Minister decided they all had to be killed. The task was given to Sir William Gull, who had sadistic tendencies anyway. His method was complicated but original; he would drive around the streets of Whitechapel in a coach until he saw his prospective victim, who would then be lured inside and disemboweled. His coachman, a man named Netley, was an accomplice. (A more recent theory suggests that Netley himself was Jack the Ripper.) And since Gull was also a Freemason, he left various clues in the form of hints of masonic ritual, such as the objects arranged so carefully around Annie Chapman and the misspelling of Jews as *Juwes*. Mary Kelly, of course, was the final victim.

It is not clear whether Knight believed this incredible farrago of nonsense. He probably did not. He knew that Gull had suffered a stroke in 1887 and would have been incapable of the murders. And a fellow investigator named Simon Wood had uncovered Annie Crook's rent book and discovered that she left the Cleveland Street address in 1886, a year before she is supposed to have been kidnapped. Moreover, the records show that she was living a perfectly normal life until 1920, when she died in a workhouse. Her religion was Church of England, not Roman Catholic. Simon Wood told Knight all of this soon after publication of *The Final Solution*, but Knight made no attempt to correct his "facts" in the paperback edition. Since his book had become something of a bestseller, it was not in his interests to admit that he had been deceived by Hobo Sickert.

It was, in fact, Hobo Sickert himself who pulled the rug out from under Knight by publicly admitting that the Jack the Ripper part of his story was pure invention. He insisted, however, that the story of Annie Crook giving birth to the Duke of Clarence's daughter—and the daughter becoming his own mother—was true. And in this he was probably being truthful. The most convincing part of Knight's book is his description of the various "clues" to the affair that Sickert slipped into his paintings.

In fact, this part of the story was confirmed—or at least strongly supported—in a book entitled *Sickert and the Ripper Crimes* (1990) by Jean Overton Fuller. It also demonstrates that Hobo Sickert did not invent his Jack the Ripper story out of whole cloth; it looks as if a remarkable coincidence led him to believe that there *was* some connection between the Duke of Clarence and the Ripper murders.

Jean Overton Fuller's mother had a friend named Florence Pash, an artist who was also an intimate of Walter Sickert. Florence had told Mrs. Fuller that Sickert knew the identity of Jack the Ripper and that he had carried some sinister secret around with him for the rest of his days—a secret that, at times, made him fear for his life. Florence Pash also confirmed that Mary Kelly *had* worked for Sickert as a nursemaid before the murders. We know that Sickert was obsessed by the Ripper murders and that he painted several pictures based on them.

All this, according to Jean Fuller, proves that Sickert was himself Jack the Ripper and that his motive was to kill the blackmailing prostitutes who knew the secret of Annie Crook.

This is obviously absurd. Why should Sickert go around murdering prostitutes because they knew that the Duke of Clarence had fathered an illegitimate child? Protecting his royal friend's good name is obviously an insufficient motive. Besides, Jack the Ripper was a sadist who enjoyed disemboweling women. Walter Sickert seems to have been one of the nastiest and most spoiled men who ever lived, but as far as we know, he was not a sadist.

What the Florence Pash evidence *does* seem to prove is that the Duke really fathered an illegitimate daughter, who became the mother of Joseph Sickert. It also confirms the unlikeliest part of Hobo Sickert's story: that Mary Kelly acted as a nursemaid to the baby. She may even have tried to blackmail Sickert. But even without the blackmail motif, we can understand why Sickert thought he was the custodian of a frightening secret. When Mary Kelly became—almost certainly by pure chance—the Ripper's final victim, he must have felt certain that the long arm of Buckingham Palace was involved. And when Hobo Sickert, the child of Walter Sickert and Annie Crook, came to hear of this tale of a royal love affair followed by murder, he understandably came to believe that the Palace was somehow involved in the murders. At least Fuller's book enables us to understand how the whole silly story came to be invented.

But that leaves us with the question: Who *was* the Ripper? In

1988, the centenary of the murders, half a dozen books propounded new theories—or old theories with a new twist.

Martin Fido's *Crimes, Detection and Death of Jack the Ripper* returned to Macnaghten's original notes, which listed three men as the chief Ripper suspects: Druitt (whom we have already dismissed), an insane Russian doctor named Ostrog (the origin of "Pedachenko"), and an insane Polish Jew named Kosminski, who was committed to an asylum in 1889. Sir Robert Anderson, the Assistant Commissioner of Police, is on record as remarking that the Ripper was a Polish Jew. Fido looked through the records of insane asylums and found a man named Aaron Kozminski, who died in 1891; but he was suffering from paranoid delusions and obviously lacked the cunning and intelligence to be the Ripper. A further search, however, uncovered a Nathan Kaminsky, treated for syphilis in March 1888, but about whom nothing more is known. Fido identifies him with David Cohen, another Polish Jew, who was committed to an asylum in December 1888 and died in the following year; Cohen was too violent to associate with his fellow patients. Fido speculates that a man who mumbled his name as "Nathan Kamin" might have been misheard as saying "David Cohen." This is true; it is also true that Cohen *might* have been Jack the Ripper. But there is not a shred of real evidence that he was.

Paul Begg, another "Ripperologist," points out in *Jack the Ripper: Uncensored Facts* that a close associate of Anderson, D. S. Swanson, wrote in the margin of Anderson's autobiography the comment that the Polish Jew died in "the Seaside Home." This would seem to rule out Kaminsky-Cohen as the Ripper.

In *The Ripper Legacy*, Martin Howells and Keith Skinner describe their fruitless investigation into an "Australian connection" mentioned by Daniel Farson: the notion that Druitt's cousin Lionel moved to Australia and wrote a pamphlet entitled "Jack the Ripper—I Knew Him." This trail led nowhere. Nevertheless, Howells and Skinner endorse Farson's conclusion that Druitt was Jack the Ripper and suggest that his "suicide" in the Thames was actually murder—that former associates from his Cambridge days, a society called The Apostles, learned that he was the Ripper and killed him in order to prevent a scandal. The book reveals their remarkable tenacity as researchers, but their theory contains as many "ifs" as Martin Fido's.

The "black magician" Aleister Crowley was convinced that the Ripper was another "magician" by the name of Roslyn D'Onston Stevenson (who preferred to be called "D'Onston"), who committed the murders as part of a ritual to gain supreme magical powers. Crowley tells a preposterous story about how D'Onston ate parts of the bodies at the scene of the crime and in so doing stained his ties with blood. The bloodstained ties were then found in a tin box under D'Onston's bed by his lesbian landlady.

In fact, D'Onston wrote a letter to Scotland Yard claiming to know the identity of Jack the Ripper: a doctor named Morgan Davies. His grounds for this belief were that he had heard Davies describing the murders to some fellow doctors and enacting the crimes with a gruesome realism that convinced D'Onston that Davies had actually committed them. The police seem to have treated it as yet another crank letter. In *A Casebook on Jack the Ripper* (1976), criminologist Richard Whittington-Egan went into the D'Onston theory at length but concluded that D'Onston was a fantasist and something of a con man.

Whittington-Egan's friend Melvin Harris decided to investigate D'Onston and discovered that Whittington-Egan had been less than just. Many of D'Onston's "fantasies" about his service in India and fighting under Garibaldi turned out to be true. Harris's *Jack the Ripper: The Bloody Truth* is an impressive piece of research. But it utterly fails to explain why a man who went to the police alleging that someone else was Jack the Ripper (on grounds that cannot be taken seriously) should himself have been the Whitechapel murderer.

Another brilliant piece of investigation was carried out by a Norwich accountant named Steward Hicks, who searched through the lunacy records for 1888 and came upon the name of a doctor named John Hewitt, who had been a patient in Coton Hill, an asylum in Staffordshire. Walter Sickert once described how he had taken a room near Camden Town and how his landlady was convinced that one of her previous lodgers, a student vet named John Hewitt, was Jack the Ripper—Hewitt had burned all his clothes in the grate (presumably to destroy bloodstains) and often stayed out all night. Hewitt's mother had finally removed him to Bournemouth, where he died of tuberculosis.

Could it be, wondered Hicks, that Hewitt's mother had actually realized he was Jack the Ripper and had had him committed to an asylum in Staffordshire? His research revealed that Hewitt had died of "general paralysis of the insane" in 1892, so he *could* be the Ripper. Hicks approached me with his theory, and I was able to help him gain access to the records of Coton Hill asylum, which had now been removed to the Staffordshire asylum. Alas, they revealed that Hewitt had committed himself to the asylum before the murders began. There was, however, still a slim hope for Mr. Hicks's theory. Since Hewitt had committed himself voluntarily to the asylum, he was allowed to go in and out as he pleased. If he had been away on the dates of the Whitechapel murders, that would constitute almost overwhelming circumstantial evidence that he was the Ripper. Regrettably, when Hicks finally gained full access to the papers in the Public Records Office, they made it clear that the dates when Hewitt was absent from the asylum were not the dates of the murders. Hicks tells me that, in spite of this, he still believes he may find evidence to show that Hewitt could have been Jack the Ripper. I wish him luck but cannot share his optimism.

Other theories that surfaced around the time of the Ripper centenary are that the killer was Frank Miles, a homosexual artist who was a friend of Oscar Wilde's (and who died insane), and that he was Joseph Barnett, the man who had lived with Mary Kelly until shortly before her murder. The Frank Miles theory—advocated by Mr. Thomas Toughill—is open to the same objection as Harrison's Stephen theory: that highly educated, "aesthetic" young poets (or artists) are not likely to turn to disemboweling. Bruce Paley, author of the Joseph Barnett theory, has a stronger case, in that whoever killed Mary Kelly locked the door behind him—yet the key is known to have been missing for some time. Barnett *could* easily have had the key. On the other hand, it may simply have turned up again before Mary Kelly was killed. And since Barnett is known to have been a mild little man, the theory that he killed five women because he was madly in love with Mary and disapproved of her habit of selling her favors is, to say the least, unlikely.

Jack the Ripper: Summing Up and Verdict, by myself and Robin Odell, also appeared during the centenary. In *Jack the Ripper in Fact and Fiction* (1965), Robin Odell had suggested that Jack the Ripper was a Jewish *shochet*, or ritual slaughterer, whose sadistic tendencies were stimulated by his profession until he began killing women. This is conceivable—except that it is hard to see why a sadist whose job involved slaughtering cattle by cutting their throats should have felt the need to kill women. And since all the records that might have enabled Odell to identify his slaughterer were destroyed during the Second World War, it seems that we must regard his theory as one more interesting might-have-been.

Since the early 1980s the phenomenon of serial murder has seized the public imagination, and careful psychological studies—particularly by the FBI's Behavioral Science Unit at Quantico, Virginia—have thrown some important new light on the phenomenon.* What can they tell us about Jack the Ripper? To begin with, the great majority of serial killers have emerged from working-class backgrounds. The middle- or upper-class serial killer is virtually unknown—presumably because the kind of frustrations that lead to multiple murder tend to spring from childhood poverty and ill treatment. This means that we can fairly confidently dismiss all the theories that involve an upper-class Ripper (or even a middle-class doctor like Matters's Dr. Stanley or D'Onston's Morgan Davies).

We must also recognize that part of the fascination of the Ripper murders lies in the mistaken notion that the murderer must have been a master criminal, a kind of Dracula who preferred to mutilate his victims rather than drink their blood. In fact, the surprising thing about most serial killers is that they tend to be ordinary, nondescript individuals. In many cases, they seem so gentle and polite that their acquaintances find it impossible to believe they were capable of murder. The Boston Strangler, Albert

---

*See Colin Wilson and Donald Seaman, *The Serial Killers* (1990).

DeSalvo, falls into this category; so does Peter Kürten, the Düsseldorf sadist, and Earl Nelson, the Gorilla Murderer—a charming young man who liked to discuss the Bible.

In many cases, the killer himself is totally unable to understand the urges that drive him to kill, and criminologists admit to being equally baffled. In September 1980 four black men were shot with a .22 rifle in Buffalo and Niagara Falls; in October two black cab drivers were stabbed to death and their hearts cut out. The killer had opened the ribcages and seemed to possess some medical skill. In December 1980 four black men were stabbed to death in New York by a man who simply approached them in the street.

The following January an eighteen-year-old army private named Joseph C. Christopher—a white—attacked a black soldier with a potato knife and then tried to emasculate himself. In custody, Christopher confessed to being the "Buffalo Slasher" as well as the .22 killer and the knife-wielding maniac of New York. People who had known Christopher in Buffalo were astounded; he was a quiet, ordinary teenager who was not known as a racist or a homosexual. (All the victims were male.) He had been raised in an Italian neighborhood by a dominant father and a passive mother—in that respect he resembled the Boston Strangler—and had adored his father, who had taught him to shoot. Christopher had been much affected by his father's death, which had occurred in 1976, when he was fourteen. He himself seemed to have no idea of why he had killed. As a "monster," Joe Christopher is a total disappointment. Yet he provides us with a more realistic image of the serial killer than the notion of a raving maniac.

The probability is that Jack the Ripper was as "ordinary" and as nondescript as Christopher. He was probably not even insane, like "Pedachenko," or violent, like Kaminsky-Cohen. So there is almost certainly no hope of establishing his identity more than a century after the murders. He was a "nobody."

Yet, oddly enough, there *is* a suspect who fits this description of a "murderous nobody." After Daniel Farson had presented his television program on Jack the Ripper in 1959, he received a letter from a man who signed himself *G.W.B.* and who explained that he was a seventy-seven-year-old who lived in Melbourne, Australia. He wrote:

When I was a nipper, about 1889, I was playing in the streets about 9:00 P.M. when my mother called, "Come in Georgie or JTR [Jack the Ripper] will get you." That night a man patted me on the head and said, "Don't worry, Georgie. You would be the last person JTR would touch." [This man was apparently Georgie's own father, who was born in 1850 and so would have been thirty-eight at the time of the murders.] My father was a terrible drunkard and night after night he would come home and kick my mother and us kids about something cruelly. About the year 1902 I was taught boxing, and after feeling proficient to hold my own, I threatened my father that if he laid a hand on my mother or brothers I would thrash him. He never did after that, but we lived in the same house and never spoke to each other. Later, I emigrated to Australia. I was booked to depart with three days' notice, and my mother asked me to say goodbye to my father. It was then he told his foul history and why he did those terrible murders, and advised me to change my name because he would confess before he died. Once settled in Melbourne I assumed another name. However, my father died in 1912 and I was watching the papers carefully, expecting a sensational announcement.

This, of course, never came. Georgie's explanation for his father's heavy drinking is that he had always wanted a daughter but that his first child—a female—was an imbecile; later children were all boys. "During the confession of those awful murders, he explained that he did not know what he was doing but his ambition was to get drunk and an urge to kill every prostitute that accosted him."

His father, Georgie explained, was a dung collector, and on one occasion, after killing a woman, he had removed his outer pair of trousers, which were saturated with blood, and hidden them in the manure. Later, while his partner went to have a meal of sausage and mash, Jack (this was the father's name) buried himself in the manure to keep warm and upon hearing a policeman asking questions about Jack the Ripper felt "scared to death."

Many sadistic killers commit their crimes only after they have been drinking heavily, and "Georgie's" account of his father rings psychologically true. A highly dominant individual, a bully who beat his wife and probably felt a contempt for all women, might well have experienced a kind of homicidal rage when accosted by prostitutes. It is also hard to imagine why a seventy-seven-year-old man should bother to write an anonymous letter from Melbourne with a completely false story. And, assuming his story to be true, it is equally hard to see why his father should have invented the story about being Jack the Ripper.

It is possible that, even at this distance in time, a check of the records of ships bound for Australia in 1902 could reveal the identity of "G.W.B." and that this in turn might lead to uncovering the identity of a man called Jack (surname probably beginning with a *B*) who was born in 1850, died in 1912, and was a manure collector in Whitechapel in 1888. We would have no means of being certain that this man was Jack the Ripper; but he would seem to me far and away the likeliest candidate.

19

Junius: Who Was the Eighteenth Century's Most Feared Satirist?

In these days of investigative journalism, it is almost impossible to imagine a man who succeeds in maintaining a secret identity when everyone in the country is agog with curiosity to know who he is. It happens only in children's comics. Yet that is precisely what happened in England in the final years of the eighteenth century. The mystery man was a writer who called himself Junius and whose murderously satirical letters set the whole country laughing at the government, and even at the King himself. As a satirist and literary stylist, Junius compares favorably with Daniel Defoe, Jonathan Swift, and Samuel Butler—all of whom published their early works anonymously. But in these famous cases, the sheer brilliance of the satire made it inevitable that the identity of the authors of *Robinson Crusoe*, *Gulliver's Travels*, and *Erewhon* should be discovered. Junius's secret went with him to the grave.

The story begins in the reign of George III, the King whose "tea tax" was to cause the American Revolution and whose General Wellington later defeated Napoléon.

George III came to the throne in 1760, and his reign was troubled almost from the beginning. Under its greatest war leader, Prime Minister William Pitt, Britain had been fighting France for four years and was winning the war. The new King was anxious to end it, to the disgust of his subjects, who wanted to see the French well and truly thrashed. And Pitt—who not only wanted to thrash the French but to go to war with the Spaniards as well—resigned in 1761. The war came to an end two years later, and the "surrender" made the King still more unpopular.

But the real trouble—which brought England close to revolution—was caused by a radical politician named John Wilkes. He was the kind of man who made every old-fashioned English gentleman foam at the mouth. He was blasphemous, ugly, cross-eyed, and a tireless seducer—but such a natural charmer that he liked to boast that he needed only half an hour's start on the handsomest man in England. He had been a member of Sir Francis Dashwood's Hell-Fire Club, a group that liked to dress as monks and invoke the Devil; Wilkes had terrified them when he introduced a sooty baboon into one of their orgies and they mistook it for Satan.

When Wilkes was elected to Parliament in 1757, he became a supporter of William Pitt. And when the King appointed his old tutor, a Scot named Lord Bute, as Secretary of State, and Bute began making peace with the French, Pitt resigned in disgust. Wilkes naturally regarded Bute as an enemy. Besides, most of the English detested the Scots—it was less than twenty years since Bonnie Prince Charlie had marched on London. So Wilkes founded a violently anti-Scottish newspaper called *The North Briton*. (A north Briton was, of course, a Scot—it was rather as if someone had founded an anti-Semitic newspaper called *The Israelite*.) Among other things it hinted that Lord Bute had gained his position by sleeping with the Queen Mother, an accusation that made the King apoplectic. The smear campaign was so successful that Bute resigned.

But now Wilkes went too far and put into the King's mouth a satirical speech—supposedly written by Bute—that amounted to an accusation of base betrayal of Britain's allies in the war. Wilkes was seized and thrown into the Tower of London, which—inevitably—boosted his popularity with the disgruntled populace. Wilkes claimed "Parliamentary privilege"—whereby a Member of Parliament has a right to speak his mind freely on political issues—and was released after a week. He now proceeded to make the King and his government still more embarrassed by suing Lord Halifax, the Secretary of State, for trespass. (He was backed financially by Lord Temple, Pitt's brother-in-law, who had also financed *The North Briton*.) Wilkes won his case; he was awarded vast damages—£5,000—and the Secretary of State lost his job.

The King was now out for Wilkes's blood. To anybody with any sense, it should have been obvious that his administration was accident-prone and had better keep its head down. Instead, the new Secretary of State, Lord Sandwich,* decided to make Wilkes pay for his victory. The House of Commons voted that Wilkes's attack on the King had been a "seditious libel." They also bribed a printer to hand over a pornographic poem—entitled "An Essay on Woman"—that Wilkes was having printed, and some of its juicier passages were read aloud in the House of Lords. The Lords thought it a joke, for everyone knew that Lord Sandwich had looser morals than Wilkes. (When Sandwich told Wilkes that he would either die of the pox or on the gallows, Wilkes retorted, "That depends on whether I embrace your mistress or your principles.") But Parliament was shocked and voted that Wilkes had no right to Parliamentary privilege after all. Wilkes was forced to flee abroad to avoid prison, but this only increased his popularity with the mob. The printer who had handed over the "Essay on Woman" could find no one to employ him and committed suicide.

The King's next choice as Prime Minister was George Grenville, a former ally of Pitt. He was capable enough but proved to be a bore who was inclined to deliver long lectures; the King got rid of him in 1765. But it was under Grenville that the government first stirred up revolution in the American colonies by imposing a Stamp Act—a tax on newspapers, advertisements, and legal documents. This met with such violent resistance in America that the next administration was forced to repeal it. It was a "dry run" for the Boston Tea Party seven years later.

Grenville had been one of the chief persecutors of John Wilkes.

---

*This was the man who invented the sandwich; rather than interrupt his gambling, he would eat a piece of meat between two slices of bread.

Now the King turned to a defender of Wilkes, the Marquis of Rockingham, who had friends on both sides, Whig and Tory. Wilkes decided to return to England, and the King's troubles began all over again. Wilkes stood for a London Parliamentary seat and was soundly beaten. Since he was an outlaw, the government did its best to have him arrested. He evaded them and got himself elected MP for Middlesex. Then he gave himself up. If the King had had any sense, he would have pardoned him. Instead, Wilkes received two years in prison and a fine of a thousand pounds. Wilkes instantly became the most popular man in England. An angry crowd rescued him from the officers of the law. He gave himself up again and was put in jail. A mob gathered and looked as if it would storm the jail; troops fired and killed five, wounding fifteen.

Wilkes wrote a violent article attacking the use of force against the rioters; Parliament voted it libelous and expelled him again. He got himself reelected by rebellious voters; Parliament threw him out again. He became the most popular cause of his time; there had been nothing like it since Daniel Defoe had got himself stuck in the pillory—for the same kind of offense—in 1703 and was pelted with flowers instead of rotten eggs. The well-meaning King, with his pathetic desire for popularity and his determination to be a "true Briton" (like all the Hanovers, he was a German by parentage), was stumbling from disaster to disaster.

Rockingham resigned; party quarrels were too much for him. Now the King had an idea that he must have regarded as brilliant and foolproof: to persuade Pitt to take over again. That ought to undo all the squabbling and bitterness of the past six years. Unfortunately, Pitt's manic depression was turning into madness. When the King made him Earl of Chatham, Pitt virtually retired to the House of Lords, and the administration was left in the hands of a much younger man, Lord Grafton. The country was in a state of chaos.

And it was at this point that Junius stepped into the picture.

Now whoever Junius was, he was a man who, for some reason, detested the King and his political allies and was a supporter of Pitt and Wilkes. He had a particular antipathy toward Lord Grafton, who had by now quarreled with Pitt. In 1768 Pitt and Grenville—who had also quarreled—received letters signed Junius, urging them to make up and unite against Grafton. In fact, Pitt resigned shortly afterward. Now Junius decided to take his case to the public.

His first letter was sent to a newspaper called *The Public Advertiser*, owned by Henry Sampson Woodfall. Newspapers were still something of a novelty in England. They had begun about fifty years earlier; by Junius's time there were eleven of them in London alone. Most of their profit came from advertisements, but readers' letters were also immensely popular—in fact, Junius's first letter, dated January 21, 1769, was held up for several days while a backlog of letters was printed.

The style of Junius's letters is not immediately appealing to a modern audience; it seems rather ponderous and pedantic. As far as his contemporaries were concerned, however, that was an advantage; they could see that he was a serious-minded man who knew how to turn a good phrase. And the very first sentence of his first letter makes it clear that what concerns him is the freedom of the British people and the feeling that designing politicians like Prime Minister Grafton were trying to steal it. Junius starts with a contentious but rather dull statement: "The submission of a free people to the executive authority of government is no more than a compliance with laws which they themselves have enacted." The English, he goes on to say, are a generous and good-natured people, who naturally respect the law and love their King. So it fills him with indignation to see these good qualities abused by schemers: "The situation of this country is alarming enough to rouse the attention of every man . . . " So far, his readers must have stifled a yawn. But a few sentences later they were startled into attention: "The finances of a nation, sinking under its debts and expenses, are committed to a young nobleman already ruined by play." To accuse the King's Prime Minister of being a dissolute gambler was strong stuff.

Next, Junius turned his attention to Britain's most popular soldier, the Marquis of Granby, whose victories in the seven-year war with France had fired British patriotism and led hundreds of pubs and inns to call themselves the Marquis of Granby. At the battle of Minden, Granby wanted to charge the French, but his superior, Lord Sackville, ordered him not to. It later became obvious that if Granby had been allowed to charge, the French would have been utterly routed. Sackville was dismissed and Granby took his place.

But like many fine soldiers, he was out of his depth in politics, and when he was made peacetime commander-in-chief, he was less than brilliant. Even so, when Junius remarked with suave malice: "Nature has been sparing of her gifts to this noble lord," it was as shocking as if someone had dismissed Winston Churchill or General Eisenhower as a dithering idiot after the Second World War. And when Junius went on to accuse Granby of using his position to "heap promotion on his favourites and dependants" and ignore merit in the rest of the army, he was virtually accusing Britain's war hero of being a crook.

It is not clear whether Junius made these accusations to produce shock and outrage. But he could hardly have chosen a better way to make himself famous—or infamous. For one of Granby's most distinguished fellow soldiers, Sir William Draper, quickly leapt to his defense and wrote an indignant letter to *The Public Advertiser*, whose owner must have been rubbing his hands with glee. Draper began by furiously accusing Junius of being a "felonious robber of private character," a "cowardly base assassin" who did not have the courage to sign his real name. Then Draper went on to defend his commander-in-chief, saying, in essence, that he was a "decent chap" whom everybody liked and who was too generous for his own good.

This kind of thing must have made readers groan with boredom. As to not keeping his promises—another of Junius's slanders—there were some cases, said Draper, where it was better not to keep promises. He was obviously thinking of some scheming friend of Granby's who had persuaded the general to make rash promises when he had had too much to drink—a person, says Draper indignantly, "who would pervert the open, unsuspecting moments of convivial mirth into sly, insidious applications for preferment . . . and who would endeavour to surprise a good man who cannot bear to see anyone leave him dissatisfied."

Junius, of course, had achieved his goal. He was being treated seriously by a famous soldier, and the delighted public was being allowed to witness their squabble. Junius's next letter began with deceptive benevolence and generosity: "Your defense of Lord Granby does honour to the goodness of your heart." He went on to praise Draper's "honest unreflecting indignation"—although the word *unreflecting* gave warning of what was to come. Then he took the gloves off and went straight for the chin: "It is you, Sir William, who makes your friend appear awkward and ridiculous, by giving him a laced suit of tawdry qualifications which nature never intended him to wear." And he became positively murderous when he answered Draper's ill-advised remarks about promises made in "convivial mirth." "It is you, Sir William Draper, who have taken pains to represent your friend in the character of a drunken landlord, who deals out his promises as liberally as his liquor, and will suffer no man to leave his table sorrowful or sober. None but an intimate friend, who must have seen him frequently in these unhappy, disgraceful moments, could have described him so well."

Draper must have winced. But he lacked the common sense to see that he was giving Junius exactly the kind of publicity he wanted. Besides, he had been an academic and felt he could exchange urbane insults with the best of them. So back he came for more, this time accusing Junius (probably correctly) of being a bitter and disappointed man who "delights to mangle carcasses with a hatchet." Then he took up the impossible task of defending his friend Granby against the hatchet, failing to realize that he was only succeeding in making him look like a helpless dummy. He went on to answer Junius's charges that he had feathered his own nest and entered into precise details about his income that only revealed how much Junius had him on the defensive.

Junius came back in his smoothest and deadliest form: "I should justly be suspected of acting upon motives of more than common enmity to Lord Granby, if I continued to give you fresh materials or occasion for writing in his defense." But then he proceeded to indulge in another of his favorite tricks: an appearance of omniscience. He went on to talk about Draper's income and career as if he knew more about them than Draper did. Then he accused Draper of being a money-grubbing liar who had turned his back on the army in exchange for a pension—which

Junius called a "sordid provision for himself and his family."

Now we can begin to see Junius's technique. There can be no doubt that he *was* bitter and twisted. He was a man with a grievance, and his specialty was libelous accusations that would cause maximum suffering to the accused, as well as maximum glee to the general public. One gets the impression that he was a kind of sadist who didn't care what he said so long as it hurt; but he was clever enough to make his accusations sound plausible—as if he was an insider with a secret source of knowledge.

The general public, of course, loves to see authority attacked and ridiculed. Things have not changed in the slightest in the two centuries or so that have passed since the days of Junius; any kind of scandal about a politician can still sell newspapers. In present-day America, politicians have no legal redress against libel—provided malice cannot be established—so that journalists can invent virtually what they like. After the Kennedy assassination, a play called *Macbird* accused Lyndon Johnson of being the murderer; it was pure invention, but its author, a dissident academic, must have been bewildered when it became the hit of the season on Broadway. In England, a magazine called *Private Eye* has specialized since the sixties in libelous and insulting stories that might have been concocted by Junius; but although the magazine has been sued to the verge of bankruptcy, it continues to flourish as the public appetite for malicious "dirt" remains insatiable. Junius was simply the first to discover that there is a permanent demand for "dirt."

The naïve Draper went on to increase Junius's fame by writing more pained and explanatory letters; Junius continued to treat him with ferocious contempt. In his third letter he dismissed him patronizingly: "And now, Sir William, I shall take my leave of you for ever. . . . In truth, you have some reason to hold yourself indebted to me. From the lessons I have given you, you may collect a profitable instruction for your future life."

Junius ignored Draper's third reply and turned his attention to the Prime Minister, the Duke of Grafton. True to form, Junius accused him of being a scheming politician who preferred his own interests to the public good. Then he turned his attention to a recent scandal concerning the Middlesex by-election, which the government had fervently hoped that Wilkes would lose—and which, in fact, Wilkes had won with the aid of a drunken rabble. (Wilkes was now, of course, in jail.)

A man named Clarke had been killed in a brawl, and an Irishman named MacQuirk, a local chairman of the anti-Wilkes party, was accused of his murder, together with another man named Balf. Both were sentenced to death, but this was obviously unfair; the evidence against Balf was weak, and MacQuirk had obviously not intended to commit murder. Both were pardoned by Grafton. Junius pretended to think that this was an outrageous interference in the course of justice, a deliberate tampering with the evidence; a murderer went free because he was against Wilkes. He ended by asking: "Has it never occurred to you that, while you were withdrawing this desperate wretch from justice . . . that there is another man, who is the favourite of the country, whose pardon would have been accepted with gratitude?"

He meant, of course, John Wilkes, and he went on to use his favorite technique of invention: "Have you quite forgotten that this man was once your Grace's friend?" Grafton was to protest again and again that Wilkes was only a casual acquaintance; Junius ignored him and went on repeating his charge: that Grafton had stabbed his friend in the back. Subsequent investigation by historians indicates that Grafton was telling the truth. But Junius never let the truth spoil a good accusation.

What so alarmed the government—and the King—was that Wilkes's imprisonment had made him potentially the most dangerous man in England. Junius went on to accuse Grafton of fleeing London for two nights during the Wilkes riots and leaving the city to be defended by two of his incompetent underlings. Grafton had apparently spent those two nights with his mistress, Nancy Parsons, and Junius jeered at her "faded beauty"—although he later pretended to be shocked when Grafton broke with her and married someone else, declaring: "His baseness to this woman is beyond description or belief." When Grafton married, Junius sneered at him as a reformed rake who had tired of debauchery.

Junius's next letter to Grafton reached new heights of malice: "Let me be permitted to consider your character and conduct," he wrote ominously, "merely as a subject of curious speculation." And after calling him lazy, dishonest, and inconsistent, he added generously: "For the sake of your mistress, the lover shall be spared. I will not lead her into public, as you have done, nor will I insult the memory of her departed beauty. Her sex, which alone made her amiable in your eyes"—he is implying that Grafton will mount anything that wears a skirt—"makes her respectable in mine."

He went on to give what he claimed to be a sympathetic account of Grafton's ancestors—"those of your Grace . . . left no distressing examples of virtue"—and of his own career—"grave and plausible enough to be thought fit for business; too young for treachery." But, he claimed, Grafton lost no time in stabbing his patron William Pitt in the back, then grabbing power under Rockingham and betraying his friend Wilkes. Like Dr. Goebbels, Junius felt that the best way to make people believe a lie was to repeat it.

After more than two centuries these insults make us smile. But if we try to put ourselves in the place of his victims, we can see that they must have felt choked with hopeless rage. Junius was not a man so much as a scorpion. When one angry victim challenged Junius to a duel, Junius declined politely: "You would fight, but others would assassinate." He was probably right. The sheer malice and unfairness of his attacks would have led some of his victims to make sure he was stabbed in the dark.

In December 1769 Junius shocked everyone, including his own supporters, by launching an attack on the King himself. His success in evading exposure had obviously given him the confidence to risk imprisonment. In earlier letters he had been careful to speak of the King with the deepest respect, referring to him in a letter to Grafton as "an amiable, accomplished prince." Now he addressed the King directly, reminding him of one of his earliest utterances when he came to the throne: "I glory in the name of Briton." The King undoubtedly meant that he regarded himself as a Briton rather than a German; Junius pretended to think that he was deliberately making a distinction between Britons and Englishmen, to emphasize his affection for the Scots: "While the natives of Scotland are not in actual rebellion, they are undoubtedly entitled to protection; nor do I mean to condemn the policy of giving some encouragement to the novelty of their affections."

He patronizingly told the King that he attributed his blunders to inexperience. He went on to defend Wilkes and to describe the King's campaign against him as mean and ridiculous. After taking swipes at the King for oppressing the Irish and the Americans, he warned him against the "fawning treachery" of the Scots. Finally, he told him condescendingly that "the affections of your subjects may still be recovered" but that this would mean ceasing to be driven by petty resentments. The King, wrote Junius, should face his subjects like a gentleman and "tell them you have been fatally deceived" by crooked ministers. He ended on a note of warning that sounded dangerously like sedition. The people were loyal to the House of Hanover, he wrote, because they expected justice. The House of Stuart—to which Bonnie Prince Charlie belonged—was "only contemptible," but armed with royal power it would become formidable. "The prince who imitates their conduct should be warned by their example" (i.e., by King Charles losing his head), "and while he plumes himself upon the security of his title to the crown, should remember that, as it was acquired by one revolution, it may be lost by another."

That made everyone gasp. The novelist Horace Walpole—son of a former Prime Minister—described it as "the most daring insult ever offered to a prince but in times of open rebellion." The printer, Woodfall, was arrested on a charge of seditious libel. The jury refused to convict, and he was released on payment of costs. Recognizing his own danger, Junius warned Woodfall to take every possible precaution, as "I would not survive a discovery three days."

How *had* he survived discovery for so long? By an elaborate system of concealment. It was easy to get his letters to the *Public Advertiser*—he could send them by messenger or by post. But communications from the newspaper were altogether more dangerous. Many people wrote to Junius and sent him "sensitive" information. Junius had letters addressed to him, via the printer, under various pseudonyms at various coffeehouses (there were literally hundreds), and the printer would signal that a letter was waiting by inserting a coded advertisement in the newspaper.

Junius frequently changed his poste restante address at short notice, informing Woodfall with messages like: "Change to the Somerset Coffee House, and let no mortal know the alteration." And he obviously spent some time worrying about what would happen if Woodfall became careless: "I am persuaded that you are too honest a man to contribute to my destruction."

Junius also corresponded with Wilkes, who was released from jail in 1770 and promptly returned to Parliament; Wilkes made a few tactful attempts to persuade Junius to reveal his identity but respected his determination to have no confidantes.

In fact, Junius was beginning to feel tired; the sheer strain of taking on opponent after opponent, like a masked swordsman, was obviously beginning to tell. Besides, when Grafton resigned in 1770—undoubtedly rattled by Junius's insults—and Wilkes was released in the same year, Junius had achieved his basic purpose. The King refused to be stampeded into making more concessions to the Libertarian Party and appointed the efficient and good-natured Lord North as his First Minister. Junius had earlier attacked Lord North: "It may be candid to suppose that he has hitherto voluntarily concealed his talents; intending, perhaps, to astonish the world when we least expect it." But he proved wrong, and Lord North developed into an excellent administrator.

Junius wrote his last public letter in January 1772. When, a year later, Henry Woodfall did his best to induce Junius to return to the fray with hints in the *Public Advertiser*, Junius replied: "If I were to write again I must be as silly as any of the horned cattle that run mad through the City. . . . The cause and the public—both are given up." In fact, the world had heard its last of Junius—although his collected letters, in book form, achieved considerable popularity. In this collection Junius wrote: "I am the sole depository of my own secret, and it shall perish with me." And as far as we know, he kept his word.

So who was Junius? In the days of Rockingham's Prime Ministership, the chief suspect was the brilliant Irishman Edmund Burke, who was passionately liberal—although by no means radical, like Wilkes. He was a friend of Dr. Johnson, Oliver Goldsmith, Sir Joshua Reynolds, and David Garrick (the most famous actor of his time). Like Wilkes, he wanted to curb the corrupt practices in the royal court and so was detested by the King. He argued strongly against the King's policies in America, suggesting—correctly—that they would lead to revolution, and after the Boston tea party he argued for the repeal of the tea tax. If Burke had been listened to, America might well still be a British colony. He was later horrified by the French Revolution and became one of its most passionate opponents, thus endearing himself to all his former enemies.

Burke was brilliant enough to have written the Junius letters. But he was also a man of immense integrity. So when he wrote to a friend, Charles Townshend, "I now give you my word and honour that I am not the author of Junius," we may take it to be the truth.

In the nineteenth century book after book about Junius appeared; speculations about his identity became as popular as speculations about the identity of Jack the Ripper did a century later. (In his edition of the Junius letters, Professor John Cannon offers a "short list" of sixty-one names.) An obvious possibility is Wilkes himself; but the exchange of letters between Wilkes and Junius that later came to light makes it clear that this is out of the question.

One writer announced confidently that Junius was George III himself, averting revolution by giving his subjects a chance to let off steam. Another writer identified Junius as the historian Edward Gibbon, resting his case upon the sheer absence of evidence, which, the writer claimed, only went to prove how far the historian had gone to conceal his guilty secret. Another staked the claim of Lord George Sackville, the military commander who had been dismissed after the battle of Minden in favor of the Marquis of Granby; certainly, Junius's attacks on Granby make this plausible, if unlikely. (Sackville was a warm supporter of the King.) Lord Chesterfield, the author of the famous *Letters to His Son*, is another candidate; but his health at the time was so poor—he was half-blind and bedridden—that it is virtually impossible that he was Junius. Perhaps the unlikeliest nominee was Thomas Paine, the author of *The Rights of Man* (1791), a polemic directed at Burke. At the time of the Junius letters, Paine was still struggling to make a start in life—as a grocer, a tobacconist, a schoolmaster, and an exciseman—and still had a number of

years to go before he learned to write; it was not until 1774 that
Benjamin Franklin persuaded him to emigrate to America.

All this seems to suggest that Junius was one of the lesser-
known names of the period. Charles Everett, the editor of the
1927 edition of the letters, devotes a long introduction to proving
that Junius was Lord Shelburne, a member of the opposition and
later Prime Minister; the historian Sir Lewis Namier destroyed
that case in a brief review in which he pointed out that Shelburne
was on the Continent in the summer of 1771 when Woodfall
received two private letters from Junius that had to have been
written in London. Shelburne's private secretary, Laughlin
Macleane, has been strongly suggested by two recent academics,
one of whom has claimed to have a statement, signed by Shelburne, identifying Macleane as Junius. The chief problem here is
that Macleane was attacked by Junius, who made fun of his
stammer. This could have been a deliberate attempt to mislead;
but Junius did not use his own name in this attack but another of
his pseudonyms, Vindex. And since no one but Woodfall knew
that Vindex was Junius, this seems to dispose of Macleane—
whether or not Shelburne believed his secretary to be Junius.
Besides, Macleane was an ardent Scottish patriot, and Junius
clearly loathed the Scots, losing no opportunity to jeer about their
corruption, stupidity, and cowardice.

This brings us to the chief suspect: Sir Philip Francis, who was
at the time a twenty-eight-year-old senior civil servant in the War
Office. Francis came under suspicion in 1812, when the private
letters of Junius to Woodfall were published in a new edition. They
revealed that Junius used various other pseudonyms, including
Vindex and Veteran. These letters pay close attention to the
affairs of the War Office and indicate that Junius knew far more
about it than any outsider could learn.

In 1772, the year the Junius letters ceased, Francis went to
India, where he clashed with Warren Hastings—the chief servant
of the East India Company, which virtually governed India. On his
return to England, he entered Parliament as a Liberal, was
knighted, and pursued Hastings with considerable vindictiveness,
being largely instrumental in having him impeached for corruption and exceeding his powers.

In 1813, when he was seventy-three, Francis was identified as Junius in a book by a man named John Taylor. He flatly denied it, calling the accusation "silly and malignant." Yet when he married again in the following year, he gave his wife the Junius letters as a wedding present. He also gave her Taylor's book on the mystery of Junius. His wife took the hint; she had no doubt that he was Junius. And Francis was aware of this. He had only, she remarked, to deny it, and she would have given up the idea; but he never did.

Professor Cannon has no doubt whatever that Francis was Junius. He points out that in 1772—before Francis was posted to India at the huge salary of £10,000 a year—Junius changed his pseudonym to *Veteran*. In 1771 Christopher D'Oyly, a friend of Francis, told him he intended to resign as Deputy Secretary of War; it is obvious from their correspondence that both disliked their chief, Lord Barrington. Francis hoped to succeed D'Oyly but was passed over in favor of a man named Chamier. "Veteran" was soon writing to his printer: "Having nothing better to do, I propose to entertain myself and the public with torturing that bloody wretch Barrington. He has just appointed a French broker his deputy. I hear from all sides it is looked upon as a most impudent insult to the army. Be careful not to have it known to come from me. Such an insignificant creature is not worth the generous rage of Junius." In which case, why bother with such small fry?

In March 1772 Francis resigned his post. Junius wrote to the printer: "The enclosed is fact, and I wish it could be printed tomorrow. The proceedings of this wretch are unaccountable. There must be some mystery in it, which I hope will soon be discovered to his confusion. Next to the Duke of Grafton, I verily believe that the blackest heart in the kingdom belongs to Lord Barrington." The "enclosed" declared: "I desire you will inform the public that the worthy Lord Barrington, not contented with having driven Mr. D'Oyly out of the War Office, has at last contrived to expel Mr. Francis."

Handwriting evidence also links Francis and Junius. In 1771 a Miss Giles in Bath was the recipient of some polite verses, and the handwriting on the cover was that of Junius. In 1870 a handwriting expert, Charles Chabot, identified the verses as being written by Francis's cousin, Richard Tilman. Francis's second wife later produced copies of the verses in her husband's handwriting, saying that he had given them to her as examples of his own early verses. In letters discovered in the late nineteenth century, Francis's authorship was confirmed by his cousin.

This raises an obvious question: Surely we have only to compare the handwriting of Junius with that of Francis to have our solution? But it is not as simple as that. Junius must have known that unless he went to considerable lengths to disguise his handwriting, it could be his downfall. It was only after careful study that Charles Chabot concluded that the handwriting of Junius was a disguised version of Francis's.

Another piece of evidence emerged in 1969, when French research revealed that a French ambassadorial report sent to Louis XVI in the 1770s attributed the letters to one Thaddeus Fitzpatrick, a man-about-town. Now in fact, we know this is impossible because Fitzpatrick died in 1771, while Junius was still writing. But the report declares that Fitzpatrick obtained his information from his friend Philip Francis, a clerk in the War Office.

Fitzpatrick had quarreled with the actor David Garrick and with Lord Chief Justice Mansfield, two men who were savaged by Junius. So there is a strong case to be made for Fitzpatrick being a collaborator of Junius. This does not contradict Junius's assertion that he was "the sole depository of his own secret," since this was made in the year after Fitzpatrick's death.

Wherever the French ambassador obtained his information—information that seems to have been denied to his British colleagues—it certainly has the ring of plausibility. One of the reasons that posterity has found the Junius problem so fascinating is that he seems to be a solitary outsider figure, a man with a truly awesome gift for savage invective and the cut and thrust of polemic, who succeeded, like the Scarlet Pimpernel, in keeping his light hidden under a bushel. It is a fascinating and romantic conception, but the major objection to it is that it is too romantic. Scarlet Pimpernels exist only in the imagination of novelists.

What seems far more plausible is that a middle-aged man-about-town, who nurses powerful grudges against people he actually knows, should decide to deliver some sharp rebukes under the cloak of anonymity and should take into his confidence a sarcastic and disaffected young clerk from the War Office who can provide inside information. (One of Francis's jobs was to report speeches in the House of Lords, so he had the opportunity to overhear much political gossip.) The picture of two men chuckling and egging one another on is somehow more believable than the picture of a solitary misanthrope nursing his own secret. Moreover, if Thaddeus Fitzpatrick was the initiator of the project, this would also explain why the later Junius letters—those that followed his death in 1771—show a falling off in quality. The rear end of the pantomime horse found himself sadly missing his partner.

This could also explain Francis's curious attitude toward the book that accused him of being Junius. More than forty years after the smoke of battle had cleared and most of his victims were dead—including Grafton himself—surely there could have been no harm in acknowledging that he was Junius? But if this meant acknowledging that he was merely a *half* of Junius—and the lesser half at that—then it would obviously be far better to keep silent and allow his contemporaries—and posterity—to give him the full credit, while continuing to deny it in a manner that convinced nobody. It was a way of having his cake and eating it.

Certainly, everything we know of Francis indicates that he could have been Junius (or half-Junius). Cannon describes him as "a man of fierce animosities, harsh and sarcastic." He quarreled with most of his friends and benefactors, says his biographer Herman Merivale, with all "those who wished well to him, defended him, showered benefits on him." All "appear . . . in his written records, branded with some unfriendly or contemptuous notice, some insinuated or pronounced aspersion." Francis broke with two of his former patrons, Henry Fox and John Calcraft, and when they quarreled, made his typically stinging and ungenerous assessment of them: "There was not virtue enough in either of them to justify their quarreling. If either of them had common honesty he could never have been the friend of the other." The phrase has the typical Junian ring. Dining with Francis in the last year of his life, Cannon reports, the philosopher Sir James Mackintosh was led to comment,"The vigorous hatreds which seemed to keep Francis alive were very amusing."

In other words, Francis had a streak of paranoia. And this is how Cannon summarizes Junius: "Junius believed . . . that it was necessary to save the constitution from violation, but the desperate plot to destroy the liberties of the subject existed only in his own mind."

There is not enough space here to describe the affair of the impeachment of Warren Hastings and Francis's part in it; but it confirms that Francis was a man who, like Junius, was a good hater with little generosity.

Finally, in the 1950s, a Swedish philologist, Alvar Ellegard, undertook a computer analysis of the writing of Junius and of forty of his contemporaries, looking for recurrent words, tricks of style, and so on. Ellegard began by being a skeptic about Francis; he ended by being totally convinced that he was Junius: "The statement that Sir Philip Francis was Junius may henceforth be allowed to stand without a question mark."

But does the identity of Junius *matter*? The answer must be yes, for he appeared at a vital moment in history. When George III came to the throne, British politics was notoriously corrupt; it was taken for granted that a man went into the House of Commons to make his fortune. He expected to take money in exchange for favors. It was not even regarded as reprehensible— merely as normal and natural. The King himself spent his vast "privy purse"—more than a million pounds—in bribing Members of Parliament. (At least he was not, like some of his European counterparts, an absolute monarch who could merely order them to vote as he pleased.) Junius lost no opportunity to jeer at this corruption.

Newspapers had begun in the reign of Queen Anne (1702–14), but they were little more than entertainment. Junius changed all that. His outrageous letters revealed that you did not have to be a King or a Member of Parliament to exert pressure on the government. Under Queen Elizabeth or Charles I, such attacks would have been regarded as high treason; there would have been torture and executions by the dozen. Woodfall's trial and acquittal

(1770) revealed that even Parliament lacked the power to silence criticism.

Newspapers began to report Parliamentary debates and laid themselves open to prosecution. In 1771 a newspaper referred to a Member of Parliament, Colonel George Onslow, as "the little scoundrel" and "that paltry, insignificant insect." When he complained, the House ordered the arrest of the printers. The printers fought back, arrested the men sent to arrest them, and hauled them in front of the Lord Mayor and two aldermen (one of whom was Wilkes, recently out of jail). When the Lord Mayor countermanded the arrest order, Parliament ordered that he be committed to the Tower of London. His supporters rose up and rioted; they hissed the King, invaded Parliament, and attacked the carriages of MPs. The Lord Mayor was hastily released. And the newspapers took advantage of this triumph to resume their reports of Parliamentary debates.

Parliament itself was forced to order publication of its debates in full—the first "Hansard" (named for Luke Hansard, the publisher) appeared in 1774. From then on, a free press was taken for granted, and the opinions of the people became as important as the opinions of the King and his ministers. Bribery and corruption became the exception rather than the rule.

Junius, of course, cannot take all the credit for this revolution; Wilkes had started it with his *North Briton* article, which in turn was inspired by Pitt and his brother-in-law. But Junius added yeast to the mixture; he stirred up the issues and raised a spirit of rebellion that looked, at one point, as if it would lead to a revolution like the one that swept France two decades later.

It is difficult to feel much sympathy for Junius as a man; he was obviously a thoroughly unpleasant character: mean, envious, and paranoid. His rage was not generous but vindictive. But his formidable literary talent, comparable to that of Swift, changed the course of British history, creating a spirit of freedom that went on to change the course of world history. It is impossible to think of any historical figure of comparable influence whose identity has remained unknown. But then, as Junius himself remarked smugly: "The mystery of Junius increases his importance."

20

The Death of Meriwether Lewis: Suicide or Murder?

O n October 11, 1809, Meriwether Lewis, Governor of the Louisiana Territory and one of the most celebrated explorers in American history, was shot to death at an isolated inn on the Natchez Trace trail in Tennessee. He was only thirty-five years old. To this day controversy continues as to whether he was assassinated, committed suicide, or was simply murdered in the course of a robbery.

At the turn of the nineteenth century much of the North American continent remained unsettled and unexplored. What information there was about the interior—provided by trappers and friendly Indians—remained sketchy and uncertain. Yet this kind of information was vital to the developing United States as its settlers pushed westward.

In 1804 the thirty-year-old Lewis, who was then a Captain in the U.S. Army, headed (together with his friend Lieutenant William Clark) a government-sponsored expedition through the newly purchased Louisiana territories along the Missouri River to its headwaters, then followed the Columbia River to the Northwest Pacific coast. In just over two years Lewis and Clark led their party across the Great Plains and the Rocky Mountains—exploring vast unknown areas including the natural wonderland of the

Yellowstone Valley—to the far side of the continent and back again.

Although the Lewis and Clark party was not the first to cross the North American continent, they were the first military-based, scientific expedition to do so. They made maps of the areas they explored and notes and sketches of the flora and fauna they encountered, discovering many previously unknown species. They traded with Indian tribes and noted their social organizations and lifestyles. When they finally returned home they brought invaluable information for those settlers who would later follow their trail. To their contemporaries, their expedition was as epoch-making as the first voyage to the moon.

On their return two years later Lewis and Clark were awarded $1,228 and 1,600 acres of public land each by a grateful Congress. Most people had given up hope of ever seeing the expedition again, and the senators were relieved to see the men they had sent into danger return alive.

Congress felt that the explorers should be offered suitably important public posts, and President Thomas Jefferson, a friend of Lewis's, was happy to comply. Clark was made a Brigadier General and Superintendent of Indian Affairs (based in St. Louis), and his subsequent career was long and distinguished.

As to Meriwether Lewis, the president was able to offer him the governorship of the Louisiana Territory, which had become available due to a decline in the political fortunes of the previous Governor, General James Wilkinson. Wilkinson was a dubious adventurer and something of a crook. He had taken a secret oath of allegiance to Spain, which paid him $4,000 a year for plotting to split off the southern states of America and ally them with Spain. Another political adventurer, former Vice President Aaron Burr, joined in the conspiracy after he had ruined his own career by killing a political opponent, Alexander Hamilton, in a duel. (Hamilton deliberately fired low, but Burr shot to kill.) When news of the conspiracy leaked out, Wilkinson decided to betray Burr to save his own skin. The move was successful; Burr was arrested and tried (and Lewis was sent as an observer to the trial). He was found not guilty of treason, but his political career was at an end. Wilkinson escaped indictment but was disgraced and in 1812 was dismissed from his command due to his failure to take Montreal.

By sending a hero like Lewis to govern Louisiana, Jefferson hoped to increase his popular support in that territory. But he was handing Lewis an impossible task. Many of his subordinates had been close to Wilkinson and Burr and may well have been involved in the conspiracy. He was forced to make wholesale dismissals, which made him many enemies. Lewis was also expected to cope with a host of inherited problems while tightfisted bureaucrats in Washington kept him on a shoestring budget. There was trouble between the original French population and the new American settlers. There were endless disputes over land claims—French, American, and Spanish—especially mining titles. There were difficulties with squatters and white hunters who set up house on government and Indian lands with cheerful indifference to the law. Traders made immense profits supplying the Indians with weapons and cheap liquor. Meanwhile, the British did their best to stir up an Indian war by sending agents provocateurs.

Lewis was convinced they had succeeded, and in May 1809 he called out five companies of militia. Historians have acknowledged that he was probably correct in his assessment of the situation and that his prompt action almost certainly averted bloodshed. His contemporaries at the time felt he had overreacted; Washington complained about the expense, the militia men grumbled about being dragged away from their homes for two months, and Lewis's political enemies rejoiced.

Lewis's personal life was also far from satisfactory. One might have expected a national hero to be irresistible to women; in fact, he seems to have been an ineffectual romantic who admired from a distance without declaring himself. His loneliness was compounded by continuing ill health, fueled by the pressures of his job. Unsuccessful business speculations added financial embarrassment to his other worries.

When Washington bureaucrats, in a fit of penny-pinching, began to find fault with his official expenditures, Lewis was subjected to new indignities. In 1809, on finding that a draft for eighteen dollars had been rejected, Lewis commented, "The fate of other bills drawn for similar purposes to a considerable amount cannot be mistaken." He paid off several of the rejected drafts out of his own dwindling resources but recognized that the situation was now becoming impossible.

By 1809 Jefferson had been replaced by James Madison. When the Secretary of War refused a draft of $500—equivalent to a quarter of Lewis's annual salary—he added in his letter to Lewis: "The President has been consulted and the observations herein contained have his approval." The new President was clearly on the side of the bureaucrats.

News of his financial problems destroyed Lewis's personal credit. His creditors forced him to sell almost all the property he had acquired in Louisiana. Finally, Lewis had so little cash that he was unable to pay his doctor's bill. In desperation, he decided to travel to Washington and plead his case in person. He left St. Louis by boat on September 4, 1809, hoping to return early the next year. His enemies made no secret of their hope that he would not be reappointed Governor and that they had seen the last of him.

During the river voyage, he made out his will. He seems to have been overtaken by immense depression and made two suicide attempts. When the boat arrived at Chickasaw Bluffs—later re-named Memphis—he had a fever and seemed to be mentally deranged. There he wrote again to President Madison. The letter was written in a sprawling uncertain hand, quite unlike his usual handwriting.

In Chickasaw Bluffs, Lewis drank too much with some old army comrades and became even more depressed. Captain Russell, the post commander, took him into his own quarters, where he was obliged to "keep a strict watch over him to prevent his committing violence on himself."

It seems obvious that Lewis was not fit to travel. He left Chickasaw Bluffs in the company of Major Alexander Neeley, a former army officer now in the Indian Service. They halted for two weeks at Fort Pickering and then traveled through Indian country along the Natchez Trace. Lewis now seemed in reasonably good spirits, although Neeley later stated that the governor appeared on certain days "somewhat deranged in mind."

Seventy-two miles southwest of Nashville, where the trail

emerged from Indian country and into U.S. territory, they encountered an isolated group of buildings called Grinder's Stand, consisting of two cabins and a stable. The owner, Robert Grinder, had squatted the site a year before and made his living selling food, liquor, and shelter to travelers. After two weeks of sleeping in the open, Lewis must have welcomed the opportunity to spend the night with a roof over his head.

Lewis was not actually accompanied by Neeley when he reached Grinder's Stand. Two of the horses had escaped into the woods, and Neeley had stayed behind to round them up. Lewis arrived at Grinder's Stand ahead of his two servants and was met by Mrs. Grinder and her children. Also present were two young slaves and a maidservant, Polly Spencer. Robert Grinder was away hunting. Lewis was given the second cabin, and his two servants—Pernia and Captain Tom—were lodged in the stable.

Lewis asked for liquor but drank very little, and paced up and down, muttering to himself, as supper was prepared. Somebody later said that they overheard him say, "They have told lies on me and want to ruin me." When supper was served he ate little and then suddenly jumped up, his face flushed "as if it had come to him in a fit." He quickly calmed down and went to sit by the open door with a lit pipe, remarking quietly to Mrs. Grinder, "Madam, this is a very pleasant evening."

When Mrs. Grinder started to prepare a bed for him, Lewis declared that he would rather sleep on the floor and sent one of his servants to collect his bearskins and buffalo robe. At this point he discovered that his pocketbook, containing some ready cash, was missing. Everybody searched for it, but without success. Lewis spent the rest of the evening cleaning his pistols and continuing to mutter to himself.

During the night a shot was heard from Lewis's cabin. Mrs. Grinder later declared that she had heard Lewis cry, "Oh, Lord!" Then came a second shot, and possibly a third. Minutes later Lewis staggered from his cabin to the locked kitchen door and begged Mrs. Grinder to give him water and dress his wounds. Mrs. Grinder refused to help or even to open the door—she later explained she was afraid, in spite of the fact that she had five other people with her.

Lewis was left alone in agony for most of the night. At dawn his servant, Pernia, told Mrs. Grinder that Lewis was threatening to cut his throat if he was not given water. Mrs. Grinder finally left her cabin and went with Pernia to Lewis's cabin. At this point the two women's statements differ, one claiming that he was lying on the bed, the other that he was crawling toward the door begging for water. Again he was heard to moan, "They are telling lies and trying to ruin me."

Part of Lewis's forehead had been blown away, exposing the brain. He was also wounded in the side, either from two bullets or one that passed straight through. There were several razor wounds on his neck and wrists. After drinking the water, Lewis begged the women to shoot him and then added, "I am no coward; but I am so strong, so hard to die." These words are almost a direct quotation from a remark in his expedition journal concerning a dying grizzly bear. Mrs. Grinder then asked him why he had attempted suicide and reported that he replied, "If I had not done it, someone else would."

Later that morning an army postrider named Smith came down the Natchez Trace and found Lewis's corpse lying on the trail, 100 to 150 yards from Grinder's cabins. It seems incredible that no watch had been kept over the dying man, but the occupants of Grinder's Stand claimed that Lewis had staggered away without their noticing. The postrider said later that from his cursory examination of the body he was sure that the wound in the side was caused by a bullet entering from behind, passing through the body, and exiting through the front. He also claimed that he had found a piece of gun wadding that, in his opinion, had come from the firing of a musket. It was lying halfway between the stable and Lewis's corpse.

Major Neeley arrived later that day, examined the body, and took statements from all concerned. A coroner's jury was assembled and an inquest held almost immediately. The verdict was "death by suicide."

The evidence certainly suggests that Meriwether Lewis committed suicide in a state of deep depression. But many doubts have been expressed, and in Tennessee it is still widely believed that he was murdered. An amateur historian, William J. Webster, writing at the turn of the nineteenth century, claimed to have seen a document that described the verdict as "possible suicide." And according to historian F. C. Frierson, Samuel Whiteside, the jury foreman, commented that "the jury were cowards and were afraid to bring in a verdict of murder, which they all knew was what they should have done . . . someone said that the murderers had Indian blood in their veins, and they were afraid they would meet a similar fate."

It certainly seems odd that there was no official investigation into Lewis's death. Such an investigation might have raised the question of why no one reported seeing powder burns on Lewis, although the muskets of that time would certainly have produced obvious burns. If there were no powder burns, the implication would be that Lewis was shot from some distance.

But if Lewis had been shot by someone else, would he not have said so? Not necessarily. Head wounds tend to produce states of dissociation, and Lewis certainly had a fever. A twentieth-century British murder case provides a relevant parallel. In March 1926 Mrs. Bertha Merrett was found with a bullet wound in her head. When she recovered consciousness, she was asked how she was shot; she said that her son Donald was standing beside her when she had heard a loud bang. Yet although she lived for two weeks more, and was even able to write checks during that time, everyone assumed that she had shot herself and no one thought to press her for details. Her son was eventually accused of her murder after it was discovered that he had been forging checks in his mother's name. (Even so, he was acquitted.)

Lewis had so many enemies by this time, so many people who were anxious not to see him back in St. Louis, that the notion that he was murdered for political reasons is perfectly plausible. In that case, he could have been killed by an assassin who took advantage of the fact that he was alone for the first time since he left Chickasaw Bluffs. Or the killer could, conceivably, have been Neeley himself. His absence that night was certainly convenient, and his explanation about the horses has struck many writers about the case as unconvincing. Neeley and Lewis had two servants—why were they not left behind to round up the horses? Neeley had left Chickasaw Bluffs with Lewis because he felt Lewis was unfit to travel alone; why, then, did he abandon him at this point?

The other favorite theory is that Lewis was killed in the course of a robbery. There are many possible candidates here: his own servants (who complained that he underpaid them), Robert Grinder, and any number of outlaws and bandits in the area. The one thing that is certain is that *someone* took Lewis's money. He left Fort Pickering with more than two hundred dollars; only twenty-five cents was found after his death. There was also local gossip to the effect that Robert Grinder had returned from his hunting trip during the night and killed Lewis. Two years later Grinder purchased a farm that was said to be beyond his means.

Finally, all that can be said with certainty is that one of the greatest explorers in America's history died under mysterious circumstances in the middle of nowhere and that there was no investigation into his death. Meriwether Lewis was buried in a plain pine box close to the place where his body was found. That, at least, seems appropriate—he was a man who preferred the wilderness to the city.

21

Fedor Kuzmich: Did the Tsar Die an Unknown Monk?

In 1836 a sixty-year-old beggar named Fedor Kuzmich was arrested as a vagrant near the town of Krasnophinsk, in the province of Perm, Russia, and was sentenced to twenty blows of the knout (whip). Then he was sent to Siberia—Russia's penal colony. There, at Nerchinsk, near Tomsk, he became a hermit and acquired a reputation for saintliness.

Fedor Kuzmich impressed all who saw him. He was tall and broad-shouldered, and of majestic appearance, producing in everyone a sense of awe and veneration. His voice, too, seems to have been that of an educated man, and his speech was gentle and deliberate. In spite of his gentleness, however, there were times when he became impatient and imperious, and the peasants who approached him felt the urge to fall to their knees.

Kuzmich always turned aside inquiries about his early life. But occasionally, he made some remark that suggested he had fought in the Russian Army against Napoléon; he spoke of the campaign of 1812 and of the victorious entry into Paris of the Russians and their allies on March 31, 1814. The meticulous tidiness of his cell suggested army training.

Kuzmich had remarkable powers as a healer, and people came to see him from all over Siberia. And according to his biographer,

Schilder (author of a pamphlet that became immensely popular in the 1890s), two former servants from the Tsar's palace were among these visitors—they had been exiled to Siberia, and when one of them fell ill, his companion decided to go and see the healer, to ask if he could help his sick comrade. According to Schilder, the man entered the cell alone, leaving a guide—probably a monk—outside; and when he saw the hermit, he felt obliged, like so many others, to fall to his knees. The old man raised him to his feet and began to speak; with astonishment, the man recognized the voice of Tsar Alexander I. And as he stared at the white-bearded features, he recognized the face of his former master. He fell down in a swoon. The guide outside heard his cry and came in; Fedor Kuzmich told him gently, "Take him back home. And when he regains his senses, warn him not to tell anybody what he saw. Tell him that his friend will recover." Kuzmich proved to be right.

The story that Alexander had been recognized by one of his former servants soon spread all over Russia and was the subject of some official correspondence. Alexander's biographer, Maurice Paleologue, described (in *The Enigmatic Tsar*, 1938) how an old soldier who had been sent to the prison of Nerchinsk saw the hermit and instantly stiffened to attention, saying, "It's our beloved Tsar Alexander Pavlovich!"

Fedor Kuzmich died in 1864 at the age of eighty-seven—precisely the age Alexander I would have been if he had lived.

Is it conceivable that a modern Tsar of Russia, the man who defeated Napoléon, should have quietly vanished and become a hermit? It is true that Ivan the Terrible abdicated in his mid-thirties and retired to a monastery; his subjects had to go and beg him to return. But that was in 1564, in a Russia that was still virtually medieval, not in the enlightened nineteenth century. To understand how it might be possible, we need to know a little of Russia's appallingly bloody and violent history.

The first absolute Tsar was Ivan the Terrible, who came to the throne in 1547 and who was a paranoid maniac. He began his reign by having his chief adviser torn apart by his hunting dogs—Ivan was in his teens at the time. He then embarked on a career of rape, murder, and torture—he regarded every woman in Moscow as a member of his private harem. Marriage seemed to reform him, but when his wife died, he became more paranoid than ever and went on to perpetrate some of the most appalling cruelties in history. While besieging the city of Novgorod, he had a timber wall built around it so that no one could escape. When the city fell, he directed a massacre that went on for five days; husbands and wives were forced to watch one another being tortured; mothers saw their babies ill treated before they themselves were roasted alive. Sixty thousand people were executed. When he besieged Weden, in Livonia, hundreds of citizens preferred to blow themselves up in a castle rather than fall into his hands; he had all the remaining townsfolk tortured to death.

Ivan was the worst of the Tsars, but only just. Even rulers we like to think of as "enlightened"—Peter the Great, Catherine the Great—were capable of ordering mass executions and torture. Peter the Great's niece earned herself the title of Anna the Bloody, while Catherine's son Paul—the child of her first lover, Saltykov—was a madman who oppressed the peasantry in a way that made them feel Ivan the Terrible was back. (Since 1649—the year Charles I was executed in England—Russian peasants were not allowed to leave their owners' estates and were merely "property.")

By 1801 the paranoid Tsar Paul was living in seclusion in a newly built palace that was surrounded by canals and had imposed a nine o'clock curfew on St. Petersburg—whose reaction to it was much as it would have been in London or Paris. On March 23 the regiment of his son Alexander was guarding the palace. Alexander had suffered greatly from his father's arbitrary despotism and had imbibed liberal ideas from Europe; he agreed with his father's chief adviser, Count Pahlen, that Paul had to be deposed. He is supposed to have insisted that Paul's life should be spared, but few historians believe that he meant it. A group of conspirators was admitted to the palace after dark and entered the Tsar's bedroom; he was ordered to abdicate, then strangled with a scarf. The people of Russia went mad with joy when Alexander became their Tsar; they felt that a nightmare was over.

It certainly looked as if it was. The handsome, charming young Tsar met every day with a group of liberal friends to discuss over coffee the way to regenerate his country through freedom of the individual. He quickly made peace with the English—to the disgust of Napoléon. He had no doubt that the first major step was the abolition of serfdom; but that was easier said than done. His minister Speransky, the son of a village priest, was asked to draft a constitution for a democratic Russia; but even he advised against freeing the serfs at one blow. Alexander had to be contented with a decree that allowed anyone to own land, a right that had previously been restricted to the nobility. He also made a determined effort to increase the number of schools and universities. He allowed students to travel abroad, lifted the ban on the import of foreign books, and closed down the secret police department.

A first step toward the liberation of the serfs was left in suspension while Russia went to war with Persia over Russia's annexation of Georgia—a war Russia eventually won. But Alexander's chief problem, of course, was Napoléon, with whom his father, Paul, had been on friendly terms. In 1805 Alexander joined England, Austria, and Sweden in an alliance against Napoléon. Britain defeated Napoléon's fleet at Trafalgar, but the Russians and Austrians were defeated by Napoléon at Austerlitz. A series of treaties with Napoléon followed, and Alexander became Napoléon's ally under the Treaty of Tilsit (1807). Alexander went on to fight successful wars against Turkey and Sweden, acquiring Bessarabia and Finland. The starry-eyed liberal was becoming a conquering hero.

By 1812 it was obvious that Napoléon and Alexander disliked each other too much to remain allies; in June Napoléon's Grand Army, strengthened by Italians, Poles, Swiss, Dutch, and Germans, invaded Russia. It looked like the end for Alexander. Smolensk fell; the Russians were defeated at Borodino; in mid-September the French entered Moscow. The next day the city burst into flames. Alexander declined to make terms, and a month later, Napoléon began his disastrous retreat. Besieged by the Russians and by the Russian winter, the French troops died in droves; Napoléon fled to Paris, leaving behind half a million corpses. The Prussians now deserted Napoléon and joined the Russians. And although Napoléon raised another army and had some remarkable victories, he could not prevent the allies from entering Paris in March 1814. In April, Napoléon abdicated and was exiled to Elba.

Alexander had defeated the "Corsican monster"; he was adored by all his subjects. If history were predictable, he would have completed his reforms and become the most popular monarch in Europe. Unfortunately, Alexander's ten years of war had turned him into a realist and made him repent of the liberal delusions of his youth. Under the influence of a dubious visionary named Julie de Krüdener, he dreamed up an idea called the Holy Alliance, in which the heads of Europe would unite under Christian principles of faith and justice; British statesman Castlereagh called it "sublime mysticism and nonsense." Yet it was deeply typical of Alexander. He had always struck those who knew him well as a self-divided man, and it is said—although it is not clear with how much truth—that he never ceased to reproach himself for the murder of his father. Alexander was a famous charmer, as well as a man of sentiment; but the continual exercise of his charm must have made him wonder sometimes whether he was a man or a mouse. To begin with, he continued to live up to his liberal pledges, conferring a constitution on Poland and emancipating the serfs in the Baltic provinces. But in Russia itself, he took care to maintain the status quo. He began to tighten the screws on education, placing conservatives in charge of universities. Censorship was introduced and liberal professors were purged.

One of Alexander's chief problems was the army. Understandably, he felt that a huge standing army was necessary. But this was enormously expensive. He devised what he considered a brilliant solution to the problem: military colonies. Local peasants had to maintain the army units, and the soldiers had to work the land like peasants. These units were a combination of barracks, collective farms, and concentration camps. They were the most hated feature of Alexander's reign.

Yet, oddly enough, he encouraged the flowering of literature that was taking place, becoming the personal patron—and in some ways the jailer—of the great romantic poet Alexander Pushkin. (One reason for this may have been his desire to get Pushkin's lovely wife into bed—Alexander, like most of the Russian

Tsars, lost no opportunity to seduce a pretty girl.) Under Alexander, Russian literature began to develop into one of the great literatures of the world.

It was this combination of freedom and repression that nurtured the Decembrist revolution that would break out three weeks after his death.* Young officers who had imbibed liberal ideas in Europe joined together in 1816 to form a literary discussion group called the Faithful Sons of the Fatherland. It struck them as outrageous that Russia should be drifting back into despotism, and they began to talk revolution. In 1820 Alexander's own Semyonovsky regiment mutinied against a harsh commander; Alexander proceeded to post its officers to other parts of Russia. Alexander soon became aware that his officers were conspiring against him, yet he seemed oddly indifferent and disillusioned. In his mid-forties, he felt the irony of the situation: a liberal Tsar who had conquered Napoléon, he had become a symbol of oppression to the very officers who had once regarded him as Russia's brightest hope. For many years, his marriage to the beautiful Empress Elizabeth had been a marriage in name only; they were childless, and he took a succession of mistresses. Life seemed curiously empty. When told of the proliferation of secret societies he said wearily, "I myself have shared and encouraged these errors and delusions . . . I have no right to punish them." A stronger and more ruthless man would have had all the conspirators arrested and tried; Alexander had no stomach for a bloodbath. He began to speak longingly of abdicating, of becoming a private citizen in Switzerland, or a botanist on the Rhine.

When informed of the death of his child by his Polish mistress, Marie Naryshkin, he burst into tears in front of his officers. A few days later, he began to travel feverishly all over Russia and covered three thousand miles in four months—an achievement that arouses no astonishment nearly two centuries later but which, in those days of bumpy carriages and roads full of potholes, was a considerable feat. Back in St. Petersburg in November 1824, he witnessed a major disaster: the river Neva flooded half the city.

---

*The Decembrist conspiracy was easily suppressed; most of the conspirators were executed.

When he heard a man crying desperately, "It's a punishment for our sins," he replied, "No, it's a punishment for my sins."

Revolt was everywhere. Pushkin said, "Holy Russia is becoming uninhabitable." The Tsar's favorite aide-de-camp died, and the Empress fell ill; Alexander felt that his life was falling apart. And when the Empress decided to try to recuperate in Taganrog, on the Sea of Azov, the Emperor announced that he would go with her. People were puzzled about the choice of Taganrog, which was not a health resort but a small fortress town in wild and swampy country. Why did she not choose Italy?

Before the Emperor set out from the capital, he attended a service at a monastery, then spent some time with an old hermit who was greatly revered. They had a long talk, and when Alexander left he remarked, "I have heard many sermons, but none has moved me as much as that old monk. How sorry I am not to have known him sooner."

He went to Taganrog, and the Empress—whose illness prevented her from hurrying—arrived ten days later. For a month they lived simply and peacefully together, and it seemed that their love had achieved an Indian summer. Then Alexander was again seized by his wanderlust and set out on a tour of the Crimea. When he returned to Taganrog on November 16, he was feverish.

And, according to the history books, he died there on December 1, 1825. Four eyewitnesses vouch for it: the Empress herself, his aide-de-camp, Prince Volkonsky, his personal physician, the Englishman Sir James Wylie, and the court physician, Tarassov. So why should we not accept this as the truth?

To begin with, because the diaries and letters of the witnesses contradict one another; for example, one says he is getting steadily worse, while another states that he is feeling much better and is gay and smiling. One thing that *is* certain is that the Tsar consistently refused all medicines during his last illness.

November 23, 1825, seems to have been the crucial day. In the morning, after sleeping well, the Tsar sent for his wife and remained in conversation with her for about six hours. They were evidently discussing something of considerable import. She wrote to her mother: "When you think you have arranged everything for the best, there comes an unexpected trial which makes it impossible for you to enjoy the happiness surrounding you." Happiness, when her husband was seriously ill? Does it not sound, rather, as if she is now certain that he is recovering and that after their reconciliation, she is now looking forward to a new and intimate relation with her husband—and then, suddenly, some new obstacle has arisen that has dashed her hopes? Could it be that her husband has confided to her that he sees this illness as an opportunity to put into practice his scheme of "disappearing"?

Moreover, after writing this letter, there is a sudden gap in her diary. Paleologue suggests that the diary entries were destroyed by Tsar Nicholas I—Alexander's younger brother—when he came to the throne. This is plausible, since Nicholas I is known to have destroyed many papers belonging to his older brother, as well as the Empress's diary. But if the Empress had just been told by her husband that he intended to disappear, this would be a still better explanation; it is surely unlikely that she would have continued to keep her diary, with the incriminating evidence.

Another curious incident occurred. Prince Volkonsky recorded in his diary that Alexander had suggested that his illness should be made known to his younger brother, the Grand Duke Constantine, who was heir to the throne. (In fact, he declined it and allowed Nicholas to take over.) Volkonsky gave the date for this request as November 21—then amended it to November 23, the day of the Tsar's long talk with his wife. It may have been a genuine error. Or it may have reflected a desire to support the story that the Tsar began to deteriorate on November 23. That he was not in an enfeebled state is proved by the fact that after his six-hour talk with his wife, he then wrote a long letter to his mother, the Dowager Empress Marie—a highly dominant woman—*which has since disappeared*. Nicholas I later destroyed the diary of the Tsar's mother, as well as all papers relating to Alexander's last years. The evidence is purely circumstantial, but it certainly fits the hypothesis that November 23 was the day on which Alexander told his wife that he intended to abdicate; the day on which he relayed this news to his mother and to his aide-de-camp and physicians—with instructions to falsify their diaries.

Four days later the parish priest of Taganrog, Father Fedotov, arrived to give Alexander Communion. Four days after that, Alexander died. Is it credible that he failed to ask the priest to come again? We would expect the opposite from a man of his religious and mystical tendencies—that is, that when he believed he was dying, he would have kept the priest by him most of the time. Neither were there any last rites, such as all the previous Tsars had received. Instead, Alexander apparently died without any of the comforts of religion—which sounds as absurd as a pope dying without the final sacrament.

Ten doctors signed the autopsy report on the day after the Tsar's death. This report provides the most positive evidence that the corpse was not that of the Tsar and that another corpse had been found during the thirty-two hours that had elapsed since his death. Alexander is reported to have died of malaria, which causes the spleen to hypertrophy. But the spleen of the corpse was quite normal. Examination of the brain revealed that the man had suffered from syphilis. But Alexander, says Paleologue, was known to be immune to syphilis. He had had many mistresses, and his favorite mistress, Marie Naryshkin, had many lovers. His promiscuity must have led him to consult his physicians about the possibility of venereal disease on several occasions; medical reports show that he had always remained immune.

The back and loins of the corpse were brownish-purple and red; this might be expected of a peasant who took no care of his skin—or who had been recently flogged—but hardly of a Tsar.

But where could the corpse have been obtained? There is no difficulty in answering this question if we recall that Taganrog was a garrison town full of soldiers. Maurice Paleologue (who was the French ambassador at the court of Nicholas II, the last of the Tsars) reports that there is some evidence (he agrees that it is "faint," because such matters were kept secret) that the head physician of the military hospital, Dr. Alexandrovitch, happened to have in his hands the body of a soldier who was roughly the same height and size as the Tsar. If the body was that of a soldier—possibly a Tatar—it could explain why the skin of the loins and back was purple; soldiers were often beaten.

Oddly enough, Dr. Tarassov, the royal surgeon, later declared that he had not signed the autopsy report. Yet the report *is* signed by Tarassov. Why did Tarassov think he had not signed it? Was it because he did not wish to put his name to a document he knew to be false? On the other hand, an unsigned autopsy report would confirm suspicions if any question of the Tsar's "survival" arose, and it would therefore be logical for someone to forge Tarassov's signature.

It is also known that when the Tsar's remains were exposed to public view—as they had to be by custom—in the church at Taganrog, everyone who looked at the face said the same thing: "Is that the Tsar? How he has changed."

Another curious event occurred when the coffin was on its way back to St. Petersburg—or rather, to the summer palace in Tsarskoe Selo—in the following March. (In the freezing Russian winter, the body was perfectly preserved, as if it had been kept in a deep freeze.) When the coffin reached Babino, fifty miles from its destination, the Dowager Empress Marie Feodorovna came—alone—to see it. She ordered the coffin to be opened, took a long look at the body, and then left. It seems odd that she should have made the journey to Babino when she could just as easily have seen the body in St. Petersburg. It is recorded that she had recently received "a very grave confidence" from Princess Volkonsky, wife of the Tsar's aide-de-camp. If that confidence was that the corpse was not that of the Tsar, it would certainly explain her visit in midwinter. If we assume that the letter of November 23 had simply told her that Alexander had decided to abdicate, and the next news she received was of his death, then it becomes understandable that she was anxious to find out as quickly as possible whether it was true that her son was still alive. She did not want to see the body in the presence of other people.

Alexander was taken to the summer palace in Tsarskoe Selo, although it might have been expected that he would lie in state in St. Petersburg so that his subjects could see him for the last time. Instead, only the royal family filed past the coffin in the chapel. As the Dowager Empress did so, she made the curious remark, "Yes, that is my dear son Alexander" and kissed the brow of the corpse. The body was then taken to the Peter and Paul Fortress and placed in a tomb.

Forty years later the new Tsar, Alexander II, heard the rumors that the hermit Fedor Kuzmich, who had died in the previous year, was actually Tsar Alexander I. He ordered the tomb to be opened. This was done at night, under the direction of the minister of the imperial court, Count Adlersberg. The coffin proved to be empty. The tomb was then resealed without the coffin. Paleologue records that the tomb was opened again in the reign of Tsar Alexander III and that the coffin was missing. In contradiction to this, the historian R. D. Charques records, in a footnote in his *Short History of Russia* (1956), that the coffin was opened again by the Bolsheviks in the 1920s and found to be empty.

But in his introduction to Tolstoy's *Death of Ivan Ilyich* (which contains his story "Fedor Kuzmich"), Tolstoy's translator, Aylmer Maude, states that in 1927 the Soviet government had the imperial tombs opened and that that of Alexander I contained only a bar of lead. This sounds altogether more likely. It suggests that Paleologue's account is the correct one and that Charques wrote *coffin* when he meant *tomb*. In fact, a completely empty coffin would not be placed in the tomb, since it would be evident to those who lifted it that it was empty; something would almost certainly be placed inside to give it weight, and that something might well be a bar of lead. When the coffin was found to be empty by Count Adlersberg, this might well have been left behind in the tomb.

Tolstoy was intrigued by the story of Fedor Kuzmich and, as already noted, sketched out a story—unfinished at the time of his death—about it. Tolstoy's "Fedor Kuzmich" purports to be the diary of Alexander I. The protagonist describes himself as "the greatest of criminals," the murderer of hundreds of thousands of people as well as of his own father. In Taganrog, he says, he received a letter from his minister, Arakcheyev, describing the assassination of Arakcheyev's voluptuous mistress; this, he says, filled him with lustful thoughts. Early the next morning he walked out alone, heard the sound of drums and flutes, and realized that a soldier was being made to run the gauntlet—that is, to run half-naked between lines of colleagues who would beat him with rods. The thought of the murdered girl and of a soldier being beaten with rods "merged into one stimulating sensation." He then realized that the soldier who was being beaten bore a striking resemblance to himself; it was a man named Strumenski, who was sometimes jokingly called Alexander II. He had been in the Tsar's old regiment and was now being punished for attempted desertion. Two days later the Tsar made inquiries and learned that Strumenski was dying. It was when his chief of staff was telling him about various conspiracies that the desire to abdicate again came upon him with tremendous force, and he realized that the death of Strumenski would provide him with the opportunity he needed. And when, the following day, he cut himself badly while shaving, and collapsed on the floor, he decided that the time had come to put his plan into operation.

Tolstoy's version assumes that Alexander decided to vanish on impulse in Taganrog; Paleologue suspects that he chose Taganrog because he had already planned his disappearance.

Oddly enough, Paleologue doubts whether Fedor Kuzmich *was* Alexander I—he cites a story to the effect that an English lord picked up the Tsar in his yacht and that Alexander died as a monk in Palestine. This is, in a sense, more logical than the notion that he became a wanderer in Russia, where he would have been easily recognized.

Many historians, including Charques, dismiss the notion that Alexander I survived his "death" in Taganrog. In *The Court of Russia in the Nineteenth Century* (1908), E. A. Brayley Hodgetts cites the report of Sir James Wylie, the Tsar's English doctor, who examined the body and diagnosed that the death was due to "bilious remittent fever." But if Alexander "disappeared," then Wylie was undoubtedly part of the conspiracy. And the doubts about the disappearance theory must be balanced against the evidence of the empty tomb and against the whole strange story of Alexander's final illness and death. It now seems unlikely that anyone will ever prove that Alexander I arranged his own disappearance. But the reason that it is unlikely—that all the relevant diaries and letters have mysteriously vanished—suggests that it is true.

22

Glenn Miller: The Strange Disappearance of a Bandleader

On December 24, 1944, an official press release stated that "Major Alton Glenn Miller, Director of the famous United States Army Air Force Band, which has been playing in Paris, is reported missing while on a flight from London to Paris. The plane in which he was a passenger left England on December 15 and no trace of it has been found since its take-off."

Glenn Miller's rise to fame and wealth had not been an easy one. Born in Clarinda, Iowa, in March 1904, he learned to play the trombone at thirteen and helped to pay his way at the University of Colorado by playing with local dance bands. He joined Ben Pollack's band at the age of twenty and over the next ten years became known in New York as an arranger as well as a trombonist, playing with Red Nichols, Smith Ballew, and the Dorsey brothers. A dance orchestra he organized for Ray Noble in 1934 became popular through its broadcasts, but Miller's own orchestra, organized in 1937, was a failure. A second orchestra, organized in the following year, did little better.

The breakthrough came in March 1939, when the band played at the Glen Island Casino in a suburb of New York and the audience was overwhelmed with enthusiasm at this new, distinctive, Glenn Miller sound, with its smooth, almost syrupy, brass. Radio broadcasts spread the fever across the country, and Miller was soon a rich man. Although he lacked the sheer inventive genius of other jazzmen of the period—Benny Goodman, Duke Ellington, and Count Basie, for example—the "seamless and rich" perfection of numbers like "Moonlight Serenade" made him the favorite of the American middle classes, while "hot" numbers like "In the Mood" and "Tuxedo Junction" made him popular with a younger generation that was learning to jive. He went to Hollywood and made two classic films, *Orchestra Wives* (1941) and *Sun Valley Serenade* (1942). During this period he became a friend of actor David Niven—a friendship that, as we shall see, plays an odd part in the mystery of Glenn Miller's disappearance.

In 1942, as a patriotic gesture, Miller joined the air force. He soon assembled another band and was assigned to entertaining the troops abroad. He was sent to London. David Niven had also joined up—but in the British Army. Since he was a famous show-business personality, he was also given an important post in armed-forces entertainment, and one of his jobs was to organize Glenn Miller's tours. He was, in effect, Miller's boss. The man actually in charge of organizing the details of Miller's tours—hotel and travel arrangements—was Lieutenant Don Haynes, Miller's former booking agent, now also in the U.S. Air Force.

In November 1944 Niven organized a six-week tour for Miller's band, starting on Saturday, December 16. The band was due to fly to Paris on that day. But on December 12, as Don Haynes and Miller were walking back to their London hotel, Miller told Haynes—according to Haynes's later story—that he wanted to go a day early because he had a social engagement. Haynes said he would book Miller on a flight from RAF Bovingdon, northwest of London, the usual takeoff point for Continental flights.

The following day, Wednesday, December 13, Haynes claims he left Miller in London and drove back to Bedford, where the band was housed in billets, to arrange their flight. The following morning, he claims, he ran into Lieutenant-Colonel Norman Baessell, who was special assistant to the station commander at RAF Milton Ernest, near Bedford. Baessell mentioned that he would be flying to Paris the next day—Thursday—and offered Haynes a lift. Haynes declined, saying he would be flying with the band on

Saturday, but mentioned that Glenn Miller would like a lift. Haynes telephoned Miller, who accepted the offer; Haynes went to London to collect him and took him back to RAF Milton Ernest.

The next morning Haynes collected Miller and Baessell and took them to the nearby airfield, Twinwood Farm. At about 1:40, their plane arrived—a small American prop-driven plane called a Norseman, piloted by Flight Officer John R. S. Morgan. In spite of appalling weather conditions, they took off five minutes later— and vanished.

We now know what happened to the plane. It flew across the channel toward Dieppe but began to experience engine trouble; the pilot was forced to ditch in the sea only six miles west of Le Touquet, which is some distance north of Dieppe. The plane was located in 1973 and examined by an independent diver seven years later. Its propeller was missing. This suggested a leak in the hydraulic system, which failed to adjust the blades to the required speed; the propeller "oversped" and probably fell off.

Now as strange as it sounds, no one at the time seems to have realized what had happened. On Monday (the flight was delayed by bad weather) the band arrived at Orly Airport, near Paris, and Haynes was puzzled when Miller failed to turn up to meet them. Haynes spent the rest of Monday, and the whole of the following day, searching Paris—which had recently been liberated—for the bandleader. He finally contacted General Ray Barker, who was in charge of all U.S. military personnel in Paris. Two days later, when the band played its first Paris engagement, the audience was simply told that "Major Miller could not be with the band." Miller's death was announced three days later.

That was the story. But Miller's wife, Helen—the childhood sweetheart whom he had married—didn't want to believe it. To begin with, she hoped that he had been taken prisoner. And when, after the end of the war, it became clear that this was a forlorn hope, she began instituting inquiries that involved searching war cemeteries, hoping that at least she could find a grave that she could visit. In February 1946 a certain Colonel Donnell wrote in answer to her inquiry to tell her that her husband had not been flying in one of the passenger planes but in a combat aircraft not designed for passengers. This aircraft, he said, was cleared to fly from Abbotts Ripton Field, near Huntington, *to Bordeaux*. Now Bordeaux is long way short of Paris, and Helen Miller must have found herself wondering whether her husband was supposed to walk the extra distance. Of course, the Norseman could have been intended to land at Paris and then go on to Bordeaux; but if so, the clearance would have said as much. The letter concluded by telling her firmly that no further information was available.

The rumor that there had been some sort of cover-up in the case led various researchers to try to track down the official documents. One of these, an ex–RAF officer named John Edwards, dismissed the cover-up theory and set out to prove that Glenn Miller *had* been on board the Norseman when it crashed. It was simply, he thought, a matter of getting the official form—called a 201—about Miller's death from the Washington file where it must be kept. But he found it to be a less simple task than he expected. The Records Office in Washington denied all knowledge of the file. The National Personnel Records Center in St. Louis said they thought the records had been lost in a fire. It began to dawn on Edwards that *somebody* had a reason for sitting on the evidence.

Another RAF man, Squadron Leader Jack Taylor, decided to have a try. He succeeded in obtaining the MACR (Missing Air Crew Report) but found that the signature was illegible and the typed details so blurred as to be almost unreadable. Two other documents he succeeded in obtaining showed only that no kind of search for Glenn Miller had been instituted at the time. This in itself seemed odd, for the Allies were by then in control of most of France, and there would have been nothing to prevent a thorough search for the famous bandleader.

It was Taylor who approached another ex–RAF pilot named Wilbur Wright, who had become a highly successful novelist and therefore had time to spare. It was true that, by 1986, most of the witnesses were dead; but Wright reasoned that it ought to be straightforward enough to obtain whatever records existed. If there was any difficulty, he could invoke the Freedom of Information Act. And so Wilbur Wright took a deep breath and wrote to the United States Air Force Inspection and Safety Center in Norton, California, for the accident report on the missing plane.

The reply stated that they had no record of an accident involving a Norseman on that date. A second letter drew from them the reply that no Norseman airplanes had been reported missing in December 1944. But Wright had a way of checking this—a document called the Cumulative Loss Listing. And this told him that there had been no fewer than *eight* Norseman airplanes lost in December 1944.

Wright began to smell a rat. And when letters to the Washington Records Office, the Army Casualty Division, and the Air Force History department met with similar blanks, one thing at least became obvious. This was not vagueness or incompetence; he was being deliberately stonewalled. Another letter to the Casualty Division in Alexandria, Virginia, brought a fascinating revelation. They admitted plaintively that they had been trying for years to obtain the Glenn Miller file from Washington and had been totally ignored.

Over the next month or so Wright kept up a furious barrage of letters to various agencies. He even wrote directly to President Reagan, asking him to intervene. He secured one grudging admission from Military Reference, admitting that there were several documents in the Miller file and listing them. But the Washington Records Office continued to insist that all documents had been lost or mislaid. In January 1987 Wright telephoned the records office and demanded to talk to the "top man." He was put through to a Mr. George Chalou, and he explained that he was a professional author and wanted to see the Glenn Miller burial file. He added that he had written repeatedly and gotten nowhere and that the Casualty Division people in Alexandria complained that Washington would not give them the file. "Right!," said Mr. Chalou, "and there's no way they'll get them back either. Those files have been under lock and key for years, and that's how they'll stay." Wilbur Wright, who was recording the conversation, stared at the phone in dumbstruck astonishment. At last he had an admission that the file was being kept under wraps.

He went on to mention that he had written to Ronald Reagan— but did not mention that so far he had received no reply. That drew a gasp of *"You didn't!"* followed by a demand for Wright's telephone number. But there was no return telephone call—only more letters assuring Wright that he had now received all the information that was available. But further pressure elicited the reply that the missing file had now been found and that when Wright came to visit the office, he would see the "original MACR." That confirmed what Wright had already deduced: that the MACR obtained by Squadron Leader Jack Taylor was a fake.

The Washington Records Office then decided to send the file to the Casualty Division in Virginia, assuring them that it had only just been located. Virginia wrote to Wright telling him that they had now mailed him a copy of the missing file. And eventually, weeks later, the file finally arrived.

This—as might be expected—included no astounding revelations; if it had, presumably it would not have been sent. But it confirmed one thing: the Missing Air Crew Report obtained by Taylor was not the original; close study revealed that it had been altered. Moreover, only page 1 had been included; page 2, which should have contained the signature, was missing. And when, with his usual incredible persistence, Wright obtained the missing page—which turned up in the pilot's Burial File—it had no signature. The later "signed" version *was* a fabrication. So why had the original unsigned version not been given to Taylor—or released soon after the accident? Obviously, because it had *not* been signed, and this would have caused suspicion. Because Captain Ralph S. Cramer, who should have signed it, must have known that he would have been putting his signature to something that was untrue, he preferred not to.

All this, Wright realized, sounded inconclusive; perhaps Cramer was in a hurry and forgot to sign it; perhaps the Washington Records Office genuinely mislaid the file. But there was one other piece of evidence that Wilbur Wright felt was far more striking: The actor David Niven had been a friend of Miller's since they had met in Hollywood in the early 1940s. As mentioned earlier, he was Miller's "boss" when Miller came to London as a member of the U.S. Air Force, and he arranged that final tour, which was never made. Yet in his bestselling autobiography, *The Moon's a Balloon*, Niven did not even mention Glenn Miller. And he also failed to say anything about him to his biographer, Sheridan Morley.

There is an equally odd omission in Niven's autobiography. He
was in Paris at the time of Miller's disappearance, arranging a
tour for Marlene Dietrich, another old friend—in fact, she, Niven,
and Miller met for dinner whenever they could. The Battle of the
Bulge—in which the Germans tried to relaunch the offensive
against the Allies—began on the day after Miller "disappeared,"
and Marlene Dietrich (who was, of course, German, and could
have been shot as a traitor if captured) had to be hastily evacu-
ated to Paris. Niven made a frantic phone call to a colleague in
England, Colonel Hignett, to try to borrow a squad of "rough-
necks" (commandos) to go and rescue Miss Dietrich. Hignett had
to refuse, since all his men were on red alert. Then why did Niven
fail to mention this important episode in his autobiography? He
mentions the period but says he was elsewhere, at a place called
Spa, two hundred miles from Paris. And a biography of Marlene
Dietrich confirms that she and Niven were together on the day
before Miller "disappeared" and that she was "rescued" from the
German advance and returned to Paris.

Wright's conclusion was that Niven knew exactly what had
happened to Glenn Miller and that whatever it was, it was not a
drowning accident off Le Touquet. But if Miller was not on the
Norseman when it crashed, where was he? Presumably in Paris,
where he was supposed to be—and with Niven and Marlene Dietrich.

Assuming that that was correct, and that Miller flew to Paris—
either on Thursday (the 14th) from Bovingdon, or on the following day—then what happened to him in Paris that led to a cover-
up?

Wright's lengthy investigation—far too lengthy to describe in
detail—led him to study many possible scenarios. He lists these in
his book *Millergate* (1990). Miller's brother Herb was convinced
that Glenn never left England but that he died of cancer. This
obviously raises the question of why a cover-up would have been
necessary. There is nothing disgraceful about dying of cancer.

Another theory studied by Wright was that Miller's plane was
shot down by German fighters. But the weather over the Continent on December 15 was so bad that all planes were grounded.
Moreover, the Luftwaffe records make no mention of a plane

being shot down over the Channel. Oddly enough, Wright's investigations revealed that the weather over Twinwood Airfield was still good and not, as Haynes claimed, appalling. The inference was that Haynes had invented the appalling weather to make his story more convincing.

Another rumor alleged that Miller had been taken prisoner and died in a prisoner-of-war camp. Wright dismisses this theory, pointing out that the Germans would have announced the capture of Glenn Miller to undermine Allied morale.

A more promising lead was connected with Lieutenant-Colonel Norman Baessell, who proved to have an extremely dubious reputation as a drug smuggler. Wright investigated a rumor that Baessell had been smuggling drugs to an airstrip in northern France on that fatal flight, that Glenn Miller had objected, and that Baessell had shot him and concealed the body; on their way back, the plane crashed. Wright's research revealed that Baessell was certainly a swashbuckling character, macho and aggressive, who would have been perfectly capable of drug smuggling. But there is not the slightest piece of confirmatory evidence that this is what happened.

One of the most interesting stories was told by a man named Dennis Cottam, who had gone to Paris in 1954 to pick up a car. In a place called Fred's Bar, not far from the Hotel Olympiades in Montmartre, where the Miller band had stayed, Cottam was told by the bartender, "You English think Glenn Miller died in the Channel on December 15, 1944, yet he was drinking in here that same evening." He told Cottam that if he wanted confirmation of this story, he should go to a blue-painted door on the other side of the street and ask the lady there about Glenn Miller. The door turned out to be that of a brothel, and the Madame there told Cottam that in 1944 her boyfriend had been a Provost Marshall Captain and that he had told her that he saw and identified the body of Glenn Miller. But why was he killed? Cottam wanted to know. "Because he knew too much about the Black Market."

That was certainly interesting. But would Black Marketeers really kill a famous bandleader who had only been in Paris for twenty-four hours or so—scarcely enough time to learn much about the Black Market?

Interviews with researcher John Edwards also brought some interesting insights. He obtained a tape made by a BBC engineer named Teddy Gower, who claimed that he had flown to Paris (Orly) with Glenn Miller from Bovingdon on Thursday, December 14, the day Miller had actually *wanted* to fly. Don Haynes had admitted that Miller wanted to fly to Orly on the 14th, and that he (Haynes) had promised to arrange a flight from Bovingdon, the usual airfield for Continental flights. Yet, according to Haynes, he had changed his mind and accepted Baessell's offer to give Miller a lift to Paris on the following day, Friday.

But why *should* Miller prefer a "lift" in a small plane (Miller hated small planes) on Friday to a comfortable trip in a larger Dakota on Thursday? Wright had already found many inconsistencies in Haynes's story that led him to believe that he was lying. For example, Haynes claimed that he had driven back to Bedford on the Wednesday afternoon in thick fog, when Wright was able to uncover evidence that he and Glenn Miller had spent that evening at the Milroy Club with a group of officers and a girl singer. This, and much other evidence, convinced Wright that Haynes was closely involved in the cover-up. Miller *had* flown to Paris on the Thursday in a Dakota and had probably been met by David Niven, who was certainly in Paris that day.

John Edwards had another rather odd story to tell Wilbur Wright. Because of the publicity given to his search for Glenn Miller, he had received many letters. One of these was from a World War II veteran who claimed that he had not only known Major Glenn Miller but had been with Miller in a military hospital in Columbus, Ohio, when the bandleader died of head injuries. That sounded so absurd that Edwards had not even followed up the story but had thrown the letter into the wastebasket.

Edwards also told Wright about an American doctor named David Pecora who claimed to have been present at the time Glenn Miller died. With his usual incredible persistence, Wright finally succeeded in tracing Pecora. The result was disappointing— Pecora agreed that he had been in France at the time but said he had no knowledge of Glenn Miller.

Nevertheless, this false lead was to prove productive. Tracking down Pecora had involved much letter writing to New Jersey, the state where Miller had lived before he joined the U.S. Air Force. Wright decided to write to the State Registrar in New Jersey, asking if they had any record of the death of a Major Alton Glenn Miller; he gave all the necessary family details, including place and date of birth. But by accident he gave Miller's state of birth as Ohio instead of Iowa. He was astonished to receive a letter confirming that Alton Glenn Miller had died in Ohio in December 1944. A telephone call to the registrar in New Jersey confirmed that Alton Glenn Miller, later a resident of New Jersey, had died in Ohio. At this point, Wilbur Wright made a mistake. Instead of asking for further details of where Miller died, he told the woman on the other end of the telephone, "You realize we are talking about *the* Glenn Miller who vanished in Europe in 1944?" After a long silence, the woman said, "We'll call you back." In fact, she called back two days later to say that the typist had made an error. They had sent him Glenn Miller's place of birth instead of his place of death.

Wright was baffled. How could they confuse a place of birth in 1904 with a place of death in 1944? What's more, Wright said to the woman, Miller was born in Iowa, *not* Ohio. "It was a typing error," the woman insisted. "And anyway, Ohio, Iowa—it's the same state." Samuel Goldwyn is known to have confused the two, but it sounded strange coming from an employee of a State Registrar.

There was, Wright discovered, another oddity that needed explaining. In 1949 Helen Miller, who had moved to Pasadena, California, had purchased a six-grave burial plot in nearby Altadena. But the family consisted of only herself and the son and daughter she and Glenn had adopted; there were also her parents, who were, in due course, buried in the plot. Who was the extra grave for? The cemetery authorities were asked to deny that Glenn Miller was buried in the plot; it took them fifteen months to do so. They also sent Wilbur Wright's "confidential" inquiry to Glenn Miller's adopted son, Steve, whose response was to write an angry letter to Glenn's brother, Herb—who had replied to Wright's inquiries—saying: "Get this guy off our backs."

Then what *did* happen to Glenn Miller? By far the most persistent rumor Wright encountered was that Miller had received a fatal blow on the head in a brawl in a brothel in Pigalle, Paris. (Pigalle is known as the prostitute's area.) In a 1976 newspaper article, John Edwards speculated that Miller was murdered in Paris on the Monday that the band finally arrived. The article summarized, "Mr. Edwards believes that Miller, who was a bit of a lad with the ladies, died of a fractured skull."

Wright was originally skeptical about this story, because he was able to disprove some of the other details given by Edwards—for example, his assertion that a Lieutenant-Colonel Corrigan was able to confirm the "murder." Wright traced Corrigan, who denied it. Edwards also claimed that an American doctor in Paris had signed the death certificate; this was presumably Dr. Pecora, who denied all knowledge of Miller's death. Yet the sheer persistence of the story—which surfaced in Paris as early as 1948—suggested that it could be true. And it certainly fits in with the rest of the information that Wilbur Wright accumulated.

This, then, is the outline of Wright's scenario of what happened to Glenn Miller:

Miller decided to go to Paris two days before the band in order to do some "socializing"—which included buying female companionship. He had arranged to meet his old friend David Niven, who would be there on December 14 to arrange Marlene Dietrich's tour. Niven's autobiography makes it clear that he was not averse to female companionship either, having been a flatmate of Errol Flynn. Niven probably met Miller off the Dakota that brought him from Bovingdon on Thursday, December 15. Two days later Niven had to rush off to rescue Marlene Dietrich from becoming a victim of the Battle of the Bulge, but the two of them returned to Paris two days later and may well have joined Miller for a meal.

Miller went to a brothel in Pigalle, became involved in some kind of brawl, and was struck on the head. When Don Haynes arrived at Orly, he was puzzled that Miller wasn't there to meet him. He claims that he spent two days searching for Miller in Paris, but (as Wright points out) that would not have been necessary. He must have known where Miller was staying and checked there—probably discovering that Miller had been missing all night.

The badly injured Miller was located; it seemed clear that he might die. How could his death by violence be explained without a scandal? The cover-up began. Miller was flown to a military hospital in Columbus, Ohio. Meanwhile, the disappearance of the Norseman provided the perfect opportunity for explaining his nonappearance at the Paris concerts. When the disappearance of the Norseman was announced nine days after it had happened, Glenn Miller was already dead in Ohio. He was probably buried there. His wife, Helen, was informed that he had died in the Norseman, but she did not believe it. And eventually, the military authorities decided to tell her what had happened—presumably before she purchased the six-grave plot in Altadena.

Some time thereafter, Glenn Miller was transferred from his unmarked grave in Ohio to his resting place in Altadena. Helen joined him there in 1966. His friend Niven, one of the few who knew the secret, maintained an entirely uncharacteristic silence about Miller for the rest of his life, not even mentioning him to his second wife. Don Haynes later published his diaries, which appeared to confirm his story that Miller had flown to Paris from Twinwood on the morning of Friday, December 15, in exceptionally bad weather. Wright's investigations revealed that the weather was reasonable on that date *but that the airfield was closed.*

Glenn Miller's records are as popular as ever, and their smooth, seamless sound is still one of the delights of the swing era. Perhaps, after all, Niven and Haynes were right when they decided that, as far as posterity was concerned, Miller had died in a mysterious airplane accident rather than in an undignified brawl in a Paris brothel.

23

The Missing Link:
The Unsolved Mystery
of Human Evolution

One day in 1908, an amateur archaeologist named Charles Dawson, who made his living as a solicitor, was walking along a farm road near Piltdown Common in East Sussex, England, when he noted some peculiar brown flints that had been used to mend the road. When he learned that they had been found in a gravel bed on the farm, he went along to take a look at it. Two workmen were digging, and Dawson asked them if they had found any fossils; they said no. But when Dawson returned later, one of them handed him a piece of a human skull. Three years later, in the same place, Dawson found another piece.

In the following year, 1912, Dawson decided to show the pieces to his friend, Dr. Arthur Smith Woodward, the keeper of the Department of Geology at the British Museum, and during that summer, Smith Woodward came to look at the site, bringing another geologist, the French priest Pierre Teilhard de Chardin (who was to become famous four years after his death, in 1955, for his book *The Phenomenon of Man*). They quickly discovered what Dawson described as a "human mandible" (lower jaw) with two molar teeth. Prehistoric animal bones and primitive human tools in the same gravel pit seemed to date the jaw as being about half a million years old. Part of a human skull also turned up in the pit.

This was a matter of great excitement, for man himself is only about half a million years old. At any rate, the sudden expansion of the brain that has become known as "the brain explosion" began—for reasons no one understands—half a million years ago. (The "first man," *Homo erectus*, dates back about one and a quarter million years but had a brain the size of an ape's.) What was so startling about this find was that the jaw was definitely apelike, yet it fit the cranium. They had apparently discovered something that science had been seeking for almost half a century—what Charles Darwin had called "the Missing Link," the definitive proof that man is descended from the ape.

It's hard for us to understand the scandal that had been caused by the publication of Darwin's *Origin of Species* in November 1859. Most of us take the notion of evolution for granted and regard biblical fundamentalism as an absurd joke. In 1859 Darwin's conclusions seemed to shake the foundations of Christianity, and therefore the foundations of British society. The first edition of the book actually sold out on its first day. And in spite of the caution with which he had phrased his conclusions—that all species emerge through natural selection due to the survival of the fittest—Darwin was soon being accused of atheism and downright wickedness. In 1859 most British people accepted that the account of creation in Genesis was entirely factual, and most accepted Archbishop Usher's estimate of the date of creation (worked out from the Bible) as 4004 B.C.

Admittedly, Sir Charles Lyell had disproved this almost thirty years before in his *Principles of Geology*, in which he showed that the earth must be millions of years old. But somehow, this did not bother the Church too much—after all, if God created the rocks, he may well have created them with million-year-old fossils, in much the same way that you might stock a new library with old books. But Darwin was saying that man was not the "Lord of Creation," merely a latecomer descended from the ape. In a speech in Parliament, Disraeli made the famous comment that in the controversy about whether man was an ape or an angel, he was on the side of the angels.

The historic battle—evolutionism's equivalent of the Battle of Hastings—took place in Oxford on June 30, 1860, and the two leading debaters were Bishop Samuel Wilberforce—known as

"Soapy Sam" because of his unctuous manner—and "Darwin's bulldog," biologist Thomas Henry Huxley. After Soapy Sam had given a humorous and satirical account of the theory of evolution, he turned politely to Huxley and "begged to know, was it through his grandfather or his grandmother that he claimed his descent from a monkey?" He sat down to roars of laughter and applause.

It is reported that Huxley slapped his knee and whispered to his neighbor, "The Lord hath delivered him into my hands." Huxley rose to his feet and spoke quietly and gravely, explaining Darwin's theory in plain and simple language. He concluded by saying, "I would not be ashamed to have a monkey for my ancestor, but I *would* be ashamed to be connected with a man who used his great gifts to obscure the truth." The applause that followed was as thunderous as the applause that had followed Wilberforce's attack. One woman fainted. And Wilberforce was so stunned that he declined the opportunity to have a final say.

Eleven years later, in 1871, Darwin declared his belief that archaeology would turn up the proof of his theory in "the Missing Link." Darwinians were eager to have the honor of fulfilling that prophecy. And in 1912 it looked as if Charles Dawson had suc- ceeded triumphantly.

Other finds followed. Teilhard de Chardin found a human ca- nine in the debris that had been thrown out of the pit; it fit the skull. An elephant bone shaped into a club—the earliest known weapon—was also found. And when, in 1915, another "Piltdown cranium" was found two miles away, even the doubters were convinced. This "proved" beyond all doubt that man was the descendant of an ape.

Dawson had only a year longer to live; he died in 1916, at the age of fifty-two, in a glow of celebrity. Woodward had christened his discovery *Eoanthropus dawsoni*—Dawsonian dawn man. And in due course a statue of Dawson was erected near the gravel pit.

The problem was that Dawson's dawn man did not seem to fit into the emerging picture of human evolution. For example, Neanderthal man, which had been discovered in 1857, had a receding jaw; so did the much older Heidelberg man, discovered in 1907 (and also dated at about half a million years old). So did

Java man, discovered in 1891. But these all looked much more humanoid, less apelike, than dawn man. In short, Piltdown dawn man was far too late to be the Missing Link.

The bubble finally burst in 1953, when the Piltdown skull was subjected to the latest scientific tests at the British Museum by Dr. Kenneth Oakley. These included fluorine analysis. (Fluorine accumulates in buried bones, so the older a bone, the more fluorine it contains.) The Piltdown skull proved to be a mere 50,000 years old, while the jawbone proved to be that of a chimpanzee; both had been stained with iron sulphate and pigment. The Piltdown skull, which had figured in so many books on the evolution of man, was a hoax. But who was responsible for it?

The obvious suspect was Dawson himself. Evidence began to accumulate that he was not as honest as everyone had supposed. Dr. J. S. Weiner, the author of a book entitled *The Piltdown Problem* (1955), went down to Sussex, and in a cabinet of fossils belonging to a contemporary of Dawson's, Harry Morris, found a flint described on its accompanying card as "stained by C. Dawson with intent to defraud." In fact, Dawson is known to have stained the bones with bichromate to preserve them—or at least that is the reason he gave Woodward. Local historians had criticized Dawson for basing his *History of Hastings Castle*, without acknowledgment, on an earlier history. And there was a story that he had bought a house that was being considered for the site of the headquarters of the Sussex Archaeological Society by using his membership to snatch it from under the society members' noses. Whoever "salted" the gravel pit with primitive tools, and bones of hippopotamus, rhinoceros, and deer, had access to this kind of material. And the same person placed the second "Piltdown skull" two miles away to silence the skeptics. Dawson was certainly in a position to do these things.

On the other hand, Francis Vere, author of *The Piltdown Fantasy*, is convinced that Dawson did *not* have sufficient knowledge to carry out the fraud—for example, enough knowledge of dentistry to grind down the teeth. He believes that the hoaxer was one of the many local amateur geologists—like Harry Morris (who is known to have been an embittered man).

But *why* was it done? If Dawson did it, then the reason may have been either the desire for personal aggrandizement or the desire to prove Darwin right once and for all. Fifty years after the publication of *The Origin of Species*, the world was still full of fundamentalists who could not accept Darwinism. In 1925 a schoolteacher named John Scopes was put on trial in Dayton, Tennessee, for teaching his pupils the theory of evolution. Scopes was found guilty and fined $100.

In a pamphlet entitled *Lessons of Piltdown* (published by the Evolution Protest Movement in 1959), Francis Vere even suggests that Teilhard de Chardin could have been responsible for the Piltdown hoax. Vere's protest is also directed at the notion that man is descended from the ape, and he suggests that what the scientists ought to be trying to explain is the "gift to Man from God—the mind." Vere's protest is in the spirit of the complaint of Samuel Butler—another anti-Darwinian—who claimed that the theory of natural selection had "banished God from the universe." Bernard Shaw took up his protest in the preface to *Back to Methuselah*, in which he argued that the failure of Darwinism lies in its rigid determinism, its failure to recognize the part played in evolution by the *will* of the individual.

What, in fact, has happened since the 1950s is that the objections of historians like Vere—and even of the townsfolk of Dayton—have been justified by new discoveries that prove, once and for all, that there is no connection between human beings and apes. Some ninety million years ago, in the age that succeeded the dinosaurs (who lived from about 250 to 150 million years ago), the ancestor of both the apes and man was a tiny insect-eating creature that resembled a mouse or shrew and that lived in the steaming forests that covered the earth. At about this time, these creatures felt confident enough to emerge from the under-growth and take to the trees, where they ate seeds and tender leaves and a new development called fruit, rather than insects. It was probably as a consequence of living in trees that the "mouse" developed a "hand" with a thumb and four fingers, rather than a paw with all the digits side by side. Many of these creatures were exterminated by their cousins the rodents, who had one major advantage—their teeth never stopped growing and so never wore down. But they survived in Africa—or rather, in the vast continent that included Africa and South America, before they drifted apart forty million years ago. By this time, the tree shrew had turned into a monkey—so in that sense, man *is* descended from a monkey.

For some reason, monkeys had their eyes in front of their heads, rather than on either side, as rodents have. This enabled them to develop depth perception, which in time would mean that they could handle tools. (If you try driving a car with one eye closed, you will find it far more difficult to judge your distance from the hedge.) As the earth became dryer, and the lush African forests became savannahs, the primates split into two lines, the apes and the monkeys. The earliest ape seems to have been a creature we call *Aegyptopithecus*, which lived about twenty-eight million years ago. Then came *Dryopithecus*, a baboonlike creature, which spread out of Africa and across Europe. About fifteen million years ago, one line of *Dryopithecus* took to the trees and became the ancestor of the modern ape—the kind we encounter in the Tarzan stories.

Next came the ape we call *Ramapithecus*, found in 1934 in northern India. This was so humanlike that paleontologist G. E. Lewis classified it as a hominid. *Ramapithecus* seems to date back between eight and fourteen million years and has a claim to be the "first man."

In 1924, in the part of Africa now called Botswana, miners who were blasting rock discovered fossil bones near a railway station known as Taungs; further investigation revealed the skull of a child; it still had milk teeth and thus was reckoned to be about six years old. The brain case was much smaller than that of a human child, yet the teeth were definitely human. Professor Raymond Dart concluded that this was one of the earliest "true men" yet discovered and called it *Australopithecus africanus*, or southern ape man. This creature was a meat eater and is nowadays referred to as a "Dartian." Another type of *Australopithecus* was discovered some time later, a vegetarian with a more robust build; he was labeled *Australopithecus robustus*.

Dart's fellow scientists were unwilling to accept that his meat-eating ape-man was an important link in the evolutionary chain, but discoveries made by the paleontologist Robert Broom in the second half of the 1930s left no doubt that the "Dartians" were a truly human species that had originated in Africa. Some dated as far back as three million years ago, others a mere three-quarters of a million years. The "Dartians" seem to have given way to the creature we call *Homo erectus*, the immediate predecessor of *Homo sapiens*, while *robustus* seems to have died out.

At some of the australopithecine sites, Dart found baboon skulls with a kind of double depression in the back. And the discovery of antelope front-leg bones (*humeri*) at these sites suggested to Dart that these early ape-men had used the bones as clubs. It led him to publish, in 1949, a highly controversial paper entitled "The Predatory Transition from Ape to Man," which argued that human intelligence had developed through the use of weapons. Wielding a club, Dart maintained, requires a certain degree of coordination between the hand and the eye. In short, Dart was suggesting that man evolved because he was the descendant of some primitive killer ape, while his more peaceful brothers stayed in the trees and developed into modern gorillas, orangutans, and so on. Dartian man went on to develop tools—stones with their edges chipped off to make primitive axes, which could be used to extract marrow from bones—about two million years ago.

Dart's version of human evolution was popularized in 1961 by the playwright-turned-anthropologist Robert Ardrey, in a book entitled *African Genesis*. This, briefly, is how Ardrey sees human development: About fifteen million years ago, in the Miocene era, Africa was still covered with lush forests. Twelve million years ago the rains stopped, and the Miocene gave way to the long droughts of the Pliocene era. At some point in the Pliocene era, our human ancestors descended from the trees to take their chance on the savannahs. These became the two types of *Australopithecus*— the meat-eating "Dartians" and the vegetarian *robustus*. During this period, Ardrey believes, the "Dartians" learned to use weapons like bone clubs.

Then, about a million years ago, the rains came, and the Pleistocene era began. It was the bad weather, Ardrey thinks, that led man to develop his intelligence. Pebble tools made their appearance. So did hand axes. The gentle *robustus* vanished as rains gave way to periodic droughts, but "Dartian" man, the "bad-weather animal," survived. And because his chief evolutionary advantage was his aggression, his killer instinct, he gradually became the most dominant species on earth. This, Ardrey suggests, is why his greatest problem in our modern world is that he will exterminate his own species.

It is a gloomy picture, and it can hardly hold any comfort for antievolutionists who are pleased that we are *not* descended from the ape. But it is not necessarily the last word. Richard Leakey, son of the eminent anthropologist Louis Leakey (whom Ardrey quotes extensively), has argued that all the evidence shows that our primitive ancestors were peaceable creatures and that it was not until he began to create cities—with their overcrowding and other problems—that man became cruel and destructive. And the Finish paleontologist Björn Kurtén developed his own views in a book entitled—significantly—*Not from the Apes* (1972). This, in summary, is his view:

Our tree-living Ramapithecine ancestors of about fifteen million years ago (in the Miocene era) were furry creatures about the size of a modern-day five-year-old child; but they had forward-looking eyes and human teeth. Kurtén suggests that these highly social creatures developed a "call system"—of warnings and so on—that developed into language. They became capable of "simple thought processes."

With the coming of the droughts—and the savannahs—of the Pliocene era, these creatures came down from the trees—not because they were driven down but because the savannahs offered a richer way of life. The baboons descended from the trees at about the same time. But the baboons remained four-legged herbivores, while the manlike primates became two-legged carnivores. Their upright posture allowed them to see farther into the distance—an advantage for hunters. The need for periods of violent activity—chasing small animals for example—led to the gradual loss of fur.

Since the wandering life was hard on women and small children, the band was inclined to find itself a semipermanent home. The men went hunting while the women remained behind. Family life developed, and two-parent families became the nucleus of the population. Sex played an increasingly important part in their lives, instead of being a "sideshow" (Ardrey's phrase), as it is for animals in the wild. Thinner fur made skin contact more sensuous. Because they walked upright, face-to-face mating gradually replaced sex from the rear. Lips became fuller and female breasts developed. (Kurtén acknowledges that he owes this idea to Desmond Morris's *Naked Ape*.) And at this point, Kurtén agrees that the ability to manipulate weapons caused a development of intelligence. Something very like speech evolved from the "monkey chatter."

Homo erectus came into being about two or three million years ago and coexisted with Dartian man. But while Dartian man had a brain size of about 500 cc, the brain of *Homo erectus* slowly developed until it reached 1,000 cc around 400,000 years ago. There it stopped, and *Homo erectus* gradually faded out.

But about half a million years ago a new species, *Homo sapiens*, came on the scene—no one quite knows how. (One scientist, Allan Wilson, has even suggested that *Homo sapiens* developed from *Homo erectus* in Australia.) What we do know is that his brain developed from *Homo erectus*'s 1,000 cc to modern man's 1,800 cc in such a short period (in evolutionary terms) that scientists speak of "the brain explosion."

What caused this brain explosion? We now know enough about evolution to know that things do not just "happen." Evolution is not "natural"; the shark has remained unchanged for 150 million years. Kurtén has nothing much to suggest, except to point out the obvious—that our evolutionary capacities are drawn out of us by changes in the environment (like the bad weather of the Pleistocene). But as far as we know, there have been no such changes in the past half million years, except a succession of ice ages. It is possible, of course, that these "pressured" man into developing his brain; but it seems more likely that they would favor the development of fur or hair. Ardrey even suggests the possibility that the brain explosion may have been connected with a huge meteor that exploded over the Indian Ocean about seventy thousand years ago (its remains, called *tektites*, can still be found scattered over twenty million square miles) and caused a reversal in the earth's magnetic field. He suggests that if the earth had no magnetic field for a brief intervening period, a rain of cosmic rays may have caused genetic changes in human beings.

Another anthropologist, Otto Kiss Maerth, devoted a book entitled *The Beginning Was the End* (1971) to the theory that human evolution was due to cannibalism—discoveries near Peking in 1929 seemed to show that the ape-men of six hundred thousand years ago ate the brains of their enemies. Maerth suggests that eating brains stimulates both the intelligence and the sexual instinct and that this explains the brain explosion. The objection to this theory is that there is not enough widespread evidence for cannibalism and the eating of brains to account for human evolution.

Ardrey has a more plausible basic hypothesis, which he calls "the hunting hypothesis"—the notion that men had to learn social cooperation because they had to learn to hunt together. But Ardrey had originally suggested that Dartian man became a carnivore during the Pleistocene era (in the past million years), when droughts made vegetation scarce. When Louis Leakey discovered evidence at Fort Ternan, in Kenya, that *Ramapithecus* was a meat eater nearly fifteen million years ago, that view was undermined; yet it only increased Ardrey's conviction that the "hunting hypothesis" explains human evolution. What he failed to explain was why wolves and other animals who hunt in packs have not evolved to the human level.

In fact, this problem has almost certainly been solved by an experimental psychologist named Nicholas Humphrey, who studied the brains of mountain gorillas in Rwanda, in central Africa, and wondered why they had such large brains when their lives are so crudely simple—eating, sleeping, and moving on to new feeding grounds. The answer came as he observed the gorillas closely and noticed their incredible sensitivity to one another's feelings. The most important thing in a gorilla's life is its relation to other gorillas. A gorilla's family life is the equivalent of a university education; it learns to react delicately to the moods, feelings, and reactions of other gorillas. If Humphrey is correct, then the size of the brain has something to do with the complexity of social relations.

The "Humphrey theory" of evolution, then, would run like this: As man became increasingly successful because of his prowess as a hunter, his numbers increased, and social intercourse with other groups became increasingly important. As sensitivity and cooperation became survival factors, the brain flourished.

Yet the "hunting hypothesis" may pave the way to the next step in the argument. If Kurtén is correct in his belief that Dartian man ceased to be a wanderer in the Pliocene era and began to leave the women and children behind while he went hunting, then this would apply even more so to *Homo sapiens* during the great droughts and ice ages of the Pleistocene. Most anthropologists seem to recognize that sex played a basic part in human evolution—from Kurtén and Morris to Maerth, with his brain-eating theory. As Ardrey points out, sex is a sideshow in the world of nature. Wild animals only become interested in it when the female experiences her periodic cycle. But at some point in his evolution, human sexual desire became independent of that cycle, and man began to have sex at all times *except* when the female was menstruating. It seems logical to explain this in terms of the hunting hypothesis. If a hunter had been away from home for weeks, then he would expect to make love to his mate when he returned, whether she was "in heat" or not. Some females would naturally object to this; but they would have fewer offspring than the females who had no such objection—or swallowed their dislike—and eventually, the objectors would die out.

What no one seems to have recognized so far is the importance of sex as an "internal" factor in evolution. When an animal has nothing else to do, it lies down and yawns. When a man has nothing else to do, his thoughts turn as often as not to sex. If there is a pretty girl in the vicinity, he may begin to brood on seduction—even if he happens to have a wife already. If he is too shy or otherwise inhibited, then he may simply daydream about sex. From being a "sideshow," sex has become one of the central interests of human existence.

Now if we imagine Stone Age hunters in a period of scarcity, we can see that they may have had to have spent longer and longer periods away from the women and children of the tribe; a hunting expedition might have lasted a month or longer. Back at home, women were now permanently receptive and were consequently beginning to develop the sexual characteristics males found exciting—larger breasts, full lips, rounded buttocks. When the males came back from a long expedition, some skinny adolescent girls had suddenly begun to change into desirable women. The presence of these unattached females must have introduced an element of competition and excitement. Young men now had good reason for wanting to become successful hunters and fighters—it gave them the pick of the girls.

We note another interesting thing about human beings: that from babyhood onward they have a tendency to idealize possible mates. Little boys fall in love with the prettiest girl in the class and daydream of being cowboys who rescue her from a band of marauding Indians. We do not know, of course, whether dogs and cats experience these emotions, but it seems unlikely. As far as we can see, it seems to have been sex that taught human beings to use the imagination.

This means that, to a large extent, sex provides us with goals and objectives, even when there are no other stimuli. It is an "internal" factor in evolution, a psychological drive that operates most of the time. It could be the factor that explains why man became an "evolutionary animal," an animal who went on striving even when he had a full belly.

Kurtén seems to skirt these ideas when he remarks: "Another semi-solution [to the problem of evolution] was the idea of an inner force of evolution, the *élan vital*, which would automatically carry us forward to new heights of nobility and spirituality. Unfortunately there is no evidence whatever for the existence of such a force." But sex is precisely such a force, as Goethe recognized when he wrote: "The eternal feminine draws us upwards and on."

In the previous paragraph Kurtén had dismissed another possibility: that by improving themselves, human beings produce better offspring. This is known as "the inheritance of acquired characteristics" and is a theory of evolution that was suggested by Darwin's predecessor, Lamarck. The simplest illustration of the difference between the two theories is the problem of how the giraffe came to have a long neck. According to Darwin, food shortages due to drought caused the original short-necked giraffes to become extinct. But the giraffes who, *by chance*, happened to have longer necks, were able to reach the leaves on higher branches and so survived. And eventually, all giraffes had long necks. Lamarck's view was that when food became scarce, giraffes had to make strenuous efforts to reach higher branches, and these efforts gradually lengthened their necks.

The discovery of the genes (by Mendel) made it look as if Darwin was right and Lamarck wrong. For genetics seemed to prove that, even if a giraffe could stretch its neck by effort, it could not transmit this long neck to its children, whose genes would ensure that they had short necks.

In the twentieth century some biologists wondered whether perhaps genes do not mutate at random but in some way that is useful to the organism. But this theory was disproved by the study of bacteria, which showed that genes always mutate at random. At least, healthy and well-nourished bacteria mutate at random. And that is as one would expect. Why should they want to change if they are comfortable and well fed?

But in the late 1980s Dr. John Cairns of Harvard decided to study starving bacteria and concluded that some of them *could* deliberately mutate to utilize a new food source. His results have been confirmed by Professor Barry Hall at the University of Rochester, New York. When he deliberately starved his bacteria of an amino acid essential to their survival, some of them mutated so they could manufacture the missing acid, until whole colonies of the mutated bacteria came into existence. It seems, then, that Lamarck was probably right after all. As, incidentally, was Samuel Butler, who objected to Darwin on precisely these grounds (see chapter 15).

But even on a more down-to-earth level, the rigidly Darwinian view is questionable. We all know that efforts made by parents *can* be passed on to their children—that, for example, parents who have educated themselves can pass on their love of learning to their children. The truth is—as Kurtén recognizes—that the brain has a huge *dormant capacity*, which can be awakened by the right stimuli. Man had developed a "modern size" brain long before he had books and music and philosophy to put in it.

Kurtén also recognizes this when he says that our ancestors

may have come down from the trees not because there was no longer enough food in the forests but because they were excited by the *possibilities* of the wide savannahs. Again, he is recognizing an evolutionary force, a craving for adventure, for a fuller and richer mode of existence. *Not from the Apes* is devoted to the thesis that man's uniqueness may date back as far as thirty-five million years, when our lineage split off from that of our cousins the apes. In the beginning, that split may have been due to natural selection and survival of the fittest. But in the past half million years or so—perhaps far longer than that—the evolutionary urge seems to have acquired its own momentum, so that even a convinced Darwinian like Sir Julian Huxley (grandson of T. H. Huxley) can state that man has finally become "the managing director of evolution."

We can see, then, that the whole Missing Link controversy was based on simple misunderstanding. Darwin appeared to be saying that man is merely a more intelligent ape and that his intelligence developed by chance. That clearly implies that individual effort counts for nothing. We struggle because we *have* to struggle; that is part of the rat race. But our "higher aspirations" are so much nonsense. We are mere apes.

Human evolution proves the contrary. Man has become an evolutionary animal, an animal who *expects* to change. Striving has become his second nature—a striving based upon his intense romanticism, the same romanticism that made the Greeks romanticize Helen of Troy, that made the troubadours romanticize their chosen "lady," that made Malory romanticize Queen Guinevere and Isolde. And there is every reason to expect our evolution to continue. The dormant capacity that changed Dartian man into modern man lies inside our heads. The brain developed through social intercourse and cooperation, but its excess size meant *dormant capacity*. In other words, *Homo sapiens* developed a modern brain but had very little use for it.

Brain physiologists tell us that, in spite of science, philosophy, art, and technology, modern man still only uses one-fifth of his brain capacity. When he learns to use the other four-fifths, there is every reason to believe that he will be as different from modern man as you and I are from our australopithecine ancestors.

24

Joan Norkot:
The Case of the Bleeding Corpse

When Sir John Mainard, known as "a gentleman of great note and judgment of the law," died in 1690, there was found among his papers an account of an incredible case in which a woman's corpse accused her murderers. The whole document was printed in *The Gentleman's Magazine* of July 1851, a copy having been taken by a lawyer named Hunt. The events it describes are so extraordinary that the magazine took the precaution of heading it: "Singular Instance of Superstition." Yet Mainard's account makes it clear that the event was witnessed by a crowd of people standing in a graveyard, including two clergymen.

The trial in which the evidence was heard took place at Hereford Assizes in Herefordshire in "the fourth year of the reign of King Charles I" (1629), more than sixty years before Mainard's death. Mainard's account is printed in full in the Reverend Montague Summers's *The Vampire in Europe* (1929). An account written by Valentine Dyall in *Unsolved Mysteries* (1954)* is also based on the court records, which it admits are "tantalizingly

---

*Researched by Larry Forrester and Peter Robinson.

scanty." The account has an irritating lack of dates, and even of names, but the general outline is clear enough.

There had been, it seems, some trouble between Arthur Norkot and his wife, Joan, one suggestion being that he suspected her of infidelity. It may have been simply overcrowding that caused their disagreements, for Joan lived in a two-room cottage with her husband and baby, as well as with her mother-in-law, Mary Norkot, and her sister- and brother-in-law, Agnes and John Okeman.

One morning Joan was found dead in her bed, with her throat cut; the baby was lying—unharmed—beside her. A bloodstained knife was sticking in the bare floorboards.

Her husband had been away from home that night, according to the relatives. He had gone to visit friends near Tewkesbury. The others swore that it was impossible that Joan Norkot could have been murdered, for anyone entering the cottage would have had to pass through the room in which they slept before entering her bedroom.

At the inquest that followed, it was admitted that there had been "a great deal of trouble" between husband and wife and that Joan had been in "a sour temper with some despondency" before she went to bed. But when the knife was tried in the small hole in the floor that its point had made, it was observed that its handle pointed toward the door and that it was some feet from the bed. If Joan had thrown the knife down after cutting her throat, surely the handle would have been pointing toward the *bed*? In spite of this, a verdict of *felo-de-se* (suicide) was returned, and Joan was duly buried, presumably in unhallowed ground.

It may have been the knife evidence that caused unpleasant rumors to circulate (Mainard merely says "observations of divers circumstances"). The coroner was asked to reopen the case and agreed to a reinvestigation. The body was exhumed, and it was found that the neck was broken. Clearly, the woman could not have broken her own neck. It was noted, moreover, that there was more blood on the floor of the room than on the bed, which seemed odd if Joan had cut her throat in bed. Moreover, Arthur Norkot's alibi collapsed when his friends in Tewkesbury declared that they had not seen him for three years. Altogether, the evidence against the accused was so strong that the prosecution decided not to mention the strangest and most incredible piece of evidence at their trial. But for some reason, the jury did not think it was conclusive, and the four were acquitted. The judge, a man named Harvey, was incredulous and "let fall his opinion that it were better an appeal were brought than so foul a murder should escape unpunished."

This could only be done in the name of Joan Norkot's baby. Accordingly, the four were retried in front of Justice Harvey. And it was at this retrial that a nameless clergyman—the minister of the parish—presented the evidence that the corpse had accused her murderers. The incredulous judge asked if anyone else had seen it, and the old man replied, "I believe the whole company saw it."

What had happened, it seemed, was this: Thirty days after she was buried, the body of Joan Norkot was taken from the grave and the coffin placed beside it, almost certainly on trestles. It must have been an unpleasant sight, since the severed jugular vein would have drained her of most of her blood. Then, in accordance with an ancient superstition, each of the accused was asked to touch the body. According to the superstition, if a corpse is touched by its murderer, the wounds will bleed afresh. Mrs. Oke-man fell to her knees and prayed to God to grant proof of their innocence. Then, like the others, she was asked to touch the corpse.

The clergyman deposed the following:

The appellers did touch the dead body, whereupon the brow of the dead, which was all a livid or carrion colour . . . began to have a dew or gentle sweat, which reached down in drops upon the face, and the brow turned and changed to a lively and fresh colour, and the dead opened one of her eyes and shut it again, and this opening the eye was done several times. She likewise thrust out the ring- or marriage finger three times and pulled it in again, and the finger dropt blood from it on to the grass.

It was at this point that the judge expressed his doubts, and the clergyman then turned to his brother, the minister of the next parish, who had also been present. The brother repeated the evidence: that the brow had begun to perspire, that its color had changed from livid (i.e., a bruised color) to fresh and normal, that the eye had opened, and that the finger had three times made a pointing motion. (This seems to have been taken to imply that only three of the four accused were guilty.)

What followed was a repetition of the main evidence that had already been presented at the first trial. The body of Joan Norkot lay "in a composed manner" in the bed, the bedclothes undisturbed and her baby beside her. This in itself was evidence enough to convict someone of murder, for it was obviously impossible that she could cut her throat elsewhere in the room—the floor was heavily bloodstained—then lie down and carefully cover herself up. Moreover, the broken neck seemed to indicate that considerable force had been used against her. It is just about possible for a person to break her own neck but not to cut her throat afterwards. It is equally impossible to cut the throat first and then break the neck.

What had happened, quite clearly, was that the husband and wife had quarreled violently and that he had ended with his hands around her throat. She had fallen and struck her head against something, breaking her neck. Now in a panic—for the death was almost certainly accidental—Arthur Norkot conferred with his mother and sister about what could be done, with his brother-in-law, John Okeman, an unwilling participant. To hide the bruises on Joan's throat and her broken neck, the solution seemed to be to cut her throat. But they were in such a panic that they did this on the floor of the room instead of in the bed. Then Joan Norkot was arranged in her bed and the baby—who had probably slept through it all—placed beside her. Someone left a bloodstained fingerprint and thumbprint on her hand. (Chief Justice Hyde, who heard the case, seems to have been so inexperienced in such matters that he had to ask how they could distinguish the prints of the left hand from those of the right.) And as they were leaving the room, someone tossed the bloodstained knife—which probably lay near the door—back into the room, so it stuck in the floor a few feet from the bed. Then Arthur Norkot hastily washed off his bloodstains and took his leave, instructing his mother to "find" the body the next morning and explain that her son was away in Tewkesbury.

It is clear that the attempt to make the murder look like suicide was so bungled that a moderately intelligent investigator could have seen through it right away. But in 1629 scientific crime investigation was unknown. It would be almost another two centuries before Britain even had a police force. If someone was suspected of a crime, the standard method of "investigation" was to torture him until he either confessed or died. No one, it seemed, felt that the evidence against the Norkot family was sufficiently strong for an accusation.

This brings us to the most difficult question of all. Did the corpse really "revive" and accuse the criminals? Any reader who has studied chapter 26 in this volume may concede that the evidence for the "survival" of the human personality is at least plausible. It would even seem that spirits can, under certain circumstances, "possess" the living and cause unexplained movements of material objects ("poltergeist" effects). And in one extraordinary case, the spirit of a murder victim seems to have returned to accuse her killer (see chapter 3). It seems just as conceivable that Joan Norkot was momentarily able to "repossess" her old body in order to accuse her attackers. But it must be immediately admitted that there are no other known examples in the history of paranormal research.

In his *Unsolved Mysteries*, Valentine Dyall suggests a common-sense solution: that the two doctors who presided over the exhumation decided to shock the suspects into a public confession. A tiny pouch of some dark red fluid was stuck to her left hand and a fine thread attached to its stopper. The thread was passed through the wedding ring. Another thread was tied to one of the eyelashes. Then both threads were attached to the coffin handles. When the "touching test" was suggested, each doctor (standing on either side of the coffin) pulled on a thread. The eyelid twitched, the ring-finger jerked, and the "blood" was released so that it ran down the side of the corpse and out of a crack in the bottom of the badly made coffin. The bleeding wound "proved" that Joan had been murdered by someone who had just touched her. The evidence states that someone put his finger into the blood and testified that it was real; but this, Dyall suggests, would obviously have been one of the doctors themselves.

It might be just possible, although one would think that in broad daylight the threads would surely have been visible. And what about the evidence of both clergymen that the face lost its "dead" color and seemed to come to life? Pure imagination? That is also possible—except that they claimed that this was the *first* thing that happened, before the eye opened or the finger twitched. The imagination theory would be more acceptable if the face had "come to life" *after* the corpse "winked."

Whatever the explanation, the evidence of the two clergymen convinced the court. Arthur Norkot, together with his mother and sister, was sentenced to death. For reasons that Sir John Mainard (who was Sergeant Mainard when he took part in the trial) does not explain, the jury decided to acquit Norkot's brother-in-law, John Okeman. When sentenced, all three repeated, "I did not do it." In fact, Agnes Okeman was reprieved when she was discovered to be pregnant. Mary and John Norkot were hanged. Mainard concludes: "I inquired if they confessed anything at execution, but they did not, as I was told."

25

The *Oera Linda Book*:
The Forgotten History of
a Lost Continent

In 1876 there appeared in London a bewildering work entitled the *Oera Linda Book* and subtitled *From a Manuscript of the Thirteenth Century*. It was published by Trubner and Co., one of the most respectable names in publishing, so there could be no suggestion that it was a hoax. And the fact that the original text in Frisian (the language of Friesland, a part of northern Holland) was published opposite the English translation offered scholars the opportunity to check for themselves. Yet if the claims of the *Oera Linda Book* were true, then the history of the ancient world had to be completely rewritten. It suggested that in the third millennium B.C., at about the time the Great Pyramid and the original Stonehenge were built, there was a great island continent in northern Europe that was inhabited by a highly civilized race. In 2193 B.C. this island was destroyed, like the legendary Atlantis, by some immense catastrophe. But enough of its inhabitants escaped to carry their civilization elsewhere—including ancient Egypt and Crete. In fact, the *Oera Linda Book* suggested that the legendary King Minos of Crete (creator of the Labyrinth) was a Frisian and that the same ancient civilization gave democracy to Athens.

All this seemed so extraordinary and so confusing that the first reaction of Dutch and German scholars was to suggest that the book was a forgery. Yet they seem to have agreed that it was not a modern forgery and that it was probably a century to a century and a half old. But that would date it roughly to the 1730s. And it is hard to imagine why anyone would have *wanted* to forge such a document in the 1730s. A century later, in the Romantic era, there would have been some point in creating this mysterious narrative with its marvelous hints of a golden age in the remote past. But it is virtually impossible to imagine why, in that rather dull era of Frederick the Great and the Prince of Orange-Nassau (dull, at any rate, from the literary point of view), anyone should have bothered. It is true that a famous forgery of "ancient" Gaelic poetry—the works of "Ossian," actually written by James Mac-Pherson—became immensely popular in England and on the Continent in the 1760s; but if the *Oera Linda Book* was inspired by MacPherson's Ossian, why did the forger put it in a drawer and forget about it until 1848, when it finally saw the light of day?

According to its Introduction, written in 1871, the *Oera Linda Book* had been preserved in the Linden (or Linda) family from "time immemorial" and was written in a peculiar script that looked a little like Greek. It began with a letter from one "Liko oera Linda," dated A.D. 803, in which he begged his son to preserve the book "with body and soul," since it contained the history of their peoples. The manuscript was inherited by a certain C. Over de Linden—a modernized version of Oera Linda—in 1848, and a learned professor named Verwijs asked if he could look at it. He immediately recognized its language as ancient Fries, a form of Dutch. The manuscript examined by Verwijs had been copied in 1256 on paper manufactured from cotton and written in a black ink that did not contain iron (which eventually turns brown).

According to the Introduction (by Dr. J. O. Ottema), the *Oera Linda Book* records the history of the people of a large island called Atland, which was roughly on the same latitude as the British Isles, in what is now the North Sea (in other words, off the coast of modern Holland). Dr. Ottema seems to think that Atland is Plato's Atlantis,* which most commentators have placed some-where in the mid-Atlantic. But since Plato says only that it was "beyond the Pillars of Hercules" (what is now Gibraltar), Ottema could be correct.

According to the *Oera Linda Book*, Atland had an excellent climate and an abundance of food. And since its rulers were wise and deeply religious, it was a peaceful and contented land. Its legendary founder was a half-mythical woman named Frya—obviously a version of the Nordic *Freya*, the moon goddess, whose name means "a lady." (In the same way, *frey* means "a lord.") Its people worshiped one God, under the (to us) unpronounceable name of Wr-alda. Frya was one of three sisters, the other two being named Lyda and Finda. Lyda was dark-skinned and be-came the founder of the black races; Finda was yellow-skinned and became the founder of the yellow races. Frya was white.

All of this is obviously legend. But the *Oera Linda Book* then goes on to describe historical events.

In the year 2193 B.C., a great catastrophe of some sort struck Atland, and it was overwhelmed by the sea. Logic suggests that the same catastrophe must have struck the British Isles, since they were so close; but if Atland was as low and flat as Holland, we can understand why it was submerged. (The Dogger Bank, where Atland would have been situated, is the shallowest area of the North Sea.)

According to Plato, Atlantis had been destroyed in a great catastrophe more than nine thousand years earlier. But one modern authority, Professor A. G. Galanopoulos, has argued that all the figures associated with Atlantis (which were recorded by Egyptian priests) were about ten times too great—for example, Plato says that the moat around the royal city was ten thousand stades (more than a thousand miles) long, which would make the royal city about three hundred times larger than Greater London or Los Angeles. If we divide nine thousand years by ten, we get nine hundred. The Egyptian priests told the Athenian lawgiver Solon about Atlantis around 600 B.C., which would make the date for the destruction of Atlantis about 1500 B.C. (nine hundred

---

*See "Atlantis" in my book *The Encyclopedia of Unsolved Mysteries* (1988).

years earlier). This is roughly the date of the explosion of the volcano of Santorini (north of Crete) that devastated most of the Mediterranean, and Galanopoulos argues that the island of Santorini was Atlantis. The only problem is that Plato placed Atlantis beyond the Pillars of Hercules—in which case, Atland is certainly a contender.

Another reason for the relative neglect of the *Oera Linda Book* is that its narrative seems so unfamiliar and its names are so strange; in this respect it resembles the *Book of Mormon* or that extraordinary work entitled *Oahspe*, which was "dictated" to an American medium named J. B. Newbrough at roughly the same time the *Oera Linda Book* was published. But these two documents claim some kind of "divine" origin, while the *Oera Linda Book* purports to be a historical document.

Nevertheless, the people mentioned in it are not pure invention. A later book speaks at length about a warrior named Friso, an officer of Alexander the Great (born 356 B.C.), who is described in other Nordic chronicles. (The *Oera Linda Book* also speaks at length of Alexander the Great.) These chronicles state that Friso came from India. The *Oera Linda Book* says that Friso was descended from a Frisian colony that settled in the Punjab about 1550 B.C.; moreover, the Greek geographer Strabo mentions this strange "Indian" tribe, referring to them by the name *Germania*. The *Oera Linda Book* even mentions Ulysses and recounts how he went in search of a sacred lamp—a priestess had foretold that if he could find it, he would become king of all Italy. After an unsuccessful attempt to buy the lamp from its priestess-custodian, the "Earth Mother" (using treasures looted from Troy), he sailed to a place named Walhallagara (which sounds oddly like Valhalla) and had a love affair with a priestess named Kalip (obviously Calypso), with whom he stayed for several years "to the scandal of all who knew it." From Kalip he obtained a sacred lamp of the kind he wanted, but it did him no good, for he was shipwrecked and had to be picked up, naked and destitute, by another ship.

This fragment of Greek history, tossed into the *Oera Linda Book* is interesting for two reasons. It dates this adventure of Ulysses about 1188, which is about fifty years later than modern archaeology would date the fall of Troy (see chapter 15). But the *Oera Linda Book* could be correct. And it states that the nymph Calypso was actually a *burgtmaagd* (a word meaning "borough maid"—literally, a virgin priestess in charge of vestal virgins). This is consistent with the central claim of the *Oera Linda Book*: that after the "deluge," the Frisians sailed the globe and became the founders of Mediterranean civilization, as well as settling in India. It is obvious why scholars have ignored the book. To take it seriously would mean virtually rewriting ancient history. If, for example, we accept that Calypso's island, Walhallagara, was the island of Walcheren, in the North Sea (as the commentary on the *Oera Linda Book* claims it was), then Ulysses sailed right out of the Mediterranean. It is certainly simpler to accept Homer's version of the story.

After nearly a century of neglect, the *Oera Linda Book* was rediscovered by an English scholar named Robert Scrutton. In his fascinating book *The Other Atlantis*, Scrutton tells how, in 1967, he and his wife—a "sensitive" with strong psychometric powers*— were walking over Dartmoor when she experienced a terrifying vision of a flood: great green waves higher than the hills pouring across the land.

Eight years later he found legends of a great deluge in ancient poetry known as the Welsh Triads (which also speak of King Arthur). The Triads explain that long before the Kmry (the Welsh) came to Britain, there was a great flood that depopulated the entire island. One ship survived, and those who sailed in it settled in the "Summer Land" peninsula (which Scrutton identifies as the Crimea—still called Krym—in the Black Sea). These peoples decided to seek other lands, because their peninsula was subject to flooding. One portion went to Italy and the other across Germany and France and into Britain. (In fact, this account does not contradict the little we know about the mysterious people called the Celts, whose origin is unknown.) So the Kmry came back to Britain—probably around 600 B.C.—and brought their Druidic religion, which involved human sacrifice.

---

*See "Psychometry—Telescope into the Past" in my book *The Encyclopedia of Unsolved Mysteries* (1988).

Scrutton went on to uncover many other legends concerning a great catastrophe in ancient Welsh poetry and in the Icelandic Eddas (where it was known as Ragnarok). It is worth mentioning that Ignatius Donnelly, whose book *Atlantis: The Antediluvian World** caused a sensation in 1882, went on to write another classic, *Ragnarok: The Age of Fire and Ice* in the following year; in this volume he attempted to study catastrophe legends of the northern hemisphere and created a remarkable theory of continental drift that later proved to be totally accurate.

Scrutton's research led him to rediscover the *Oera Linda Book* and to become absorbed in its strange yet credible account of ancient history. The first question he asked himself was: What was the precise nature of the catastrophe that destroyed Atland and depopulated Britain? In *The Other Atlantis* (1977) he suggests that it was a giant meteor or asteroid that struck the earth somewhere in the region of the North Pole; the force of the explosion had the effect of tilting the earth's axis into a more upright position, so lands that had formerly had long, hot summers now developed arctic conditions. The Greeks have their legends of the Hyperboreans, a people who live in idyllic conditions in the far north, and Scrutton identifies these with the Atlanders.

This projectile, Scrutton suggests, produced the crater known as the Arctic Ocean—which, he claims, would look like one of the enormous craters of the moon if its water was drained away. Many stones and rocks that modern scientists believe were moved by glaciers were actually, Scrutton suggests, hurled by the explosion. But this part of his theory is open to a simple objection. The opening section of the *Oera Linda Book* says that during the whole summer before the flood "the sun had been hid behind the clouds, as if unwilling to look upon the earth." There was perpetual calm, and "a damp mist hung like a wet sail over the houses and marshes." Then, "in the midst of this stillness, the earth began to tremble as if she was dying. The mountains opened to vomit forth fire and flames."

That seems clearly to be a description of a volcanic catastrophe of the kind that is supposed to have destroyed Atlantis, not a tidal

*See "Atlantis" in my book *The Encyclopedia of Unsolved Mysteries* (1988).

wave caused by a meteor. Does this mean that the meteor theory must be abandoned? Not necessarily. A meteor that struck in the region of the North Pole would certainly have produced a tidal wave, but if the polar cap itself was covered with ice, it may not have been great enough to cause a tidal wave that would submerge Britain and Atland. But the volcanic activity that would almost certainly follow such an impact *could* produce a mighty tidal wave, like the one caused by the explosion of Santorini (and later of Krakatoa).

Scrutton also mentions a description in the Finnish epic the *Kalevala* of a time when the sun vanished from the sky and the world became frozen and barren, and quotes a modern introduction that places this at a period when the Magyars (Hungarians) and the Finns were still united—at least three thousand years ago.

Scrutton believes that the "maps of the ancient sea kings" described by Professor Charles Hapgood (and discussed in chapter 28) confirm his view of the catastrophe that destroyed Atland. Once again, there is an objection. Core samples taken in Queen Maud Land (in the Antarctic) show that the last time the South Pole was unfrozen was around 4000 B.C. So the great maritime civilization that Hapgood believes was responsible for the "ancient maps" must have flourished before then.

This, of course, does not rule out a catastrophe some two thousand years later—perhaps the civilization of Atland lasted for two thousand years, like that of the Egyptians. But if Hapgood is correct, and his great maritime civilization existed more than six thousand years ago and then was either forgotten or destroyed in a great catastrophe, it certainly becomes difficult to reconcile the two theories.

There is, however, one way of reconciling them that is no bolder—or more absurd—than the theories themselves. Hapgood believed that the ancient maps were evidence of a *worldwide* maritime civilization that existed long before Alexander the Great. Let us, then, posit the existence of such a civilization that began sometime after the last great ice age—say, around 10,000 B.C. Six thousand years later this civilization is highly developed in the Antarctic and in Atland. In other parts of the world—like the Middle East—it is less highly developed, although there are already cities, and the plow has been developed. For unknown reasons—no one knows what causes ice ages—the cold returns, and the Antarctic civilization freezes up, so its peoples are forced to go elsewhere—notably to Egypt. The Atland civilization, being in more temperate latitudes, is not affected. Then, in 2192 B.C., comes the "great catastrophe" that tilted the earth's axis. Now, like the inhabitants of the South Pole, the Atlanders are also forced to move—and of course they move south, to regions that have not been affected by the great catastrophe—like India and the Mediterranean. If this scenario is correct, then both Hapgood and Scrutton could be right.

One thing seems clear: that the ancient maps prove the existence of a great maritime civilization that flourished before Alexander the Great. Like the maps, the *Oera Linda Book* also points to the existence of such a civilization. Even if the *Oera Linda Book* proved to be a forgery, the evidence of the maps would be unaffected. But at the present time, there is no evidence that it is a forgery. In this case, it deserves to be reprinted in a modern edition and carefully studied by historians—as well as read by the general public for its fascinating tales of murder and battle. If it proves to be genuine, the *Oera Linda Book* could revolutionize our view of world history.

26

Possession by the Dead:
Myth or Reality?

In 1924 the National Psychological Institute in Los Angeles published a book with the arresting title *Thirty Years Among the Dead*, by Carl A. Wickland. It was not, as one might have supposed, the memoirs of a mortuary attendant but an account by a respectable doctor of medicine of his psychological research into Spiritualism. Inevitably, it aroused a great deal of scorn among the medical fraternity, one fortunate result being that first editions are still fairly easy to find in the "occult" sections of secondhand bookshops. Yet this is hardly fair to a work that proves, on closer examination, to be a sober and factual account of Dr. Wickland's theory that a great deal of mental illness is caused by "spirit possession."

Wickland, born in Leiden (Sweden) in 1861, had emigrated to Chicago, where he earned his medical degree; he became a member of the National Association for the Advancement of Science and a medical adviser to the Los Angeles branch of the National Psychological Institute. It seems likely that he decided to burn his boats and publish his book because at age sixty-three he was on the verge of retirement anyway, and ridicule would make no difference.

Ridicule was inevitable. Twelve years before Wickland had been born, in 1849, the movement called Spiritualism had been launched in the Corinthian Hall in Rochester, New York, and within a few years, the new "religion" had swept across the Christian world.

It had all started two years earlier in the small town of Hydesville, where strange banging and rapping noises had kept the Fox family awake all night. Mrs. Fox asked the unseen knocker whether it was a spirit, and if so, to make two raps; she was answered by two thunderous bangs. Later "communications" in a code of raps seemed to establish that the knocker was the ghost of a peddler who had been murdered by a previous tenant and buried in the basement. (The previous tenant denied it indignantly, but more than half a century later, human bones were unearthed in the basement, behind a makeshift wall.) The raps and bangs turned into typical poltergeist phenomena,* which followed the two teenage sisters, Kate and Margaretta, even when they were separated. In the Fox home, bloodcurdling groaning noises and sounds like a body being dragged across the floor made James Fox's hair turn white. Eventually, a "spirit" spelled out a message to the effect that "this truth" must be proclaimed to the world, which led to the launch of the Spiritualist movement in November 1849.

Suddenly, hundreds of "mediums" discovered that they could communicate with spirits; some "physical mediums" could even cause them to "materialize." Scientists were furious and denounced the movement as a revival of medieval superstition; even the foundation of the Society for Psychical Research in London in 1882—by serious-minded scientists, philosophers, and statesmen—failed to provide Spiritualism with an air of respectability.

So even as late as 1924 Wickland was inviting ridicule with a title like *Thirty Years Among the Dead.* Yet the book's opening chapters soon make it clear that his interest sprang from medical curiosity and was that of a medical man rather than a "believer."

It all began, he explained, with a patient whom he calls Mrs. Bl—, who began to practice automatic writing and who soon

---

*See "Poltergeists" in my book *The Encyclopedia of Unsolved Mysteries* (1988); and my book *Poltergeist: A Study in Destructive Haunting* (1981).

began to have fits of derangement in which she used vile language and claimed she was an actress; she had to be committed to an asylum. Another woman, "an artist and lady of refinement," became convinced that she was a damned soul and knelt in the mud to pray at the top of her voice. Yet another woman, who owned a millinery shop, posed in her window in her nightclothes, declaring that she was Napoléon, and had to be removed by the police.

At this time (in the mid-1890s) it was generally believed that mental illness could be explained in purely physical terms; many a head physician in a mental home was appointed because he had a working knowledge of brain anatomy. Freud himself was an early convert to this theory (known as *organicism*), his professor, Dr. Theodore Meynert, being one of its chief advocates. (Meynert later turned his back on Freud when the latter returned from Paris espousing a new "psychological" explanation of neurosis based on the idea of the unconscious mind.) In America, the favorite theory of mental illness was that it was due to poisons in the system resulting from such causes as infected tonsils or decayed teeth. But Wickland was intrigued by the case of a youth named Frank James who, after a fall from a motorcycle at the age of ten, changed from an affectionate, obedient boy to a juvenile delinquent who spent many terms in reformatories and jails. Declared hopelessly insane, James succeeded in escaping from the criminal asylum and during his recapture was hit on the head with a club. On awakening, he had once again reverted to his earlier personality—gentle and good-natured.

This convinced Wickland of the inadequacy of the "toxemia" theory. And while he was still a medical student, his marriage to a woman who proved to be an excellent "medium" soon provided him with evidence of an alternative theory. One day Wickland was dissecting a leg in medical school, and on his return home, was alarmed when his wife, Anna, seemed to be about to faint. He placed his hand on her shoulder and was startled when she drew herself up and said threateningly, "What do you mean by cutting me?" After a few questions it became clear that he was speaking to the spirit of the owner of the leg he had been dissecting. Wickland guided Anna to a chair, and the spirit objected that he had no right to touch "him." When Wickland replied that he was touching his wife, it retorted, "What are you talking about? I am no woman—I'm a man." Eventually, Wickland reasoned the spirit into recognizing that it was dead and that dissecting its old body would do it no harm. When it asked for a chew of tobacco or a pipe, Wickland had to explain that his wife was a nonsmoker. (The next day he observed that the teeth of the corpse were heavily stained with tobacco.) More detailed explanation finally convinced the man that he was dead, and he left.

This showed Wickland that a "ghost" may believe that it is still alive, particularly if death came unexpectedly. He also encountered a case that seemed to demonstrate that spirits did not need to manifest themselves through a "medium." When he was alone one day, dissecting a female corpse, he thought he heard a distant voice shout, "Don't murder me!" A newspaper on the floor made a rustling noise, as if it was being crushed. Some days later, at a séance, a spirit who gave her name as Minnie Morgan claimed that it was she who had shouted "Don't murder me!" and crushed the newspaper. Minnie also had to be convinced that she was no longer alive.

At séances, entities who spoke through his wife later explained to Wickland that such "homeless spirits"—those who are unaware that they are dead—are attracted by the warmth of the "human aura"—a kind of energy sphere that is supposed to surround the human body—and, under certain circumstances, may attach themselves to the owner of the sphere as a kind of mental parasite. In effect, such spirits are in a state of sleep, in which dreams and reality are confused, and, as in sleep, the dreamer is unaware that he is dreaming.

In one case—of a female musician who had suffered a nervous breakdown—the woman spoke in a "wild gibberish" of English and Spanish (a language of which she was ignorant). Eventually, Wickland succeeded in learning that she was possessed by three spirits: a girl named Mary, and two rival lovers. One had murdered Mary, then the two men had killed each other in a fight; the three spirits were unaware that they were dead and had found themselves able to "possess" the musician, who was psychically weakened. (Wickland's experience was that people who are insane or on the verge of a nervous breakdown are vulnerable to these psychic parasites.) Before the woman was finally cured, another spirit—that of a little girl who had been killed in the San Francisco earthquake—was "removed" from her (by a mild shock treatment involving static electricity generated by a Wimshurst machine, which Wickland found highly effective in "dislodging" these uninvited visitors).

Wickland's book contains so many cases in its 460-odd pages that it is impossible to summarize. But one typical case will illustrate why he was so convinced that he was dealing with real spirits and not with some strange form of hysteria on the part of his wife. In 1904, at a séance in Chicago, Mrs. Wickland began to clutch her throat and cry out, "Take the rope away. I am in the dark!" When the "spirit" had been soothed into speaking normally, she declared that she was a sixteen-year-old girl named Minnie Harmening, who had committed suicide by hanging herself in a Chicago suburb called Palatine (Wickland misheard it as Palestine). She had, she said, encountered the spirit of a big man with a black beard in the barn, and he had "hypnotized" her and made her hang herself.

Wickland and his wife were on a visit to Chicago at that time and had not heard of what had become known as the Harmening suicide, which had taken place six weeks earlier. The girl's suicide had baffled her family because it had been without apparent cause (although, Wickland adds, "the girl had always been peculiar," implying that she was mentally deficient). Moreover, there were some suspicious circumstances—the clothes around the neck had been torn, and there were scratches on her throat. The suicide had taken place—as the girl had said—in Palatine, Cook County, Illinois.

The spirit appeared again at the next séance and in reply to questions, explained that as soon as she had kicked the box away, she "came to her senses" and clawed at her clothes, tearing them as she tried to loosen the rope.

Wickland cites many such cases in which he was able to corroborate the evidence of "spirits." But what is obviously of chief interest in this case is that the girl claimed to have been "hypno- tized" (she may simply mean strongly influenced) by a black-bearded spirit and induced to kill herself. That is to say, she had, in effect, been "possessed" by the black-bearded spirit.

Unfortunately, Wickland was not generally concerned with the kind of corroboration he provides in this case, with the result that his book is seldom mentioned by modern scientific investigators of the paranormal. (Wickland's own excuse is that the spirits were usually in such a state of confusion that they could not give precise names and dates.) What he might have done is illustrated by his friend F. Lee Howard, a congregational minister, who attended a session in which the Wicklands were attempting to treat the daughter of one of Howard's friends. Howard questioned a "possessing spirit," which declared itself to be that of a suicide victim, and he obtained the name and date. A check with the coroner's records confirmed that such a person had committed suicide on the given date. In another case, a reader of Wickland's book wrote to say that the details given by one of the spirits convinced him that it was his father's cousin.

Another objection raised by modern researchers is that Wickland is often naïve and that he is inclined to mistake mental illness for "spirit possession." For example, the case of Frank James, the boy who became a juvenile delinquent after a fall from a motorcycle, would nowadays be explained in terms of the science of "split-brain physiology." This is based upon the recognition that when the *corpus callosum,* the knot of nerves joining the two cerebral hemispheres of the brain, is severed—as it is sometimes to cure epilepsy—the patient turns into two different people, each of whom resides in a separate hemisphere of the brain. (See also chapter 17.) The normal "everyday self," the person one thinks of as "me," lives in the left hemisphere and is basically a logical and practical person, the one who copes with daily chores. The person who lives in the right is a stranger and seems to be altogether more intuitive and instinctive; he seems more concerned with what goes on inside us. You could say that the left-brain self is objective, the right brain subjective; one is, in effect, a scientist and the other an artist. Most of us are unaware of this "other" (right-brain) self, even though we are connected to it by the *corpus callosum.* In split-brain patients, the "other self" can be studied by directing stimuli to the left eye (actually, the left visual field) or the left side of the body; for some odd reason, the left side of the body is connected to the right brain, and vice versa.

In a well-known case of the 1870s, a French youth named Louis Vivé was bitten by a viper and became paralyzed in both legs for three years; during this time he was quiet and well behaved. One day he had a "hysterico-epileptic" attack, followed by a fifteen-hour sleep; when he woke up, the well-behaved youth had given way to a violent, aggressive, and dishonest delinquent. But, unlike Frank James, Vivé's two personalities continued to alternate. This new "criminal" self had a speech defect and was paralyzed down the right side of his body. After receiving a conviction for theft, Vivé was sent to an asylum at Rochefort, where two doctors became interested in his case. At this time there was considerable interest in the influence of magnets and of various metals on physical ailments like paralysis, and the doctors tried stroking his right side with steel. It had the effect of transferring the paralysis to the left side and restoring the patient to his previous quiet and well-behaved personality. All his memories of the "criminal" period vanished, and he could recall only his "own" earlier self—although his "other self" could be brought back by hypnosis.

Here it seems clear that the "criminal" Vivé was a condition associated with his right brain—hence the speech disorder. (Speech is controlled by the left side of the brain.) Another well-known case of "dual personality," that of Clara Fowler (described by Dr. Morton Prince in his book *Dissociation of a Personality*—Prince calls her Christine Beauchamp) seems to illustrate the same point. An old friend of Clara's father made a sexual advance that so upset her that she began to suffer from depression and nervous exhaustion. When Prince placed her under hypnosis, another personality emerged, a mischievous child who called herself Sally. From then on, Sally would frequently "take over" the body and play practical jokes, such as going for a long walk in the countryside, then vacating the body and leaving Clara to walk home. Typically, Sally had a bad stutter, suggesting that, like Vivé's alter ego, she was associated with the right brain. (It has been noted that left-handed people who have been forced to learn to write with the right hand often develop a stutter.)

But while it is tempting to explain Wickland's cases in terms of "multiple-personality disorder" and split-brain physiology, it proves in practice to be an impossible enterprise; we can see that, in the case of the Minnie Harmening suicide, no amount of split-brain physiology can explain how Mrs. Wickland was able to describe a case of which she had no knowledge.

In fact, Wickland's findings had been anticipated by half a century. In 1855 a French educator named Denizard Hyppolyte Léon Rivail was introduced to a *somnambule*—a person who "channeled" trance communications when hypnotized—named Celina Bequet, through whom the spirit of the famous hypnotist Franz Mesmer was alleged to speak. Accepting without question that he was in touch with the spirits of the dead—a reasonable assumption under the circumstances—Rivail asked hundreds of questions about life after death and published the result in an influential work entitled *The Spirits' Book.* (He used the pseudonym Allan Kardec, suggested to him by "spirits.")

According to *The Spirits' Book,* man consists of body, "aura," intelligent soul, and spiritual soul. The aim of human life, according to the spirits, is evolution, and this comes about through reincarnation—rebirth into new bodies. People who die suddenly, or are unprepared for death by reason of wasted lives, are often unaware that they are dead and become homeless wanderers on the earth, attracted by human beings of like mind, and sharing their lives and experiences. They are able, to some extent, to influence these like-minded people and to make them do their will through suggestion. Some "low spirits" are activated by malice; others are merely mischievous and can use energy drawn from human beings to cause physical disturbances—these are known as *poltergeists.* When Kardec asked, "Do spirits influence our thoughts and actions?" the answer was, "Their influence upon [human beings] is greater than you suppose, for it is very often they who direct both." Asked about possession, the "spirit" explained that a spirit cannot actually take over another person's body, since that belongs to its owner; but a spirit can assimilate itself to a person who has the same defects and qualities as himself and may dominate such a person. In short, such spirits could be described as "mind parasites."

According to Wickland, one of the most famous murders of the early twentieth century was due to "spirit influence." On the night of June 25, 1906, a wealthy young rake named Harry Thaw sat beside his wife on the roof of Madison Square Garden, watching a new revue. Before her marriage, Mrs. Thaw had been Evelyn Nesbit, a beautiful model and showgirl, whom Thaw had persuaded to accompany him to Europe. Thaw was addicted to flogging, and on one occasion, he whipped Evelyn so severely that she was confined to bed for two weeks. When she admitted to him that she had been seduced at the age of fifteen by Stanford White, the architect of Madison Square Garden, Thaw had become almost insane with jealousy. On the night of June 25, as they were leaving the roof show, Thaw saw White sitting alone at a table, walked up to him, and shot him three times with a pistol.

At Thaw's murder trial, Evelyn gave lurid details of her seduction by the architect (who was more than thirty years her senior), describing how he had taken her virginity after getting her drunk on champagne. ("When I came to I found myself in the bed, naked except for an abbreviated pink undergarment.")* The jury was unable to reach an agreement. At the second trial, Thaw was found not guilty by reason of insanity and confined to an asylum, from which he escaped in 1913; later that year a jury found him to be sane and authorized his release.

Three weeks after the murder, on July 15, 1906, Mrs. Wickland fell to the floor during the course of a séance and when moved to a chair, shouted in a brusque voice, "Waiter, bring me a drink!" Asked where she thought she was, she replied, "In Madison Square Roof Garden, of course." Then she began to tremble, explaining that she could see "dead people," and rushed about the room. As soon as this spirit ceased to "possess" Mrs. Wickland, another spirit took over, exulting, "I killed the dog!" But this was not Harry Thaw; in reply to questions the spirit said that his name was Johnson and that he had caused Thaw to shoot Stanford White because "he had trifled too long with our daughters." (In fact, White was a famous seducer of chorus girls, keeping a special apartment for that purpose; but then, Thaw shared his taste.)

---

*Evelyn Nesbit, *The Untold Story* (1934).

Next, a spirit who claimed to be Thaw's father appeared, begging the people present to "save my boy." (Thaw senior had been dead for some years, and Thaw's mother was overindulgent.) He went on to explain that Thaw had been obsessed by "vengeful spirits" when he killed White and that his son was a "psychic sensitive."

There is nothing in the two books on the case, or in Evelyn Nesbit's book, *The Untold Story,* to suggest that Thaw may have been psychic. But Nesbit's book makes it clear that Thaw was mentally little more than a child. One account states: "Had Thaw been a poor man, he probably would have been in an asylum." At his trial, evidence was presented of insanity in his family—in fact, his elder brother, Horace, had died in an asylum. Evelyn Nesbit's accounts of his violent tantrums—for example, if a waiter dared to try and brush crumbs off the tablecloth he would jerk the cloth away, hurling the dishes to the floor—make it clear that he was mentally disturbed. (The tantrums would vanish with equal suddenness, and Thaw's face would dissolve into a charming and sunny smile.) While this does not support the case for "obsession" by vengeful spirits, it *does* support Wickland's contention that Thaw was the type of person whose mind was open to invasion because he was "not all there."

There *is* one small piece of evidence that suggests that the "spirit" of Thaw's father was what he claimed to be. He begged Wickland to "write to my wife and my attorney, Mr. Olcott," and in fact, Judge Olcott *was* Thaw's attorney, a fact that was unknown to the Wicklands.

The classic study of "possession," *Possession, Demoniacal and Other* (1921), is by a Tübingen professor, T. K. Oesterreich. Oesterreich totally discounts the "spirit" explanation, insisting that possession is always a case of hysteria or mental illness. He will not even accept the hypothesis of multiple personality, since he cannot believe that the human personality can "split." One of his most impressive pieces of evidence for the hysteria theory is a lengthy account of the famous case of "Achille," described by the psychiatrist Pierre Janet. Achille, a moderately successful businessman, came from a peasant background and married early. In the winter of 1890, when he was thirty-three, Achille returned from a business trip in a depressed condition, then suddenly went dumb. One day he sent for his wife and child, embraced them despairingly, then went into a cataleptic state for two days. When he awoke he was suffering from delusions; he seemed to think he was in Hell and that demons were burning him and cutting him in pieces. The room, he said, was full of imps, and he was possessed by a devil. After a number of suicide attempts he was sent to the Salpêtrière Hospital in Paris, under the care of the famous physician Charcot. The latter placed Janet in charge of the case.

Janet watched with interest as Achille displayed all the signs of demoniacal possession, as described in the Middle Ages: in a deep voice he cursed God, then in a shrill voice protested that the Devil had forced him to do it.

At first all of Janet's efforts to communicate were a failure; Achille refused to listen to him and resisted all of the doctor's attempts to hypnotize him. Janet saw the solution when he observed that Achille was extremely absentminded—he compared him to someone searching for an umbrella that he holds in his hand. While Achille was raving, Janet quietly inserted a pencil in his hand, then tried ordering him, in a whisper, to make writing movements. The pencil wrote: "I won't." "Who are you?" asked Janet, and the pencil wrote: "The Devil." "I shan't believe you," Janet replied, "unless you can give me proof. Can you make Achille raise his left arm without knowing it?" "Of course," came the answer—and Achille raised his arm. "Why are you doing that?" Janet asked Achille in his normal voice, and Achille looked at his raised arm with astonishment.

The demon went on to demonstrate his powers by making Achille dance, stick out his tongue, and kiss a piece of paper. Finally, Janet asked him if he could put Achille into a deep sleep. Moments later, Achille was in a trance. Now Janet was able to question him about the cause of his illness. He quickly learned that Achille had been unfaithful to his wife while away on his business trip and that deep and intense guilt had caused the depression and other symptoms. Now that he was able to induce hallucinations, Janet made Achille believe that his wife was in the room and had forgiven him for his infidelity. (It is not quite clear from Janet's account whether the wife actually came to the hospital.) After this, Achille's psychological problems soon cleared up.

This is certainly a remarkable case. Yet as a refutation of the "spirit" theory, it is obviously open to one serious objection. According to Wickland, people suffering from nervous traumas or states of intense guilt and misery are more likely to become "obsessed" by spirits than normal healthy persons. Wickland would point out that Achille may have been genuinely "obsessed" by a mischievous spirit and that as soon as Janet had made him feel that he was forgiven, the spirit was "driven out."

In her introduction to Oesterreich's *Possession,* Anita Gregory, an investigator of the paranormal, has some harsh words to say about Wickland and his *Thirty Years Among the Dead.* She points out that there is a basic sameness to all his cases—he always has to convince a spirit that it is dead—and his account of how the spirits of Madame Blavatsky and Mary Baker Eddy expressed contrition for their false doctrines is almost laughable. She also points out that Oesterreich's rationalism is often crude and unconvincing and that he deals with subtleties by ignoring them.

Perhaps the most obvious example of Oesterreich's failure to allow facts to speak for themselves is in his account of one of the most famous of all cases of "possession," that of "the Watseka wonder," a girl named Lurancy Vennum. In July 1877 thirteen-year-old Lurancy, of Watseka, Illinois, had a fit, after which she became prone to trances. In these trances she became a medium, and a number of disagreeable personalities manifested themselves through her. On February 11, 1878, placed under hypnosis by a local doctor, Lurancy stated that there was a spirit in the room named Mary Roff, and a Mrs. Roff who was also present exclaimed, "That's my daughter." Mary had died twelve years earlier, at the age of eighteen. Lurancy then stated that Mary was going to be allowed to take over her body for the next three months.

The next day Lurancy claimed to be Mary Roff. She asked to be taken back to the Roff's home, and on the way there, she recognized their previous home, in which they had lived while she was alive and which was unknown to Lurancy. She also recognized Mary Roff's sister, who was standing at the window. And during the next few weeks, "Mary" showed a precise and detailed knowledge of the Roff household and of Mary's past, recognizing old acquaintances and toys and recalling long-forgotten incidents. On May 21, the day she had declared she had to leave, she took a tearful farewell of her family, and on the way home, "became" Lurancy again. The case was investigated by Richard Hodgson, one of the most skeptical members of the Society for Psychical Research, who was convinced of its genuineness.

Readers of Hodgson's account of the "Watseka wonder" will find it very hard to find loopholes; Mary provided such detailed proof of her knowledge of her early years, and of the family background—recognizing unhesitatingly anyone Mary had known—that the notion of trickery or delusion becomes untenable; it is perhaps the single most convincing case of "possession" in the history of psychical research. But Oesterreich merely quotes William James's summary of the case (from *The Principles of Psychology*), making no attempt to analyze it and passing on quickly to other matters—in spite of the fact that James himself had spoken of "the plausibility of the spiritualistic interpretation of the phenomenon." And Anita Gregory concludes her introduction by admitting that she is unable to declare that all the people in Oesterreich's book are frauds, dupes, lunatics, and psychopaths, ending with the words: "So I shall conclude . . . that the phenomena described by Oesterreich are very much in need of an explanation."

Oesterreich's *pièce de résistance* is a long account of the famous case of the "devils of Loudun," which, in 1952, was made the subject of a full-length study by Aldous Huxley. In 1633 Urbain Grandier, the parish priest of the small French town of Loudun, was charged with bewitching the nuns in a local convent and causing them to be possessed by demons, so that they screamed blasphemies and obscenities and writhed about on the floor displaying their private parts. Grandier had become notorious for his immoralities—he had impregnated two of his penitents and seduced many others—and had made many enemies. Inquisitors claimed to find "devil's marks" on his body, and in a trial that was a travesty of justice, he was found guilty and sentenced to be burned alive. Even under torture, and later at the stake, Grandier maintained his innocence. His death made no difference, and the nuns continued to be possessed by "demons" for many years.

Oesterreich, like Aldous Huxley, takes the view that all this could be explained simply in terms of hysteria, while another authority, Rossell Hope Robbins, goes even further in his *Encyclopedia of Witchcraft and Demonology* and attributes the manifestations to outright imposture. But a careful reading of Huxley's own book makes either of these explanations seem implausible. It is easy to see how sex-starved nuns could deceive themselves into believing that they were possessed by devils—the Mother Superior of the convent, Sister Jeanne des Anges, admits in her autobiography that she made no real attempt to combat the possession because she enjoyed the sexual stirrings aroused in her by the demons.

But it is far more difficult to understand what then happened to the exorcists themselves. Brother Lactance, who had overseen the torture, became "possessed" and died insane within a month; five years later Brother Tranquille died of exhaustion after months of battling against the "invaders" of his psyche, and was amazed to witness his body writhing on the ground and hear himself uttering blasphemies that he was powerless to prevent. Brother Lucas, another of Grandier's persecutors, met the same fate. The "witch pricker," Dr. Mannouri, also died in delirium. Brother Jean-Joseph Surin, a genuinely saintly man, who was called to Loudun to try and exorcise the nuns after Grandier's execution, himself fell victim to the "devils" and became periodically insane for twenty-five years.

It is difficult to believe that ordinary hysteria could produce such results. Surin described in a letter how the "alien spirit" was united to his own, "constituting a second me, as though I had two souls." Considering these facts, the skeptical Anita Gregory admits that "one is probably not justified in assuming that . . . the Loudun pandemonium [was] necessarily nothing but collective delusion." And bearing in mind Kardec's comment that "a spirit does not enter into a body as you enter into a house . . . he assimilates himself to a [person] who has the same defects and the same qualities as himself," the hypothesis that the Loudun "pandemonium" was caused by Wickland's earthbound spirits seems, on the whole, more plausible than the religious-hysteria theory.

It is difficult to draw a clear dividing line between "possession" and poltergeist manifestations. Poltergeists are "noisy ghosts" who cause objects to fly through the air, and scientific observation of dozens of cases has established their reality beyond all doubt.* The most widely held current view is that they are a form of "spontaneous psychokinesis" (mind over matter) caused by the unconscious mind of an emotionally disturbed adolescent, but this theory fails to explain how the unconscious mind can cause heavy objects to fly through the air. (In laboratory experiments, "psychics" have so far failed to move any object larger than a compass needle.) According to Kardec's "informants," poltergeists are earthbound spirits who are, under certain conditions, able to draw energy from the living and make use of negative energies "exuded" by the emotionally disturbed and the sexually frustrated.

In the Amherst case of 1878, poltergeist phenomena began to occur in the home of an unmarried girl named Esther Cox, who lived with her sister and her sister's husband, Daniel Teed. After an attempt at abduction and rape, Esther's boyfriend had hastily left the area, and Esther was deeply upset. A few days later, rustling noises—sounding like a mouse—came from a box under her bed; a few nights after that, following a hysterical fit, Esther's body began to swell like a balloon. There were then two loud bangs, and she ceased swelling and fell asleep. All of this was repeated a few days later; the bedclothes also flew off the bed, and the pillow inflated. As the family stood around the bed, there was a scratching noise above it, and an invisible hand or claw traced on the plaster the words: *Esther, you are mine to kill.* At a later stage of the manifestations, Esther turned into a human magnet—knives stuck to her—and some iron spokes in her lap became too hot to touch. When spontaneous fires broke out, Esther was accused of causing them and sentenced to four months in jail. By the time she was released, the manifestations had ceased.

Ten years later, in 1889, a farm in Quebec province run by a

---

*See "Poltergeists" in my book *The Encyclopedia of Unsolved Mysteries* (1988).

man named George Dagg became the scene of equally bizarre
poltergeist manifestations: milk pans overturned, small fires
started, windows smashed, and water poured on the floor. In this
case, the "focus" (or the person who seemed to be causing it) was
a young girl named Dinah McLean, an orphan. The poltergeist
often attacked Dinah, making her scream; like Esther Cox, she
also seemed to be able to hear it, although no one else could.
Later, it began to talk in a gruff voice, uttering violent obscenities
and alleging that it was the Devil. But after some dialogue with
George Dagg—during which it admitted to causing the fires and
throwing stones—it declared its willingness to leave the following
Sunday. Crowds of neighbors gathered, and the poltergeist talked
freely, seeming to have an intimate knowledge of their lives. (The
Fox poltergeist had also been able to supply all kinds of personal
information to the neighbors.) It also alleged that it was not the
"Devil" of the previous day but an angel sent by God; but it
proceeded to contradict itself and then lost its temper and used
foul language. Finally, it declared that it would leave the following
morning after taking leave of the village children. The next
morning, the children rushed in from the yard to say that they
had just seen a beautiful man in white, who had picked up two of
them—Mary and Johnny—in his arms and declared that Johnny
was a fine little fellow, then put them down and ascended into the
sky. After this, the manifestations ceased.

In both these cases, the poltergeist masqueraded as some kind
of demonic entity but was clearly nothing of the sort—an observation that seems to suggest that poltergeists, like the devils of
Loudun, are probably also "earthbound spirits."

Another investigator who came to believe that "possession" was
due to spirits was Max Freedom Long, an American schoolmaster
who arrived in Hawaii in 1917, at the age of twenty-seven, and
began to make a study of its native "magicians," the kahunas or
"keepers of the secret"—the last representatives of the ancient
Huna religion.* According to Huna belief, Long discovered, man
has three "selves": the "low self," the "middle self," and the "high

---

*See "The Curse of the Pharaohs" in my book *The Encyclopedia of Unsolved
Mysteries* (1988).

self." The low self is basically emotional and corresponds roughly to Freud's unconscious mind. The middle self is our ordinary, everyday consciousness. The high self might be called the super-conscious mind and can foresee the future. After death, the three selves may become separated, and it is the low self that sometimes becomes a poltergeist, and the middle self may become a "ghost." In his book describing these investigations—offputtingly entitled *The Secret Science Behind Miracles*—Long also discusses the phenomenon of multiple personality and expresses the view that this is often due to "possession," either by a low self or a middle self or a combination of the two. He describes the case of a California girl with a secondary personality that took over the body for years at a time. When doctors tried to amalgamate the two under hypnosis, a third personality appeared, who told them that the girl should be left as she was, with two spirits sharing the body. This third personality warned that if they persisted, it would withdraw and leave them with a corpse; Long believed this third person to be the girl's "high self."

Two more eminent American investigators came to accept the possibility of "possession." The philosopher William James was converted from his early skepticism to a belief in "spirits" through the mediumship of Mrs. Leonore Piper, whose "control," Phinuit, was able to tell him all kinds of things that he could not possibly have learned by normal means. James was to agree that if a medium could be "possessed" by a spirit, then it was possible that other people might be and that this could explain cases of "demo-niacal possession."

James's close friend, Professor James Hyslop, was another skep-tic who was "converted" by Mrs. Piper. But he had a more practi-cal reason for becoming convinced of the reality of "possession." When Hyslop was president of the American Society for Psychical Research in 1907, he was visited by a goldsmith named Frederick Thompson, who believed that he had become "possessed" by the spirit of a painter named Robert Swain Gifford, whom he had met on a few occasions. After Gifford's death, Thompson had begun to hear Gifford's voice urging him to draw and paint—something he had never done before—and although he had no artistic training, Thompson began to paint in Gifford's style. What convinced

Hyslop was that Thompson painted accurate pictures of places that he had never seen but that Gifford *had.* Some of these proved to be identical to Gifford's final sketches—which Thompson had never seen—and when Hyslop visited the New England swamps and coastal regions, he recognized them as the subject of these sketches.

Hyslop consulted a neurologist, Dr. Titus Bull, about Thompson. And Bull himself went on to conclude that many cases of mental illness really involved "possession." In one case, the patient, who had suffered a head injury, claimed that he had been "taken over" by the spirit of a painter named Josef Selleny, who had been a friend of the Emperor Maximilian and who was "forcing" him to paint. (Wickland, as we know, believed that such accidents as head injuries could provide opportunity for alien "entities" to invade.)

Lengthy research by Bull's assistant, Helen Lambert, finally uncovered the existence of a real Josef Selleny (the encyclopedias mistakenly spelled his first name *Joseph,* but the patient spelled it correctly), who had, indeed, been a friend of the Emperor Maximilian. A medium who worked with Dr. Bull was able to reveal that the patient was being possessed by several "entities," one of whom seized possession of her body and grabbed Bull by the throat.

Eventually, the various entities were dislodged or persuaded to go away. Mrs. Lambert's account, later published in her book *A General Survey of Psychic Phenomena,* sounds remarkably like many cases described by Carl Wickland. The few available cases make it clear that Bull's name deserves a distinguished place in the annals of psychical research; unfortunately, most of his records have been lost.

Clearly, views like those of William James and Titus Bull will find no acceptance with the majority of doctors and scientists. Yet in recent years, belief in "possession" as a cause of some mental illness has received support from two eminent psychiatrists, Adam Crabtree and Ralph Allison. In his book *Multiple Man* (1986), Crabtree asserts that he has come to accept, merely as a convenient working hypothesis, the notion that certain multiple personalities are "possessed" by spirits, inviting us to believe that he is waiting for someone to suggest an alternative psychological theory that will cover all the facts. But the cases he describes make it virtually impossible to imagine such a hypothesis.

Crabtree's first experience with "possession" involved a young patient named Sarah Worthington, who was in a condition of suicidal depression. In a semitrance state, Sarah spoke in a completely different voice, which sounded like that of an older woman used to exercising authority. This "voice" identified herself as Sarah's grandmother and explained that she wanted to "help Sarah." It began to emerge that the grandmother also had a problem: many years earlier, she had left her seven-year-old son alone in the house, then rushed back when she heard that the neighborhood was on fire. Her son had, in fact, been removed to a safe place by neighbors, but she had spent a traumatic hour searching for him. Later, her indifference to her daughter, Sarah's mother (she greatly preferred her son), had created psychological problems, which had been inherited by Sarah. Now the grandmother believed that she was trying to help Sarah, who had always felt rejected; in fact, her presence was troubling the girl, who was intuitively aware that she had been "invaded." The case sounds oddly similar to many described by Carl Wickland. But in this case, it was unnecessary to persuade the "spirit" to go away; when Sarah realized that the obscure inner presence she felt was her grandmother, she came to accept it, and all her suicidal impulses vanished.

In another case, a girl named Susan was convinced that she was "possessed" by her dead father, who had been killed in a car crash. He had always been sexually obsessed with her, creeping into her bedroom when she was asleep to fondle her genitals; her unconscious knowledge of what was going on made her contemptuous of him. But the close rapport between them meant that when he died, he had found refuge in his daughter's body, unaware that he was dead. When Crabtree was able to persuade him to leave her, her problems vanished.

But from the point of view of "demoniacal possession," perhaps the most interesting case in Crabtree's book is that of a history professor whom he calls Art. About to be married for the second time, Art was experiencing strange feelings of reluctance, as if "under great pressure from some inner force that he could not control." A censorious inner voice would criticize anyone whom he liked. Art's own theory was that some negative aspect of his personality had unconsciously assimilated the critical attitudes of his mother, Veronica, who was now living in Detroit. When Crabtree placed Art in a light trance, he was able to open a dialogue with the "mother," and she told him, "Art is mine and his life is mine. . . . I have to make sure Art knows how kooky all these friends of his are."

Art's description of his mother revealed that she was sexually obsessed with her son. Until he was in his late teens, she would call him into her bed when her husband had left for work and arouse him into a state of sexual excitement that she refused to satisfy. Oddly enough, the Veronica who "possessed" Art was also aware of herself as "Veronica who lived in Detroit," and she described the life of her alter ego as drab and dull. Crabtree suggested that life might become more interesting if she spent more time with "Veronica in Detroit," and the entity agreed to try it. When Art's mother had an operation to remove a cancerous growth, the entity realized that it had been robbing her of vitality by concentrating on Art and began spending less time with Art. The real Veronica's life now underwent a remarkable transformation, and she began seeing more of people and enjoying herself. Art, surprisingly enough, found he missed the censorious inner voice and recognized how much he had encouraged it, using it as an excuse for not making his own decisions. As he faced this fact, his problems vanished.

Here we may assume either that Art himself was suffering from delusions—a reasonable enough hypothesis, under the circumstances—or that, in some odd way, his mother *was* somehow "possessing" him from a distance, in spite of the fact that she was still alive. This, admittedly, sounds farfetched—until we take into account the mother's transformation after her operation. And if Art's mother *was* somehow "in two places at once," the implications are very strange indeed.

Can one person "possess" another? In Frederic Myers's classic *Phantasms of the Living,* there is an interesting account of a girl who was convinced that a man she scarcely knew was taking control of her dreams and trying to force her into sexual slavery (see chapter 31). If this is possible, and if disembodied "spirits" exist, then it would seem to follow that, under certain circumstances, "possession" by a spirit is a possibility.

Although Crabtree claims to treat the notion of "possession" merely as a working hypothesis, it can be seen that his work lends support to the views expressed by Wickland. This is even more so in the case of the California psychiatrist Ralph Allison, whose *Minds in Many Pieces* (1980) is a major work in the field of multiple personality disorder (usually shortened to MPD). Allison had been practicing for almost a decade when he encountered his first case of MPD—a woman named Janette who had tried to kill her husband and children. A colleague advised Allison that he thought Janette was a case of MPD, and when Allison induced her to relax deeply and asked if he could speak to the "other person," a woman with a harsh, grating voice emerged and identified herself as Lydia. At one point, Janette had been raped in the hospital by several orderlies; now, as Lydia mentioned her interest in "drinking, dancing, fucking," and placed herself in a provocative position, Allison began to suspect that the orderlies may not have been entirely to blame. Eventually, a third personality named Karen emerged—a balanced, sensible woman—and with her help, Allison was able to cure Janette. (He came to call such personalities "the inner self-helper.")

In this case, the basic hypothesis of multiple personality covered the facts: that a traumatic childhood had caused the "prime personality" to withdraw from the problems of life, like an ostrich burying its head in the sand. But Allison's next patient, a girl named Carrie, forced him to take the "possession" hypothesis seriously. Carrie was another "multiple" with a history of childhood traumas, including a gang rape. Even without hypnosis, an alter ego named Wanda emerged and talked to Allison. But it seemed clear that Wanda was not responsible for the suicidal impulses Carrie was experiencing. When told that a "psychic" claimed that Carrie was possessed by the spirit of a drug addict who had died of an overdose in New York in 1968, Allison decided to "give the concept of spirit possession a try." Under deep hypnosis, Carrie agreed that the drug addict was influencing her life, and Allison's makeshift "exorcism"—performed with a swing-ing crystal ball on a chain—apparently succeeded. Unfortunately, it failed to dislodge two other personalities, and Carrie eventually committed suicide.

Yet Allison continued to reject the notion of "spirit possession" until he encountered a girl named Elise, who revealed several personalities under hypnosis. Most of these were able to describe their history—what traumas had caused them to be "born." But one of them claimed to be a man named Dennis, who explained that he had entered Elise's body when she was experimenting with black magic as a teenager and that he enjoyed remaining there because he enjoyed having sex with another of Elise's personali-ties, a girl named Shannon. The sex was not, as might be sup-posed, a bodiless intercourse between two "spirits"; when Shan-non took over Elise's body and had sex with a man, Dennis would enter the man's body. And although Elise and Shannon shared the same body, Dennis was not interested in having sex with Elise, only with Shannon. Eventually, with the help of another "inner self-helper," Elise was cured. It was this case that finally convinced Allison that multiple personality may sometimes be a case of spirit possession.

Another case confirmed this. In curing a girl named Sophia (by "integrating" her various personalities), Allison discovered that two personalities remained "left over." Under hypnosis, Sophia was regressed to birth and described how the doctor who had been her mother's lover had suffocated two triplets at birth but had been interrupted before he could dispose of the third—Sophia. The other two children had then moved into Sophia's body. Armed with this knowledge, Allison was able to rid Sophia of her two sisters and cure her.

Allison concluded that there were many possible causes of multiple personality, such as compulsive neurosis and violent traumas. But he also listed "possession" by another living per-son—as in the case of "Art" and his mother—possession by a dead person—as in Dr. Bull's case of the painter Gifford—and possession by a "nonhuman spirit." By this he was referring to what would once have been called "demoniacal possession." In a paper on multiple personality, the parapsychologist Stanley

Krippner reveals that an increasing number of psychiatrists accept the "spirit hypothesis."*

What, then, is to be made of this bewildering mass of evidence
about "possession," which most doctors would dismiss as childish
fantasy? Belief in possession depends, clearly, on the prior assumption that "spirits" actually exist and that what happens at
séances, for example, is genuine "possession" by the dead. This is
doubted by many eminent parapsychologists and even by some
mediums themselves; they prefer to believe that all that is involved
in such cases is telepathy and some form of extrasensory perception (ESP). But, as we have seen, William James himself was
finally convinced by Mrs. Piper. So was Richard Hodgson, who
had her shadowed by private detectives to see how she acquired
her information—and who learned nothing whatever. But he was
staggered when Mrs. Piper told him about a girl named Jessie, to
whom he had been engaged in Australia and who had subsequently died; Mrs. Piper's "control," Phinuit, was able to report to
Hodgson a conversation with Jessie about which no one else
knew.

Hyslop himself was inclined to believe that that mediumship
was a matter of "super ESP" until he was finally convinced by
William James—many years after James's death. Hyslop received
a letter from an Irish medium, telling him that a spirit who called
himself William James (and of whom the medium had never
heard) had asked him to contact Hyslop and remind him of the
"red pajamas." James had once agreed with Hyslop that whichever
of them died first should try to communicate with the other. At
first, the message about red pajamas meant nothing to Hyslop.
Then he suddenly remembered. When he and James had visited
Paris as young men, their luggage had failed to arrive, and Hyslop
had been forced to go out and buy some pajamas. All he had been
able to find at short notice was a bright red pair, and James had
teased him for days about his poor taste in pajamas. It was this
message that finally convinced Hyslop of the survival of the dead.

If, like Hyslop, we can accept the notion of "survival," and if,

---

*Several of these are described in my book *Beyond the Occult* (1988), part 2,
chapter 3.

like Kardec, we can accept that spirits can, under certain conditions, share the human brain, then it is hard to see why we should
not also accept that they can influence people's actions—that is,
"possess" them. It is important to note that "spiritualists" are in
general agreement that such "possession" is rare, since it is
impossible for a spirit actually to dislodge the incumbent, or even
to share the body, unless there is a close affinity between "posses-
sor" and "possessed."

The Loudun case seems to provide support for this view. Kardec states that poltergeists can only manifest themselves by
stealing human energy, particularly sexual energy. Sister Jeanne's
autobiography makes it clear that her own sexual frustrations
alone could have provided a host of "entities" with the necessary
energy. And by the time a dozen or so nuns were writhing on the
floor and making suggestions that caused even hardened roués to
blush, the convent must have been awash with sexual energy. Most
cases of possession in nunneries seem to involve the same feverish sexuality. Two decades before the Loudun case, fourteen-year-
old Madeleine de Demandolx de la Palud was seduced by Brother
Louis Gaufridi, twenty years her senior; the liaison was broken up
and she was sent to a nunnery at Aix-en-Provence. Two years later
Madeleine began to see devils and smashed a crucifix. Her hysteria soon spread to the other nuns; Madeleine accused Gaufridi
not only of seducing her but of introducing her to various diabolic
practices. Gaufridi was asked to try and exorcise the demons, and
when he failed, was put in prison.

At his trial, Madeleine declared that her allegations were all
imaginings, after which she began to move her hips back and
forth in a lascivious manner. The judge chose to disbelieve her;
Gaufridi was tortured until he "confessed," then was burned at the
stake.

It is important to realize that fornication among the clergy was
a commonplace occurrence in the seventeenth century and that
seduction of nuns by their confessors was far from rare. In 1625
a French orphan named Madeleine Bavent was seduced by a
Franciscan priest, appropriately named Bonnetemps. In the following year she entered a convent run by Brother Pierre David,
who secretly belonged to the Illuminati—a sect that believed that

the Holy Spirit could do no harm and that therefore, sex was perfectly acceptable among priests. David apparently insisted that Madeleine should strip to the waist as he administered communion; other nuns, she later claimed, strolled around naked. She claimed that she and David never engaged in actual intercourse—only mutual masturbation—and that when David died in 1628, his successor, Brother Mathurin Picard, continued to caress her genitals during confession.

It was after Picard's death in 1642 (when Madeleine was thirty-five) that the nuns began to manifest the usual signs of possession: writhing on the ground, contorting their bodies, and making howling noises like animals, as they alleged they were being ravished by demons. Fourteen of the fifty-two nuns exhibited these symptoms, and all put the blame on Madeleine.

Madeleine then told the full story of David, Picard, and the latter's assistant, Brother Boulle. She claimed that Picard and Boulle had indulged in various "magical" acts involving communion wafers and menstrual blood and eventually in "sabbats," in which a Black Mass was recited. The priests had draped their erections with consecrated wafers with a hole cut in the middle and "thus arrayed gave themselves to the women present"—Madeleine being favored five or six times.

Madeleine was accused of being a witch and was discharged from the order; Picard's corpse was dug up, excommunicated, and tossed onto a refuse heap. This led the priest's brother to create a scandal, and the result was a trial that ended with Boulle being tortured and burned alive, together with another priest named Duval. Madeleine, confined in a convent and brutally treated, made several suicide attempts and finally died at the age of forty. The nuns were all dispersed to other convents.

Madeleine's descriptions of sabbats and Black Masses sound like pure invention. But half a century later the notorious *chambre ardente* ("lighted chamber") affair revealed that many priests did, in fact, take part in such practices. When Louis XIV was informed by his chief of police that many women were asking for absolution for murdering their husbands, he ordered an investigation. It revealed that an international poisoning ring, organized by men of influence, existed. A number of fortune-tellers provided their clients with poisons and love philters, while priests performed Black Masses involving the sacrifice of babies and magical ceremonies in which they copulated with women on altars. These facts duly emerged in secret sessions of the "lighted chamber," and were recorded in detail. (The king later ordered all records to be destroyed, but the official transcript was overlooked.) One hundred and four of the accused were sentenced, thirty-six of them to death, while two of the fortune-tellers were burned alive. It is difficult for us to understand why the Church was involved in this wave of demonology—the likeliest explanation is that seventeenth-century rationalism was undermining its authority and that the protest against this authority took the form of licentiousness and black magic. Whatever the explanation, the *chambre ardente* transcripts leave no doubt but that it really happened.

One interesting question remains: whether, as Ralph Allison believes, there is such a thing as possession by "nonhuman" entities—i.e., whether some form of "demoniacal possession" is a reality. Of all these cases involving "possession," the Loudun affair remains the most puzzling. Even if we can accept Wickland's belief that human beings can be influenced by "earthbound spirits," it is difficult to understand how five of the exorcists became victims of the demonic possession and four actually died of it. None of the patients described by Wickland, Crabtree, or Allison was driven to this extreme.

One possible clue is provided by a curious little book that appeared in Cape Town, South Africa, in 1972. It is entitled *Who Are the Dead?*, and the author is listed as Helen Quartermaine—which is not, apparently, her real name.

The author's view, briefly, is that in addition to the physical body, all human beings possess a "personality body"—also known as the psyche—which is made of a finer matter than the physical body. This personality body permeates the physical body—the author uses the image of a ball of wool soaked in water to illustrate how the personality body "imbues" the physical body. The points of contact between the two bodies, she says, are the seven endocrine glands, also known as the seven chakras of Hinduism.

So far, Helen Quartermaine is simply echoing the "occult tradition," in which the personality body is sometimes called the astral body. (Occult tradition also recognizes the human "aura," or etheric body, which might be regarded as its "life field"—the equivalent of a magnet's magnetic field.) But she goes on to make some far more startling assertions. Our problem, she says, is to keep these three "bodies" in alignment. In most people the two "higher bodies" tend to jut out of the right side. This lopsidedness means that the left side is unprotected and can easily be "invaded" by other disembodied personalities. When people get angry or upset, she explains, the personality receives a shock and is displaced sideways. And it may remain this way for a long time. Life force drains away into the physical body, and the result is serious depletion. She goes on to say: "Considering the endless list of trifling incidences which can cause a person to be malpositioned within his three bodies . . . it follows that *all* of us play host to our dead, by leaving the door of our physical bodies open to admit them. Worse follows, however, for we must also leave ourselves open to their mental, physical and emotional sicknesses."

She goes on to describe how the dead may attach themselves to those they love. Thus far she is in basic agreement with Wickland. But she then states: "Sometimes, of course, the motivating force is quite the opposite, and hate becomes the destroying power. There are many well-known cases of revenge striking from beyond the grave."

Ms. Quartermaine next cites the case of Barbara Graham, executed in the gas chamber at San Quentin in June 1953 for her part in the murder of an elderly widow, Mabel Monahan, in the course of robbery. By 1953 Barbara, then thirty, had become a gangster's moll as well as an alcoholic and drug addict. On March 9 she agreed to help the gang enter Mrs. Monahan's house in Burbank, California, by knocking on the door and asking to use the phone to contact a garage. Her four accomplices, Jack Santo, Baxter Shorter, Emmett Perkins, and John L. True, rushed into the house behind her and tied up the sixty-three-year-old widow while they searched the house for the fortune she was supposed to be guarding for the owner of a gambling casino. What actually happened is uncertain; the body of the woman, strangled with a strip of bedsheet, was found three days later by the gardener; her head, wrapped in a pillowcase, had been battered by a heavy blunt instrument.

The case was puzzling, since the victim's purse contained $500, and $10,000 worth of jewelry was untouched. But after questioning various underworld figures, the police called on Baxter Shorter, who—under a promise of complete immunity—told them that Santo, Perkins, True, and Barbara Graham had been involved. (A man named William Upshaw had also agreed to take part but had backed out.) Barbara, he said, had rung the doorbell, and when the old lady opened the door, True and Perkins had rushed in. When Shorter finally went in to see what was taking them so long, he saw Barbara pistol-whipping Mrs. Monahan. Santo had tied the pillowcase around her head and Perkins had strangled her. A search of the house failed to reveal the gambler's hoard, and they left empty-handed.

Shorter's story was accepted and he was released. But he was soon kidnapped by Perkins—who was still free—and murdered. Later, Perkins, Santo, and Barbara Graham were arrested in a motel. Barbara denied that she was present in the Monahan home; whether or not this was true, it is certain that many people in court did not believe that she had done the beating, as True alleged. But the main evidence against her was that she had attempted to bribe a fellow prisoner—in fact, a police officer—to provide her with an alibi for $2,500. She had also told the policeman that Shorter had been "well taken care of."

Barbara Graham was tried, together with Santo and Perkins (her lover). Mainly on True's evidence, she was found guilty. She died in the gas chamber on the same day as Santo and Perkins (who had been sentenced to death for a second time for the murder of a whole family committed during the course of robbery).

Helen Quartermaine states:

[Barbara Graham] swore she was innocent, but when the verdict found her guilty she pledged herself to see that all the men concerned with her conviction would also, like herself, die prematurely. This list included the three men who were said to be her accomplices.

The first to die after her execution was the one who had turned prosecution witness and whose evidence damned her; he was involved in the collision of two boats on the Mississippi and killed outright. The other two men were retried at a later date and found guilty; they were also executed. This was only the beginning. The District Attorney in charge of her prosecution died very suddenly and unexpectedly from cancer. The fear grew when the warden of San Quentin prison . . . was struck dead by heart failure. Next came the abrupt death, again from cancer, of the Superior Court Judge who sentenced her. In February 1958, the man who informed the police against Mrs. Graham was crushed to death on a journey by cars piling up. Another informer on the lady's catalogue of revenge has since disappeared, and police have strong reason to suspect he may have been murdered.

This account has several minor inaccuracies. Santo and Perkins died the same day, not "at a later date." John True died in January, not February, 1958, when a Dutch freighter rammed a small craft in a fog. William Upshaw was not the man who informed the police on Barbara Graham—but he certainly died when he drove into a road obstruction in California. The "other informer"—Shorter—had died long before Barbara Graham.

Helen Quartermaine is convinced that these deaths were actually caused by Barbara Graham's "personality body," out for revenge. Wickland, as we have seen, believed that such influence is possible and that Harry Thaw killed Stanford White under the influence of an entity—or entities—seeking revenge. Helen Quartermaine argues that the kind of lapse of attention that caused William Upshaw to drive his car into an obstruction, or that caused the Dutch freighter in the fog to run down the boat carrying divers (including John True), could easily be induced by a "vengeful spirit."

John True and William Upshaw were responsible for the death sentence that sent Barbara Graham to the gas chamber. The

Loudun inquisitors were responsible for the torture of Urbain Grandier and for his agonizing death at the stake. Helen Quartermaine would undoubtedly regard the possession of the Loudun inquisitors as the revenge of Urbain Grandier on his tormentors.

Whether plausible or not, the suggestion may be regarded as a disturbing footnote to Wickland's *Thirty Years Among the Dead*.

27

Richard III:
Murderer or Scapegoat?

In 1674 King Charles II ordered that part of the Tower of London—the fortress that had held so many famous prisoners—should be demolished and cleared for safety reasons. This included a staircase that ran up the outer wall of the Tower's central building, the White Tower. Under the bottom stair, ten feet down, the workmen discovered a wooden chest containing the skeletons of two children; one lay on its back, while a smaller one lay facedown on top of it, as if it had been tossed roughly into the chest. King Charles had no doubt of the identity of these pathetic skeletons: they were the two "Princes in the Tower," murdered almost two centuries earlier.

The man believed to be responsible for their murders was their uncle, King Richard III. The two Princes were the children of his elder brother, the late King Edward IV, whose health had been undermined by overeating and sexual excesses. When King Edward died in 1483, the future Richard III became Protector of the Realm—that is, a temporary regent until Edward's eldest child, also named Edward, was old enough to be crowned King.

What actually happened, according to William Shakespeare's *Richard III*, is that the wicked uncle—who was Duke of Gloucester at the time—decided to murder the Princes and seize the throne for himself. He ordered his servant, Sir James Tyrell, to carry out the deed; the Princes were smothered in the Tower by two of Tyrell's henchmen. Two years later Richard III was killed at the Battle of Bosworth (crying, according to Shakespeare, "A horse, a horse, my kingdom for a horse!"), and Henry Tudor, a distant cousin of Richard's, became King Henry VII.

It all sounds very plausible. But is it true? Almost as soon as he came to the throne, Henry issued a proclamation that accused Richard of every kind of wickedness—yet, for some odd reason, he does not mention the murder of the Princes in the Tower. It was twenty years later that Tyrell was sentenced to death on another charge—treason—and confessed to the murder of the Princes before his execution. The King's official historian, a man named Polydore Vergil, then issued the first account of the murder of the Princes.

Shakespeare, of course, had not the slightest doubt of Richard's guilt; he took his history from the *Chronicles* of the Elizabethan historian Raphael Holinshed, who described how the Princes were smothered with pillows and buried at the bottom of the stairs under a "great heape of stones." Shakespeare, writing for a sensation-hungry audience, threw subtlety to the winds and introduced his ugly, humpbacked villain, rubbing his hands and chortling, "I am determined to prove myself a villain," and describing himself as "subtle, false, and treacherous." (Tolstoy was convinced that the notion that Shakespeare as a great genius was a strange delusion, and there are times when it is hard not to agree with him.*) In fact, Richard was neither humpbacked nor ugly; it is true that one of his shoulders was higher than the other, but on the other hand, one of his dancing partners had once described him as "the handsomest man in the room."

As the years went by it became clear that history had wronged Richard III in more ways than one. The famous eighteenth-century letter writer Horace Walpole argued against his guilt in *Historic Doubts on Richard III*, and in 1906 a historian named

---

*Tolstoy's essay "Shakespeare and the Drama" should be required reading for all drama students; in fact, it is hidden away in a volume entitled *Recollections and Essays* and is seldom referred to.

Sir Clements Markham wrote a book entitled *Richard III: His Life and Character*, in which he pointed out that Richard seems to have been a rather nice man and that there is no evidence whatever that he murdered his two nephews. Markham claims that the two historians who accused him of the murder were both, so to speak, in the pay of the opposition.

But the real turning point came in 1951, when the mystery writer and playwright Josephine Tey—whose account of Elizabeth Canning is described in chapter 4—published a highly successful novel entitled *Daughter of Time*, which is a vindication of King Richard. The novel's protagonist is a bedridden detective who becomes interested in historical whodunits and spends his days studying histories of Richard III. He concludes that Richard has been badly maligned—that none of the evidence would stand up in court. Josephine Tey's novel was a tremendous success and marked the beginning of a new attitude toward Richard III. Today, very few historians would be willing to say outright that Richard was guilty. And in 1984 London Weekend Television staged a two-hour trial of Richard III, with real barristers and judges, and when all the evidence had been presented, the jury found him innocent.

What, then, are the facts?

The father of the murdered Princes was King Edward IV, who came to the throne in 1461 after deposing King Henry VI. The latter was a weak, gentle character who, as one writer remarks, would have made a good monk but made a rotten king; he also had periodic fits of insanity.

Edward's seizure of the throne came about as a result of the long series of conflicts known as the Wars of the Roses, which was basically a quarrel between two families, the Yorks (white roses) and Lancastrians (red roses), for the throne of England. Henry VI was a Lancaster, and after Edward toppled him from his throne, he spent the last six years of his life in the Tower of London; in 1471 he was pretty certainly murdered.

Edward was a total contrast to his predecessor. Henry was pale, shy, and monkish; Edward was tall, handsome, and lustful. And it seems that, when he set his mind on a girl, he wanted her so badly that he was willing to marry her if there was no other way of getting her into bed. At about the time he came to the throne, he was forced to use this technique to seduce Lady Eleanor Butler. It is not quite certain that he married her; he may have simply plighted his solemn troth, but since, in the fifteenth century, this was just as binding as marriage, we may simplify matters by saying that he married her and that the motive was purely sexual. Having—we may assume—surrendered her virginity and been abandoned, she entered a nunnery, where she died five years later.

Even before her death, Edward experienced the same urgent desire to possess a beautiful twenty-seven-year-old widow named Elizabeth Woodville and was forced to marry her to gain his objective. The marriage—in May 1464—was at first kept secret. But the lovely—and apparently timid and sweet—Elizabeth was made of tougher material than Eleanor Butler was and persuaded her husband to announce the marriage publicly. It caused an immense scandal—comparable to the scandal of Edward VIII and Mrs. Simpson in 1936—and the whole country was outraged. Edward's mother reproached him with bigamy. Having gained his objective, Edward returned to his routine of seducing every pretty girl who attracted his attention, and the Queen solaced herself by pushing her brothers into exalted positions and betrothing them to rich heiresses, as well as marrying off her sisters to Dukes and Earls. Her ambition was to make quite sure that her sons (the first born in 1470) became heirs to the throne and that her family should be the most powerful in the land. She very nearly succeeded.

Her husband had two younger brothers: George, Duke of Clarence, and Richard, Duke of Gloucester (who would become Richard III). The Queen had a particular hatred for Clarence. To begin with, he was heir to the throne (at least until she gave birth to her first son). He made no secret of his dislike of her and went around saying that she had used sorcery to seduce Edward. Clarence was immensely popular with the people; he was tall, good-looking, articulate, and charming; he was also shallow, vain, and envious. Rumors floated around that this elder brother, Edward, was illegitimate—in which case, Clarence should have been King. Clarence certainly thought so.

Edward's marriage to Elizabeth Woodville also enraged one of the most powerful men in the kingdom, the Earl of Warwick, known as the "King maker." His dream was to destroy all the Woodvilles. He persuaded Clarence—then his son-in-law—to join him in a rebellion against the King. It was very nearly successful; they captured Edward after the Battle of Banbury in 1469, but he escaped. Clarence then changed sides and supported his brother at the Battle of Barnet two years later, when Warwick was killed.

During all this time, the future Richard III remained loyal to Edward. If Clarence was the bad brother, Richard was the good one: courageous, steadfast, affectionate, and (like his brother Edward) tolerant and forgiving. So when Edward finally lost all patience with Clarence and introduced a bill of attainder against him (to be "attained" meant to be found guilty of treason), Richard rushed back from Scotland, where he was defending the Marches against the Scots, and begged for his brother's life. Their mother, the Duchess of York, also tried hard to reconcile the brothers, but to no avail. This time Edward had had enough. In 1478 the Duke of Clarence was killed in the Tower—the traditional story is that he was asked how he would like to die and replied jokingly that he would like to be drowned in a butt of Malmsey wine; he was taken at his word. (Shakespeare shows him being stabbed, then dragged off to the butt of Malmsey in the next room. He also makes Edward send a last-minute pardon, which arrives too late. But then, Shakespeare's intention is to show Edward and his Queen as good, decent people, and Richard as the worst kind of villain.)

The Queen, Elizabeth Woodville, was naturally delighted—she had played her part in persuading her husband to carry out the sentence. But it seems possible that they both had another motive for getting rid of Clarence: Clarence knew about Edward's earlier marriage to Lady Eleanor Butler. Eleanor was now dead, but since Edward had married Elizabeth Woodville in 1464, his second marriage was bigamous, and their children were therefore bastards, with no title to the throne.

Inevitably, there was one more party to the secret: the clergyman who had married Edward and Eleanor Butler. This was a cleric named Robert Stillington, who became Bishop of Bath and Wells. By an interesting coincidence, Stillington was arrested almost immediately after Clarence's death and thrown into the Tower. The charge against him was never made public. Whatever it was, he seems to have been able to reassure the King that he could keep a secret, and he was released.

Five years later, in 1483, Edward paid the penalty for his years of gorging, boozing, and womanizing and experienced a sudden and total collapse of health. It started in March; by April 9 he was dead. His will appointed his brother Richard Protector of the Realm and guardian of his two children and declared that neither his Queen nor any of her family should play any part in the government. It was as if he had seen through her at the end.

Richard was in York when he heard the news. His first act was to make the local nobles swear allegiance to Prince Edward (who was, in fact, now King Edward V although as yet uncrowned). But he also realized his danger. Edward was now in Ludlow, being looked after by the Queen's brother, Lord Rivers. The Queen would not take kindly to the idea of Richard being Protector of the Realm. (In fact, the Woodvilles lost no time in declaring the appointment null and void.) She had been looking forward to this moment—when she and her family could take over England—for a long time. By making Richard the Protector, King Edward had also made him a prime candidate for murder. Richard had to move fast.

Fortunately, he was capable of swift and decisive action. The Queen's brother had already reached Northampton with the young King. When he heard that Richard was close by, Rivers sent the boy on ahead by a secret route, while he stayed on in Northampton to delay Richard with an exchange of courtesies. Richard saw through the trick and had him arrested. Then he sent his men after the boy King and had him brought back. When the Queen realized that her plot had been foiled, she fled to her sanctuary at Westminster. Richard came to London with the boy and went ahead with arrangements for the coronation.

What happened next is not clear. Shakespeare, of course, has no doubt that Richard had no intention of allowing the boy to be crowned. But it seems far more probable that Richard's mother, the Duchess of York, now let him in on the secret of the bigamous marriage. (Richard had gone to stay with her in London.) If

Edward was illegitimate, then he could not become King. There was no other candidate except Richard himself. Three days after Edward was supposed to have been crowned—on June 23, 1483—Parliament asked Richard to become King. Later that day, Richard took the oath of allegiance.

The two young Princes were placed in the royal apartments in the Tower of London—not as prisoners but as guests (after all, the Tower was a royal residence). Richard's primary goal was undoubtedly to keep them out of the hands of the Woodvilles, who would use them as pawns in the power game. With the Princes in his hands, he had a certain guarantee of the ex-Queen's good behavior.

He was being naïvely optimistic. In fact, the Woodvilles lost no time in plotting against him. Now that it was clear that Elizabeth Woodville's children could never claim the throne, the Woodvilles turned to a Lancastrian named Henry Tudor, who was living in exile in Brittany. His claim to the throne was extremely tenuous; he was a descendant of the widow of Henry V. The Woodvilles proposed that he marry the ex-Queen's eighteen-year-old-daughter, Elizabeth. Henry had nothing to lose; in October of the same year he sailed for England to join a rebellion organized by supporters of the Woodvilles—the Duke of Buckingham and the Bishop of Ely. But a storm dispersed his fleet and he was forced to return home. Richard III demanded his extradition and Henry fled. Two more years of plotting ended in his invasion of England. On August 22, 1485, his army met Richard's at the Battle of Bosworth, and Richard was killed.

The crown was found on a bush and placed on Henry's head. He became King Henry VII, father of Henry VIII and grandfather of Queen Elizabeth I—which helps to explain why Shakespeare chose to turn Richard into one of his nastiest villains.

According to most historians, the two Princes had now been dead for two years. Richard had given way to temptation and had them murdered in the Tower by Sir James Tyrell. Yet—as already noted—there is at least one strong reason to doubt this story. One of Henry's most urgent pieces of business was to draw up an act of attainder against his predecessor, to justify his own seizure of the throne. It leaves no stone unturned in depicting Richard as a murderous villain—except one. It does not mention the murder of the Princes in the Tower.

Why? One obvious possibility, of course, is that they were not dead when Henry came to the throne. In fact, why should they have been? Richard had no reason to fear them. Parliament had passed an act called Titulus Regius, which declared that Richard was lawful King because the two Princes in the Tower were bastards. Bishop Stillington had declared that he had married King Edward to Lady Eleanor Butler.

On the other hand, Henry VII had a rather particular reason for wanting them dead. One of his first acts as King was to repeal the Titulus Regius act. This is understandable, if he intended to marry their sister (as he did). But in reversing her illegitimacy, he was also reversing that of the boys. They would now have a valid title to the throne, and he, Henry, would be the usurper.

Henry's solution to this problem was to order that the Titulus Regius act should be destroyed *unread* and that anyone found harboring a copy should be punished. He was very nearly successful; in fact, a single copy survived by accident. But why such secrecy—unless he was anxious not to draw attention to the fact that the Princes were now legitimized? And why worry about that if they were already dead?

This may hardly seem a good enough reason for murdering your bride's little brothers; but there is other evidence. If Henry had wished to discredit Richard by publicizing the murder of the Princes, then the simplest way to have done it would have been to put Tyrell on trial and get him to admit the murders publicly. Yet far from persecuting Tyrell, Henry VII heaped rewards on him. Tyrell was appointed Constable of Guisnes, in France, then sent as Ambassador to Rome. He had originally been given a grant for life of the revenues of some land in Wales, but Henry inexplicably changed his mind and gave him the revenues of Guisnes instead.

In her book *The Princes in the Tower* (1978), Elizabeth Jenkins (who is convinced of Richard's guilt) explains that the reason Henry did not include a charge of murdering the Princes in his denunciation of Richard was that "he did not know where the bodies were." This is absurd. If Tyrell killed the boys, then he certainly knew where the bodies were, and all the King had to do was ask him.

Seventeen years later Tyrell finally made a false step: he was too friendly with the Earl of Suffolk, Edmund de la Pole, who was involved in a French conspiracy against Henry. With an under-handedness that seems typical, Henry lured Tyrell away from his stronghold at Guisnes with a promise of safe conduct and then simply broke his promise. With his servant John Dighton—who is supposed to have been one of the actual murderers of the Princes (Tyrell only supervised)—he was charged with treason and exe-cuted. But before his execution he is reported to have made a full confession to killing the Princes on Richard's orders. The odd thing is that no confession was actually published—as we might expect. It was Henry's tame historian, Polydore Vergil, who re-ported the confession. So did Sir Thomas More (who was mar-tyred under Henry VIII) in his *History of Richard III.* But we know that Sir Thomas obtained all his material from one of Richard's bitterest enemies, John Morton, Bishop of Ely. Many parts of More's account have been shown to be false, and the fact that More left it unfinished suggests that he himself recognized that he had been duped.

So what was the truth about the Princes in the Tower? The logical inference would seem to be that the Princes were still alive after Richard's death at Bosworth and that Henry lost no time in having them murdered—by Tyrell and Dighton—soon after he became King. Tyrell was rewarded with the Welsh income, but Henry decided that he would be still safer across the Channel and exchanged it for Guisnes. When his chance came to destroy Tyrell, he leapt at it. Guisnes was besieged; but rather than risk Tyrell escaping and repeating his story all over Europe, Henry lured him to his death with treachery. Then Polydore Vergil was ordered to write the story of the "confession."

According to Vergil, Richard "lived in continual fear" that his nephews would supplant him and ordered the lieutenant of the Tower, Sir Robert Brackenbury, to kill them. Sir Robert refused with horror, saying he would rather die himself. So the King sent Tyrell instead. Oddly enough, he made no attempt to punish or remove Brackenbury. And just before the Battle of Bosworth, Brackenbury rode more than a hundred miles at great speed to join Richard and fight on his side. (Brackenbury was also killed at Bosworth.) This hardly sounds like the action of a man who had indignantly refused to murder the Princes, then seen them killed by Tyrell. (Vergil records that Brackenbury's priest buried the bodies.)

Two of Richard's defenders, Sir Clements Markham and Josephine Tey, insist that there were no rumors during Richard's lifetime about the murder of the Princes; Elizabeth Jenkins points out that an Italian named Dominic Mancini—a spy in the pay of Louis XI of France—had, in fact, recorded such a rumor in December 1483, four months after Richard's coronation. But Josephine Tey has argued convincingly that the source of that rumor was Richard's enemy Morton, Bishop of Ely, who also gave Sir Thomas More his material.

Altogether, then, it seems clear that all the circumstantial evidence indicates that Richard was not the murderer and Henry was. All we know of Henry's character—his deviousness, his vengefulness—makes him a prime candidate. The affair of Tyrell's execution is typical of Henry's method. And Henry and his successor—Henry VIII—went on to use a series of judicial murders to get rid of anyone who might be regarded as a Yorkist sympathizer. Typical of these is the way in which Henry got rid of Clarence's son, the Earl of Warwick. In 1497 a youth named Perkin Warbeck claimed to be one of the murdered Princes in the Tower—the younger one, Richard. He seems to have been basically a dupe of the Yorkists, and when his "rebellion" failed, he surrendered to Henry on a promise of pardon. He was imprisoned in the Tower. Another youth, Clarence's son—the Earl of Warwick—was also there. The King encouraged them to get together, then used agents provocateurs to encourage them to plot an escape. Both were then executed.

So why does *anyone* still believe that Richard was guilty? There is, unfortunately, one apparently damning piece of evidence. In 1933 Professor William Wright, Dean of London Hospital, was asked to examine the bones, which had been kept in an urn since the time of Charles II. He was assisted by Dr. George Northcroft, ex-president of the British Dental Association. According to their findings, the bones were those of two boys (although they admitted the possibility that they might have been girls), aged about ten and twelve.

If they were correct, Richard must be guilty. For the boys were, respectively, ten and twelve in 1483, the year of Richard's coronation. Henry did not come to England until two years later.

Thomas B. Costain devotes the end of his book, *The Last Plantagenets*, to the question of the bones. One of his main points is that both skeletons were unusually tall for boys of ten and twelve. Edward, the elder, was four feet nine and a half inches, while his brother was four feet six inches. (Height can be estimated from the long bones.) Costain then quotes a textbook giving average heights of children for various ages, which states that the average height for a boy of twelve is just under four feet seven inches. By this reckoning, Edward was more than two and a half inches too tall—and in an age when, on average, men were far shorter than today (as we can see by looking at old suits of armor). It is true, of course, that his father was tall. But we know that most boys suddenly "shoot up" during puberty, not as early as twelve. If Edward was murdered in 1483, he would not yet have reached puberty.

Costain goes on to quote many books by experts: Gradwohl's *Legal Medicine*, Thomas Dwight's *Human Skeleton*, and Wentworth and Wilder's *Personal Identification*. All agree that the dating of skeletons is still a perfunctory matter and that considerable variation must be allowed. As to the dental evidence, Northcroft declared that Edward's teeth showed him to be between twelve and thirteen. But Wright diagnosed Edward as suffering from the bone disease osteitis, which can retard the growth of teeth for up to a year. This, admittedly, poses a problem. If we are suggesting that Edward was murdered on the orders of Henry VII, then it could not have been before August 1485, when he was nearly fifteen. If osteitis could retard tooth growth by a year, and Edward had been murdered in 1485, then we might expect the dental examination to reveal his age as nearly fourteen, not nearly fifteen. This is a matter to which we shall return in a moment.

Costain goes on to quote a recent report on bone formation in American children. Three knee bones, apparently belonging to children of the same age, turned out to belong to a mature six-year-old, an average eight-year-old, and a retarded ten-year-old.

In an article on dental identification in *Papers from The Criminologist* (1971), Professor Gosta Gustafson describes how age is determined from teeth: a thin slice from the middle of the tooth is ground down into a transparent layer, so it can be examined under a microscope. Having described the method, he then tells of how a tooth from a body that had been almost totally destroyed in a fire was estimated by this method, revealing its "owner" to be an elderly man who had recently vanished from a lunatic asylum. The examination, he says, showed that the tooth was "approximately" the age of the vanished man.

This word *approximately* occurs frequently in accounts of determination of age from teeth and bones. For example, the same volume contains an essay by Dr. Thomas E. A. Stowell on the bones of St. Edward the Martyr, and after explaining that it is possible to determine age from "the skeleton as a whole," Stowell goes on to say that he assesses the bones "as those of a young man over seventeen years old and probably not above the age of twenty-one."

Gustafson's comment on the Princes in the Tower is interesting:

> For English readers interested in history it may be pointed out that the two princes thought to have been killed in the Tower of London in June 1483—Edward V and Richard, Duke of York—were found in 1674; the remains were investigated in 1934 [sic] when their ages were estimated from the development of the teeth, and identity reasonably well proved.

What the paragraph inadvertently manages to suggest is that the remains were already assumed to be those of two boys, aged ten and twelve, murdered by Richard III, and that examination confirmed this. We do not know, of course, whether the two professors began by assuming that they were looking at boys of ten and twelve. Perhaps they maintained an attitude of rigid detachment, determined not to be influenced by their expectations. But it raises the question of what results they might have achieved had they been told that they were looking at the bones of two boys murdered by Henry VII in 1485, and therefore of about twelve and fourteen.

In *The London Archaeologist* of spring 1987, yet another piece of evidence appeared. Dr. Theya Molleson of the Natural History Museum had examined the bones again and concluded—understandably—that they were indeed the bones of the Princes. The boys were "prepubescent"—which, in the case of the older of the two, certainly suggests an age of less than fourteen. And according to Dr. Molleson, the teeth prove that the boys died in 1484, not 1483. That would seem to be final. Richard was on the throne in 1484 and Henry was still in France; Richard *has* to be the murderer. But then we may recall Dr. Wright's evidence about osteitis, which can retard the teeth for up to a year. In that case, the date of Edward's death could well be 1485, not 1484.

We may also recall that in December 1483 the spy Mancini was reporting rumors that the Princes had been murdered. Dr. Molleson's dating of the deaths in 1484 clearly disproves that. Richard, at least, was innocent of killing them at the time Mancini reported he was believed to have done so.

The evidence of bones, as we have seen, can be somewhat ambiguous. If Edward was a sickly boy, as we know he was, then he may well have been "prepubescent" at the time of his death, even if that took place in 1485. Since he was suffering from osteitis, his teeth may well have suggested the date of his death as a year earlier than it was. Since the disputed period is a year, not two years, absolute precision is essential. But the teeth of his brother should be able to establish beyond all doubt whether he died in 1484 or 1485. Clearly, what is needed at this point is a reexamination of the bones, bearing all these facts in mind.

Until that happens, we must maintain an open mind. But if the bones *should* prove to date from 1484, we would be faced with yet another mystery: why on earth did Richard kill the two boys when, by that time, he was firmly established on the throne and had Henry to fear rather than his nephews? If a man could be acquitted on purely circumstantial evidence, Richard would undoubtedly be found innocent.

28

The Sea Kings of 6000 B.C.: The Maps That Contradict the History Books

In 1966 Charles Hapgood, a professor of the history of science, caused something of a scandal when he published a book entitled *Maps of the Ancient Sea Kings*. For what Professor Hapgood was arguing, with a logic that was difficult to fault, was that civilization may be far, far older than historians now recognize: that as long as twelve thousand years ago, when man was still a wandering hunter, ancient seafarers may have been sailing across the Atlantic. These conclusions were not the outcome of wild speculation; they were the logical result of the study of old maps that had been available for centuries.

The story began in 1956, when a cartographer named M. I. Walters, at the U.S. Navy Hydrographic Office, found himself looking at a copy of a strange map that had been presented to the Office by a Turkish naval officer. It was obviously very old—in fact, it was dated 919 in the Muslim calendar, which is A.D. 1513 by Christian reckoning. It was basically a map of the Atlantic Ocean, showing a small part of North Africa, from what is now Morocco to the Ivory Coast, and all of South America. These were in their correct longitudes, a remarkable—in fact, almost unbelievable—achievement for those days, when most maps were laughably crude. (One of the most famous medieval maps shows

Italy joined to Spain; another shows the British Isles shaped like a teapot.) It was also, for 1513, an astonishingly accurate map of South America. And what was even more surprising was that it apparently showed Antarctica, which was not discovered until 1818. Oddly enough, it also showed the mid-Atlantic ridge, which seems an unbelievable piece of knowledge for any period before the invention of sonar depth soundings—unless, of course, it had been observed while it was still above water.

The original mapmaker had been a Turkish pirate named Piri Re'is (Re'is means "admiral"), who had been beheaded in 1554. He had been the nephew of a famous pirate, Kemal Re'is, and had held a high post, equivalent to the governorship of Egypt. Piri Re'is had made the interesting statement that he had based his map on twenty old maps, one of them made by Christopher Columbus and others from the great library of Alexandria, destroyed by invading Arabs in A.D. 640.

In fact, the Piri Re'is map had been known since 1929, when it had been discovered in the Topkapi Palace museum in Istanbul, and there was already a copy in the Library of Congress. But thus far, no one had paid much attention to it. Walters decided to try and remedy that and showed the map to his friend, Captain Alington H. Mallery, a navigator who was devoting his retirement to studying old maps. Mallery was allowed to borrow the map, and when he brought it back, he had some startling—indeed, incredible—comments. Mallery agreed that the land shown to the south was Antarctica; what was more, the map had apparently been made before the Antarctic continent was covered with ice. But that seemed absurd. The coast of Antarctica had certainly been covered with ice in the time of Alexander the Great; the last time men could have seen it without ice was many thousands of years ago, long before the earliest known maritime civilizations. And that could only mean one of two things: either that ships had sailed the seas at a time when, according to historians, our ancestors were living in caves, or—what sounded equally outrageous—that there had once been a flourishing civilization on Antarctica itself, whose men made maps that were copied down through the ages, up to the time of Alexander the Great.

These suggestions caused considerable controversy, which

came to Hapgood's attention. He was interested because it sounded as if the Piri Re'is map might support some of the conclusions he had drawn about the movements of the earth's crust—and published in a book entitled *Earth's Shifting Crust* in 1958. Hapgood's starting point had been the puzzle of the great ice ages, which are still unexplained by science. Hapgood's own suggestion was that, for some unknown reason, the amount of sunlight varies from age to age. Ice caps form unevenly at the poles, and this lack of balance affects the rotation of the earth—just as an off-balance wheel begins to vibrate as it spins. This, Hapgood suggested, causes masses of ice to dislodge, as well as the tectonic plates to which they are stuck. And the movement of these plates causes a catastrophic shake-up of the earth's crust. Hapgood estimated that the last such catastrophic movement took place between ten and fifteen thousand years ago. Before that, he suggested, Antarctica was 2,500 miles closer to the equator than it is today and had a temperate climate. Albert Einstein wrote an introduction to the book, in which he declared that Hapgood's theories deserved careful attention.

When Hapgood learned of Mallery's views on the Piri Re'is map, he decided that, instead of arguing about whether it was genuine, it would be more sensible to subject it to careful, detailed study. He therefore assembled a group of students at Keene State College in New Hampshire and set them the task of studying a number of ancient maps, including that of Piri Re'is.

Hapgood's first surprise was that the maps known as *portolans*—those used by seafarers in the Middle Ages (the word means "from port to port")—had been known to scholars for centuries and that no one had paid much attention to them, even though some showed, for example, that Cuba had been known before Columbus "discovered" it in 1492. His next surprise was that these portolans were often as accurate as modern maps. It seemed odd that land-based mapmakers should have been content with crudities when their marine counterparts were so sophisticated.

Hapgood also noted that A. E. Noderskiold, a leading scholar whose study of early maps had appeared in 1889, believed that the portolans of the fifteenth and sixteenth centuries were based on far older maps that dated back centuries before Christ. One of Noderskiold's main reasons for this belief was that the great geographer and astronomer Ptolemy, who was active in Alexandria around A.D. 150, made maps that were less accurate than these medieval portolans, even though he had the greatest library in the world at his disposal. Was it likely that ordinary medieval seamen, working by rule of thumb, could surpass Ptolemy unless they had some ancient maps to guide them?

The arguments Hapgood uses to support this thesis, based on the research of his students, are too long and too technical to describe at length here. But one thing that was obvious was that although Piri had combined the twenty maps he admitted using to the best of his ability, he had often allowed them to overlap—or fail to overlap. He had shown the Amazon river twice but had left out a nine-hundred-mile stretch of the coastline. The problem was to try to understand how these errors had come about.

One error could be pinned down to the Greek astronomer Eratosthenes, the first man to calculate the size of the earth with accuracy. He knew that on June 21 the sun at midday was reflected in a certain well in Syene, on the Nile, and that towers did not cast a shadow. But in Alexandria, they did. He had only to measure the length of the shadow of a tower in Alexandria at midday on June 21 to calculate the angle of the sun's rays. This proved to be 7½°. Since he knew the distance from Syene to Alexandria, he could easily work out how many miles were required for 360°. Due to a miscalculation of distance, Eratosthenes increased the circumference of the earth by about 4½°; but it was an amazingly accurate calculation for 240 B.C. Hapgood discovered that if he allowed for this 4½° error, Piri's map became even more accurate. This was an additional piece of evidence that Piri's map was based on ancient Greek models.

Another problem is the obvious one known to all geographers—that the earth is a sphere, and a map that is flat is bound to distort it. Today mapmakers use a "projection" based on division into latitude and longitude. But the old mapmakers, it seemed, used a simpler method. They chose a center, drew a circle around it, then subdivided this into sixteen segments, much like dividing a cake into sixteen slices. Along the outer edge of every "slice" they

drew various squares—a complicated method, but one that
worked well enough. The original center of the Piri Re'is map was
actually off the map, but calculation indicated that it had to be in
Egypt. At first, Alexandria seemed the obvious place. But more
careful calculation showed that the place had to be further north.
When it turned out to be Syene, Hapgood knew he was on the
right track.

But this in itself, Hapgood realized, had some interesting implications. When the geographers of Alexandria made their maps—
which included Eratosthenes's 4½° error—it is unlikely that they
sailed off to visit the various places they were mapping. They
presumably used older maps. And those older maps must have
been incredibly accurate—without the 4½° error. This suggests
that the older mapmakers possessed a more accurate and advanced mapmaking science than the Greeks.

In fact, there is one interesting piece of evidence that this is so.
Toward the end of the second century B.C. the Greek grammarian
Agatharchides of Cnidus, who was a tutor to one of the Ptolemy
kings of Egypt, was told that, according to ancient tradition, the
base of the Great Pyramid—built around 2500 B.C.—was precisely one-eighth of a minute of a degree in length—that is, it was
that part of the earth's circumference. (A minute is a sixtieth of a
degree.) The pyramid's base is just over 230 meters. If 230 is
multiplied by 8, then by 60, then by 360, the result is just under
four hundred thousand kilometers, or just under twenty-five thousand miles—a remarkably accurate estimate of the length of the
equator. Now it is possible, of course, that whoever designed the
pyramid chose the length of its base at random and that some
later geographer, after Eratosthenes, worked out that it was an
eighth of a minute. But our knowledge of the ancient Egyptians,
and the importance they attached to sacred geometry, suggests
that they knew exactly what they were doing—and that they knew
the circumference of the earth in 2500 B.C.

When Napoléon invaded Egypt in 1798, one of the learned
men he took along with him, Edme François Jomard, studied the
Great Pyramid carefully and made some important discoveries:
The four sides of the pyramid point to the four points of the
compass—north, south, east, and west—with incredible accuracy.

The pyramid is ten miles from Cairo, which is at the base of the Nile Delta—so called because it is a triangle of streams running into the sea—and if diagonals are drawn from the pyramid, they neatly enclose the delta. Moreover, a line drawn from exactly halfway along the north face slices the delta into two exact halves. All of these facts indicate that the ancient Egyptians had some extremely precise method of measuring long distances and did not do it by rough guesswork.

The French meter is supposed to be precisely one ten-millionth of the distance from equator to pole. Jomard's study of the pyramid convinced him that the Egyptians had also used a measure based on the earth's size—in this case, 1 divided by 216,000.

All of this is staggering. How could a fairly primitive agricultural civilization know the size of the earth? What is equally hard to understand is why this knowledge had to be rediscovered by Eratosthenes more than two thousand years later—until we recall that until Columbus sailed to America, there was a general belief that the earth is flat. Knowledge can be lost very easily.

Hapgood made another interesting discovery from his study of the Piri Re'is map: that the original maps from which it was drawn must have used a slightly different length for the degree of latitude than the degree of longitude. Why? Well, presumably because if you are trying to project the surface of a sphere onto a flat sheet of paper, the lines of longitude get shorter as they draw toward the poles, while the lines of latitude (since they run parallel across the globe) are less affected. The first European to use this projection method was Gerardus Mercator, in 1569. It looked as if the ancient mapmakers had already used the same method.

Hapgood concluded that the "evident knowledge of longitude implies a people unknown to us, a nation of seafarers, with instruments for finding longitude undreamed of by the Greeks."

What was equally impressive was Hapgood's confirmation of Mallery's conclusion that the coast of Queen Maud Land, on the Antarctic continent, had been drawn without the ice sheets. In 1949 an expedition mounted by Norway, Britain, and Sweden was able to establish the outline of the land under the ice by various sophisticated techniques for taking depth soundings through the ice caps. This indicated that Piri Re'is probably based his map on

some original map of the Antarctic before the Ice Age—which, as
we recall, Hapgood had placed (in *Earth's Shifting Crust*) between ten and fifteen thousand years ago.

The Piri Re'is map was not the only one examined by Hapgood
and his students. Hapgood asked the Library of Congress to allow
him to look at all the old maps of the period and was startled to
find hundreds of them laid out for his inspection. It was a 1531
map by one Oronteus Finaeus that filled him with a conviction
that he had made a discovery equal in importance to the Piri
Re'is map. It showed the South Pole—which was amazing enough
for a date nearly three centuries before its official discovery. What
was positively staggering was that it was a map of the whole polar
cap, as if drawn from the air, showing a remarkable resemblance
to the pole as we know it today. And again, all the evidence
suggested that it had been made in the days before the pole was
covered with ice—it, too, showed the coast of Queen Maud Land
and mountain ranges now under the ice, as well as rivers flowing
into the sea. Certain mistakes on the map reappeared in all other
contemporary maps, suggesting that all of them had been based
on some old map, possibly dating back to Alexander the Great.
But the 1949 core samples left no doubt that the Antarctic was
covered with ice at the time of Alexander the Great (356-23 B.C.).
So the original maps must have been much older.

How much older? The core samples showed that the last warm
period in the Antarctic ended six thousand years ago, or around
4000 B.C., so the "Antarctic civilization" posited by Hapgood
must have flourished before this. Now this, in itself, is not particularly astonishing. Man was fishing ten thousand years ago and
began to farm soon after that. Jericho, the oldest market town so
far discovered, was fortified between eight and ten thousand years
ago, and its inhabitants used polished limestone dishes because
they had not yet learned to bake pottery. On the other hand,
writing was not invented until about 3500 B.C., in Sumeria.
Domestication of camels and donkeys was to cause an expansion
in trade about five hundred years later. So the Oronteus Finaeus
map suggested that some kind of writing—because it is hard to
conceive of a map without "labels"—must have existed nearly
three thousand years earlier. Besides, mapmaking is a sophisti-

cated science requiring, among other things, some knowledge of geometry—and the earliest knowledge of geometry seems to date from Babylon about 1500 B.C., nearly five thousand years later than the "Antarctic civilization."

A Turkish Hadji Ahmed map of 1550 (fourteen years before the birth of Shakespeare) shows the world from a northern "projection," as if hovering over the North Pole. Again, the accuracy is incredible. But what may be its most interesting feature is that Alaska and Siberia *seem* to be joined. Since this projection shows a heart-shaped globe, with Alaska on one side of the "dimple" and Siberia on the other, this could merely indicate that the mapmaker did not have enough space to show the Bering Strait which divides the continents. If this is not so, the consequences are staggering: we know that a land bridge *did* exist in the remote past, but it may have been as long as 12,000 years ago.

Other early portolans were equally remarkable for their accuracy. The "Dulcert Portolano" of 1339, for example, shows that the cartographer had precise knowledge of an area from Galway to the Don Basin in Russia. Others showed the Aegean dotted with islands that do not now exist—they were presumably drowned by melting ice; an accurately drawn map of southern Great Britain, but without Scotland and with indications of glaciers; and a Sweden still partially glaciated.

Perhaps the most interesting piece of evidence uncovered by Hapgood is a map of China that he found in Needham's *Science and Civilisation in China*, dating from A.D. 1137 and carved in stone. Hapgood's studies of Piri Re'is and other European portolans had made him familiar with the "longitude error" mentioned above; now he was astonished to find it on this map of China. If he was correct, then the Chinese had also known the "original" maps on which Piri Re'is's map was based.

And this, of course, suggested the staggering idea that some worldwide seafaring civilization had existed before Alexander the Great and that it had disappeared while the civilization of Mesopotamia was still primitive and illiterate. This is the suggestion that Hapgood—shunning all academic caution—outlines in his book's last chapter, "A Civilisation That Vanished." He points out that we had to wait for the eighteenth century to develop an

accurate method of measuring longitude and the circumference
of the earth, and until the nineteenth for the exploration of the
Arctic and Antarctic. According to Hapgood: "The maps indicate
that some ancient people did all these things." And this civilization disappeared, either in some catastrophe or over a long period
of time, and was simply forgotten. If it existed in Antarctica—and
possibly the Arctic—then its disappearance is easily explained by
the return of the ice cap about six thousand years ago.

And what does all this mean? Hapgood was content simply to
postulate a maritime civilization that sailed the seven seas when,
according to historians, the only seafarers were fishermen who
hugged the coasts of the Mediterranean. But others were anxious
to dot the *is* and cross the *ts*. They saw his "advanced civilization
of the Ice Age" as a proof of the real existence of Atlantis, supposedly destroyed in some great prehistoric catastrophe, while
others seized upon it as proof that the earth had been visited by
"spacemen" at some remote epoch in the past. The "ancient
astronaut" theory (see chapter 8) was popularized in books like
The Morning of the Magicians (1960) by Louis Pauwels and
Jacques Bergier, and *Chariots of the Gods?* (1957) by Erich von
Däniken. All these speculations—popularized in the 1968 film
2001: A Space Odyssey—had the same effect on the scientists of
the 1960s that the Spiritualist explosion of the 1860s had on their
nineteenth-century predecessors. Serious inquiry was undermined by "guilt by association." Hapgood ceased to be taken
seriously, even by a minority of his fellow academics.

In 1979 a revised edition of *Maps of the Ancient Sea Kings:
Evidence of Advanced Civilisation in the Ice Age* made reviewers
aware that Hapgood did not deserve to be tarred with the same
brush as von Däniken. It is perfectly conceivable that some of his
arguments may prove to be false and that the mistakes of un-
skilled mapmakers may explain the extra islands in the Aegean,
the missing upper half of England, the mid-Atlantic ridge, and
even the land bridge across the Bering Strait. But his main argument remains unaffected. Portolans of the Middle Ages show
Antarctica long before it was explored, and the skill with which
they are drawn suggests that they are based on far older maps.
Perhaps the resemblance between the Chinese map of 1137 and

the portolans is coincidence, and there was no "worldwide maritime civilization." But at the very least, there must have been some fairly sophisticated civilization long before the so-called birth of civilization in Mesopotamia or China—perhaps buried beneath Antarctic ice.

Hapgood is inclined to undermine his own case with specious arguments. For example, he points out that in *Gulliver's Travels* (1726), Swift gives a strangely accurate description of the two moons of Mars, which were not discovered for another century and a half. Hapgood suggests that Swift was relying on "some ancient source," when the true explanation is probably the curious serendipity that can be found so often in the history of art and literature. (I point out in my book *Starseekers* that in *Eureka*, Poe anticipated the Big Bang theory of the origin of the universe, as well as the discovery that atoms can be broken down into positive and negative particles.) In other words, we are dealing with something closer to Jung's "synchronicity."

To be fair to von Däniken and *The Morning of the Magicians*, it must also be admitted that Hapgood's carefully argued analysis of the portolans *does* offer some support for the "ancient astronaut" theory. The Oronteus Finaeus map *does* look as if it has been based on an aerial view. So does the 1550 Hadji Ahmed map of the world seen from above the North Pole. Moreover, it is still difficult to see how the lines and the vast drawings on the desert floor at Nazca could have been drawn by people who were unable to look down on them from the air—although primitive balloons would have been as effective as spacecraft for that purpose.

But the theories that have appealed to Hapgood's findings for support (including those based on the *Oera Linda Book*, discussed in chapter 25) cannot be regarded as evidence either for or against his findings. All that *is* quite certain is that Hapgood's evidence for an ancient maritime civilization that preceded any of those we know is virtually incontrovertible.

29

Sea Monsters:
Unknown Giants of the Deep

On October 10, 1848, the *Times* of London carried the following report: "When the *Daedalus*, frigate, Captain M'Quhae, which arrived on the 4th inst., was on her passage from the East Indies between the Cape of Good Hope and St. Helena, her captain, and most of her officers and crew, at four o'clock one afternoon, saw a sea serpent."

The report brought a flood of angry letters from naval men who felt that the *Times* was failing in its duty to the public by printing such rubbish. Understandably, the public took a different view, and newspapers all over the country seized upon the story. A conference was hastily called at the Admiralty, which concluded that an immediate investigation was required.

The first step was to contact Captain Peter M'Quhae, to find out whether there was any substance to the story. To the embarrassment of Admiral Sir W. Gage, who was in charge of the investigation, M'Quhae replied that despite certain glaring inaccuracies, the *Times* story was essentially correct: he had indeed seen a sea monster. He had noted the event in the ship's log and had planned to report the incident through normal channels.

His story was as follows: At five o'clock on August 6, 1848, while the *Daedalus* was between the Cape of Good Hope and St.

Helena, one of the midshipmen reported a strange creature swimming slowly toward them off the starboard bow. Most of the crew
were at supper, and there were only seven men on deck, including
the captain, the watch officer, and the ship's navigator. All of
them witnessed what M'Quhae described as "an enormous serpent"—judged to be about 100 feet long—as it swam in a straight
line past the frigate, apparently oblivious to its existence. The
captain judged it to be traveling at around twelve to fifteen miles
an hour and described how it had remained within the range of
their spyglasses for nearly twenty minutes. Although the afternoon was showery and dull, M'Quhae stated that it was still bright
enough to see the creature clearly and that it swam close enough
that "had it been a man of my acquaintance I should have easily
recognized his features with the naked eye."

He described the large, distinctly snakelike head projecting just
above the waves on a neck about fifteen inches thick, followed by
sixty feet or so of serpentine back, which crested above the
surface of the water. The color was uniformly dark brown, apart
from the throat, which was a yellowish white. To M'Quhae it
seemed to slip through the water effortlessly, without the aid of
fins or the undulatory swimming typical of snakes and eels. This
odd fact may be explained by a mane of hair or seaweed that ran
along its back and that may have obscured its means of propul-
sion. At no point did the creature open its mouth to reveal "large
jagged teeth" (as the *Times* had reported). The witnesses had all
agreed that it appeared neither frightened nor threatening but
rather that it was traveling forward "on some determined purpose." M'Quhae had made a sketch of the creature which, at the
admiral's request, he converted into a larger drawing to accompany his statement.

To the credit of the Admiralty, it quickly made the controversial
report publicly available. On October 13 the *Times* printed the
report in full, and fifteen days later the *Illustrated London News*
printed several pictures of the "*Daedalus* sea serpent" based on
M'Quhae's drawing. The "purposeful" sea monster became a
subject of sometimes heated national debate.

The other six witnesses named by M'Quhae backed his version
of events, but it was clear from the outset that there was some

difference of opinion on details. The magazine *Zoologist* published an extract from the journal of the watch officer, Lieutenant Edgar Drummond, covering the day of the sighting. Drummond had judged the head to be about ten feet long—rather large for a sixteen-inch neck to support. He estimated the visible part of the body at about twenty feet long, and although he mentioned that the captain claimed to see another twenty feet of tail just beneath the surface, this still came short of M'Quhae's estimate of sixty feet of wave-cresting body. Drummond also disagreed about what his captain referred to as a "mane" on the creature's back, preferring to describe it as some sort of dorsal fin.

Few skeptics were rude enough to accuse the witnesses of being downright liars, but many hinted that this was their view. One wrote to the *Times* asking why M'Quhae did not order his men to put about and give chase to the creature. Another, perhaps with tongue in cheek, demanded why he had not fired a broadside at it.

A more useful contribution to the discussion was a letter in the *Literary Gazette* that pointed out that the description of the *Daedalus* monster was remarkably like that of a sea serpent described by the Danish Bishop Pontoppidan in his influential zoological study, *A Natural History of Norway* (1753). It continued: "One might fancy the gallant Captain had read the old Dane, and was copying him, when he tells of the dark brown colour and white about the throat, and the neck clothed as if by a horse's mane or a bunch of sea-weed, the exact words of the historian." Through all this M'Quhae maintained a dignified silence. It took the intervention of one of Europe's leading men of science to persuade him to comment.

Sir Richard Owen, curator of the Hunterian Museum, an anatomist, naturalist, and paleontologist of immense reputation, came forward to lead the crusade of *Daedalus* sea-serpent debunkers. Owen was considered by many people to be the greatest living authority on zoology. Pugnaciously conservative, he would later become Darwin's most bitter and most venomous opponent.

Owen began by sending the *Times* a copy of a lengthy letter he had written to a friend who had inquired whether the *Daedalus* sea serpent might not be a survival of the Saurian age—one of the most popular theories that had emerged during the controversy.

Owen dismissed M'Quhae's suggestion that the creature was a giant sea snake, implying that the captain should leave scientific deductions to the experts. After a careful consideration of M'Quhae's statement, Owen came to the conclusion that the creature was almost certainly a mammal of some sort, and—since his analysis was based on the preconceived idea that the sighting was of some species already known to science—he went on to suggest one that might fit the bill: the *Phoca proboscidea* or sea elephant. (The level of Owen's expertise on sea serpents may be judged from his remark that alligators are often encountered by vessels at sea; in fact, alligators are relatively weak swimmers and cannot even live in turbulent stretches of river.)

The sea elephant is, in fact, an enormous seal (it may grow to twenty feet in length) that is native to the seas around Antarctica. Owen's suggestion was that one of these creatures might have been swept north on an iceberg, from which it would swim periodically to eat fish. When the ice melted, it would have been forced to swim until its strength gave out. Perhaps, he wrote, it was dying when the *Daedalus* encountered it, thus explaining its lack of interest in them. In his opinion, what M'Quhae had mistaken as a forty-foot stretch of semisubmerged reptilian body was, in fact, the turbulence its horizontal tail made as it swam along in a straight line. The "mane" that the captain noted was, Owen pointed out, typical of bull sea elephants—also known as Anderson's sea lions. He then went on to deny the existence of all sea serpents on the grounds that science had found no evidence of them and concluded with the assertion: "A larger body of evidence from eye-witnesses might be got together in proof of ghosts than of sea-serpents."

In a letter to the *Times* M'Quhae replied, a little testily, that the creature seen that day had not been a sea elephant, which he would have quickly recognized, or for that matter a seal of any kind. As an experienced sailor he was quite capable of telling the difference between water turbulence and the passage of a large, solid body. He also insisted that he had not heard of the account of a sea serpent given by Bishop Pontoppidan until it had been mentioned by the *Literary Gazette* correspondent and that therefore it could not have influenced him to embroider the account of what he had seen.

Finally, he ended by stating categorically that there had been no hysterical excitement among the witnesses and that he himself was certain that no kind of optical illusion could have misled them about the details given in the report. His statement, he concluded, would stand as it was "until some more fortunate opportunity shall occur of making a closer acquaintance with the 'great unknown'—in the present instance assuredly no ghost." The letter was his final word on the controversy, and its general tone was one of a man sick to death of the whole subject.

Ten years after the *Daedalus* sighting, a Captain Frederic Smith wrote to the *Times* describing how his lookout on the *Pekin* had sighted what they took to be a sea serpent with a "huge head and neck, covered with a long shaggy-looking kind of mane," but that had proved to be a twenty-foot length of seaweed. The letter ended by concluding that the *Daedalus* serpent was almost certainly a piece of seaweed as well. This drew a reply from an officer of the *Daedalus* in which he stated that the "serpent" was "beyond all question a living animal, moving rapidly through the water." He went on to describe how they had observed it at close quarters for some time. Again, the circumstantial details of the report are impressive.

At least the British Admiralty indicated their belated support for M'Quhae's story by placing his report in their official records, the first such claimed sighting to be dignified in this way.

In fact, there had been dozens of sightings of sea serpents before 1848—Bernard Huevelmans's book *In the Wake of the Sea Serpents* (1968) lists about 150 between 1639 and 1848. The 1639 sighting is secondhand, but there are dozens of other reports that are as circumstantial as M'Quhae's. For example, Captain George Little, of the frigate *Boston*, described how, in May 1740, he was lying in Broad Bay, off Maine, when "I discovered a large Serpent or monster coming down the Bay, on the surface of the water." A cutter full of armed men went off to take a closer look, but "when within a hundred feet . . . the serpent dove. He was not less than from 45 to 50 feet in length; the largest diameter of his body, I should judge, 15 inches; his head nearly the size of a man, which he carried four or five feet above the water. He wore every appearance of a common black snake."

Huevelmans quotes 587 sightings between 1639 and 1966. One of the 1966 sightings was made by two Englishmen, John Ridgeway and Chay Blyth. Ridgeway wrote in *A Fighting Chance*:

> I was shocked to full wakefulness by a swishing noise to starboard. I looked out into the water and suddenly saw the writhing, twisting shape of a great creature. It was outlined by the phosphorescence in the sea as if a string of neon lights were hanging from it. It was an enormous size, some thirty-five feet or more long, and it came towards me quite fast. . . . It headed straight at me and disappeared right beneath me. . . . I was frozen with terror at this apparition.

And Huevelmans concludes his chapter—and his sightings—with a report by two vacationers near Skegness in eastern England, who saw "something like the Loch Ness monster" a hundred yards out to sea: "It had a head like a serpent and six or seven pointed humps trailing behind."

Huevelmans goes on to quote Sir Arthur Conan Doyle as saying that if one okapi had been shot in Africa, its existence might be doubted. If ten men shoot an okapi, the evidence would be strong. If fifty men shoot one, "it would become convincing." So 587 sightings—even if some are dismissed as fraud or genuine mistakes—undoubtedly deserve to be classified as convincing. Huevelmans then analyses the sightings and classifies them into seven basic types: the "super-otter," with a flat head and long, otterlike body; the many-humped serpent, with its row of regular humps; the many-finned serpent, with pointed projections along both sides; the merhorse, a creature with a mane; the long-necked serpent, with a long, slender neck like a prehistoric diplodocus; and the "super-eels," which resemble giant snakes. He toys with a classification called the "Father-of-all-the-turtles"—looking, as one might suppose, like a giant turtle—but finally dismisses it as suspect and doubtful. The first five he believes to be mammals, while the super-eel—on the evidence of body fragments—seems to be a fish.

Bishop Pontoppidan, whom we have already encountered, was not the first to describe the sea serpent. As early as 1539 a Swedish bishop named Olaf Mansson (Latinized as Olaus Magnus) published in Venice a map of the north that clearly showed two sea serpents. And in a *History of the Goths, Swedes, and Vandals*, published in 1555, he describes a "serpent 200 feet long and 20 feet thick" that lives in the sea caves off Bergen. This story, accompanied by terrifying pictures of serpents devouring ships, was cited by many subsequent encyclopedists. Two hundred years later Bishop Pontoppidan devoted a chapter of his *Natural History of Norway* to various monsters, including the sea serpent, the kraken, and the mermaid. In the case of the sea serpent he took the trouble to obtain a firsthand account by one Captain Lorenz von Ferry, who ordered a boat to pursue the creature, and was able to describe in some detail the horselike head with a white mane and black eyes, and the many coils or folds—he thought there were seven or eight, with about a fathom (six feet) between each fold.

The main interest of Pontoppidan's comments at this juncture is that his book aroused considerable skepticism in Britain when it was translated in 1765 and that a Captain (later Admiral) Charles Douglas, who tried to find out what he could about such monsters, took a distinctly skeptical view of the evidence of some witnesses. Oddly enough, he recorded that while many Norwegians believed in the existence of "Stoor worms" (sea worms), they were inclined to dismiss the kraken, a giant octopus, as a myth. And it continued to be dismissed as a myth until its existence was finally accepted by science in the 1970s. т legends of the kraken—a vast octopoid monster that sometimes attacked swimmers, ships, and even coastal villages—can be traced back as far as the ancient Roman scholar Pliny, who described a "polyp" with thirty-foot-long arms that climbed ashore to steal fish being salted at Carteia in Spain and that was killed only after a violent encounter. Yet it should be noted that just about every seagoing culture in the world has had its equivalent of the kraken myth.

By comparison, Bishop Pontoppidan's kraken seemed relatively harmless. He notes that local fishermen had discovered that there was a certain place off the coast of Norway where the recorded depth of eighty to one hundred fathoms would at times diminish to twenty or thirty fathoms, and that during these times the sea around would become turbid and muddy and the fishing in the area spectacularly abundant. This, they believed, was due to the kraken, a vast tentacled beast a mile and a half in circumference, which swam up from the seabed and attracted the fish by venting its excrement. The monster posed no danger to men provided they removed their boats from the area before it came to the surface. This kraken seemed to be curiously passive—it looked like a group of surfacing islands interconnected by a weedlike substance and surrounded by waving "horns," some "as high and as large as the masts of middle-siz'd vessels." After eating its fill of the fish "beached" on its immense bulk, it would sink to the bottom again.

By the end of the eighteenth century science had dismissed such creatures as mythical. But the large number of nineteenth-century sightings of sea serpents off the coast of America began to erode the skepticism, while huge sucker marks found on sperm whales, and fragments of enormous tentacles found in their stomachs, made it clear that the giant squid was no myth either.

In November 1861 crewmen on the French gunboat *Alecton* saw a giant squid near Tenerife and tried to harpoon it. The creature was clearly dying, since they were able to slip a noose around it; but it broke in two as they tried to heave it aboard. The squid was about twenty-four feet long, and the mouth measured eighteen inches across. The *Alecton* arrived at Tenerife with enough of the monster to leave no possible doubt of its existence, and an account of it was read before the French Academy of Sciences on December 30, 1861. Yet a zoologist named Arthur Mangin still expressed disbelief and wanted to know why the creature had not simply dove below the surface. It was more likely, he thought, that everybody concerned in the report was a liar.

But in the 1870s so many giant squids expired on the beaches of Newfoundland and Labrador that it became impossible to doubt their existence. And in 1896 an enormous though muti-

lated corpse was washed up on the beach in St. Augustine, Flor-
ida, and photographed and examined by Dr. DeWitt Webb. It took
four horses, six men, and a block and tackle to move the six- or
seven-ton bulk farther up the beach. The experts decided that it
was a dead whale. But seventy-five years later, scientific examination of the few pieces that had been preserved demonstrated that
it was a giant octopus (not a squid) that must have been about 200
feet across—big enough that its bulk would have occupied most of
Picadilly Circus or Times Square.

Fortunately, actual encounters with such monsters have been
rare. But some of the most vivid accounts date from the Second
World War. On March 25, 1941, in a remote part of the South
Atlantic, the Allied vessel *Britannia* was attacked by a German
raider flying the Japanese flag. The Germans fired on the vessel
until she was ablaze, then gave the crew five minutes to abandon
ship before they sank her. Because the *Britannia* had an insufficient number of lifeboats, many of the crew found themselves
clinging to fragile rubber rafts in the open ocean, hundreds of
miles from land and well off the normal shipping lanes. One of
these was overloaded with twelve exhausted men, among whom
were Lieutenants Rolandson and Davidson of the Royal Navy and
Lieutenant R. E. Grimani Cox of the Indian Army, who survived
to give an account of their experiences.

They had no food or water and no shelter from the sun. To avoid
swamping the raft they had to take turns hanging precariously
from its sides, where they had no defense against the attacks of
Portuguese men-of-war, which Cox later described as "stinging
like a million bees." By the second day some of the men had
become delirious; on the third the sharks started to close in. For
three days the wounded and thirst-maddened survivors were
picked off one by one. Then, to the sailors' joy, the circling sharks
suddenly disappeared.

One of the survivors gazed into the ocean depths and saw, to
his horror, a huge shape surfacing beneath them. An enormous
tentacled creature surfaced beside them and flailed its "arms"
over the raft. It grabbed an Indian sailor, "hugging him like a
bear," and dragged him into the sea. Satisfied with its prey it

moved off but later renewed its attack. Lieutenant Cox's arm was badly mauled by a grasping tentacle, but this time the sailors managed to fight it off. Several days later Cox, Rolandson, and Davidson, the only survivors of the original twelve, were rescued by a Spanish ship.

When, in 1943, Cox was examined by the British biologist, Dr. John L. Cloudsley-Thompson, the latter observed a number of circular scars on Cox's arm showing that disks of skin and flesh, each measuring about one and a quarter inches in diameter, had at some time been savagely gouged out of it. In Cloudsley-Thompson's opinion the injuries closely resembled those made by the serrated suckers of a squid; and from their size he deduced that the squid in question would have had to have been approximately twenty-three feet long. Richard Owen and his fellow skeptics would have regarded this as a monster of unprecedented proportions, but the only surprise for Cloudsley-Thompson was that a giant squid so "small" could abduct a full-grown man.

Another account of a giant squid also dates from the war years. J. D. Starkey describes how he would lower a cluster of electric bulbs over the side of an Admiralty trawler to attract fish, which could then be easily caught. One night in the Indian Ocean he found himself gazing at a "green unwinking eye." Shining a powerful torch into the water, Starkey saw tentacles two feet thick. He walked the length of the ship, studying the monster, with its parrotlike beak, and realized that it had to be more than 175 feet long. The squid remained there for about fifteen minutes; then "as its valve opened fully . . . without any visible effort it zoomed into the night."

The major problem, as far as science is concerned, is that it seems virtually impossible to study sea monsters in their natural habitat. Like the notorious Loch Ness monster, they seem oddly shy. One student of "lake monsters," the late Ted Holiday, even came to believe that some of them must be regarded as paranormal phenomena—a conclusion he reached because of his observation that some of the lakes in which monsters have been observed are too small to support a large creature. Holiday's encounters with the Loch Ness monster also developed in him a conviction that it seemed to have a sixth sense about when it could show itself without danger of being photographed.*

Another "monster watcher"—Tony "Doc" Shiels—reached a similar conclusion. In 1975 and 1976 there were many sightings of a sea monster off Falmouth, in Cornwall; it was christened "Morgawr," meaning "Cornish giant." Shiels succeeded in taking an excellent photograph of Morgawr, which had the same "plesiosaur-like" shape as the Loch Ness monster—a long neck and a bulky body with "humps" on the back. Shiels subsequently went to Loch Ness and immediately succeeded in snapping two photographs of the monster. But his book *Monstrum*, subtitled *A Wizard's Tale*, makes it clear that he believes that his own monster-sightings have involved some kind of encounter with the world of the paranormal.

This need not imply that creatures like Morgawr and "Nessie" are ghosts, as Holiday was at one point inclined to believe. It may merely imply that they possess highly developed telepathic powers that have enabled them, thus far, to avoid the monster-hunters with considerable success. Which in turn may imply that those who wish to study them must also possess such powers.

The mystery of the underwater monsters is still far from solved. But at least there is now enough evidence to make it clear that Olaus Magnus and Bishop Pontoppidan deserve an apology.

---

*See "Loch Ness Monster" in my *Encyclopedia of Unsolved Mysteries* (1988).

30

The Skull of Doom:
The Strange Tale of the Crystal Skull

For the past twenty years the weirdest gem in the world has belonged to a lady who keeps it on a velvet cloth on a sideboard in her house. It is a fearsome skull, weighing 11 pounds 7 ounces (5.19 kilograms), carved of pure quartz crystal, and its owner believes it comes from a lost civilization. Its eyes are prisms and it is said, the future appears in them. It has been called the "skull of doom."

That passage from Arthur C. Clarke's television series "Mysterious World" may serve as an introduction to one of the most interesting mysteries of the twentieth century. The skull belonged to an explorer and adventurer named Albert ("Mike") Mitchell-Hedges, born in 1882. On his death in 1959 it passed into the possession of his ward, Anna Mitchell-Hedges, born in 1910, who claimed to have discovered it in a "lost city" in South America— the Mayan city of Lubaantun, in British Honduras. According to her own account: "I did see the skull first—or I saw something shining and called my father—it was his expedition, and we all helped to carefully move the stones. [Lubaantun means "place of fallen stones."] I was let pick it up because I had seen it first." It was found, apparently, underneath the altar in the ruins of a Mayan temple. The date she gives—1924—conflicts with an earlier account in which she is said to have discovered it on her seventeenth birthday, which would have been three years later. What she found was the upper part of the skull; the jaw, she says, was found three months later under rubble twenty-five feet away.

Mitchell-Hedges, according to Anna, felt that the skull belonged to the local Indians, descendants of the ancient Mayas, and he gave it to them. But when he prepared to leave for England in the rainy season of 1927, the grateful Indians returned it to him as a present for his kindness to them.

The ancient Mayas are themselves something of a mystery. Their earliest history seems to date back to 1500 B.C., but their great "classic" period extends roughly from A.D. 700 to 900. During this period they developed a high level of civilization, with writing, sophisticated mathematics, a calendar, and impressive sculptures. Then, with startling suddenness, Mayan civilization collapsed—no one knows why. Disease and earthquakes have been suggested, yet there is no evidence for either. Neither is there evidence of violence. It seems that the Mayas simply abandoned their cities and melted away into remote places. And their great civilization reverted to a far more primitive level. Their partially deciphered writings offer no clue to the mystery.

Mitchell-Hedges believed that there was a connection between the Mayas and the legendary continent of Atlantis, which is said to have vanished beneath the waves of the Atlantic Ocean in prehistoric times. Another explorer, Colonel Percy Fawcett, believed that he had evidence that survivors from Atlantis had reached South America and that the evidence lay in Brazil. Fawcett vanished without a trace on an expedition to Brazil in 1924. Mitchell-Hedges believed that the survivors had come ashore farther north, in the Yucatán Peninsula of Central America, and one of the objects of his expedition to Honduras was to look for proof of this theory. He never found it, but he *did* find clues to the lost treasures of Sir Henry Morgan, a pirate who had captured Panama (with considerable brutality) in the seventeenth century.

What, in fact, do we know about the "skull of doom"? Remarkably little. It is made from a single block of rock crystal, or clear quartz. Mitchell-Hedges declared that it was probably 3,600 years old, but that would take it back a thousand years before the earliest date suggested for the Mayas. He also suggested that it must have taken 150 years to create, by the grinding and polishing of rock with sand. In *Chariots of the Gods?* Erich von Däniken has (predictably) taken an even bolder line, explaining (mistakenly) that "nowhere on the skull is there a clue showing that a tool known to us was used!" and suggesting that it was created by the "Ancient Astronauts" who (according to von Däniken) built the Great Pyramid. A modern crystal expert, Frank Dorland, has said that he could make a similar skull in three years, but that would be with the aid of modern technology.

Inevitably, the experts are divided on the subject of the skull's origin. Most seem to agree that it was probably carved in Mexico, from rock crystal found in Mexico or Calaveras County, California, and that it could have been manufactured in the past five hundred years. But if that date is correct, then it runs counter to the claim of Mitchell-Hedges that it was found in a Mayan temple that had been abandoned for a thousand years. The Aztecs—the likeliest manufacturers of the skull—founded their capital, Tenochtitlán, around A.D 1325.

Regrettably, this is also the view of practically everybody who has looked into the matter. Mike Mitchell-Hedges was undoubtedly a very remarkable man, and Anna's total devotion to him is understandable. When he met her in Toronto in 1917, she was a seven-year-old orphan by the name of Anna Le Guillon and was in the charge of some men who intended to put her into an orphanage. Mitchell-Hedges was touched by her plight and adopted her, a decision, as she later said, that neither of them had reason to regret.

But for all his kindness and erratic brilliance as an explorer, Mitchell-Hedges was not another Captain Scott or Colonel Fawcett; his character was altogether closer to that of the swashbuckling Sir Henry Morgan. He was a man with a keen sense of humor, and he enjoyed telling—and even printing—tongue-in-cheek tall stories. His life of adventure was inspired by his childhood reading of Rider Haggard stories and Arthur Conan Doyle's *Lost World*, and his own books—with titles like *Land of Wonder and Fear* and *Battles with Giant Fish*—reflect the character of a man who was, in some respects, an overgrown schoolboy. He was not so much a liar as an Elizabethan adventurer born out of his time.

It has been suggested that Mitchell-Hedges brought the crystal skull from London to Lubaantun and "planted" it under the altar for his adopted daughter to find on her seventeenth (or fourteenth) birthday, something of which he would have been perfectly capable.

Yet his autobiography, *Danger My Ally* (1954), suggests that all was not as straightforward as Anna's account suggests. You would expect a man who had made such an important find to describe it in some detail; instead, he dismisses it in a few lines, explaining: "How the skull came into my possession I have reason for not revealing." But why not, if Anna's story about its discovery is accurate? After all, it would reflect credit on his adopted daughter. He also describes at length far less important artifacts he found in Lubaantun. Stranger still, he has removed *all* reference to the skull from the American edition of the book. There can be only one reason for this: he does not want to be caught in a lie but is still not willing to tell the truth.

Anna Mitchell-Hedges stuck firmly to the Lubaantun story. *Daily Express* journalist Donald Seaman has described how he heard it directly from her own lips. In 1962 Seaman, who was writing a book about espionage, came upon a photograph of the recently convicted spy Gordon Lonsdale that showed him posing with two middle-aged women. Careful research revealed that one of the women was Anna Mitchell-Hedges. Curious to know what she was doing with a spy, Seaman contacted her at her home in Reading and went to see her, accompanied by photographer Robert Girling.

Anna Mitchell-Hedges proved to be a stout, formidable-looking woman in her fifties, and when they arrived she was still attired in her dressing gown. The story behind the photograph proved to be innocent enough; it had been taken at a historic castle, where she and her friend had fallen into conversation with the man who later proved to be at the center of the Portland spy case; a passing commercial photographer had snapped them, extracted payment from Anna Mitchell-Hedges, and later forwarded the photograph to her. She hadn't seen Lonsdale since that time.

Perhaps feeling guilty that she had brought them to Reading on a wild goose chase, she asked them if they would like to see the "skull of doom." Neither had ever heard of it, but they politely said yes. She asked them to follow her and led them to the master bedroom, where she groped around under the bed. Seaman, who was expecting to see an object the size of an egg, was surprised when she brought out something that might have been a large cabbage, wrapped in newspapers. They accompanied her back to the sitting room, where she unwrapped it on the table.

Both Seaman and Girling stared with amazement at the magnificent and bizarre object that lay on the table. The life-size human skull seemed to be made of polished diamond—in the dim light it had a greenish hue, as if lit from the inside or from underneath. Its lower jaw moved like that of a human jaw, adding a gruesome touch of realism. They agreed later that neither had seen anything at once so beautiful and so oddly disquieting. This, Anna Mitchell-Hedges told them, was the "skull of doom," found in a Mayan temple in 1927. It had received its nickname from the local natives, who were convinced that it had magical powers and should be treated with the respect due to a supernatural being. It had become the focus of a number of legends about people who encountered misfortune after showing it insufficient respect.

She went on to tell them that in 1927 her father had been looking for the treasure buried by the pirate Henry Morgan in 1671. They had learned that in the area of the Mayan city of Lubaantun, in British Honduras, natives had names like Hawkins and Morgan. Her father was also convinced that the remains of the lost civilization of Atlantis were in the same area. But the skull was the only ancient artifact he had found.

Now that her father was dead (he died in 1959), Anna wanted to return to Honduras to look for the treasure, and in order to raise the money, she was willing to sell the skull, as well as a drinking mug that had been presented to King Charles II by Nell Gwyn (and that had been authenticated by scholars).

"How much is the skull worth?" asked Seaman.

"Probably about a quarter of a million."

"My God! Aren't you afraid to keep it in the house?"

"I think I could deal with any burglars." Anna Mitchell-Hedges opened her dressing gown, and revealed a Colt .45 revolver strapped to her waist.

There was some talk about the possibility of the *Daily Express* helping to finance the expedition to Lubaantun and allowing Seaman to go along to report on it. To his great regret, the proposal was turned down by the editor. But Donald Seaman has never forgotten that menacingly beautiful object that seemed to glow with its own light.

But, as we have seen, the Lubaantun story remains dubious. Norman Hammond, an archaeologist who also excavated Lubaantun, failed to mention the crystal skull in his book on Lubaantun, and he explained to Joe Nickell, a skeptical investigator (who figures in the introduction to this book) that this was because the crystal skull had nothing to do with the site. "Rock crystal is not found naturally in the Maya area" he writes and goes on to mention that the nearest places where it has been found are Oaxaca, in southern Mexico, and the Valley of Mexico, where some other small crystal skulls—of Aztec manufacture—have been found. He adds that as far as the documentary evidence shows, Anna Mitchell-Hedges was never in Lubaantun. This seems to be verified by others on the expedition. (Hammond is also on record as saying, "I have always thought that it is most likely a *memento mori* [something designed to remind us that we must all die] of sixteenth- to eighteenth-century origin. While a Renaissance origin is not improbable, given the sheer size of the rock crystal block involved, manufacture in Quing-dynasty China for a European client cannot be ruled out.")

When we learn that Mitchell-Hedges himself was caught in a lie—his assertion that he served with the Mexican revolutionary Pancho Villa and fought at the Battle of Laredo—and that he lost a libel suit against the *Daily Express*, which claimed in 1928 that he had staged a fake robbery for the sake of publicity, it begins to look as if the whole crystal skull story must be dismissed as pure invention. In fact, the first reference to the skull occurs in a journal entitled "Man—A Monthly Record of Anthropological Science" in 1936, in which two experts compare the skull with another in the British Museum and refer to the former as "the Burney skull."

The Burney referred to is Sydney Burney, an art dealer, and Sotheby's records show that he put the skull up for auction in late 1943; but since no one bid more than £340 for it, Burney decided to keep it. It was then, apparently, sold to Mitchell-Hedges in 1944 for £400.

When Nickell asked Anna Mitchell-Hedges about this story, he was told that Mitchell-Hedges had left the skull with Burney as security for a loan to finance an expedition and that Burney had no right to offer it for sale. But there is not a scrap of evidence to prove that the skull was in the possession of Mitchell-Hedges before 1944. Moreover, a letter from Sydney Burney, dated March 21, 1933, to someone at the American Museum of Natural History declares that before he (Burney) became its owner, the skull had been in the possession of the collector from whom Burney bought it, and before that, in the collection of an Englishman.

So it would seem almost certain that Mitchell-Hedges invented his story of finding the skull in a Mayan temple and that his daughter has continued to support this false version out of an understandable sense of gratitude and loyalty to her adopted father. Presumably this also applies to Mitchell-Hedges's claim that the skull had been used to "will someone to death" (Anna Mitchell-Hedges explained that this should be regarded as an expression of his sense of humor) and to various other claims about the skull's supernatural powers—like the newspaper report of a cameraman who fled in terror from the darkroom when his enlarging bulb exploded as he was trying to enlarge a photograph of the skull.

It all sounds rather disappointing—particularly when we learn that traces of "mechanical grinding" have been found on the teeth. The consensus seems to be that the "mystery" surrounding the "skull of doom" is a hoax.

Yet such a view would be premature. To begin with, the other—and far less "perfect"—crystal skull, which is in possession of the British Museum (and sits at the top of the stairs in the Museum of Man, near Picadilly Circus in London), is generally accepted as genuine, and it also shows traces of mechanical grinding. The Mexican Indians used a grinding wheel driven by a string stretched across a bow. It seems relatively certain that both skulls originated in Mexico. The Museum of Man skull was bought at Tiffany's, the New York jeweler, in 1898 and cost £120.

In 1963 Anna Mitchell-Hedges allowed the aforementioned

scholar and crystal expert, Frank Dorland, to borrow the skull and take it to California for tests; he studied it for seven years. One of his most important conclusions was that the skull could well be as old as twelve thousand years, although more recent work has undoubtedly been done on it. Dorland sent the skull to the laboratory of the Hewlett-Packard Electronics company, which manufactures crystal oscillators. They suggested that the skull had taken a very long time to manufacture—perhaps three hundred years (twice as long as Mitchell-Hedges's estimate.) If this is correct, then it seems probable—almost certain—that it was a religious object, created on the orders of priests and kept in a temple. In that case, its purpose would be connected with divination. It would be kept on an altar—probably covered up (like the crystal balls of clairvoyants)—and exposed for certain ceremonies, probably lit from underneath.

Dorland also reported that he was told by friends of Mitchell-Hedges that the skull was brought back from the Holy Land by the Knights Templars during the Crusades and that it was kept in their Inner Sanctum in London until it finally found its way on to the antiques market.

This is in many ways more plausible than the Mayan temple story. The Templars, founded in 1118 by Hugh de Payens of Champagne, was a religious order whose members swore to devote their lives to the defense of the Holy Land and its Christian pilgrims. Their success was extraordinary and their wealth became legendary. This led to their downfall, for their money was coveted by King Philip IV of France, who organized a mass arrest of Templars on October 13, 1307. They were accused of black magic, of blasphemy, of renouncing Christ, and of sexual perversions. One of the major accusations was that they worshiped the demon Baphomet in the form of a stuffed head *or a human skull* and that the cords they wore around their robes were hallowed by being wrapped around this skull.

Some of the lesser accusations against the Templars are acknowledged to be true by scholars, among them the belief that they practiced ritual magic. Hundreds of Templars were executed; yet the king never succeeded in laying his hands on their fabled "treasures." Nothing seems less likely than that the "skull" worshiped by the Templars was an ordinary human skull, and the Mitchell-Hedges skull would certainly be a perfect candidate for the mysterious talisman.

And what of its "mystical" properties? Anna Mitchell-Hedges declared that Adrian Conan Doyle, son of Arthur, was unable to bear the skull and disliked even being in the same room with it. She said he could tell when it was around, even when it was not visible. Such assertions as these are usually dismissed as typical attempts at legend building. But Frank Dorland himself concluded, after seven years of contact with the skull, that it had mystical properties. He described hearing sounds of "high-pitched silver bells, very quiet but very noticeable" and sounds like an "a capella choir." And staring into the skull, he saw images of "other skulls, high mountains, fingers and faces." He stated that the first night he kept the skull in his house, he heard the sound of prowling jungle cats.

This, of course, could be pure autosuggestion. But what happened after a visit from "satanist" Anton LaVey could not be dismissed in this way. LaVey called on Dorland with the editor of an Oakland newspaper; he claimed that the skull was created by Satan and was thus the property of his church. (LaVey has a keen sense of humor as well as of publicity.) LaVey ended by playing at some length on Dorland's organ, so that when he left, it was too late to return the skull to the safe deposit box where it was kept. That night, once again, there were many strange sounds that kept Dorland and his wife awake. But when they got up to investigate, they found nothing. The next morning they found that many of their belongings had been displaced, and a crystal rod used as a telephone dialer had leapt thirty-five feet to the front door.

Dorland's theory is not that the skull itself possesses a "spirit" (or poltergeist) but that it had absorbed something from LaVey's presence—that perhaps LaVey's "vibes" and those of the skull conflicted, producing physical effects. This theory is not as far-fetched as it sounds. Clairvoyants use crystals because they claim they can absorb living energies; they keep them covered with black velvet because these energies escape when exposed to daylight. Since the time of the oldest known magical beliefs, crystals have been held in special esteem because of their powers.

Oddly enough, there is now some kind of scientific backing for this notion. For a decade or more the biologist Rupert Sheldrake has been arguing that learning among human beings and animals is "transmitted" by a process that he calls *morphic resonance.* The most famous story illustrating this process is of the monkeys on Kojima Island, off the coast of Japan, that learned to wash their potatoes in the sea because the salt improved the taste; subsequently, asserts zoologist Lyall Watson (in *Lifetide*), monkeys on other islands, with no connection with the original group, began doing the same thing. Morphic resonance might thus be regarded as a kind of telepathy, and Sheldrake believes that it plays an active part in evolution.

The strange thing is that this phenomenon applies not only to living creatures but to crystals as well. Some new chemicals are extremely difficult to crystallize in the laboratory. But once they have been crystallized anywhere in the world, the process suddenly becomes faster in all laboratories. At first it was suspected that this was because scientists were carrying traces of the crystal in their hair or clothes when they visited other laboratories; but this theory had to be discounted. It seems that crystals, like living creatures, can "learn" by morphic resonance. So the notion that they can absorb living energies and radiate them again is less outlandish than it seems.

It seems probable that we shall never know the truth about the "skull of doom," but its resemblance to the British Museum skull suggests that it was probably of Aztec manufacture. What we know of the Aztecs—and their religion of human sacrifice—suggests that it was created as some kind of religious object, possibly used for scrying (short for *descrying*)—that is, for purposes of divination, as a modern clairvoyant uses a crystal ball. But for whatever purpose it was created, most of those who have seen it seem to agree that it is one of the most beautiful manmade objects in the world.

31

Vampires:
Do They Exist?

The problem of the vampire can be stated simply. Any rational person will agree that the notion that vampires actually exist *has* to be pure superstition. Blood-drinking supernatural beings do not and cannot exist. There has to be some simpler, more sensible, explanation. The objection to this view is that a number of early accounts of vampires have such an air of sobriety and authority that it is difficult to dismiss them as pure fantasy. Here, for example, is an eighteenth-century report known as *Visum et Repertum* ("Seen and Discovered"), signed by no fewer than five Austrian officers, three of them doctors:

> After it had been reported in the village of Medvegia [near Belgrade] that so-called vampires had killed some people by sucking their blood, I was, by high decree of a local Honorable Supreme Command, sent there to investigate the matter thoroughly, along with officers detailed for that purpose and two subordinate medical officers, and therefore carried out and heard the present enquiry in the company of the Captain of the Stallath company of haiduks [Balkan mercenaries and outlaws opposed to Turkish rule], Hadnack Gorschiz, the standard-bearer and the oldest haiduk of the village. [They reported], unanimously, as follows. About five years ago, a local haiduk called Arnod Paole broke his neck in a fall from

a hay wagon. This man had, during his lifetime, often described how, near Gossova in Turkish Serbia, he had been troubled by a vampire, wherefore he had eaten from the earth of the vampire's grave and had smeared himself with the vampire's blood, in order to be free of the vexation he had suffered. In twenty or thirty days after his death, some people complained that they were being bothered by this same Arnod Paole; and in fact, four people were killed by him. In order to end this evil, they dug up Arnod Paole forty days after his death—this on the advice of their Hadnack, who had been present at such events before; and they found that he was quite complete and undecayed, and that fresh blood had flowed from his eyes, nose, mouth, and ears; that the shirt, the covering, and the coffin were completely bloody; that the old nails on his hands and feet, along with the skin, had fallen off, and that new ones had grown. And since they saw from this that he was a true vampire, they drove a stake through his heart—according to their custom—whereupon he gave an audible groan and bled copiously. Thereupon they burned the body to ashes the same day and threw these into the grave. These same people also say that all those who have been tormented and killed by vampires must themselves become vampires. Therefore they disinterred the above-mentioned four people in the same way. Then they also add that this same Arnod Paole attacked not only people but cattle, and sucked out their blood. And since some people ate the flesh of such cattle, it would appear that [this is the reason that] some vampires are again present here, inasmuch as in a period of three months, seventeen young and old people died, among them some who, with no previous illness, died in two or at most three days. In addition, the haiduk Jovitsa reports that his stepdaughter, by name Stanacka, lay down to sleep fifteen days ago, fresh and healthy, but that at midnight she started up out of her sleep with a terrible cry, fearful and trembling, and complained that she had been throttled by the son of a haiduk by the name of Milloe [who had died nine weeks earlier], whereupon she had experienced a great pain in the chest, and become worse hour by hour, until finally she died on the third day.

At this, we went the same afternoon to the graveyard, along with the aforementioned oldest haiduks of the village, in order to cause the suspicious graves to be opened, and to examine the bodies in them. Whereby, after all of them had been [exhumed and] dissected, the following was found:

1. A woman by the name of Stana, twenty years old, who had died in childbirth two months ago, after a three-day illness, and who had herself said before her death that she had painted herself with the blood of a vampire—wherefore both she and the child, which had died soon after birth and through careless burial had been half eaten by dogs—must also become vampires. She was quite complete and undecayed. After the opening of the body there was found in the *cavitate pectoris* a quantity of fresh extravascular blood. The vessels of the *arteriae*, like the *ventriculis cordis*, were not, as is usual, filled with coagulated blood; and the whole viscera—that is, the lung, liver, stomach, spleen, and intestines— were quite fresh, as they would be in a healthy person. The uterus was, however, quite enlarged and very inflamed externally, for the placenta and lochia had remained in place, wherefore the same was in complete putrefaction. The skin on her hands and feet, along with the old nails, fell away on their own, but on the other hand completely new nails were evident, along with a fresh and vivid skin.

2. There was a woman by the name of Militsa, sixty years old, who had died after a three-month sickness and had been buried ninety or so days earlier. In the chest much liquid blood was found, and the other viscera were—like those mentioned above—in good condition. During her dissection, all the haiduks who were standing around marveled greatly at her plumpness and perfect body, uniformly stating that they had known the woman well from her youth and that she had throughout her life been very lean and dried up; they emphasized that she had come to such surprising plumpness in the grave. They also said that it was she who had started the vampires this time, because she had been eating of the flesh of those sheep who had been killed by previous vampires.

3. There was an eight-day-old child which had lain in the grave for ninety days and which was also in a condition of vampirism.

4. The son of a haiduk, sixteen years old, named Milloe, was dug up, having lain in the earth for nine weeks, after he had died from a three-day illness, and was found to be like the other vampires. [This is obviously the vampire who had attacked the stepdaughter of the haiduk Jovitsa.]

5. Joachim, also the son of a haiduk, seventeen years old, had died after a three-day illness. He had been buried eight weeks and four days and, on being dissected, was found in similar condition.

6. A woman by the name of Ruscha who had died after a ten-day

illness and been buried six weeks earlier, in whom there was much fresh blood, not only in the chest but also in *in fundo ventriculi*. The same showed itself in her child, which was eighteen days old and had died five weeks earlier.

7. No less did a girl of ten years of age, who had died two months previously, find herself in the above-mentioned condition, quite complete and undecayed, and had much fresh blood in her chest.

8. They caused the wife of the Hadnack to be dug up, along with her child. She had died seven weeks earlier, her child—who was eight weeks old—twenty-one days previously, and it was found that mother and child were completely decomposed, although earth and grave were like those of the vampires lying nearby.

9. A servant of the local corporal of the haiduks, by the name of Rhade, twenty-three years old, died after a three-month illness, and after being buried five weeks, was found completely decomposed.

10. The wife of the local standard-bearer, along with her child, were also completely decomposed.

11. With Stanche, a haiduk, sixty years old, who had died six weeks previously, I noticed a profuse liquid blood, like the others, in the chest and stomach. The entire body was in the above-mentioned condition of vampirism.

12. Milloe, a haiduk, twenty-five years old, who had lain for six weeks in the earth, was also found in a condition of vampirism.

13. Stanoicka [earlier called Stanacka], the wife of a haiduk, twenty-three years old, died after a three-day illness and had been buried eighteen days earlier. In the dissection I found that her countenance was quite red and of a vivid color, and as was mentioned above, she had been throttled at midnight, by Milloe, the son of a haiduk, and there was also to be seen, on the right side under the ear, a bloodshot blue mark [i.e., a bruise] the length of a finger [demonstrating that she had been throttled]. As she was being taken out of the grave, a quantity of fresh blood flowed from her nose. With the dissection I found—as so often mentioned already—a regular fragrant fresh bleeding, not only in the chest cavity but also in the heart ventricle. All the viscera were found in a completely good and healthy condition. The skin of the entire body, along with the nails on the hands and feet, were as though completely fresh.

After the examination had taken place, the heads of the vampires were cut off by the local gypsies and then burned along with the bodies, after which the ashes were thrown into the river Morava.

The decomposed bodies, however, were laid back in their own graves. Which I attest along with those assistant medical officers provided for me. *Actum ut supra*:

L.S. [signed] Johannes Fluchinger, Regimental Medical Officer of the Foot Regiment of the Honorable B. Furstenbusch.

L.S. J. H. Siegel, Medical Officer of the Honorable Morall Regiment.

L.S. Johann Friedrich Baumgarten, Medical Officer of the Foot Regiment of the Honorable B. Furstenbusch.

The undersigned attest herewith that all which the Regiment Medical Officer of the Honorable Furstenbusch had observed in the matter of vampires—along with both medical officers who signed with him—is in every way truthful and has been undertaken, observed, and examined in our own presence. In confirmation thereof is our signature in our own hand, of our own making, Belgrade, January 26, 1732.

L.S. Buttener, Lieutenant Colonel of the Honorable Alexandrian Regiment.

L.S. J. H. von Lindenfels, Officer of the Honorable Alexandrian Regiment.

As we study this strange account (which is admittedly difficult to do without skipping), there is an obvious temptation to dismiss it as a farrago of peasant superstition. Yet this is no secondhand tale of absurd horrors; the three doctors were officers in the army of Charles VI, Emperor of Austria—that newly emerging power that was succeeding the Holy Roman Empire. They were thoroughly familiar with corpses, having been serving in the army that had fought the Turks since 1714 and that defeated them four years later.

A brief sketch of the historical background may clarify the emergence of vampires in the first half of the eighteenth century. For more than four centuries the Turks had dominated eastern Europe, marching in and out of Transylvania, Walachia, and Hungary and even conquering Constantinople in 1453. Don John of Austria defeated them at the great sea battle of Lepanto (1571), but it was their failure to capture Vienna after a siege in 1683 that caused the breakup of the Ottoman Empire. During the earlier stages of this war between Europe and Turkey, the man whose name has become synonymous with vampirism—Dracula, or Vlad the Impaler—struck blow after blow against the Turks, until they killed and beheaded him in 1477.

Vlad Tepes (the Impaler), king of Walachia (1456-62, 1476-77), was, as his nickname implies, a man of sadistic temperament whose greatest pleasure was to impale his enemies (which meant anyone against whom he had a grudge) on pointed stakes; the stake—driven into the ground—was inserted into the anus (or, in the case of women, the vagina), and the victim was allowed to impale himself slowly under his own weight. (Vlad often had the point blunted to make the agony last longer.) In his own time he was known as Dracula, which means "son of a dragon" or "son of the Devil." It is estimated that Dracula had about one hundred thousand people impaled during the course of his lifetime. When he conquered Braşov, in Transylvania, he had all its inhabitants impaled on poles, then gave a feast among the corpses. When one nobleman held his nose at the stench, Vlad sent for a particularly long pole and had him impaled. When he was a prisoner in Hungary, Vlad was kept supplied with birds, rats, and toads, which he impaled on small stakes. A brave and fearless warrior, he was finally killed in battle—or possibly assassinated by his own soldiers—and his head sent to Constantinople. Four hundred twenty years later, in 1897, he was immortalized by Bram Stoker as the sinister Count Dracula, no longer a sadistic maniac but a drinker of blood.

By the time of the outbreak of vampirism in Medvegia in the early 1730s, Vlad's hereditary enemies, the Turks, had been driven out of Serbia, and the Austrians were now in Belgrade—which had originally fallen to the troops of Suleiman the Magnificent in 1521. The Austrians soon became aware of a strange superstition among the peasantry; they dug up corpses and beheaded them, alleging that they were *vampires*, or *upirs*.

Tales of the "living dead" had been current since the days of ancient Greece. The Greeks called the creature a *lamia* or *empusa* and seemed to identify it with a witch. Lamias were not blood drinkers but cannibals. The biographer Philostratus tells a story of the philosopher (and magician) Apollonius of Tyana, who instantly recognized the fiancée of his disciple Menippus as a lamia, and with a few magical words caused the whole wedding feast to disappear into thin air. The girl then admitted that it was her intention to make a meal of Menippus. (Keats sentimentalizes the story in his poem *Lamia*; unable to believe any evil of a pretty girl, he makes her a lovelorn snake and Apollonius the cold, rational philosopher who destroys their happiness.)

Tales of the "undead"—known as *vrykolakas*—persisted in Greece down through the centuries, and on January 1, 1701, a French botanist named Pitton de Tornefort visited the island of Mykonos and was present at a gruesome scene of dissection. An unnamed peasant, of sullen and quarrelsome disposition, was murdered in the fields by persons unknown. Two days after his burial, his ghost was reported to be wandering around at night, overturning furniture and "playing a thousand roguish tricks." Ten days after his burial, a mass was said to "drive out the demon" that was believed to be in the corpse, after which the body was disinterred and the local butcher given the task of tearing out the heart. His knowledge of anatomy seemed to be defective, and he tore open the stomach and rummaged around in the intestines, causing such a vile stench that incense had to be burned. In the smoke-filled church, people began shouting "vrykolakas" and alleging that some of the smoke poured out of the corpse itself. Even after the heart had been burned at the seashore, the ghost continued to cause havoc until the villagers finally burned the corpse on a pyre.

De Tornefort took a highly superior attitude about all this, convinced that it was simply mass hysteria: "I have never viewed anything so pitiable as the state of this island. Everyone's head was turned; the wisest people were stricken like the others." Although the year was only 1701, de Tornefort's attitude was that of a typical French rationalist of the eighteenth century.

Twenty years later, after the Turks were driven out of eastern Europe, western Europe was astonished by these gruesome tales of disinterments—of which the one quoted above is so typical. And now it was no longer possible to take an attitude of amused superiority, since many of the accounts were firsthand. An account of what happened when a man named Peter Plogojowitz was exhumed dates from 1725, seven years before the story of the vampires of Medvegia. It is recounted by another official:

After a subject by the name of Peter Plogojowitz had died, ten weeks past—he lived in the village of Kisilova, in the Rahm district [of Serbia]—and had been buried according to the Raetzian custom, it was revealed that in this same village of Kisilova, within a week, nine people, both young and old, died also, after suffering a twenty-four-hour illness. And they said publicly, while they were yet alive, but on their deathbed, that the above-mentioned Peter Plogojowitz, who had died ten weeks earlier, had come to them in their sleep, laid himself on them, and throttled them, so that they would have to give up the ghost. The other subjects were very distressed and strengthened even more in such beliefs by the fact that the dead Peter Plogojowitz's wife, after saying that her husband had come to her and demanded his opanki, or shoes, had left the village of Kisilova and gone to another. And since with such people (which they call vampires) various signs are to be seen—that is, the body undecomposed, the skin, hair, beard, and nails growing—the subjects resolved unanimously to open the grave of Peter Plogojowitz and see whether any such above-mentioned signs were to be found on him. To this end they came here to me, and, telling of these events, asked me and the local pope, or parish priest, to be present at the viewing. And although I at first disapproved, telling them that first the praiseworthy administration should be dutifully and humbly informed, and its exalted opinion about this should be heard, they did not want to accommodate themselves to this at all but rather gave this short answer: I could do what I wanted, but if I did not accord them the viewing and the legal recognition to deal with the body according to their custom, they would have to leave house and home, because by the time a gracious resolution was received from Belgrade, perhaps the entire village—and this was supposed to have happened once before when it was under the Turks—could be destroyed by such an evil spirit, and they did not want to wait for this.

Since I could not hold such people from the resolution they had made, either with good words or threats, I went to the village of Kisilova, taking along the Gradisk pope, and viewed the body of Peter Plogojowitz, just exhumed, finding it, in accordance with thorough truthfulness, that first of all I did not detect the slightest odor that is otherwise characteristic of the dead, and the body—except for the nose, which was somehow sunken—was completely fresh. The hair and the beard—even the nails, of which the old ones had fallen away—had grown on him; the old skin, which was somewhat whitish, had peeled away, and a new fresh one had emerged under it. The face, hands, and feet, and the whole body, were so constituted, that they could not have been more complete in his lifetime. Not without astonishment, I saw some fresh blood in his mouth, which according to the common observation, he had sucked from the people killed by him. In short, all the indications were present (as remarked above) as such people are supposed to have. After both the pope and I had seen this spectacle, while the people grew more outraged than distressed, all the subjects, with great speed, sharpened a stake—in order to pierce the corpse of the deceased with it—and put this at his heart, whereupon, as he was pierced, not only did much blood, completely fresh, flow also through his ears and mouth, but still other wild signs (which I pass by out of high respect) took place. [He means that the corpse had an erection.] Finally, according to their usual practice, they burned the aforementioned body, *in hoc casu*, to ashes, of which I (now) inform the most laudable administration, and at the same time would like to request, obediently and humbly, that if a mistake was made in this matter, such as is to be attributed not to me but to the rabble, who were beside themselves with fear.

Imperial Provisor, Gradisk District

Here again we have a respectable official vouching for the fact that the corpse looked remarkably fresh and had fresh blood in the mouth.

Let us consider these accounts in more detail. To begin with, it seems clear that the vampire is not a physical body that clambers out of its grave—as in *Dracula*—but some sort of ghost or spectral "projection." In the long account of the Medvegia vampires signed by Dr. Fluchinger et al., we find that the vampire lies down beside its victim and throttles her; a mark on the girl's throat seems to indicate that this is what happened. There is nothing here of the Draculalike vampire who sinks his pointed fangs into the victim's flesh. What the villagers allege is that the body has been *taken over* by a demonic entity, which attacks the living and somehow drains their vitality. The corpse that is the home of the demonic entity then flourishes in the grave and even continues to grow new skin and nails. The detail of blood in the chest seems a little puzzling, until we look again at the account and see that the blood is found in the breast cavity (*cavitate pectoris*) of the woman named Stana, while the lungs are mentioned separately later in the same sentence; in other words, when the breast was opened up, exposing the heart, fresh blood was found. There is no reason, in this particular instance, to suppose that this is the blood of the victim; it is presumably the vampire's own.

The many skeptics who have written on the subject of vampires usually produce the same rationalizations. These are typified by the long article on vampirism in Rossell Hope Robbins's *Encyclopedia of Witchcraft and Demonology* (1959). He points out that there must have been many premature burials and that when the grave of such an unfortunate was opened, the corpse would be found in a contorted position that suggested that it had come to life. He also points out that "the existence of maniacs who crave for blood" could have given rise to the legend of the vampire. The sudden deaths of a large number of people in a space of weeks is explained by plague or other unknown forms of illness. Paul Barber, in *Vampires, Burial and Death* (from which the above translations have been quoted), takes much the same line, although he admits that the premature burial theory fails to explain the Medvegia "outbreak." But he goes on to point out that different bodies decay at different rates and that therefore, there is nothing surprising in the description of a two-month-old body that remains as fresh as when it was buried.

All this is plausible enough. But if we read straight through the accounts by Fluchinger and the Gradisk provisor (a steward to a religious house), we see that these rationalizations simply fail to provide an adequate explanation of what has taken place. It is true that the account of Arnod Paole, the soldier who became a vampire, is secondhand, having occurred five years before the officers went to investigate the new outbreak of vampirism. We may therefore doubt whether he gave an "audible groan" as they drove a stake through his heart, and all the other details of the hearsay account. But even if we suppose that some plague was really responsible for the deaths of the seventeen villagers, it is hard to explain why eleven of the corpses were undecayed, while only four corpses were decomposed in the manner one might expect.

In fact, the real problem with all these debunkers of the vampire theory is that they do their debunking piecemeal; that is, they concentrate on some small point that they feel they can disprove and then behave as if they have produced a total explanation that makes any further discussion unnecessary. Those people who—like myself—find their theories inadequate might well agree that vampires *cannot* really exist. But they simply cannot agree that the skeptics have proved their point and produced a convincing explanation for the many highly detailed stories.

Paul Barber also cites an interesting case known as the Shoemaker of Breslau. He takes his version from an 1868 collection of Prussian folklore by J. Grasse, but there is an earlier version of the same story in Henry More's *Antidote Against Atheism* (1653). This describes how, on September 21, 1591, a well-to-do shoemaker of Breslau, in Silesia—one account gives his name as Weinrichius—cut his throat with a knife and soon after died from the wound. Since suicide was regarded as a mortal sin, his wife tried to conceal it and announced that her husband had died of a stroke. An old woman was taken into the secret, and she washed the body and bound up the throat so skillfully that the wound was invisible. A priest who came to comfort the widow was taken to view the corpse and noticed nothing suspicious. The shoemaker was buried on the following day, September 22, 1591.

Perhaps because of this unseemly haste, and the refusal of the wife to allow neighbors to view the body, a rumor sprang up that the shoemaker had committed suicide. After this, his ghost began to be seen in the town. Soon it was climbing into bed with people and squeezing them so hard that it left the marks of its fingers on their flesh. This finally became such a nuisance that in the year following the burial, on April 18, 1592, the council ordered the grave to be opened. The body was complete and undamaged by decay but "blown up like a drum." The skin had peeled away from the feet, and another had grown, "much purer and stronger than the first." He had a "mole like a rose" on his big toe—which was interpreted as a witch's mark—and there was no smell of decay, except in the shroud itself. Even the wound in the throat was undecayed. The corpse was laid under a gallows, but the ghost continued to appear. By May 7 it had grown "much fuller of flesh." Finally, the council ordered that the corpse should be beheaded and dismembered. When the body was opened up, the heart was found to be "as good as that of a freshly slaughtered calf." Finally, the body was burned on a huge bonfire of wood and pitch and the ashes thrown into the river. After this, the ghost ceased to appear.

Barber agrees that "much in this story is implausible" but points out that so many details—notably the description of the body—are so precise as to leave no doubt "that we are dealing with real events."

But what are these "real events"? Before we comment further, let us consider another well-known case from the same year, 1592 (which is, of course, more than a century earlier than the famous vampire outbreak we have been discussing). This case has also been discussed by both More and Grasse and concerns an alderman of Pentsch (or Pentach) in Silesia named Johannes Cuntze (whose name More Latinizes to Cuntius). On his way to dinner with the mayor, Cuntze tried to examine a loose shoe of a mettlesome horse and received a kick, presumably on the head. The blow apparently unsettled his reason; he complained that he was a great sinner and that his body was burning. He also refused to see a priest. This gave rise to all kinds of rumors about him, including that he had made a pact with the Devil.

As Cuntze was dying, with his son beside the bed, the casement opened and a black cat jumped into the room and leapt onto Cuntze's face, scratching him badly; he died soon after. At his funeral on February 8, 1592, "a great tempest arose"; it continued to rage as he was buried beside the altar of the local church.

Before he was buried, there were stories that his ghost had appeared and attempted to rape a woman. After the burial the ghost began to behave like a mischievous hobgoblin, throwing things about, opening doors, and causing banging noises so that "the whole house shaked again." On the morning after these events animal footprints or hoof marks were found outside in the snow. His widow had the maid sleeping in her bed; the ghost of Cuntze appeared and demanded to be allowed to take his proper place beside his wife. And the parson of the parish (who is mentioned as the chronicler of these events) dreamed that Cuntze was "squeezing" him and woke up feeling utterly exhausted. The spirit was also able to cause a nauseating stench to fill the room.

The conclusion is much as in the story of the shoemaker of Breslau. Cuntze was finally disinterred on July 20, six months after his burial, and was found to be undecayed, and when a vein in the leg was opened, the blood that ran out was "as fresh as the living." After having been transported to the bonfire with some difficulty—his body had apparently become as heavy as a stone—he was dismembered (the blood was, again, found to be quite fresh) and burned to ashes.

In fact, there are even earlier accounts of the walking dead. The French expert on vampires, Jean Marigny, remarks:

> Well before the eighteenth century, the epoch when the word "vampire" first appeared, people believed in Europe that the dead were able to rise from their graves to suck the blood of the living. The oldest chronicles in Latin mention manifestations of this type, and their authors, instead of employing the word "vampire" (which did not yet exist) utilized a term just as explicit, the word *sanguisugae* (Latin for "leech," or "bloodsucker"). The oldest of these chronicles date from the twelfth and thirteenth centuries and, contrary to what one might expect, are not set in remote parts of Europe, but in England and Scotland.*

Marigny goes on to cite four cases described by the twelfth-century chronicler, William of Newburgh, author of *Historia rerum Anglicarum*. These are too long to cite here (although they can be found in full in Montague Summers's *The Vampire in Europe*). The first, "of the extraordinary happening when a dead man wandered abroad out of his grave," describes a case in Buckinghamshire, recounted to the chronicler by the local archdeacon. It describes how a man returned from the grave the night after his burial and attacked his wife. When this happened again

---

*"La Tradition Legendaire du Vampire en Europe" in *Les Cahiers du G.E.R.F.* (Groupe d'Etudes et de Recherche sur la Fantastique, Grenoble University of Languages and Letters, 1987).

the following night, the wife asked various neighbors to spend the night with her, and their shouts drove the ghost away. Then, like Cuntze and Weinrichius, the ghost began to create a general disturbance in town, attacking animals and alarming people. That he *was* a ghost, and not a physical body, is proved by the comment that some people could see him while others could not (although they "perceptibly felt his horrible presence"). The archdeacon consulted the bishop, Hugh of Lincoln, whose learned advisers suggested that the body should be dug up and burned to ashes. Hugh of Lincoln felt this would be "undesireable" and instead wrote out a charter of absolution. When the tomb was opened, the body proved to be "uncorrupt," just as on the day it was buried. The absolution was placed on his chest and the grave closed again; after that, the ghost ceased to wander abroad.

William of Newburgh's other account sounds slightly more like the traditional vampire in that the ghost—of a wealthy man who had died at Berwick on Tweed—had an odor of decomposition that affected the air and caused plague. The body was exhumed (it is not recorded whether it was undecayed) and burned.

The third story concerns a priest, chaplain of a lady of rank, at Melrose Abbey, whose life had been far from blameless; after death, his ghost haunted the cloister and appeared in the bedchamber of the lady of rank. The body was exhumed and burned.

In the fourth story, a dissolute lord of Alnwick Castle, in Northumberland, spied on his wife's adultery by lying on top of the "roof" that covered her four-poster bed. The sight of his wife and her lover "clipping at clicket" so incensed him that he fell down and injured himself, dying a few days later without absolution. He also returned as a ghost to haunt the district, his stench causing a plague that killed many people. When the corpse was exhumed, it proved to be "gorged and swollen with a frightful corpulence"; when attacked with a spade, there gushed out such a stream of blood "that they realized that this leech had battened on the blood of many poor folk." The body was cremated and the haunting ceased.

These stories have the touches of absurdity that might be expected from an ecclesiastical chronicler of that period; yet their similarity to the other chronicles cited suggests that they have some common basis. The same applies to another work, *De nugis curialum* by Walter Map (1193), also cited at length by Summers.

All these cases took place long before western Europe heard tales of vampires from former Turkish dominions, and, except in the case of the "leech" of Alnwick, there is no suggestion of blood drinking. But in most ways, the revenants behave very much like Peter Plogojowitz and the vampires of Medvegia. They haunt the living, climb into bed with people when they are asleep, and then throttle them, leaving them drained of energy. And when the bodies are disinterred, they are found to be undecayed. It seems very clear that there is no basic difference between the vampires of 1732 and the revenants of 1592. And when we look more closely into the accounts of the vampires, we discover that they are energy suckers rather than blood suckers. Peter Plogojowitz has fresh blood in his mouth, but it is merely a matter of hearsay that he sucked the blood of his victims—the account mentions only throttling. Otherwise, these earlier revenants behave very much like the paranormal phenomena known as poltergeists—they throw things and create disturbances.

One of the earliest accounts of poltergeist activity can be found in a document known as *Sigebert's Chronicle*, by one Sigebert of Gembloux (Belgium), which dates from the ninth century. One passage runs as follows:

There appeared this year [858] in the diocese of Mentz [near Bingen, on the Rhine] a spirit which revealed himself at first by throwing stones, and beating against the walls of houses as if with a great mallet. He then proceeded to speak and reveal secrets, and discovered the authors of several thefts and other matters likely to breed disturbances in the neighborhood. At last he vented his malice upon one particular person, whom he was industrious in persecuting and making odious to all the neighbours by representing him as the cause of God's anger against the whole village. The spirit never forsook the poor man but tormented him without intermission, burnt all the corn in the barns, and set every place on fire where he came. The priests attempted to frighten him away by exorcisms, prayers, and holy water, but the spectre answered them with a volley of stones which wounded several of them. When the priests were gone he was heard to bemoan himself and say that he was forced to take refuge in the cowl of one of the priests, who had injured the daughter of a man of consequence in the village. He continued in this manner to infest the village for three years together, and never gave up until he had set every house on fire.

The account in another document, the *Annales Fuldenses*, from which Sigebert of Gembloux condensed this account, mentions that the man the spirit tormented was a farmer and that the spirit accused him of adultery and of seducing the daughter of his overseer.

Now at this point, oddly enough, we leave the realm of superstition—if the vampire is indeed superstition—and enter that of actuality. For the poltergeist is undoubtedly one of the best-authenticated of all psychical phenomena; there are hundreds, perhaps thousands, of accounts on record. Poltergeists specialize in mischief and seem to be the juvenile delinquents of the psychic world. They drive people to distraction with their pranks, causing objects to fly through the air (and sometimes change course abruptly in midflight) and often making a racket that can be heard for miles. Allowing for the exaggerations of the medieval chronicler, the above case from Sigebert has the ring of authenticity. It is true that speaking poltergeists are unusual; nevertheless, there *are* a number of cases on record.

Generally speaking, poltergeists do no harm; Giraldus Cambrensis remarks of a Pembrokeshire poltergeist of A.D. 1191 that it seemed to intend "to deride rather than to do bodily injury." Again, however, there are a few exceptions. The psychical investigator Guy Lyon Playfair mentions a Brazilian case in which the poltergeist drove a girl to suicide by tormenting her. And the poltergeist known as the "Bell witch," whose malign activities continued from 1817 to 1821 in Robertson County, Tennessee, fixed its attentions on one particular man, farmer John Bell, and—like Sigebert's poltergiest—"tormented him without intermission," beating him black and blue and finally poisoning him.

What exactly is a poltergeist? Writers like Sigebert and Giraldus Cambrensis took the understandable view that it was a spirit. Modern psychical research is inclined to find such a view embarrassing. Frank Podmore, one of the founders of the Society for

Psychical Research, concluded in 1890 that they are mischievous children throwing stones. But conscientious investigators soon realized that such a view was untenable. In the mid-twentieth century they finally came to terms with the poltergeist by deciding that it was an example of "recurrent spontaneous psychokinesis" (RSPK) or "mind over matter." A few gifted psychics are able to move small objects, such as pins, compass needles, or scraps of paper, by concentrating on them. No one has yet succeeded in doing anything more spectacular with "mind force"—even something as modest as throwing a stone.

On the other hand, it was soon noticed by investigators that nearly all poltergeist occurrences seemed to center around an emotionally disturbed adolescent or one on the point of puberty. If these individuals were somehow causing the poltergeist effects, then they must be doing so unconsciously. One of the strongest advocates of this theory was the Freudian psychiatrist Nandor Fodor, who was also a distinguished psychical investigator. Fodor argued that the Freudian unconscious is to blame for the "spontaneous psychokinesis" and that the energies involved are the powerful sexual energies of puberty. Neither Fodor nor any other adherent of the theory could explain how the unconscious mind could cause heavy objects to fly through the air and even cause them to penetrate solid walls. But the theory had a satisfyingly scientific ring and was soon generally accepted.

In the early 1970s, however, one investigator came to have strong doubts about this theory. He was Guy Lyon Playfair, a Cambridge graduate who had gone to teach English in Rio de Janeiro. He became interested in the paranormal after a personal experience of "psychic surgery" and joined the Brazilian Institute for Psycho Biophysical Research (IBPP). In Brazil, a large proportion of the population are adherents of a religion known as Spiritism, based on the writings of the Frenchman Allan Kardec, which accepts communication with the dead and the active role of spirits in human existence. After engaging in a number of poltergeist investigations, Playfair was less inclined to dismiss Spiritism as nonsense—in fact, he concluded that Kardec is correct in asserting that poltergeists are spirits. His investigations into the Brazilian form of voodoo, known as *umbanda*, also convinced him that it actually works and that *umbanda* practitioners often perform their "magic" by means of spirits. The experiences that led him to these conclusions are described in his book *The Flying Cow*.

In a book entitiled *Poltergeist*, I have described how my own investigations led me to conclude that Playfair was correct (see also chapter 9) and how the "spontaneous psychokinesis" theory simply fails to cover all the facts. After being a convinced adherent of this theory, I found myself forced by the evidence to accept the embarrassing view that poltergeists are spirits. Since that time I have met many psychical researchers—particularly in America—who are at least willing to entertain that possibility.

The same (as we shall see elsewhere in this volume) applies to the closely related field of "possession," the notion that human beings may be possessed by "unclean spirits." The standard view is stated in Aldous Huxley's well-known study, *The Devils of Loudun*, in which it is taken for granted that the nuns who writhed on the ground and uttered appalling blasphemies were in the grip of sexual hysteria. Here, even more than in the case of the poltergeist, it seems natural to assume that we are dealing with psychological illness—and no doubt in many cases this is so. Yet a number of American psychiatrists—among them Morton Prince, Ralph Allison, and Adam Crabtree—have produced studies of "multiple personality" in which they admit that it is difficult to explain certain cases except in terms of possession by the spirit of a deceased person. (See chapter 26.)

Another piece of interesting evidence for this view of possession can be found in Professor Ian Stevenson's study, *Twenty Cases Suggestive of Reincarnation*. He describes the case of a Hindu boy named Jasbir Lal Jat, who apparently died at the age of three in 1954. Before he could be buried, he revived—but with a new personality completely unlike the old one. This new Jasbir claimed to be a man named Sobha Ram, who had died in the village of Vehedi after a fall from a cart. He claimed to be of Brahmim caste and made difficulties about his food. The family dismissed his claims as childish imagination. But when Jasbir was six, a Brahmin woman from Vehedi came to the village, and Jasbir insisted that she was his aunt. She was, in fact, the aunt of a man named Sobha Ram who had died of a fall from a cart at precisely the same time Jasbir had revived. Taken to Vehedi, Jasbir showed an intimate knowledge of the place and of Sobha Ram's relatives, convincing his own father and mother that he was telling the truth. The conclusion must be that *if* Jasbir was Sobha Ram, then the "spirit" of the latter took possession of the vacant body at the moment Jasbir "died."

In his classic work, *Human Personality and Its Survival of Bodily Death*, Frederic Myers, one of the founding members of the Society for Psychical Research, devotes a chapter to "Trance, Possession and Ecstacy." He begins by acknowledging that when spiritualist "mediums" go into a trance, they are "taken over" by spirits and that this constitutes the phenomenon that was once called "possession." He adds that in some cases, the spirit messages may be deceptive and that "they suggest—nor can we absolutely disprove the suggestion—a type of intelligence inferior to humans, animal-like, and perhaps parasitic." This is as far as he is willing to go in conceding that possession may occasionally be nonbenevolent. But he goes on to cite many cases of what he calls "psychic invasion"—that is, cases in which someone has seen the "spirit" of another person, often someone who has died at exactly that moment. In other cases, the person who "appears" is still alive. A Mrs. T., living in Adelaide, recounts how, lying in bed but still wide awake, she saw a former lover standing in the bedroom, as well as another man, whom she felt to be a cousin who had "been the means of leading him astray." The former lover, who looked very pale, told her that his father had just died and that he had inherited his property. Because her husband was skeptical about this vision, she wrote it down. Some weeks later she heard that her lover's father had died at exactly the time of the vision and had left him his property.

Another case, cited in *Phantasms of the Living* (which Myers coauthored), has a slightly more sinister touch. A nineteen-year-old girl described how she had begun having dreams of a man with a mole on the side of his mouth, and how these filled her with repugnance. The dreams always began with a feeling of some kind of "influence" coming over her. (In spite of her reticence, it is clear that these dreams were of a sexual nature and that the man was forcing her to participate in sex acts.) Two years later, at a party in Liverpool, she felt the same "influence" and turned around to find herself looking into the face of the man with the mole. She was introduced to him, and he insisted that they had met before, which she denied. But when he reminded her of a Birmingham music festival, she suddenly remembered that she had experienced the same unpleasant sense of "influence" there and had then fainted. After this the man began to pursue her and even began talking about the dreams. She felt instinctively that if she admitted to these, she would be in his power; therfore, she pretended not to understand. Eventually, she left Liverpool and ceased to see him.

Here it seems clear that the man had recognized her as the kind of person over whom he was able to exercise some psychic "influence" and had somehow invaded her dreams. If we can once concede the possibility of such "invasion," as well as the possibility of "spirits," then the notion of vampires suddenly seems less absurd.

In a remarkable book entitled *Hungry Ghosts*, the British journalist Joe Fisher has described his own strange experience of "spirits." Fisher had written a book about reincarnation, in the course of which he had become convinced of its reality. One day, after being interviewed on the radio in Toronto (where he lives), he received a phone call from a woman who explained that she had accidentally become a mouthpiece of "discarnate entities." She was being hypnotized in an attempt to cure her of leukemia, and various "spirit guides" had begun speaking through her mouth. (Myers points out that a "spirit" can only enter a body when the usual "tenant" is absent, a point to note when considering that early accounts of vampires involve attack *during sleep*.)

The first time Fisher went to the woman's house, a "spirit" named Russell spoke through her mouth with a reassuring York-shire accent and told him that he had a female "guide," a Greek girl named Filipa, who had been his mistress in a previous existence three centuries earlier. This struck Fisher as plausible, since he had always felt some affinity with Greece. He began attending the séances regularly and devoting some time every morning to relaxing and trying to contact Filipa. Eventually he succeeded;

buzzing noises in his ears would be succeeded by a feeling of bliss and communication. Filipa was a sensual little creature who liked to be hugged, and Fisher implies that, in some sense, they became lovers. It broke up his current love affair; his live-in girlfriend felt she was no match for a ghost.

Other people at the séances were told about their "guides" or guardian angels. One guide was an ex-RAF pilot named Ernest Scott, another an amusing cockney named Harry Maddox. Fisher's disillusionment began when, on a trip back to England, he decided to try and verify Ernest Scott's war stories—having no doubt whatever that they would prove genuine. The airfield was certainly genuine; so was the squadron Ernest claimed to have belonged to; the descriptions of wartime raids were accurate; so were the descriptions of the squadron's moves from airfield to airfield. But there had been no Ernest Scott in the squadron, and a long search in the Public Record Office failed to turn up his name. Fisher went back to Canada in a bitter mood and accused Ernest of lying. Ernest strenuously denied it. Anyway, he said, he was due to reincarnate in another body, so had to leave. The "guide" Russell later told Fisher that Ernest had been reborn in England and gave the name of the parents and date of birth. Oddly enough, when Fisher checked on this it proved to be accurate. He even contacted the parents, who were intrigued but decided they had no wish to get more deeply involved.

With Russell's approval, Fisher tried to track down the farm in Yorkshire where Russell claimed he had lived in the nineteenth century. Here again, many of the facts Russell had given about the Harrogate area proved to be accurate; but again, the crucial facts were simply wrong. It seemed that Russell was also a liar. And so, upon investigation, was the lovable World War I veteran Harry Maddox. His accounts of World War I battles were accurate; but Harry did not exist.

Finally, Fisher took his search to Greece. In spite of his disillusion with the other guides, he had no doubt whatever that Filipa was genuine. She possessed, he states early in the book, "more love, compassion and perspicacity than I had ever known." The problem was that all his attempts to locate Theros—a village near the Turkish border—in atlases or gazetteers had failed. Yet that could be because it had been destroyed by the Turks in the past three centuries. But a town called Alexandroupoli, which Filipa had mentioned, still existed. After a long and frustrating search for the remains of Theros, Fisher went to Alexandroupoli, a city that he assumed had been founded by Alexander the Great. But a brochure there disillusioned him. Alexandroupoli was a mere two centuries old; it had not even existed at the time when he and Filipa were supposed to have been lovers. Like the others, Filipa was a liar and a deceiver.

In a chapter entitled "Siren Call of the Hungry Ghosts," Fisher tries to analyze what has happened to him. The answer seems simple. He had been involved with what Kardec called "earthbound spirits," spirits who either do not realize they are dead or have such a craving to remain on earth that they remain attached to it:

> These earthbound spirits or, in Tibetan Buddhist phraseology, *pretas* or "hungry ghosts," are individuals whose minds, at the point of physical death, have been incapable of disentangling from desire. Thus enslaved, the personality becomes trapped on the lower planes even as it retains, for a while, its memory and individuality. Hence the term "lost soul," a residual entity that is no more than an astral corpse-in-waiting. It has condemned itself to perish; it has chosen a "second death."

Fisher also quotes Lieutenant Colonel Arthur E. Powell's book entitled *The Astral Body*:

> Such spooks are conscienceless, devoid of good impulses, tending towards disintegration, and consequently can work for evil only, whether we regard them as prolonging their vitality by vampirising at séances, or polluting the medium and sitters with astral connections of an altogether undesirable kind.

And Fisher cites the modern American expert on out-of-the-body journeys, Robert Monroe:

> Monroe tells of encountering a zone next to the Earth plane populated by the "dead," who couldn't or wouldn't realize they were

no longer physical beings. . . . The beings he perceived "kept trying to be physical, to do and be what they had been, to continue being physical one way or another. Bewildered, some spent all of their activity in attempting to communicate with friends and loved ones still in bodies or with anyone else who might come along."

Kardec had insisted that most human beings can be unconsciously influenced by spirits, since they can wander freely in and out of our bodies and minds. And a psychical investigator named Carl Wickland, whose *Thirty Years Among the Dead* is a classic of Spiritualism (see chapter 26), declared that "these earthbound spirits are the supposed 'devils' of all ages; devils of human origin. . . . The influence of these discarnate entities is the cause of many of the inexplicable and obscure events of earth life and of a large part of the world's misery." Wickland states that these entities are attracted to the magnetic light emanating from mortals; they attach themselves to these auras, finding an avenue of expression through influencing, obsessing, or possessing their victims.

Such spirits can easily be contacted by means of an Ouija board, a smooth tabletop with letters arranged in a semicircle; the "sitters" place their fingers on an upturned glass, which moves of its own accord from letter to letter, spelling out words. Anyone who has ever tried it will have noticed that the "spirits" seldom tell the truth. G. K. Chesterton devotes several pages of his *Autobiography* to experiments with an Ouija board, and while he concedes that the force that moves the glass is, in some sense, "supernatural," he nevertheless concludes: "The only thing I will say with complete confidence about that mystic and invisible power is that it tells lies."

This is interesting, because Chesterton became a Roman Catholic convert, and the Catholic church has always been strongly opposed to "Spiritualism." This is not because the Church rejects life after death, but because it is deeply suspicious of the kind of entities that "come through" at séances, taking the view that spirits have no reason to hang around the "earth plane," any more than adults want to hang around their old childhood schools. Unlike H. G. Wells, Julian Huxley, or other modern rationalists, Chesterton did not reject "spirit communication" as a fraud or delusion; but, like Joe Fisher, he was unable to accept the "spirits" at face value.

If we can at once concede the possibility of "psychic invasion," as well as the possibility of "spirits," then the notion of vampires suddenly seems less absurd. In *The Magus of Strovolos*, an American academic, Kyriacos C. Markides, has described his friendship with a modern Cypriot mystic and "magus," Spyros Sathi, known as Daskalos, who lives in Nicosia. Daskalos, like Myers and Fisher, takes the actual reality of spirits for granted, but he also speaks without embarrassment of possession and vampirism.

Some of Markides's stories of Daskalos are so extraordinary that most readers will suspect him of extreme gullibility. Yet Daskalos's teachings, as quoted by Markides, make it clear that he deserves to be classified with such twentieth-century teachers as Steiner and Gurdjieff. And Markides offers many examples that seem to leave no doubt whatsoever of the genuineness of Daskalos's psychic powers. He was able to describe Markides's house in America in remarkable detail, although he had no way of learning such details. On another occasion, when Markides and a friend were searching for Daskalos, Markides remarked jokingly that perhaps he was visiting a mistress; when they found him and asked where he had been, Daskalos snapped, "Visiting a mistress," then went on to say that he had overheard all their "silly conversation." It becomes clear that Daskalos takes "possession" for granted, and Markides tells a number of stories, in some of which he was personally involved.

There are, Daskalos claims, three kinds of possession: by ill-disposed human spirits; by demonic entities; and by elementals (the latter being human thoughts and desires that have taken on a life of their own). He goes on to describe a case of spirit possession of the first type. Daskalos was approached by the parents of a girl who claimed that she was being haunted by the spirit of her dead fiancé. Although they had lived together, she had refused to allow him to possess her until they were married. He died of tuberculosis, haunted by unfulfilled cravings. "Each night before she would go to bed he would semi-hypnotise her and induce her to keep the window of her room open. He would then enter inside a bat and would come to her. The bat would wedge itself on her neck and draw blood and etheric [energy]." The local priest told Daskalos how to deal with the situation. He must wait in the next room, and when he heard the bat entering, should go in and quickly shut the window; then, since the bat would attack him, he must stun it with a broom. Then he must wrap the bat in a towel and burn it in a brazier [stove]. Daskalos did this, and as the bat burned, the girl screamed and groaned. Then she calmed down and asked, "Why were you trying to burn me?" The "haunting" ceased thereafter.

Daskalos told another story that has elements of vampirism. On a journey in southern Greece he had encountered another girl who was being haunted by a former lover, a shepherd who had been in love with her and had died in a motor accident. Five years later, when looking for some goats, the girl saw the shepherd— whose name was Loizo—and he followed her, finally making her feel so sleepy that she felt obliged to sit down. He then "hypnotized" her and caused her to experience intense sexual pleasure. When she reported the incident, she was medically examined and found to be a virgin. But three days later the shepherd came to her bed and made love to her. Medical examination revealed that she was no longer a virgin. Daskalos noticed two reddish spots on her neck. The girl told him: "He kisses me there, but his kisses are strange. They are like sucking, and I like them."

The doctor who examined the girl believed that she had torn the hymen with her own fingers; Daskalos seems to accept this but believes that Loizo made her do this.

Daskalos claimed that two days later, he saw the shepherd coming into the house and greeted him. Loizo explained that he had wanted the girl for many years and had never had sexual relations with a woman—only with animals like donkeys and goats. Now that he was possessing her, he had no intention of letting her go. He refused to believe it when Daskalos told him he was dead. Daskalos warned him that if he persisted in possessing the girl, he would remain "in a narcotised state like a vampire." His arguments finally convinced the shepherd, who agreed to go away.

These two cases, taken in conjunction with the others we have considered, offer some interesting clues about the nature of the vampire. According to Daskalos, the "earthbound spirit" of the dead fiancé was able to enter an ordinary bat and then to suck her blood. This was an expression of his sexual desire, his desire to possess her. There have been many cases of so-called Vampirism in the history of sex crimes. In the early 1870s an Italian youth named Vincent Verzeni murdered three women and attempted to strangle several more. Verzeni was possessed by a powerful desire to throttle women (and even birds and animals). After throttling a fourteen-year-old girl named Johanna Motta, he disemboweled her and drank her blood. Verzeni admitted that it gave him keen pleasure to sniff women's clothing, and "it satisfied me to seize women by the neck and suck their blood." So it is easy to imagine that the earthbound fiancé mentioned by Daskalos should enjoy drinking the girl's blood. But we can also see that his desire to "possess" her was also satisfied in another way—by somehow *taking control of her imagination.*

Again, in the case of Loizo, we can see that the shepherd had entered the girl's body and taken possession of her mind so that he could cause her to tear her own hymen with her fingers. This implies—as we would expect—that the lovemaking was not on the physical level, since Loizo possessed no body. (Joe Fisher seems to hint at something similar when he describes his relationship with Filipa.)

All of this has interesting implications. The act of lovemaking seems to involve a paradox, since it is an attempt at the mingling of two bodies, an attempt that is doomed to failure by their separateness. In the *Symposium*, Plato expresses the paradox in an amusing myth. Human beings were originally spherical beings who possessed the characteristics of both sexes. Because their sheer vitality made them a challenge to the gods, Zeus decided that they had to be enfeebled. So he sliced them all down the center, "as you and I might slice an apple," and turned their faces back to front. And now the separated parts spent their lives in a desperate search for their other half, and they ceased to constitute a challenge to the gods.

It is plain that, in its crudest form, the male sexual urge is basically a desire for "possession" and that the act of physical penetration is an act of aggression. (Most writers on Dracula, for example, have noted that it is basically a rape fantasy.) As a man holds a woman in his arms, he experiences a desire to absorb her, to blend with her, and the actual penetration is only a token union. So we might say that a "vampire" like Loizo is able to achieve what every lover dreams about: a possession that involves total interpenetration, union of minds.

The notion of vampirism that begins to emerge from all this is simple and (provided one can accept the notion of "earthbound spirits") plausible. Daskalos told Markides that those who commit suicide may become trapped in the "etheric of the gross material world," unable to move to the higher psychic planes. A person who commits suicide dies in "a state of despair and confusion" and "may vibrate too close to the material world, which will not allow him to find rest." He becomes a "hungry ghost," wandering in and out of the minds of human beings like a man wandering through a deserted city. In all probability, he is unaware that he is dead. (The wife of Peter Plogojowitz declared that he came to her asking for his shoes; since shoes would obviously be of no use to a ghost, we must conclude that he was unaware that his feet had "dematerialized.") Under normal circumstances, the spirit would be incapable of influencing his involuntary host or of making his presence felt; only if the host happens to vibrate with the same desires, to be "on the same wavelength," can true "possession" occur.

It also seems clear that some human beings have a greater ability than others to sense the presence of these entities; we call such people "psychic." They may be totally unaware that they are psychic unless some chance event happens to reveal it. In a book entitled *The Paranormal*, the psychologist Stan Gooch has described how, at the age of twenty-six, he attended a séance in Coventry with a friend and spontaneously fell into a trance condition. When he awoke, he learned that several "spirits" had spoken through him.

It was during this period, Gooch reveals in a later book entitled *Creatures from Inner Space*, that he had his first experience of a "psychic invasion." He was lying in bed one Saturday morning with his eyes closed when he felt a movement on the pillow beside his head, as if someone had gently pressed a hand against it. The movement continued for some time; but when he opened his eyes, he was alone.

Twenty years later, lying half awake in the early morning, he became aware that someone else was in bed with him. He felt that it was a composite of various girls he had known: "On this first occasion my conscious interest in the situation got the better of me, and the succubus [female demon] gradually faded away. On subsequent occasions, however, the presence of the entity was maintained, until finally we actually made love." He notes that "from some points of view the sex is actually more satisfying than that with a real woman, because in the paranormal encounter archetypal elements are both involved and invoked."

Oddly enough, Gooch does not believe that his succubus was real; he thinks such entities are creations of the human mind. He cites cases of hypnotized subjects who have been able to see and touch hallucinations suggested by the hypnotist, and a book entitled *The Story of Ruth*, by Dr. Morton Schatzman, which describes how a girl whose father had tried to rape her as a child began to hallucinate her father and believe that he was in the room with her. He seems to believe that his succubus was a similar hallucination. Yet this view seems to be contradicted by other cases he cites in the book.

The first of these concerns a policeman, Martin Pryer, who had always been "psychic." At one point he decided to try practicing the control of hypnagogic imagery—the imagery we experience on the verge of sleep—and soon began having alarming experiences. On one occasion, a strange entity began to cling to his back like a limpet and held on until he staggered across the room and switched on the light. On another occasion, he thought that a former girlfriend was outside the window, and when he asked what she was doing, she replied, "You sent for me." Then a female entity seemed to seize him from behind, clinging to his back; he sensed that it wanted him to make love to her "in a crude and violent manner." After some minutes it faded away.

Gooch goes on to describe the experiences of an actress friend named Sandy, who was also "psychic." One night, she woke up and felt that the spotlight in the corner of her ceiling had changed into an eye that was watching her. Then she felt an entity—she felt it was male—lying on top of her and trying to make love to her. "One part of her was quite willing for the lovemaking to proceed, but another part of her knew that she wanted it to stop." The entity became heavier, and another force seemed to be dragging her down through the mattress. She made an effort to imagine that she was pulling herself up through the mattress, and the pressure suddenly vanished. But when she went into the bathroom, she discovered that her mouth was rimmed with dark streaks, and when she opened it, it proved to be full of dried blood. There was no sign of a nosebleed or any other injury that could account for the blood.

Guy Playfair has described a similar case in *The Flying Cow*. A girl named Marcia, who had a master's degree in psychology, was on the beach at São Paolo when she picked up a plaster image of the sea goddess Yemanja, which had obviously been thrown into the sea as an offering. Against the advice of her aunt, she took it home. After this, she experienced a series of disasters. She began to feel exhausted and lose weight. Her pressure cooker blew up, burning her hands and face, and her oven exploded. She began to experience suicidal impulses. Then one night, an "entity" entered her bed, and she felt a penis entering her. It happened on several subsequent occasions. In desperation, she went to consult an *umbanda* specialist, who urged her to return the statue to the beach. As soon as she did this, the run of bad luck—and the psychic rapes—ceased.

Such cases make it difficult to accept Gooch's view that these entities are a kind of hypnotic hallucination. It seems obvious that he arrived at that conclusion because his "succubus" seemed to be a blend of previous girlfriends. But according to the "earth-bound spirit" hypothesis, we would assume that the entity simply put these ideas into his mind—that is, into his imagination. He writes: "In short, this entity, though possessing physical and even psychological attributes familiar to me, was none the less essentially its own independent self." And he agrees that the "archetypal elements" were, to some extent, "invoked"—that is, that he himself was conjuring them up. Sandy was able to free herself from the "psychic invasion" by *imagining* that she was pulling herself back up through the mattress, indicating that the entity was controlling her imagination, not her body.

We also note that these "psychic invasions" occurred when all three subjects—Gooch, Martin Pryer, and Sandy—were either asleep or hovering between sleep and waking, and therefore in a trance condition akin to mediumship.

The evidence, then, all seems to suggest that the vampire, like the poltergeist, is an "earthbound spirit," a "hungry ghost" that draws vitality from human beings. Daskalos's remark to Loizo, that "he would remain in a narcotised state like a vampire," indicates that such spirits become, in effect, drug addicts who are unable to progress to a higher level while in the grip of their addiction.

One of the few contemporary "vampirologists" is a graduate of the State University of New York named Stephen Kaplan. In his book *Vampires Are . . .* (1984) he describes how he became interested in the subject. In the course of his studies in anthropology, he noticed that "many of the customs and rituals of the primitive cultures we were studying showed striking similarities to vampire myths and legends." This led him to suppose that there might be some basis of truth in vampire legends, and in 1971 he founded the Vampire Research Center on Long Island. As a result of interviews on the radio, he received many calls, most of which were hoaxes. The first real "vampires" he encountered were a couple who liked to taste blood. (In fact, blood is an emetic, so it would be impossible to drink it in quantity.) The woman used to whip her companion until he bled, then lick the cuts. They had formed a small group that would indulge in these practices. Another woman Kaplan interviewed obtained blood by trading sexual favors.

Without exception, the people Kaplan interviewed were "sexually disturbed." (In *The Sexual Anomalies and Perversions* by Dr. Magnus Hirschfeld, there is a section devoted to vampirism, in which it becomes clear that it is related to necrophilia; Hirschfeld describes, for example, a gravedigger named Victor Ardisson who drank animal blood and performed various perverted acts on female corpses whom he disinterred.) But Kaplan suggests that genuine vampirism is "the draining of physical energy from one individual to another, often via the blood." He speaks of "psychic vampires," people who seem to drain our physical energies. He comments that the process seems to be the reverse of "psychic healing," whereby the healer is able to transfer energy to the patient.

In an article on sexual occultism in the magazine *The Unexplained,* the occult historian Francis King describes the process by which a "magician" can cause sexual arousal in a selected victim:

> The would-be lover sits as near as possible to his intended victim. He gauges her breathing by the rise and fall of her breast, and, once he has established the exact rhythm, begins to breathe in precise unison with her. The sorcerer continues this for a period of between three and five minutes, and then contracts the muscles of his anus from five to ten seconds. This, supposedly, establishes an "astral link" between the two people involved, by bringing into action the man's *muladhara chakra*, the centre of psychic activity that, according to some occultists, controls the libido. It is situated, they claim, in a part of the "subtle body" roughly corresponding to the area between the anus and the genitals. The magician then gradually increases his rate of breathing until it reaches the rate characteristic of the height of sexual activity. The "astral link" ensures that the emotions normally associated with this rapid breathing are communicated to the woman, and she immediately experiences sexual arousal. The magician then begins a conversation.

He goes on to theorize that vampirism is a way of draining "psycho-sexual energy" from the victim.

What is being suggested is that a man can establish a telepathic link between himself and a woman he desires and use it to influence her desires. In *God Is My Adventure,* Rom Landau tells a story of the philosopher and mystic George Gurdjieff, which seems to indicate that he was also able to do this. One man told Landau of an occasion when he was lunching with an attractive female novelist:

Gurdjieff caught her eye, and we saw distinctly that he began to inhale and to exhale in a peculiar way. I am too old a hand at such tricks not to have known that Gurdjieff was employing one of the methods he must have learned in the East. A few moments later, I noticed that my friend was turning pale; she seemed to be on the verge of fainting. And yet she is anything but highly strung. I was very much surprised to see her in that strange condition, but she recovered after a few moments. I asked her what the matter was. "That man is uncanny," she whispered. "Something awful happened," she continued. "I ought to be ashamed . . . I looked at your 'friend' a moment ago, and he caught my eye. He looked at me in such a peculiar way that within a second or so I suddenly felt as though I had been struck right through my sexual center. It was beastly!"

It seems likely that the "man with the mole" described in *Phantasms of the Living* possessed the same curious ability and that this explained why the girl had fainted at the Birmingham music festival; it also seems clear that, having established the "psychic link," he was able to invade her dreams in the manner of a "vampire."

Let us, then, attempt an outline of a theory of vampirism that is in accordance with the various accounts that have been quoted. The story of Arnod Paole, like so many others, makes it clear that he was not a willing vampire; the *Visum et Repertum* states that he had been "troubled by a vampire" in Turkey and had eaten earth from the grave to free himself of the affliction. This was not successful, and the earthbound spirit returned after death to vampirize people in Medvegia. If we assume that vampirism is an experience akin to sexual satisfaction, then the implication is that Paole's unquiet spirit became a vampire, much as many sexually abused children grow up to become child abusers. But this view suggests that sex itself may be regarded as a form of benevolent vampirism; the act of lovemaking, which has to rest content with an interpenetration of bodies, is an attempt at mutual absorption. In that case, the actions of sex criminals must be seen as a form of nonbenevolent vampirism. (The sex murderer Ted Bundy told police interrogators: "Sometimes I feel like a vampire.") If we can accept this view, then it is not difficult to accept that some "earthbound spirits" or "hungry ghosts" also attempt to maintain their link with the world by a form of psychic vampirism.

Only one question remains: if vampirism is a draining of psychic energy, why do so many accounts mention the drinking of blood? Stephen Kaplan suggests that genuine vampirism is "the draining of physical energy from one individual to another, often via the blood." The *Visum et Repertum* mentions that fresh blood was flowing from Paole's eyes, nose, mouth, and ears. Gooch's friend Sandy found that her mouth was full of dried blood after the "psychic attack," although she had no injury that might account for it.

But why should a "vampire" leave its own blood behind? Is it possible that the blood *was* Sandy's own and that the "incubus" (male demon) had the power to draw it from her, like a leech, without breaking the skin? This notion opens up an entirely new realm of speculation about vampires—a realm which, for lack of further evidence, we must at present leave unexplored.

32

Vortices:
The Bridge Between
the Natural and the Supernatural?

In 1839 a gray-bearded professor read a paper entitled "An Essay on the Figure of the Earth" to the Royal Society in Edinburgh; it exhibited a high order of mathematical ability, and its author had been awarded a gold medal by Edinburgh University. But the professor who read it was not, in fact, its author; the actual author was a boy of fifteen named William Thomson, and he was not allowed to read his own work because it might have embarrassed the learned audience to be lectured by a fresh-faced teenager. In due course, William Thomson went on to become one of the most celebrated scientists of his day, the discoverer of the Second Law of Thermodynamics (the recognition that the universe is "running down"), of "absolute zero," and of the moving coil galvanometer. He was also instrumental in laying the first transatlantic cable and in bringing Bell's telephone to Britain. At the age of sixty-eight he was made Lord Kelvin, and the absolute scale of temperature still bears his name.

Yet if Kelvin had been asked what he considered his most important achievement, he would undoubtedly have replied: the vortex (or whirlpool) theory of atoms—a theory that has now been totally forgotten. In fact, most of his contemporaries would have agreed; the 1875 edition of the *Encyclopaedia Britannica* carries a two-page entry on his vortex theory of atoms, written by the eminent mathematical physicist James Clerk Maxwell. The idea had come to Kelvin in 1867, in a flash of inspiration, and only a few weeks later, he delivered a paper on his theory to the same Royal Society in Edinburgh that had listened to his first paper twenty-eight years earlier.

Kelvin had been a child prodigy; the son of James Thomson, a Belfast professor of mathematics, he had started attending his father's lectures at the age of eight and had entered the University of Glasgow (to which his father had moved) at the age of eleven. A trip to Europe at the age of sixteen had introduced him to Fourier's book on the mathematical theory of heat; from then on, he was determined to become a physicist—or, as they called it in those days, a "natural philosopher."

The dazzling idea that struck him in 1867 seems to have developed from his observation of smoke rings. A simple way to create these is to introduce smoke into a box that has a round hole in one of its sides. If you give the opposite side of the box a vigorous slap (particularly if that side is made of some soft material like toweling), a smoke ring will shoot out of the hole. But if you try to stop the smoke ring with your hand, it will not dissolve like a bubble, as you might expect. It will simply bounce off your hand like a rubber ball. If you make two smoke rings collide head on, they vibrate from the impact like two charging bulls meeting head on, then bounce away from each other. In short, they behave like solid objects.

In 1803 an English chemist named John Dalton had suggested that matter is finally made up of tiny hard balls called "atoms," which are indivisible. He had borrowed the idea from the Greek philosopher Democritus but had backed it up with highly convincing evidence. Dalton's theory had led to a number of important breakthroughs in physics and chemistry, such as the recognition of how atoms fuse together to form molecules—so that two atoms of hydrogen, for example, combine with one of oxygen to form water.

That still left many problems. For example, *why* are atoms of hydrogen and oxygen quite different? You would think that if the universe were made up of primordial particles, all those particles would be the same.

Kelvin went on to explain that "vortices" of energy can form different substances because there can obviously be many different types of vortices—different sizes, speeds, and so on. Within ten years or so most physicists accepted Kelvin's view that atoms are vortices; it simply seemed to make sense. In 1882 a brilliant twenty-six-year-old Cambridge scientist, J. J. Thomson (no relation to William Thomson), won a prize for a paper on the motion of vortex rings. Yet fifteen years later, Thomson's discovery of the electron apparently made Kelvin's vortex theory obsolete. Kelvin himself intensely disliked the "new physics" that arose from the study of the disintegration of radioactive particles and declined to believe that atoms could fall apart.

The discovery of the electron led to quantum physics, to the theory of relativity, and, eventually, to the "discovery" of subelectronic particles like quarks—all of which seemed to make the vortex theory doubly irrelevant.

In 1968 a twenty-year-old science student at Kelvin's old university, Belfast, went to see his professor of zoology, Dr. G. Owen. The student's name was David Ash, and he was thinking of transferring from physics and zoology to medicine. He expected some resistance and was startled when his professor showed him to a chair and then strode about the room delivering a diatribe on the way young men believe everything their elders tell them. All they cared about, he complained, was getting a degree and a good job. Learning for the sheer joy of learning had vanished.

When Ash left the professor's study, he was fired with sudden determination. He would stop thinking about a career and devote himself to *real* learning—to inventing theories and exploring ideas for the sheer joy of it. Fortunately, his father, Dr. Michael Ash, was the author of some highly unorthodox theories of medicine and raised no serious objection. After a period as a science teacher, Ash became a consultant on nutrition and alternative medicine and devoted all his spare time to developing his own unorthodox theories of the nature of matter, based on an idea that he called "primordial spin"—or vortices. He had come across the idea in a physics textbook printed in America in 1904 that championed Kelvin's "outmoded" idea. In due course, Ash joined forces with a young science graduate, Peter Hewitt, to argue these ideas in a book entitled *Science of the Gods*—which, in spite of its catchpenny title, is a serious attempt to create a theory of the nature of matter that can transcend the serious limitations of contemporary science.

One of the most irritating of these limitations must be obvious to any reader of this book: that science seems incapable of dealing with certain fundamental mysteries of human existence. You and I have no idea of where we were a hundred years ago and where we shall be a hundred years hence. It is a real question, and it is as important as anything we could ask; yet science regards it as a pseudoquestion. Neither can modern science deal with such mysteries as precognition—glimpses of the future—second sight—glimpses of things that are happening elsewhere—or out-of-the-body experiences. If it humbly admitted that these are at present beyond its range, there would be no problem. But it insists that these problems do not exist, that they are simply a sign of human gullibility and self-deception. Yet anyone who has taken a serious look at these problems knows this to be escapist nonsense.

In the 1870s a group of British scientists and philosophers decided to form a society that would study claims about ghosts and life after death; in 1882 it was launched under the title The Society for Psychical Research. Most of its members—scientists like J. J. Thomson, literary men like Tennyson and Mark Twain, and statesmen like Gladstone—were skeptics but were willing to admit that there *was* something here that needed explaining. Lewis Carroll wrote: "That trickery will *not* do as a complete explanation of all the phenomena . . . I am more than convinced." He thought that perhaps spirits could be explained as some unknown natural force "allied to electricity." By the 1890s the Society had made important investigations of ghosts, out-of-the-body experiences, and telepathy and had proved beyond all doubt that—as Carroll suspected—they could not be explained as trickery. But at that point they got stuck. All their hopes of turning the "paranormal" into a science melted away like ghosts at cockcrow. And, more than a century later, the position is still unchanged. As far as science is concerned, the paranormal does not exist—or is, at best, a kind of crank fringe activity.

That is why David Ash and Peter Hewitt are asking one of the most important and relevant of all scientific questions: can some new approach provide science and the paranormal with a common foundation?

In the third chapter of their book, they raise the question of "the key to the supernatural." Energy, they say, is the prime reality. But is our physical universe the *only* reality? If matter and light are two forms of energy (as Einstein showed), is it not possible that there are other forms of energy, so-called nonmaterial forms? To anyone interested in the paranormal, the answer is obviously yes. The entity known as the poltergeist has been proved to have the ability to make solid objects pass through walls (so that, for example, in one case a picture fell out of its frame without either breaking the glass or the sealed cardboard at the back of the frame). Neither matter nor light can pass through solid walls; ergo, some other form of energy must exist.

If, as Kelvin believed, matter is made up of "vortices" or whirlpools, what are these whirlpools *in*? Ash replies that the very question is based on a misconception. Before Einstein, scientists believed that light was a vibration in the "ether"—an unknown fluid that pervades all space. Two physicists named Michelson and Morley showed that the "ether" does not exist. Light seems to be "pure movement," not a movement *in* something. A simple illustration might clarify this idea. Suppose I toss a book across the room—as I am always tossing books from my worktable onto the camp bed that serves as a halfway house to the bookshelf. While the book is in motion, it remains in every way the same book; a tiny Martian scientist sitting on it would detect no difference whatever. Yet its motion is undoubtedly real. You must regard its motion as a kind of invisible additive. Now try to imagine this invisible additive on its own. It is impossible, of course; but that does not prove that it cannot exist. When you look at the night sky you cannot imagine space going on forever; yet common sense tells you it does, even beyond the edge of the universe. Ash is suggesting that, just as energy is more "fundamental" than matter, so "pure movement" is more fundamental than energy.

So why should energy be restricted to the speed of light? Ash writes: "If movement could have a faster speed, it would give rise to a completely different type of energy." This he calls super-energy. (In fact, physicists have suggested in recent years the possibility of a particle called the *tachyon*, which is faster than light.)

According to Ash: "Objects of super-energy would share the same *form* as things in our world, but their *substance* would be entirely different." They would actually coexist with our physical world but would be, under normal circumstances, undetectable. And this, Ash suggests, could be the explanation of ghosts, poltergeists, "miracles" (like those of the Hindu guru Sai Baba, who can "materialize" objects out of thin air), precognition, and all other so-called paranormal phenomena.

The skeptic will ask: does Ash's suggestion bring us any closer to understanding the paranormal? In a sense, yes, it does. Most scientific theories begin as an attempt to explain some puzzling phenomenon, such as thunder and lightning. The super-energy theory can certainly help to explain a wide variety of "paranormal" phenomena.

Let us begin with an extremely simple one: dowsing. A "diviner" can hold a forked twig in his hands and detect underground water. This can be explained in purely electrical terms. Moving water produces a weak electric field, and men—and animals—seem to have an inbuilt sensitivity to this field—obviously part of our survival mechanism.

A Cambridge don named T. C. ("Tom") Lethbridge, who was also an archaeologist, often used his own dowsing abilities to detect buried objects. He also discovered that a pendulum—a weight on a piece of string—worked just as well as a dowsing rod—the pendulum would swing in a circle over things he was looking for. He then made another discovery that sounds absurd but that all dowsers will verify: that he could "ask the pendulum questions" and that it would reply in the negative or affirmative by swinging back and forth or in a circle. The theory advanced by scientists—like Sir William Barrett—is that the unconscious mind knows the answer and causes the muscles to make the pendulum move in a circle or a "swing."

During his Cambridge days, Lethbridge used the pendulum to explore a giant Celtic figure cut in a hillside but now buried beneath the turf.* And after his retirement to an old house in Devon, he continued his investigations into the "power of the pendulum." Instead of a short pendulum, he tried a pendulum made of a long piece of string, which he was able to shorten or lengthen by winding it round a stick. His first experiment was to place a silver dish on the floor and then to hold the pendulum over it and carefully unwind the string. When it reached 22 inches, it went into a circular swing. He tried it over copper; this went into a circular swing at 30½ inches. He now tried the 30½-inch pendulum in his garden and soon unearthed a small copper tube with it.

So far, Lethbridge was merely "proving" that different metals caused the pendulum to respond at different lengths. He next proved to his satisfaction that all substances have their characteristic "rate" (length of the pendulum swing): oak (11 inches), mercury (12½), grass (16), lead (22—the same as silver), potatoes (39). Many substances, of course, "share" a rate with others, but Lethbridge found that the weight "circled" a distinct number of times for each—for example, sixteen times for lead and twenty-two for silver.

Now certain that he was on to something of scientific importance, he became more ambitious. One of the strangest and most absurd phenomena connected with the pendulum is "map dowsing." It sounds preposterous, but a good dowser can locate water by swinging his pendulum over a map. At this point we have to leave "scientific" explanations behind, and fall back on ESP (extrasensory perception) or on the powers of the unconscious mind. Lethbridge reasoned that if the pendulum is equally at home with an abstraction like a map, it should be at home with abstractions in general—love, anger, evolution, death. It ought, for example, to have a different rate for male and female. He and his wife, Mina, tried throwing stones against a wall; then he tested them with the pendulum. Those Mina had thrown reacted at 29 inches, those

---

*These excavations—and Lethbridge's subsequent career—are described at length in my book *Mysteries* (1978).

Lethbridge had thrown at 22. These, it seemed, were the "rates" for male and female.

Other stones—sling stones from an Iron Age fort—showed a reaction at 40 inches. Could it be that the stones had been thrown in the course of battle, and 40 was the rate for anger? Lethbridge set his pendulum at 40 inches and thought of something that annoyed him; it immediately began to swing in a circle.

So Lethbridge had established, at least to his own satisfaction, that emotions and ideas, as well as substances, caused the pendulum to react at a definite rate. The rate for death was 40, and this was also the rate for black, cold, anger, deceit, and sleep—obviously connected ideas. When he drew a circle divided into 40 compartments, and placed each quality or object in its appropriate compartment, he found that "opposite" qualities occurred where you would expect to find them: safety at 9, danger at 29, pleasant smells at 7, unpleasant smells at 27, and so on.

In a moment of idleness, he tried placing the substances at their appropriate distance from the center—sulphur at 7 inches along line 7, chlorine 9 inches along line 9, and so on—then joined up the dots with a line—which was, of course, a spiral. Spirals (vortices) seem to play an important part in most primitive religions; they are found carved on rocks all over the world. The vortex obviously embodies some important primitive idea. And now, looking at his own spiral, it struck Lethbridge that a spiral can go on indefinitely. Why should the "dowsing spiral" stop at 40?

So Lethbridge proceeded to experiment with the pendulum extended beyond 40 inches. And he discovered that every substance now reacted at its "normal" rate, *plus* 40; sulphur at 43½, silver at 62, and so on. There was one small difference. If he held a 43½-inch pendulum over a heap of sulphur, it reacted most strongly *slightly to one side* of the heap; the same applied to everything else he tested. It was as if, in this realm beyond 40, energies were slightly diffracted, like a stone at the bottom of a fish tank that appears slightly to one side of its proper position.

When the pendulum was extended beyond 80, all the same effects occurred again, including the "diffraction effect." And when it was extended beyond 120, it was the same all over again.

Lethbridge's deduction from these observations may sound

totally arbitrary, although in his books he makes it sound reasonable enough: that since 40 is the "rate" for death, then the pendulum beyond 40 is reacting to a level of reality "beyond death" and to yet another level at 80, another at 120, and so on, possibly ad infinitum. (He found it impossible to test a pendulum at more than 120 inches because it was too long.)

One of the oddities that Lethbridge observed is that in "our" world—below 40—there is no "rate" for time; this is presumably because we are *in* it, and so time appears "stationary," as a stream would to a boat drifting along it. At the second level—beyond 40—time "registers" at 60 inches but—oddly enough—seems to have no forward motion. (I do not profess to understand what he meant.) Then, in the world beyond 80, time disappears again.

Lethbridge concluded that many "worlds" coexist on different "vibration rates." We cannot see the world "beyond 40" because it moves too fast for us, so to speak, just as you cannot read the name of a station if the train goes through it too fast. But some people—"psychics"—are better at reading fast-moving words, so to speak, and keep catching glimpses of the next level of reality.

Lethbridge is of interest in this context because he did not begin as an occultist but as an archaeologist trained in scientific method. The notion of "other realities" forced itself upon him little by little, as a result of experiences that he found hard to explain. He always declined to go further than the facts would allow, but the facts often forced him to go further than he wanted. Personal experience convinced him, for example, of the reality of ghosts, poltergeists, and what he called "ghouls"—unpleasant sensations associated with certain places where tragedies have occurred. Yet he preferred to believe that these could be explained in terms of "tape recording"—"imprints" of human emotions on some kind of electrical field.

Lethbridge died in 1971, but he would undoubtedly have approved of David Ash's vortex theory and of the notion that paranormal events can be explained in terms of super-energy (or, as he would have said, higher vibrational rates). He would probably have added that each level of reality has its own level of super-energy and that there is no obvious limit to the number of levels.

This notion of levels is fundamental to occultism. Madame Blavatsky taught that there are seven levels of reality, the first three of a descending order and the last three of an ascending order. Earth is situated at the bottom, at level four, the "heaviest" and densest of all levels. Yet the sheer density of matter means that human beings are capable of greater achievement than on any other level—just as a sculptor can create more permanent works of art out of marble than out of clay.

Another thinker who attempted to bridge the gap between science and the paranormal was Arthur Young, inventor of the Bell helicopter.* In books such as *The Reflexive Universe*, Young also speculated that there are "seven levels of existence," which include (in order) subatomic particles, atoms, molecules, plants, animals, humans, and what might be called "true humans," or human beings who have moved to the next evolutionary stage. This seventh level is also that of light.

To most scientists, such speculations will sound suspiciously "mystical." Yet the most interesting scientific development of the second half of the twentieth century has been the recognition by scientists themselves that some of the implications of relativity physics and quantum theory *are* "mystical." Consider the strange paradox of the "photon that interferes with itself" (for the sake of brevity I will quote my own book, *Beyond the Occult*):

> If I shine a beam of light through a pinhole it will form a circle of light on a screen (or photographic plate). If two pinholes are opened up side by side, the result—as you might expect—is two overlapping circles of light. But on the overlapping portions there are a number of dark lines. These are due to the "interference" of the two beams—the same effect you would get if two fast streams of traffic shot out on to the same roundabout. Now suppose the beam is dimmed so only one photon at a time can pass through either of the holes. When the image finally builds up on the photographic plate you would expect the interference bands to disappear. Instead, they are there as usual. But how can one photon at a time interfere with itself? And how does a photon flying through one

---

*For a fuller account of Arthur Young, see my book *Mysteries* (1978), pages 608-10.

hole "know" that the other hole is open? Could it possess telepathy, as Einstein jokingly suggested? . . . Perhaps the photon splits and goes through both holes? But a photon detector reveals that this is not so: only one photon at a time goes through one hole at a time. Yet, oddly enough, as soon as we begin to "watch" the photons, they cease to interfere, and the dark bands vanish. The likeliest explanation is that the photon is behaving like a wave when it is unobserved, and so goes through both holes, and interferes. The moment we try to watch it, it turns into a hard ball.

In 1957 a Princeton physicist named Hugh Everett III suggested an apparently preposterous idea to explain this apparent paradox. The "wave" we call a quantum is not a real wave. We impose reality on it because our minds work that way. It is a "wave of possibilities." (Heisenberg's famous "uncertainty principle"—that you cannot know both the speed and the position of a photon— and the amusing paradox of Schrödinger's cat—that a cat in a box can be neither dead nor alive, but in an "intermediate" state—are examples of the same notion.) If the two "holes" can somehow interfere with each other, even though there is only one photon, then the two alternative paths of the electron must exist side by side, so to speak. But where? Everett suggested that one of them exists in a parallel "alternative universe." In these parallel universes (or perhaps they are just different ways of seeing the same universe), a tossed coin could come down heads in one and tails in the other. A wave is actually two particles in two different worlds—or rather, many different worlds, for every "alternative" splits into two more, and so on.

Anyone who finds this idea absurd should study *Parallel Universes* (1988) by the physicist Fred Alan Wolf, in which the implications of the theory are developed in all their Alice-in-Wonderland complexity. The physicist Sir Fred Hoyle has suggested that the paradoxes of quantum physics can be explained only if we assume that *future* possibilities can somehow influence the present and that therefore, in some very real sense, the future has already taken place—a possibility that is already familiar to all students of precognition—those sudden flashes of foreknowledge of the future.

Clearly, the need to find a deeper foundation that can embrace science and the "paranormal" is one of the most vital notions that has emerged during the twentieth century. Yet obviously, even this way of expressing it perpetuates the misunderstanding, since it speaks of science and the paranormal as if they were separate entities, rather than part of the same whole. The philosopher Edmund Husserl was struggling toward the same insight in his last book, *The Crisis in the European Sciences*, when he pointed out that the Greeks had *divided* reality into the world of the physically real and the world of ideas. Galileo then taught scientists how to handle this physical world in terms of mathematics, and suddenly science was confined to the world of physical reality. And since scientists declined to admit any other reality, science became oddly lopsided. (This is what Alfred North Whitehead meant when he accused science of "bifurcating" nature, dividing reality into the "solid" realm of physics and the—comparatively unimportant—realm of lived experience, which includes art, religion, and philosophy.) Husserl argued that we have to take a stand against "scientific reality" and rethink science until it can comfortably include the full range of our human reality. Husserl, of course, was not remotely interested in the paranormal, and his work is doubly important because it shows how a philosopher (who began his career with a book on mathematics) can reach the same philosophical conclusions closely related to those of Lethbridge or David Ash from the other end, so to speak.

In *Science of the Gods*, Ash and Hewitt have made a brave attempt to show how the vortex theory can explain many kinds of "psychic phenomena" in scientific terms, from ghosts and miracles to reincarnation and UFOs. It is an exciting and imaginative program that—inevitably—falls short of its objective. But at least it makes us aware that when Kelvin had his flash of "vision" in 1867 and developed it into the vortex theory of atoms, he may have laid the foundation for a new and more comprehensive science of reality.

33

Zombies:
The Evidence for the Walking Dead

E ver since 1932, when Bela Lugosi starred in *White Zombie*, the zombie legend has been a Hollywood standby, challenging the vampire, the walking mummy, and the Frankenstein monster in popularity. No one who has seen a film like *King of the Zombies* can ever forget the shot of a zombie marching on like a robot while someone fires bullet after bullet into its chest.

Zombies, according to Alfred Metraux's book, *Voodoo* (1959), are "people whose decease has been duly recorded and whose burial has been witnessed, but who are found a few years later . . . in a state verging on idiocy." In Port-au-Prince, Haiti, says Metraux, "there are few, even among the educated, who do not give some credence to these macabre stories." Understandably, such tales have met with skepticism outside Haiti.

One of the first Western observers to record an actual incident of zombiism was the black ethnographer Zora Neale Hurston, who had trained in America under the great Franz Boas. In October 1936 a naked woman was found wandering in Haiti's Artibonite Valley; her name was Felicia Felix-Mentor, and she had died at the age of twenty-nine and been buried. Zora Hurston went to visit her in the hospital at Gonaïves and described her as having "a blank face with dead eyes" and eyelids "white as if they had been burned with acid."

According to Zora Hurston, people were "zombified" if they betrayed the secrets of the Haitian secret societies. No one believed her, and Metraux writes patronizingly of "Zora Houston [sic], who is very superstitious." Nevertheless, Metraux tells a story involving two members of "high society." After his car broke down, one of them was invited to the home of a little white-bearded man, a *houngan* or vodoun (voodoo) priest. Piqued by his guest's skepticism about a *wanga* (magical charm), the old man asked him if he had known a certain M. Celestin—who had, in fact, been one of the visitor's closest friends. Summoned by a whip crack, a man shambled into the room, and to his horror the visitor recognized his old friend Celestin, who had died six months earlier. When the zombie reached out for the visitor's glass—obviously thirsty—the *houngan* stopped him from handing it over, saying that nothing could be more dangerous than to give or take something from the hand of a dead man. The *houngan* told his visitor that Celestin had died from a spell and that the magician who had killed him had sold him for twelve dollars.

Other stories recounted by Metraux make it clear that he considers zombies to be people who have literally died and then been raised from the dead. Understandably, he rejects this as superstition. In fact, as we shall see, Zora Hurston was correct and Metraux was wrong.

Haiti, in the West Indies, was discovered by Columbus in 1492, but it was not until two centuries later that it became a base for pirates and buccaneers. French colonists developed Haiti's rich sugar trade, using black slaves kidnapped from Africa. The Spanish ceded Haiti (or Saint-Domingue, as it was called) to the French in 1697.

The slaves were treated with unbelievable cruelty—for example, hung from trees with nails driven through the ears or smeared with molasses and left to be eaten alive by ants. Another horrifying practice involved filling a slave's anus with gunpowder and setting it alight, an act the Frenchmen often referred to as "blasting a black's ass." In spite of the risks, slaves ran away whenever they could and hid in the mountains, until, eventually, certain mountainous regions became "no-go areas" for whites. In the 1740s a slave named Macandal, who had lost his arm in a sugar press, escaped to the mountains and taught the runaway Maroons (as the slaves were known) to use poison against their oppressors. Mass poisoning of cattle was followed by mass poisoning of the colonists. Macandal was eventually betrayed and sentenced to be burned alive (although, according to legend, he used his magical powers to escape). But from then on, the secret societies spread revolt among the black slaves. After the great revolts of the 1790s, French authority virtually collapsed, and although it was savagely restored under Napoléon, he was never able to conquer the interior of the island. A series of black emperors ruled until 1859, but the island has alternated between a state of virtual anarchy and harsh authoritarian rule ever since, both of which have nurtured the secret societies.

Zora Hurston asserted that "zombification" was effected by means of a "quick-acting poison." It was not until the early 1980s, however, that a young American anthropologist, Wade Davies, heard rumors that zombification was, in fact, a process involving certain known poisons, chief among which was that of the puffer fish—a delicacy dear to the Japanese, although it has to be prepared with extreme care. (More on this follows.)

Summoned to meet a New York psychiatrist named Nathan Kline, Davies was told of two recent cases that seemed to demonstrate beyond all doubt that zombification was not a myth. In 1962 a Haitian peasant in his forties, Clairvius Narcisse, was admitted to the Albert Schweitzer Hospital in the Artibonite Valley, suffering from fever; he died two days later and was buried the next day. Eighteen years later, in 1980, a man walked up to Narcisse's sister Angelina and identified himself as her brother, Clairvius. He asserted that he had been "zombified" by order of his brother, with whom he had been disputing about land. He had been removed from his grave and taken to work with other zombies. After two years, their master was killed and he escaped to wander the country for the next sixteen years. It was not until he heard of his brother's death that he dared to make himself known.

Narcisse's identity was confirmed, and the BBC made a short film about the case. In the same year, a group of "zombies" was found wandering in the north of the country—where Narcisse had been forced to work, confirming Narcisse's story of the escape.

In 1976 a thirty-year-old woman named Francina Illeus, known as *"Ti Femme,"* was pronounced dead. Three years later she was found alive by her mother and recognized by a scar on her temple; her coffin was found to be full of rocks. She believed that she was poisoned on the orders of a jealous husband.

In 1980 another woman, Natagette Joseph, aged sixty, was recognized as she wandered near her home village; she had "died" in 1964.

When Davies went to Haiti to investigate, his attention focused on *Datura stramonium,* known in America as jimsonweed and in Haiti as zombie's cucumber. He went to see Max Beauvoir, an expert on vodoun. He interviewed Clairvius Narcisse and confirmed his story. He also discovered that Narcisse was not simply the victim of a vengeful brother; he had been something of a Casanova and had left illegitimate children—whom he declined to support—all over the place. Davies later concluded that "zombification" is not simply a matter of malice. The secret societies had a sinister reputation, but it seemed that they were less black than they were painted and often acted as protectors of the oppressed. Zombification, it seemed, was often a punishment for flagrant wrongdoing.

Davies's research led him to a highly poisonous toad, the *Bufo marinus,* and to two varieties of puffer fish, so called because they inflate themselves with water when threatened. Both are full of deadly neurotoxin called *tetrodotoxin,* a fatal dose of which would just cover the head of a pin. Captain Cook had suffered severely after eating the cooked liver and roe of a puffer fish. The Japanese throw away all the poisonous parts of the fish and eat the flesh raw—as *sashimi*—but the deadly liver is also eaten after being cleaned and boiled.

But it was clear to Davies that the poison of the puffer fish is not the sole secret of "zombification." In his extraordinary book *The Serpent and the Rainbow* (1985), he describes his search for samples of zombie poison. His aim was to obtain samples and take them back to be tested in the laboratory. But although he

met a number of *houngans* and witnessed some remarkable
ceremonies—in a number of which he saw people "possessed" by
spirits (so that one woman was able to place a lighted cigarette on
her tongue without being burned)—his quest came to a premature end when one of his major backers died and another suffered
a debilitating stroke. But his book leaves very little doubt that the
secret of "zombification" is a poison that can produce all the signs
of death. When the body is dug up, an antidote is administered
(Davies was able to study some antidotes and concluded that the
"magical" powers of the priest seem to be as important as the
ingredients themselves), and then the victim is often stupefied by
further drugs that reduce the subject to a level of virtual idiocy.

A 1984 BBC program introduced by John Tusa confirmed that
"zombification" results from a poison that affects certain brain
centers, reducing consciousness to a dream level.

Wade Davies was left in no doubt about the reality of "zombification." But his investigation into the vodoun religion also seems
to have convinced him that not all the phenomena of vodoun can
be explained in such naturalistic terms.

Index

Abnormal Hypnotic Phenomena
(Dingwall), 187
"Achille," 303-4
Acupuncture, xvii
Æ *See* Russell, George
Alcohol, 186
Alexander I (of Russia), 244-53. *See also* Kuzmich, Fedor
death of, 248-51
Allison, Ralph, 314-15, 319
Altamira, 100, 101
American Society for Psychical Research, 310
Amityville horror, xvii
Ancient astronauts, 69-72, 345. *See also* Dogon mythology; von Däniken, Erich
Animal magnetism, 178
Antarctica, 343
Ardrey, Robert, 272-73, 275
Arthur (king). *See* King Arthur
Arthur: Roman Britain's Last Champion (Saklatvala), 8-9
Ash, David, 403-6

Atland (Atlantis), 287-88, 291
Atlantis, 288-89, 291, 359. *See also* Atland
Auras, 301, 321
The Authoress of the Odyssey (Butler), 155. *See also* Butler, Samuel
Avalon, 4. *See also* Glastonbury Abbey
Aztecs, 360, 363, 367

Baader, Andreas, 18-20, 23, 24. *See also* Baader-Meinhof gang
Baader-Meinhof gang
activities of, 22-23
death of, 17-18, 23
development of, 19-21
and Mogadishu hijacking, 15-17, 24-25
Barbados coffins (Barbados vault), xix-xxi
Basa, Teresita, 26-30
Bavent, Madeleine, 317-18
Beauvoir, Simone de, 192

"Beerhall Putsch," 126
Black Dahlia, 47
Black mass, 318, 319
Blade Runner, 61, 65
Blegen, Carl, 162-63, 167
The Blue Sense (Truzzi), xvii
Book of Mormon, 289
Boston Strangler, 211
Bottomley, Horatio, 113, 118, 122
Bourne, Lois, 93-94
Brain. *See also* Split-brain patients
    size of, 267, 274, 275, 278, 279
    two-sided, 184-86, 192-93
Brazilian Institute for Psycho
    Biophysical Research (IBPP), 384
Buffalo Slasher, 212
Bull, Titus, 311
Burke, Edmund, 226-27
Burney skull, 363-64
Burr, Aaron, 235
Butler, Samuel, 170, 270, 278
    and Homer, 150-56

Calypso, 289
Camelot, 8
Cannibalism, 275, 373
Canning, Elizabeth, 32-41
    disappearance of, 32-33
    validity of story, 34-41
"Canningites," 36-37, 38
Carpenter, William B., 180-81
Carroll, Lewis, 404
Cerebral hemispheres. *See* Mind; Split-
    brain patients
Chakras, 319, 398
Chambre ardente, 171, 318-19
Channeling, 301
Charcot, Jean-Martin, 177, 179, 304
Chardin, Pierre Teilhard de, 266, 268
Charfield train accident. *See* Railway
    Children
Chariots of the Gods? (von Däniken),
    70, 345, 360
Charles II (of England), 324
Charroux, Robert, 101

Chesterton, G. K., 77-78, 390
"Chicken Freak," 47-48
China, 138-44
Chronicles (Holinshed), 325
Chua, Remy, 27-28, 30
Churchill, Sir Winston, 117, 120, 129
Clairvoyance, 174, 187, 366, 367
Clay, Henry, 181
Clemens, Samuel (Mark Twain), 404
Cleveland torso murders. *See* Mad
    Butcher
Colburn, Zerah, xiv
Columbus, Christopher, 338, 339, 342
The Coming of the Fairies (Conan
    Doyle), 86
Committee for the Scientific
    Investigation of Claims of the
    Paranormal (CSICOP), xvii-xviii,
    88
Conan Doyle, Sir Arthur, xix, xxi, 79,
    82-83, 352
Conscious mind. *See* Mind
Cooper, Joe, 87, 88, 92-93
Corbett, Jim, xx
Corpus callosum (commissure), xv,
    185, 299. *See also* Split-brain
    patients
Cottingley fairies, 79-95
    photos of, 80-88
    questions about, 90-95
    sightings of, 79-80
Crabtree, Adam, 311-12, 313
Croiset, Gerard, xvii
Crop circles, 50-56
    "The Crop Circle Enigma"
        (symposium), 55
    explanations for, 54, 56
    eyewitness accounts of, 53
    hoaxes, 56
    varieties of, 50-53
Crystals, 366-67
Curses, 173-75

Daedalus (frigate), 347-49
Dalton, John, 402

Danger My Ally (Mitchell-Hedges), 361
Dart, Raymond, 271–72
"Dartian" man, 271–72
Darwin, Charles, 150, 267
Daskalos (Spiros Sathi), 391–92
Daughter of Time (Tey), 362
Davies, Wade, 415–17
Dawson, Charles, 266, 268, 269
Decapitation, 42, 43
Demoniacal possession. *See* Possession, demoniacal
Dental identification, 335
Devils of Loudun, 306–7, 309, 317, 319, 322–23
The Devils of Loudun (Huxley), 385
Dick, Philip K., 57–68
  early life and work, 57–60
  "possession" of, 62–65, 68
  quarrel with Ellison, 61–62
Dickens, Charles, xxii
Dietrich, Marlene, 260,264
Divine Invasions (Sutin), 57, 65
Do Androids Dream of Electric Sheep? (Dick), 61
Dogon mythology, 72–76
Dolezal, Frank, 47
Don Marcelino (de Sautuola), 99–100, 104
Dörpfeld, Wilhelm, 160–61, 162
The Downfall and Conquest of Great Britain (St. Gildas), 3
Dowsing, xi–xii, 175, 406
  with maps, 407
Dracula, 394. *See also* Vampires; Vlad the Impaler
Dracula (Stoker), 376
Draper, Sir William, 220–21
Drugs, 186
Druidism, 13, 290
Druitt, Montague John, 203–4
Dual mind, 180–81. *See also* Mind; Split-brain patients
Dual personality 300–1. *See also* Mind; Split-brain patients
Duke of Grafton, 222–24

Earth's Shifting Crust (Hapgood), 339
Easter Island, 70–71
Eddy, Mary Baker, 305
Edward IV (of England), 324, 326–27, 328–29
Edward V (Prince Edward), 329–30. *See also* "Princes in the Tower"; Richard III
Effluvia, xix, xxi
"Egyptians" (Gypsies), 37, 38
Egyptian mythology, 75–76
Einstein, Albert, 339
Ellison, Harlan, 61–62
Ensslin, Gudrun, 17–21, 24, 25. *See also* Baader-Meinhof gang
Entebbe, 16
Epic of Gilgamesh, 71
Eratosthenes, 340, 342
ESP (extrasensory perception), 317, 407. *See also* Clairvoyance; Mediums
Evans, Arthur, 161–62
Evolution, 267, 270–75. *See also* Missing link
  of bacteria, 278
  "Humphrey theory" of, 276
  through reincarnation, 301
Excalibur, 9

Fairies, 77–78. *See also* Cottingley fairies
The Fairy Faith in Celtic Countries (Wentz), 78
Fairy tales (Irish), 77
Feng Shui (Eitel), xv
Fielding, Henry, 35
Fischer, John, xviii
Fitzpatrick, Thaddeus, 230–31
The Flying Cow (Playfair), 396
Fradin family, 100–104
The Franchise Affair (Tey), 31–32, 38
Francis, Sir Philip, 228–32
Freemasons, xix–xxi
Freud, Sigmund, 179, 180, 184, 296, 384
Frya, 288

Gardner, Edward, 81–83, 85
Gardner, Martin, xvi
Garstin, Crosbie, xiii
A General Survey of Psychic
    Phenomena (Lambert), 311
Geoffrey of Monmouth, 1–6, 8–10
George (duke of Clarence), 327–28
George III (of England), 215–18,
    224–25
Ghosts, 297, 381, 409
Glastonbury Abbey, 6–7
Glozel, France
  cave paintings, 100
  excavations, 101–2
  authenticity of findings, 102–4
Gnomes, 81, 93
Goblins, 94
Gold of the Gods (von Däniken), 72
Goodrich, Norma Lorre, 10, 13, 14
Gooch, Stan, 394–95, 400
Goring, Hermann, 133, 134
Graham, Barbara, 320–22
Grail. See Holy Grail
Granby, Marquis of, 219–22
Graves, Robert, xiv, 156
Grayson, Elaine, 111, 119–20
Grayson, Victor, 105–23
  death of, 116–17
  disappearance of, 105–6
  early life and career of, 106–7,
    120–21
  election to Parliament, 108, 121
  declining influence of, 110–11
  military service of, 112
Great Pyramid. See Pyramids
Gregory, Anita, 305–6, 307
Gregory, Maundy, 112–16, 123
Grenville, George, 217–18
Grey, Anthony, 138–39
Griffiths, Frances. See Cottingley
    fairies
Grimble, Arthur, 11–12
Gulliver's Travels (Swift), 346
Guinevere, 7
Gurdjieff, George, 191, 391, 398–99
Gypsies. See "Egyptians"

Haiti, 414–15
Hall, Virtue, 34–35
Hallucinations, 66–67
Hamilton (Duke of), 125–26, 130
Hapgood, Charles, 292–93, 337, 339,
    340–41
Harris, Melvin, xvii
Hauntings, xviii. See also Poltergeists;
    Ghosts
Haushofer, Albrecht, 127, 133–34
"Head Hunter." See Mad Butcher
Henry II (of England), 5–6
Henry VI (of England), 326
Henry VII (of England), 330–31, 332–33
Herodotus, 146
Hess, Rudolf, 124–35
  early life and career of, 126–27
  identity of, 132–33
  at Nuremberg trials, 130–31
Hewitt, Peter, 404, 405
Hijacking. See Baader-Meinhof gang
Himmler, Heinrich, 134
Historia rerum Anglicarum, 380
History of the Kings of Britain
    (Geoffrey of Monmouth), 1
Hitler, Adolf, 126–27, 130, 133, 134
Hittites, 164–68
Hodgson, Richard, 306, 316
Hodson, Geoffrey, 85, 86
Holt, Harold, 136–43
  demotion of, 141
  early life and career of, 141
  as Prime Minister, 137–44
Holy Grail, 9
Homer, 145–50, 164, 170
  death of, 149
  early accounts of, 146–49
  origin of name, 148
Homer's Daughter (Graves), 156
"Honors Scandal," 105
Hope, Henry Thomas, 172. See also
    Hope Diamond
Hope Diamond, 171–73, 175
Hudson, Thomas, J., 180, 181–84
Human Personality and its Survival
    of Bodily Death (Myers), 386

Humphrey, Nicholas, 275
Huna religion, 309
"Hungry ghosts." *See* Pretas
Hungry Ghosts (Fisher), 387
Hurkos, Peter, xvii
Hurston, Zora Neale, 413-15
Husserl, Edmund, 412
Huxley, Aldous, 306, 307
Huxley, Thomas Henry, 268
Hypnosis, 176-82, 186-94, 298, 300,
    301, 315, 392, 395, 396
  with animals, 11-12
  in demoniacal possession, 304
  early history of, 178-79
  rape during, 176-77, 190-91
Hyslop, James, 310-11, 316
Hysteria, xv, 179, 303, 307

Ice age, 99, 101, 343
Iliad, 150, 157-60, 161, 163, 170
In the Wake of the Sea Serpents
    (Huevelman), 351-52
Ivan the Terrible, 243-44

Jack the Ripper, 47, 48, 195, 196-214
  American equivalent of, 42
  identity of, 202-11, 212-13
  letters from, 191-201
  origin of name, 199, 200
James, William, xix, 191, 306, 310,
    316
Janet, Pierre, 303-5
Joseph of Arimathea, 7, 9
Joyce, James, 156, 170
Judicial murders, 333
Jung, Carl, 55
Junius, 215-33
  identity of, 226-32
  letters of, 218-26

Kaplan, Stephen, 397-98, 400
Kelvin (William Thompson), 401-3
King Arthur, 1-9, 14
  accounts of, 5-6, 8
  early history of, 3-4
  remains of, 6-7

search for Holy Grail, 9
Kirkpatrick, Ivone, 128-29
Knights Templars, 365-66
Kraken. *See* Octopus, giant
Kurtén, Bjorn, 274, 276, 277, 278
Kürten, Peter, 44
Kuzmich, Fedor, 242-43, 252-53

Lady of the Lake, 13
Lamarck, 277-78
Lamias, 373-74
The Last Plantagenets (Costain),
    334-35
The Law of Psychic Phenomena
    (Hudson), 181, 184
Leakey, Louis, 273, 275
Lethbridge, T. C., xii, 406-8, 409
Lewis, Meriwether, 234-41, 238-39
"Ley lines," xv
Life of Merlin (Geoffrey of
    Monmouth), 10-11
Linear A, 162
Linear B, 162, 166, 167
Liu, V. M., 142
Lloyd George, David, 113, 119
Loch Ness monster, 342, 356-57
London, Jack, 109, 121-22
Long, Max Freedom, 309-10
Louis XIV (of France), 318
Lovecraft, H. P., 74
"Lunar knowledge," xv, xvi

Macandal, 415
Maclean, Edward Beale, 172
Mad Butcher, 42-49
  search for, 44, 46-47, 48-49
Madame Blavatsky, 305, 410
Magicians, 11-13
Magnus, Olaus, 353, 357
Mainard, Sir John, 280-81, 285
Mallery, Arlington H., 338
Man Eaters of Kumaon (Corbett), xx
Mao Tse-Tung, 141
Maps, ancient, 337-38, 344. *See also*
    Portolans
Mapmaking, 340-41, 342

Maps of the Ancient Sea Kings
(Hapgood), 337, 345
Marie Antoinette, 172
Matters, Leonard, 202
Maxwell, James Clerk, 402
Mayas, 359
Mediums, 297, 310, 386
Mein Kampf (Hitler), 126
Meinhof, Ulrike, 19–20. *See also*
Baader-Meinhof gang
Mental illness, 296, 303, 385
and possession, 294, 299, 305, 311
Menzies, Robert, 140, 142
Merlin, 9–14
early history of, 1, 2
as a title, 10
Merlin (Goodrich), 10
Merry Maidens (stone circle), xi, xii
Mesmer, Franz, 178–79, 301
Meteor striking earth, 291–92
Michell, John, xv, 55–56
Miller, Glenn, 254–65
death certificate of, 263
early career of, 254–55
file of, 258–59
Miller, Helen, 256, 263, 265
Millergate (Wright), 260
Mind
conscious and unconscious, 184,
407
dual, 184–85
objective and subjective, 182–83
Mind control, 188–89
Mind Out of Time (Wilson), xviii
Minos, 161, 286
Minotaur, 161
Missing link, 266–79
and brain size, 274, 275
and "dartian" man, 271–72
"hunting hypothesis," of 275–76
and Piltdown man, 269–70
Mitchell-Hedges, Mike, 358–59
Mitchell-Hedges, Anna, 360–61
Mitsinari (Dupreyat), 12
Mogadishu hijacking. *See* Baader-
Meinhof gang

Moller, Irmgard, 17, 23. *See also*
Baader-Meinhof gang
Mordred, 5, 6
More, Sir Thomas, 332
Morgan, Sir Henry, 359, 360, 362
The Morning of the Magicians
(Pauwels), 69, 345, 346
Morte D'Arthur (Malory), 3
Mother Wells, 34, 35–36, 39
Multiple Man (Crabtree), 311
Multiple personality, 303, 310, 311,
385. *See also* Possession
as mental disorder, 301, 314–15
and "spirit hypothesis," 316
Munich Olympics, 22
Murder by Perfection (McCormick),
115, 118, 123
The Murder of Rudolf Hess (Thomas),
132–33
Murphy, Bridey, xviii
Myrddin. *See* Merlin
Mysticism, 410–11

Naked Ape (Morris), 274
Napoléon, 245–46, 341
Narcisse, Clairvius, 415–16
National Psychological Institute, 294
Necrophilia, 397
Nelson, Nelson, 176–77
Nesbit, Evelyn, 302–3
Ness, Eliot, 44, 46, 48–49
Nickel, Steven, 47
Nickell, Joe, xvi, xviii–xxi
Niven, David, 255, 259–60, 264, 265
Nommo, 73–74
Norkot, Arthur, 281, 283, 285
Norkot, Joan, 281–85
"Normal" view, xxii. *See also* Reality
Not from the Apes (Kurtén), 273, 279

Oahspe, 289
Occultism, 410
Octopus, giant, 353–55, 356
Odysseus. *See* Ulysses
Odyssey, 150–56, 170
geography of, 153–54

Oera Linda Book, 286-93, 346
Oesterreich, T. K., 303, 305-6, 307
Ohnesorgi, Benno, 18
On the Sublime (Longinus), 149
Open to Suggestion (Temple), 190
Orderson, Isaac, xx
Origin of Species (Darwin), 267, 270
"Ossian," 287
The Other Atlantis (Scrutton), 290,
    291
Ottema, J. O., 287
Ouija board, 390
Owen, Sir Richard, 349-50, 356

Parallel Universes (Wolf), 411
Paranormal, xvii-xviii, xxi, 406
A Pattern of Islands (Grimble), 11-12
Paul (tsar of Russia), 244-45
Pendulums, 406-9
Personality body, 319, 322
Phantasms of the Living (Myers), 313
Piltdown skull, 103, 104, 268-69
Piri Re'is, 338-39
    map of, 342-43
Pitt, William (the elder), 215-17
Pixies, 93-94
Plato, 288-89
Poisons used in voodoo, 416
Polillo, Flo, 44, 45-46
Poltergeists, 89, 183, 295, 301, 308-9,
    317, 382-84, 405, 409
Poltergeist (Wilson), 89, 90, 93, 385
Pontopiddian, Bishop, 349, 353, 357
Portolans, 344
Possession, 28, 65, 297-99, 301-3,
    305-8, 310, 314-18, 385, 394
    demoniacal, 303-5, 306-7, 312-13,
        315
    and mental illness, 294
    and poltergeists, 308-9
    types of, 391-92
    in voodoo, 417
Possession, Demoniacal and Other
    (Oesterreich), 303-4, 305
Precognition, 411
Pretas ("hungry spirits"), 389

Priestley, J. B., 188
The Prime Minister Was a Spy
    (Grey), 138-39
"Princes in the Tower," 334-35. *See*
    Richard III
Prodigies, xiv
Psychic detection, xvii-xviii
Psychic healing, 398
Psychic invasions, 397
Psychics, xvii, 394, 409. *See also*
    Mediums
Psychokineses, 308, 384
Psychometry, 174, 183, 188, 290
Ptolemy, 340
Pushkin, 246, 248
Pyramids (Great Pyramid), 69, 70, 71,
    341-42, 360

Quantum physics, 403
Quest for Merlin (Tolstoy), 10, 11

Railway Children, 96-99
Rape, psychic, 396
Raspe, Jan-Carl, 17, 23, 25
Reality, 60, 409
Reinach, Salomon, 102, 104
Reincarnation, 301
Richard III (of England), 324-26, 327,
    328-29
Richard III (Shakespeare), 324-25,
    328, 329, 330
"The Ripper File" (television series), 205
Rose Merryn, xiii
Russell, George (Æ), 78-79, 94

Sacred sites, xv. *See also* Stonehenge
Sandwich, Lord, 217
Sartre, Jean Paul, 192-93
Schliemann, Henrich, 158-60
"Schrodinger's cat," 411
Science and the paranormal, xiii-xiv,
    xxi-xxii, 404, 412
Science of the Gods (Ash and Hewitt),
    404, 405, 412
Scientific reality, xxii, 412. *See also*
    Reality

Scrutton, Robert, 290–93
Sea monsters, 347–58
  giant octopus/squid, 353–56
  Loch Ness monster, 356–57
  sea serpents, 347–53
Seances, 297, 298
Secret Places of the Heart
  (Williamson), 69
The Secret Science Behind Miracles
  (Long), 310
Secrets of the Supernatural (Nickell
  and Fischer), xviii
Serial killers, 211–12
The Serpent and the Rainbow
  (Davies), 416
Sex, 307, 308, 393, 399
  in evolution, 273–74, 276–77
  in possession, 315
Sex crimes, 195–96, 393, 399
Sexual abuse, 312, 313, 314
Sexual occultism, 398
Shaw, George Bernard, 121, 156, 270
Shock treatment, 298
Sickert, Hobo, 205–7
The Sirius Mystery (Temple), 76
Skepticism, xiv
Skull of Doom, 358–67
  discovery of, 358–59
  mystical properties of, 366–67
  origin of, 360–65
Smith Woodward, Arthur, 266
Snowdon, Philip, 108, 109, 110
Society for Psychical Research, xviii,
  295, 383–84, 386, 404
"Solar knowledge," xv
Somnambule, 301
Sorry You've Been Duped (Harris),
  xvii
Sperry, Roger, xv, xvi
Spirit influence, 386–90
Spiritualism, 81, 82, 294, 295, 384,
  390
The Spirits' Book (Rivail), 301
Split-brain patients, xv–xvi, 185–86,
  299–300, 301
Squid, giant, 355–56

Squires, Mary, 34, 35–36, 38–39
Stewart, Alan, 137
Stoker, Bram, 373
Stone temples, xii. *See also*
  Stonehenge
Stonehenge, xii, xv
The Story of Ruth (Schatzman), 395
Super-energy, 406, 409
Succubus, 395, 396
Suggestion, hypnotic, 190, 193
Superself (Wilson), xviii
Sutin, Lawrence, 57, 65
Svengali, 177–78
Swedenborg, Emanuel, 68
Synchronicity, 55, 346

Telepathy, 189, 367
  in photons, 411
  in sea monsters, 357
Temple, Robert, 73–76
Tennyson, Alfred Lord, 404
Texier, Charles, 164
Tey, Josephine, 326, 333
Thaw, Henry, 302–3
Theosophical Society, 81, 92. *See also*
  Madame Blavatsky
Thermoluminescence, 103
Thirty Years among the Dead
  (Wickland), 294, 295, 305, 332,
  390
Thomas, Hugh, 132–33
Thompson, J. J., 403
Tibetan Book of the Dead, 62, 78
Tintagel, 8
Titulus Regius Act, 331
Tolstoy, Leo, 252–53, 325
Tolstoy, Nicolai, 10, 11
Tornado and Storm Research
  Organization (TORRO), 51
Torso (Nickel), 47
Torso Killer. *See* Mad Butcher
Toxemia, 296
Trilby (DuMaurier), 177
Trojan War, 145–46, 147, 157,
  162–63, 164–68
Troy, 157–61, 162–63

Truzzi, Marcello, xvii, xviii
Twain, Mark. *See* Clemens, Samuel
2001: A Space Odyssey, 69, 345
Tyrell, Sir James, 325, 330-33

UFOs, xv, 52, 55, 56, 69
Ulysses, 147, 153, 154, 289
Ulysses (Joyce), 156
Umbanda, 396. *See also* Vodoun
Uncertainty principle, 411
Undead, 374-75
The Untold Story (Nesbit), 302-3
The Untouchables (Ness), 49
Uther Pendragon, 2-3

Valhalla, 289
Vampire Research Center, 397
Vampires, 375-76, 379-80
    bodies of, 370-72
    historical background of, 372-74
    rationalizations of, 377
    theory of, 399-400
Vampires Are . . . (Kaplan), 397
Vampirism, 368-83, 392-94, 397-400
Van Dusen, Wilson, 65-68
Vere, Francis, 270
Vergil, Polydore, 332-33
Visum et Repertum, 368-72, 399
Vlad the Impaler (Dracula), 373
Vodoun (voodoo), 384, 414-15,
    416-17
Von Däniken, Erich, 70-71, 345, 346
Voodoo. *See* Vodoun
Voodoo (Metraux), 413

Vortex theory of atoms, 401-3
Vortices, 401-12
Vortigern, 1-2

Wallace, Alfred Russel, 187
Watkins, Alfred, xv
"Watseka Wonder," 305-6
Wells, H. G., xiii
Welsh triads, 290
Wentz, W. Y. Evans, 78-79, 94
White, Stanford, 302-3
The White Goddess (Graves), xiv
Who Are the Dead? (Quartermaine),
    319-20
Wickland, Anna, 296-97, 298, 302
Wickland, Carl, 294-95, 299, 312,
    390
Wilberforce, Samuel, 267-68
Wilkes, John, 216-18
Wilkinson, James, 235
Wilson, Ian, xviii
Witch Among Us (Bourne), 93-94
Witch doctors (shamans), 11-13
Wizard of the Upper Amazon
    (Lamb), 12
Woodville, Elizabeth, 327
Wright, Elsie. *See* Cottingley fairies
Wright, Wilbur, 257-64

Yeats, W. B., 77-78, 87, 94
Young, Arthur, 410

The Zetetic Scholar (magazine), xvii
Zombies, 413-17